INDIAN NATIONALISM AND HINDU

SOCIAL REFORM

Indian Nationalism and Hindu Social Reform

BY CHARLES H. HEIMSATH

PRINCETON, NEW JERSEY

PRINCETON UNIVERSITY PRESS

1964

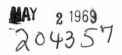

for my sons,
Carl and Peter

PREFACE

FIVE YEARS AGO, while organizing a course on modern Indian history at Yale, I discovered that very little had been written on the social reform movement in 19th century India. Indeed, I was not then aware that the references to social reform by 19th century Indian writers in fact were indications of a true movement, "a series of actions or activities directed toward a particular end," with continuity at least up to the First World War. Initial investigation in the India Office Library in the summer of 1958, under a grant from the Stimson Fund at Yale, encouraged me to seek support for further work on the social reform movement, involving travel to India and time for research and writing in this country. Fortunately, the School of International Service of The American University was initiating its area studies program on South Asia and invited me to participate, with time off for another trip to India. The Rockefeller Foundation generously supplied funds for my travel and also stipends for research carried on in London and Washington. I wish to express my gratitude to Dean Ernest S. Griffith of the School of International Service and to Chadbourne Gilpatric and Kenneth W. Thompson of the Rockefeller Foundation, all of whom made it possible for me to undertake this study and complete it. Neither The American University nor the Rockefeller Foundation has had any control over the project and thus bears no responsibility for its results.

While in India I was able to interview many persons who had knowledge of the social reform movement. Without their guidance and insight my study would frequently have strayed from the proper course, and I am afraid that even with it I may have misjudged certain matters. Needless to say, many of those whom I interviewed may find themselves in disagreement with what I have written.

In particular I would like to acknowledge, with thanks, the kind attention which the following persons gave to me when I sought their help: Professor Nilakanta Sastri of the University of Madras; Swami Swahananda of the Ramakrishna Math; S.R. Venkataraman and K.L.N. Rao of the Servants of India Society; the statesmen and scholars, C.R. Rajagopalachari and Sir C.P. Ramaswami Aiyar; Mona Hensman of Ethiraj College; V.K. Narasimhan of the *Hindu*; Professor Chandran Devenasan of Madras Christian College; Professor A.R. Desai of the University of Bombay; T.A. Kulkarni of the Gokhale Education Society; Professor N.R. Phatak, the biographer of Gokhale; Principal T.K. Tope of the Government Law College in Bombay; Professor G.B. Sardar of the Women's University in Poona; Laxman Shastri Joshi of the Pradnya Pathshala at Wai; Dr. Tara Chand, Director of the National Archives; P.M. Joshi of the Secretariat Record Office in Bombay; V.G. Dighe of the National Archives; Pundit Anandpriya of the Baroda Arya Samaj. Professor J.D.M. Derrett of the School of Oriental and African Studies kindly criticized Chapter VII in an earlier form. Selig Harrison read the chapter on nationalism and has provided a great deal of encouragement. Surjit Mansingh and Professors John R. McLane, Thomas R. Metcalf, and Baidya Nath Varma reviewed portions of the manuscript and made valuable suggestions. Dr. Horace Poleman of the Library of Congress advised me on transliterations. S. Natarajan, whose *A Century of Social Reform in India* has been of great value to me, kindly provided me with access to otherwise unavailable documents on the national social reform movement—his father was closely connected with this movement. Ravindra Tandon and Appa Ghatate helped me in various Hindi and Marathi translations.

Librarians provide the crucial link between a researcher and his materials, and I wish to thank all those who helped me, in particular Douglas Matthews of the India Office Library. Many thoughtful people at the British Museum Library, the New York Public Library, the Sterling Memorial Library at Yale, the Harvard College Library, the South Asia Regional Studies Library of the University of Pennsylvania, the Library of Congress, the Battelle Library at The American University, the International Aryan League Library in Delhi, and the Library of the University of Bombay deserve my sincere appreciation. I am grateful to Leda Natalia Heimsath, who provided valuable suggestions on the organization and sequence of ideas while reading the manuscript before it was typed. I also wish to thank two expert typists, Grace Harry and Lois Stuart. Finally, I wish to acknowledge the encouragement given to me during three years of work on this book by R. Miriam Brokaw of Princeton University Press.

Despite all this help, I have not done everything that I set out to accomplish, and there are many inadequacies in this book. The subject-matter as I have handled it is far narrower than one might suspect. I have dealt, for the most part, with the social reform movement at the level at which it had some national significance; the multifarious local reform movements, many of them in the same tradition as the national movement, were only partially investigated. I suspect, from the scattered recorded evidence that I was able to get, that the local movements were, in kind, much like the nationally significant movement. I trust that this proves to be the case, when someone reviews all the local scenes more thoroughly, through the multitudes of vernacular sources that are in existence. I have surveyed the all-India movement first since it interests me more than any particular local social reform movement. I have not disregarded the uniquenesses of the regional movements, and much of the material I collected must be viewed in its local context. But I think that attempts should be made to perceive the unities in modern Indian intellectual life, despite the obvious differences in development between the major regions of India.

The balance which I have attempted to strike in the presentation of the various movements and specific crusades is one based on estimates of their relative importance for the social reform movement as a whole and for modern Indian history. Occasionally, as in the case of Dayananda Saraswati and the Arya Samaj, I have overemphasized somewhat—in terms of space devoted to the effort—these accounts, because other easily available sources have not adequately dealt with them. The Brahmo Samaj and Bengali movements in general received less attention than they merit, because they have often been the subjects of serious studies.

Shortly after beginning the research for this book I concluded that it would greatly complicate the work if I included Muslim nationalism and Muslim social reform movements, because these were based on a modern intellectual tradition which had its origins and its development in semi-isolation from intellectual life among Hindus. I may later find myself in error, but I have now come to accept the view of Professor R. C. Majumdar, that Hindus and Muslims in 19th century India formed "two distinct communities" and that in social and cultural matters they "lived in two water-tight compartments as it were." The Muslim social reform movement is a separate subject for discussion, and it had almost nothing to do with the movement among Hindus, which is the theme of the present study.

This study extends to the First World War, the proper culmination of the 19th century in modern Indian life. The impact of Gandhi and the post First World War nationalist movement on the social reform movement was immense and requires separate analysis; to have dealt properly with Gandhi's thought and influence on social reform alone would have added more to the length of this work than I think is appropriate. I have included an Epilogue which suggests some of the developments in social reform after 1919, and I hope that a future study may present the contemporary period in its proper perspective.

The primary source materials on which this study is based are the writings and speeches of those Indians who took an interest in social reform questions. Of secondary importance are accounts of the social reform movements and the careers of the reformers. My main concern has been to expose the thinking of the modern social reformers, and to a lesser extent the ways in which their thinking was expressed in actions. I managed to survey a fair amount of the published record of the national social reform movement in India and in London; I rely especially heavily on contemporary pamphlets, many of which, however, are repetitive and therefore have not been included in the Bibliography. Apart from an effort to reinterpret the political nationalist movement largely on the basis of published works, I make no claim to have contributed to the study of Indian political developments in the 19th century. I leave this much-needed task to better qualified writers.

Chapter VII of this book, slightly reduced in length, appeared in the *Journal of Asian Studies* for August 1962, under the title,

"The Origin and Enactment of the Indian Age of Consent Bill, 1891."

I should like to make here one precautionary observation that should be kept in mind while reading what follows. Although one can discover social critics in any country at almost any time, 19th and 20th century India has had an overabundant allotment of this type of sincere but often irritating person. The self-deprecatory and chronically deflating pen—a modern Indian literary phenomenon—might well be the subject of a study in itself; Nirad Chaudhuri's *Autobiography of an Unknown Indian* is probably the best example of this kind of writing in English. A subtle and important difference between Indians and others writing social criticism lies not so much in the quantity of the output as in the approach of the writers to their subject. In the West one is not surprised to read an outraged indictment of certain social usages from which the author stands apart as critical observer; it would be a surprise, however, and in fact would create uneasiness in the reader should he come across critic after critic who places himself firmly in the society he is abusing and indicts himself along with the group. This is the usual style of Indian social criticism, and one subconsciously begins to feel that matters are even worse than the criticisms suggest since the critics themselves are personally involved. One should remember that this is a stylistic trait. It may stem from unusual objectivity in self-analysis or from humility. In either case it is wholly admirable.

CHARLES H. HEIMSATH

Washington, D.C.
July 1963

CONTENTS

xiii

CONTENTS

INDIAN NATIONALISM AND HINDU

SOCIAL REFORM

INTRODUCTION

"NEITHER politics nor war provides a key to the meaning of Indian history," writes Percival Spear; instead in society and culture are to be found the processes which give significance to India's past, and its present.[1]

The Indian social reform movement produced a multifaceted intellectual expression of the social and cultural transformations which took place under the impact of British rule. No other coherent body of thought so sensitively and profoundly exposed the mental processes of Indians as they formulated the ideas underlying the structure of their modern society as did the literature on social reform. The making of modern India, indeed, is recorded in that literature, with a richness of context and a reliable reflection of subjective truth that are nowhere else available. The intellectual history of the social reform movement is the main subject of this book.

In the 19th century—as today in India—the transformation of society began by individual revolts against prescribed ways of behaving. The established society recognized that fact, and all social rebels were derisively called reformers. When the all-India social reform movement—or movements, depending on the context—emerged in the second half of the 19th century some of its leaders were bothered by the loose definition of a reformer, which could include irresponsible iconoclasts as well as sober men holding positions of public trust. But no restrictive criteria were put forth, much less agreed upon, with which to judge whether or not a person was a true reformer, and in any province or town those known as reformers ranged from full-time social workers or teachers devoting their lives to the advancement of society, to exuberant students who lent their names and voices to any cause which offered a chance of challenging traditional authorities. Persons who publicly opposed the reform movement, often called

[1] P. Spear, *India: A Modern History*, p. 448.

3

anti-reformers, were themselves sometimes leading exemplary lives according to the standard of the reformers. The problem of definition was never solved.[2]

For the present purposes of historical analysis of an intellectual movement, social reformers were all those who were advocates of alterations in social customs which would involve a break with traditionally accepted patterns; they were those who, convinced themselves that altered ways of thinking and behaving were positive values, sought to convince others to modify or entirely transform their ways of life. Some changes that they advocated were minor, for example, elimination of an obnoxious caste regulation, and would have occurred in any case by the slow erosion of outworn customs; yet those changes often came sooner because of a vocal and influential vanguard which popularized them. Other changes were of major proportions, for example, the breakdown of the caste system itself, and were advocated by men who held a broad view of the welfare of Indian society and preached on themes of universal ethics and the potentialities of all human beings.

If this definition were extended, as it properly could be, to the sociological realm, social reformers might include all social innovators, who through necessity, opportunism, or real conviction adjusted their behavior or ideas so as better to adapt themselves to the new standards presented and sometimes enforced by British rule. This study does not, however, intend to probe that vast and complex aspect of modern Indian life known as social change. Among other omissions in the chapters which follow, very little attention is given to legal codes and their enforcement, unless the enactment of a law had an important relationship to the reform movement. Also, there is far less discussion of the Western-sponsored movements for social reform in India than their importance might justify. Indian, not Western, social reformers created the movement which is described in this study. Studies of economic changes and the spread of education, both of which inevitably caused social changes, are also omitted. In short, the social reform

---

[2] As late as 1903 the *Indian Social Reformer* (ISR) raised the question: who are the social reformers—all those who claimed to be, or only those who belonged to a social reform association? (March 8, 1903, p. 257.)

movement did not include all forces operating to produce social change; it was only one, distinct component of those forces.

As an intellectual phenomenon, whose behavioral consequences are difficult, if not impossible, to measure, the social reform movement in the 19th century was limited in its avowed leadership and most of its following to educated Indians. Educated men defined the ideals of reform, and those ideals accordingly reflected the particular needs and desires of their supporters. In India, social reform did not ordinarily mean a reorganization of the structure of society at large, as it did in the West, for the benefit of under-privileged social and economic classes. Instead it meant the infusion into the existing social structure of new ways of life and thought: the society would be preserved, while its members would be transformed. The accepted rationale of India's progress in modern times has been the idea of filtration of ideas and modes of behavior from the upper layers of society to the lower ones. Upper castes established the traditional social norms, and they were expected to act as the main purveyors of the reformed, modern ones. This essentially conservative and gradualist approach to social change was sincerely believed in by most of the social, as well as the political, reformers and was not adopted as an excuse for inaction. "The customs and institutions with which the social reformer proposes to deal," explained Chandavarkar, "are common to the higher classes of the Hindu society from whom the lower classes take their standard."[3] In fact, many of the social reform causes had almost no meaning for lower caste groups at the time that they were undertaken; they were efforts entirely devoted to adjusting the ideas and behavior of high-caste, educated men and their families to the requirements of the Western-ized culture which they desired to create for themselves.

By the beginning of the 20th century some reformers, stimulated by the ideas of a truly national awakening, were advocating the uplift of lower castes and outcasts and were repudiating the caste structure of society itself. The introduction of these ideas into the programs of the Hindu social reformers was a significant shift away from the earlier preoccupation with the advancement of individuals or restricted groups. The ideas of uplift and rehabili-

[3] N. G. Chandavarkar, *Speeches and Writings*, p. 54.

5

tation, when translated into practical action, often produced programs of a social service nature, and among Indians it was the social reformers who were chiefly responsible for inaugurating the social service movement.[4] The utopian idea of eliminating caste distinctions, reminiscent of the social messages of the medieval bhakti sects, however, could scarcely result in direct action comparable to the crusades for widow remarriage or even intercaste dining. No reformer suggested practical ways of eliminating the caste system as a whole, although many of them regarded it as the main cause of India's social ills.

During the 19th century, social, religious, and political reform movements represented the primary areas of creative intellectual endeavor for most educated Indians. Relationships between these three great reform movements were various and shifting, and a proper understanding of one of them requires knowledge of the others as well. The first chapter of this book presents some of the main features of the social revolt, both its intensity and the direction of its attack on existing society. Chapter II shows the linkage between social and religious reform and presents the argument that the social revolt and the social reform movement, which in many ways was the constructive side of the revolt, were unique in India's history, unlike other movements for social change of which records exist. Chapter III provides a summary of the early political reform movements in the three Presidencies as a background to political nationalism. It lays no claim to originality and is included chiefly as a reminder that political thought and organizations were not neglected areas of expression for educated Indians.

The discussion of the social reform movement, beginning with Chapter IV, is organized as a three-stage development during the century which ended with the First World War. These same three stages might emerge from studies of the development of Indian thought in areas other than social reform. The first stage, covered in Chapters IV and V, had its beginnings in the urge of

---

[4] "Social reform aims essentially at change—a change sometimes involving the basic values of a society, whereas social work [or service] primarily relates to welfare activities undertaken within the limits set by the existing values." *Social Welfare in India*, p. 4.

6

individuals to reshape their personal lives, in large measure in accordance with standards adopted from Western thought. The preoccupation with individual revolt and reform covered many decades and was marked by relatively slow development of organized movements. The first important evidence that this first stage, a new epoch in Indian intellectual history, had begun was the career (1815-1832) and subsequent influence of Rammohun Roy in Bengal. Roy's Brahmo Samaj established a standard for social reform movements in Bombay, Madras, and the Punjab, the most important of which rested firmly on religious reform premises.

Although Roy's ideas continued their attraction for Indian intellectuals throughout the century, a shift away from the individually oriented methods and scope of the Roy approach to reform began to take place in the 1880's. At that time, as individuals and small groups began to identify themselves with an Indian nation, the same methods and ethical ideals which prompted individual reform, methods and ideals still largely derived from the West, were applied to efforts to transform Indian society on a national basis. Simultaneously, the goal of national political advancement provided a secular basis for social reform which eliminated, for many Indians, the need to relate social to religious reformation.

Evidences that a new stage in India's intellectual life was emerging multiplied in the 1880's with the founding of the Indian National Congress (Chapter VI); Malabari's marriage reform crusade, the first all-India social reform movement (Chapter VII); and the establishment of the National Social Conference (Chapter VIII). The relationship of social reform to political reform in the context of nationalism was probably the most critical public issue during this stage of the social reform movement, and the decision reached about that relationship affected the future of both social and political reform in India (Chapter IX). The urge to unify for common purposes appeared also in the formation of subnational groups, such as provincial and caste organizations, and in the continued reform endeavors of the religious Samajes (Chapters X and XI). During this second stage, nationalism expressed the expectations of progress for the nation as well as the new desire for unity among scattered and culturally diverse individuals and groups. But those individuals and groups, with few exceptions imbued with Western ideas, were the self-appointed *representatives* of the nation, not the corporate nation itself, and their values were their own.

It might be argued that this second stage represents even today the spirit of Indian political life. But in the development of the social reform movement a third stage emerged during the latter part of the one-hundred-year period ending with the First World War. Corporate social values suited to the national society began to take precedence over the values of limited groups claiming to represent the nation, and Indian society (in fact, Hindu society), not transplanted Western society, was recognized as the proper vehicle for individual self-realization. An intellectual development was beginning in which social reform began to mean a regeneration of the traditional spirit of the nation—a regeneration, political as well as social, which was founded on religious revival. By the end of the third stage, criticism of society, frequently as harsh as in the earlier stages, was based on the failure of national social life to realize its own innate potentialities and not on its inferior performance in comparison to Western societies. Chapter XII describes the third stage.

Throughout these three stages, social reform ideas, the movement or movements embodying them, and the methods used by reformers reflected the intellectual temper of the age, and at the same time influenced contemporary thinking and the organized reform movements in the religious and political fields. Social reformers were never an isolated group, but were usually religious or political leaders as well. The integration of social, religious, and political changes by individuals and by society as a whole stands as a tribute to the versatility and adaptability of Indian minds and has made a crucial and unique contribution to the stability of the modern Indian nation.

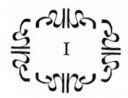

I

THE SOCIAL REVOLT IN

MODERN INDIA

INDIVIDUAL outrage against particular social customs and religious beliefs has always been a feature of Indian society, despite the high value that has always been placed on continuity, order, and the wisdom of social precedent. Long before modern times and Indian exposure to Western civilization, flexibility in customs, mobility in social relationships, and many cases of collective revolt against traditional social standards were already in existence in India. For a Hindu, an outright revolt could take the form of excluding oneself from normal social and religious requirements by adopting the role of a sannyasi, or wandering ascetic; caste laws then no longer applied, and unorthodoxy in religious beliefs and behavior was tolerated—or even revered, if it caught the popular imagination. Social and religious rebellions against the traditional authority of Brahmin priests and other high castes created new movements whose doctrines and practices differed from orthodox Hinduism; the medieval bhakti, or devotional, movements represented that form of rebellion, as did Sikhism in its early stages. Social revolts with more indirect impacts periodically emerged throughout India in the form of efforts to improve the positions of certain castes in their relations to other castes. Mobility within the caste system has always existed as a result of rebelliousness and a group's desire for change and betterment.

The special character of the 19th and 20th century revolt lay in this: much of it originated from secular motives based on rational-

9

istic critiques of society and led to secular, as well as religious, movements for social reform; it applied to all parts of India almost simultaneously; it gained the support of the political authority of the state, which resulted in legislation and administrative action; and finally, it persisted and, as a stated or implied premise of all nationalist thought, it succeeded in producing general Indian acceptance of the social ideals of the rebels—ideals which are in ascendancy today.

Indian criticisms of their own social practices and the religious beliefs which supported them was not a passing phase in response to Western rule. The suggestion of certain nationalist writers that those criticisms resulted from a temporary intoxication due to alien influences must be dismissed. Almost every Indian leader from Rammohun Roy to Jawaharlal Nehru frankly expressed at one time or another his dissatisfaction and even contempt for certain practices or failings among his own people. There have been periods when such ideas were acceptable or even laudable as evidence of a genuine concern for the welfare of the nation, and there have been times when a man risked censure and even bodily attack for expressing them. But never in the century preceding Independence was there so general and complete a tolerance of existing social conditions or so universal and unqualified a repudiation of the doctrines of reform that powerful voices were not being raised in favor of major social changes which would bring India into a closer approximation of modern society. Virtually all of the outstanding nationalist leaders who identified themselves with the revival of genuine Indian values in reaction against excessive Westernization were themselves endowed with Western training, from which the bulk of their aspirations for Indian society was derived. The vociferousness of the pleaders in behalf of traditional India could not conceal a great selectivity when they described the Indian society of traditional eras.

The beginnings of the 19th century social revolt, easily identified with the thought of Rammohun Roy (1772-1833), established the tone and substance of what was to follow. Roy vividly described the degraded state of society and acknowledged without embarrassment the virtues of Western learning, liberal legal and social institutions, and the Western social ethic. His revolt against living Hindu society and his appeal to Indians to purify their religion and reconstitute their social institutions echoed throughout the century after his death from the lips and pages of his followers, acknowledged or not, whose ideas were affected in some way by this "first modern Indian." Both Roy's proposal for a new Indian religious life and his assessment of the benefits of British rule rested on his conception of a renovated Indian society. It was impossible for him to envisage a reformed Indian religion unless it carried the message of social advancement, and both religious and social reform were prerequisites to any enhancement of India's political stature.

In a famous letter written in 1828, Roy stated his convictions on Indian political advance. "I regret to say," he wrote, "that the present system of religion adhered to by the Hindus is not well calculated to promote their political interest. The distinction of castes, introducing innumerable divisions and subdivisions among them has entirely deprived them of patriotic feeling, and the multitude of religious rites and ceremonies and the laws of purification have totally disqualified them from undertaking any difficult enterprise. . . . It is, I think, necessary that some change should take place in their religion, at least for the sake of their political advantage and social comfort."[1] Roy found "Hindus in general more superstitious and miserable, both in performance of their religious rites, and in their domestic concerns, than the rest of the known nations on the earth."[2] They were "with few exceptions, immersed in gross idolatry, and in belief of the most extravagant description respecting futurity, antiquity, and the miracles of their deities and saints."[3] Apart from the few, like himself, who could perceive the essential truth embedded in Vedic scriptures and separate that from the false accumulations of the ages, the great majority of Hindus accepted the literal teachings of idolatrous Brahmins, and "therefore continue, under the form of religious devotion, to practice a system which destroys, to the

[1] Rammohun Roy, *English Works* (J. C. Ghose, ed.), pp. 929-30.
[2] Letter to John Digby, *ibid.*, p. 929.
[3] From "An Appeal to the Christian Public in Defense of 'The Precepts of Jesus,' " *ibid.*, p. 559.

utmost degree, the natural texture of society, and prescribes crimes of the most heinous nature. . . ."[4]

Rammohun Roy's contributions to the making of modern India lay not only in his iconoclasm and in his intellectual evocations of the new era, but also in his practical work to reestablish the "natural texture of society." He founded the Brahmo Sabha (later Samaj) for the consolidation and spread of the religious tenets and forms of worship which he and a courageous group of followers held suited to India's heritage and contemporary needs. His own translations and abridgements of Hindu scriptures and the original religious writings from his pen became texts for the theistic movements which grew up in the decades to follow. Probably stimulated by evidence produced by the Christian missionaries of Serampore, in Bengal, on the extent of the practice of suttee,[5] Roy began a campaign in 1818 against that evil which culminated in a Government regulation prohibiting the custom in 1829. For Roy, English education was the portal opening the way to Indians to advance toward equality with Westerners, and he provided crucial support for private and governmental efforts to introduce higher education along European lines. He could not have been expected to inaugurate a political movement at a time when the government itself was hardly consolidated in the country. Nevertheless, his political writings on judicial reform, civil rights, the separation of administrative powers, freedom of the press, and other liberal doctrines, became standard works for the political reform movement one half century later.

In terms of practical endeavor the English-educated group of Bengalis following Roy failed even to maintain the momentum initiated by him except in the educational field, where they had the growing support of the government. But that diversified group, whether liberal or radical in politics,[6] Brahmos (i.e. Brahmo Samajists) or not in religion, were usually rebels in society. Most extreme were the students of the Hindu College at Calcutta who

[4] Preface to the "Katha Upanishad," *ibid.*, p. 45.

[5] *Sati* (Sanskrit) means a virtuous woman, or a faithful wife; it acquired the meaning of a widow who was cremated on the funeral pyre of her dead husband, in theory willingly; it also referred to the custom of widow-burning.

[6] See B. Majumdar, *History of Political Thought* . . . , for descriptions of those men.

"adopted an aggressive attitude to everything Hindu and openly defied the canons of their inherited religion, while some of them offended public opinion by their youthful exuberance, such as drinking to excess, flinging beef-bones into the houses of the orthodox, and parading the streets shouting 'we have eaten Mussalman bread.' Some of them embraced Christianity. . . ."[7] Reviewing that period, Satyavrata Mukerjee later wrote: "There was a rush for everything English, and English ideals dominated our lives and thoughts. . . . Irreligion was fearfully rampant. The Trinitarian orthodoxy of Christian bigotry as well as the exploded farrago of Hindu dogmatism were alike unsuited to the rationalist temper of the age. Immortality, licentiousness, riotous living were the order of the day. Denationalising emasculation was the prevailing characteristic. It was said of the new Bengalee of the age, that he delighted in wounding the religious susceptibilities of his countrymen, and 'in cutting his way to salvation through ham and beef and wading his way to liberalism through tumblers of beer.' "[8]

Bombay did not lag far behind Calcutta in producing young rebels, chiefly the products of the Elphinstone Institution, founded in 1827 to promote English education, on the model of the Hindu College. The Bombay Students' Literary and Scientific Society sponsored lectures, many of whose themes were as rebellious as those heard in Bengali student groups. One young speaker began by announcing: "My chief and most important object, is to denounce some of the most pernicious Customs of our people, particularly of the Hindus, my own section."[9] The Bombay social revolt, however, from those early years took a form which differed from the Bengal revolt. Despite proclamations of rebellion, secrecy in breaking caste laws and an outward guise of conformity with tradition marked the judiciousness of the Bombay approach to social dissent, in contrast to publicity-conscious Bengal, where

[7] K. A. N. Sastri, *History of India*, III, 368-69. See also "Derozio and Young Bengal," in A. Gupta, *Studies in the Bengal Renaissance*.

[8] S. Mukerjee, "Studies in Bengalee Literature I," *Hindustan Review*, May 1907, p. 480.

[9] Bhaskar Damodhar, Second Normal School Scholar, Elphinstone Institution; in "The Students' Miscellany . . . ," p. 8. Most of the speakers who followed were Parsis.

13

rebels and orthodox alike conspired to make every social deviation a notorious cause. As succeeding chapters show, Bombay's social revolt developed more surely than Bengal's into movements for general social reform.

By mid-century the social revolt spanned the subcontinent among English-educated men and made them receptive to the first social reform crusade with more than a local following. Pundit Ishwar Chandra Vidyasagar (1820-1891), a Bengali follower of Rammohun Roy, illuminated to all who could read or cared to listen the social state of Hindu widows, a subject which had received little or no attention from Roy. "Woman!" he wrote in 1856, "in India, thy lot is cast in misery!"[10] Indeed, the entire society seemed rotten to the reformer's sensitive perception: "How miserable is the present state of India! It was once known to nations as the land of virtue. But the blood dries up to think that it is now looked upon as the land of depravity. . . . From a view of its present degradation it is vain to look for a speedy reformation."[11] The crusade for emancipation of Indian women became the first tenet of the social reform movement everywhere in India. Their generally inferior status, their enforced seclusion, especially in Bengal and northern India, their extremely early marriage, and their lack of education everywhere were facts documented by Vidyasagar and reformers throughout the country. As higher educational opportunities expanded and hundreds of graduates found themselves without any feminine companionship on an intellectual level, the situation became intolerable, at least for some Indians, on personal, as well as abstract moral, grounds. The example of the educated and cultivated European wife suggested the direction in which Indians might direct their own women's progress. The Bombay Parsi, Framji Bomanji, whose community was one of the first to adopt Western modes of behavior, wrote in 1863: "We want the English language, English manners, and English behavior, for our wives and daughters; and until these are supplied, it is but just that the present gulf between the Englishman and the Indian should remain as wide as ever."[12]

[10] Vidyasagar, *Marriage of Hindu Widows*, p. 94. (See also Appendix 1 of this study.)

[11] *ibid.*, p. 93.   [12] Bomanji, *Lights and Shades of the East*, p. 94.

English education had virtually displaced traditional instruction in all important urban centers when the Universities of Calcutta, Bombay, and Madras were founded in 1857. Western ideas and ethical standards were spreading gradually throughout British India as the administrative and economic outposts of British influence grew into a network of culture contact points, and the Christian missionaries moved quietly into even remote regions. The opening of the Suez Canal in 1869 made personal connections with Britain and Europe comparatively easy for the wealthy or for those who could obtain sponsorship for their travel. Scores of men returned from England and hundreds of other vigorous Indians spread dissatisfaction with their society throughout the land. While concentrating their attacks on the treatment of women and on marriage customs, reformers took up other causes which their newly gained intellectual and social perspectives demanded: the anti-rational bases of many religious rituals; unjustifiable caste restrictions on inter-dining, diet, and overseas travel; malpractices in the management of temples and religiously sanctioned prostitution; the degrading treatment of low castes and untouchables; and infanticide. The Brahmo Samaj became a refuge for many men who needed the support of numbers or the sanction of religion for their reformed ideas and behavior. Other Samajes were established in Bombay, Madras, and the Punjab. But some reformers preferred to remain nominally Hindus while undertaking major changes in their personal lives.

In the second half of the century and in the decades when Indians were striving to create a nationalist movement, the social revolt grew in intensity and led to social reform endeavors which were based on an urgent concern for the progress of the nation. Keshub Chandra Sen (1838-1884), the leader of the Brahmo Samaj and its greatest missionary, dreamed of a great national awakening which would combine religious and social reform. Sen viewed contemporary Indian life with an eye common to many of his educated countrymen. "What we see around us today," he said, "is a fallen nation—a nation whose primitive greatness lies buried in ruins. Its national literature and science, its theology and philosophy, its industry and commerce, its social prosperity and domestic simplicity and sweetness, are almost numbered with

15

the things that were. As we survey the mournful and dismal scene of desolation—spiritual, social and intellectual—which spreads around us, we in vain try to recognize therein the land of Kalidas —the land of poetry, of science, and of civilization."[13] Sen's personal revolt and his constructive reforming efforts were the last of the great Bengali assertions of the religious and social needs of all Indians, until Vivekananda appeared at the end of the century. While Bengalis after 1880 appeared temporarily exhausted by the unsettling jolts to which their society had been subjected since Rammohun Roy, elsewhere educated men pressed the attack against social degeneracy and useless religious orthodoxy. Dayananda Saraswati (1824-1883) in northern India launched the most vigorous campaign against the Brahmin priesthood and the social customs which it supported that the 19th century witnessed in any part of the country, and the Arya Samaj was founded to continue his reformation.

In Bombay Presidency, especially in Poona, a school of thought developed with a constructive program for social and political advancement which dominated the course of the nationalist movement for several decades. Its beginnings were marked by social and religious criticism of a high intellectual caliber—unprejudiced, for the most part, by personalized philosophies of spiritual salvation. Sardar Gopal Hari Deshmukh, "Lokahitwadi" (1823-1892), almost matched Dayananda's vitriolic condemnations of the traditional Brahmin monopoly of education and religious life. As early as the 1840's he had written—in Marathi, not in English— that "The priests are very unholy because they repeat things without understanding their meaning and profanely reduce knowledge to such repetition. The Pundits are worse than priests, because they are more ignorant and also are haughty. . . . Who are the Brahmins and in what respects do they differ from us? Have they twenty hands and do we lack something in us? When such questions are now asked the Brahmins should give up their foolish concepts; they must accept that all men are equal and

[13] Sen, "The Improvement of Indian Women," in *Transactions of the Bengal Social Science Association,* quoted in McCully, *English Education and the Origins of Indian Nationalism,* pp. 251-52.

everybody has a right to acquire knowledge."[14] His attacks continued and were joined by the vigorous newspaper editor, Gopal Ganesh Agarkar (1857-1895), who also wrote in Marathi so that his words would have the greatest possible effect. Agarkar urged reason as the only proper guide to conduct and accepted the challenge of a minority faction at that time, led by Bal Gangadhar Tilak, which feared that social reform would weaken political nationalism. Calling attention to certain educated Indians who claimed that India's traditions were necessarily superior to all others, Agarkar wrote, "It is a shame that people like us whose eyes are open, who know that there are other countries beside India and who know that there exist great philosophies beside those found in Sanskrit books, should also become so narrow-minded and act like blind people."[15]

In the mainstream of the national social reform movement, whose course was defined in the 1880's in Bombay, were the Maharashtrian Brahmins, Mahadev Govind Ranade (1842-1901), Kashinath Trimbak Telang (1850-1893), Ramakrishna Gopal Bhandarkar (1837-1925), and Narayan Ganesh Chandavarkar (1855-1923). Ranade, considered a moderate reformer, provided the intellectual standard for social criticism which marked the proceedings of the National Social Conference. With an underlying moral concern reminiscent of Keshub Chandra Sen, he asked the Conference in 1893, "Are we or are we not conscious that many of us, under the narcotic influence of custom and usage, too often violate the feelings of our common human nature and our sense of right and wrong, stunt the growth of our higher life, and embitter the existence of many of those who depend on us . . . ? Are we prepared to point out any single hour of the day when we do not unconsciously commit injustice of a sort by the side of which municipal injustice is nothing, when we do not unconsciously sanction iniquities by the side of which the most oppressive tyrant's rule is mercy itself? . . . we should take due care to set our house in order, as no mere whitewashing and no plaster-

[14] Deshmukh, *A Collection of Essays* (in Marathi), pp. 44-45, quoted by D. K. Bedeker in a review for *Quest*, 1960.
[15] *Sampurna Agarkar*, 2, 72.

ing would remove these hidden sources of our weakness. The whole existence must be renovated. The baptism of fire and not of water must be gone through by those who seek a renovation of heart such as this."[16]

Four years later at the Twelfth Social Conference, Ranade again adopted the stern tone of moral outrage: "All admit that we have been deformed. We have lost our stature, we are bent in a hundred places, our eyes lust after forbidden things, our ears desire to hear scandals about our neighbors, our tongues lust to taste forbidden fruit, our hands itch for another man's property, our bowels are deranged with indigestible food. We cannot walk on our feet but require stilts or crutches. This is our present social policy, and now we want this deformity to be removed. . . ."[17] Telang echoed Ranade's judgments: "Our system is to a great extent become petrified . . . the moral conceptions which once informed it have long since vanished and . . . we are now hugging the mere outer shell."[18] Bhandarkar reduced many of society's ills to the absence of a "corporate consciousness." Sadly he admitted that " . . . we Indians are devoid of sympathy for our fellow creatures. Our benevolence is active where particular individuals have to be helped. Our feelings are stirred at the sight of individual human beings in distress. But we are devoid of the sense of public duty. . . . We cannot yet work with perseverance for objects that are to benefit not certain specific individuals, but the body public."[19] And Chandavarkar perhaps summed up the spirit of revolt: " . . . in all conscience, there is very little fun in the kind of death-in-life that we have been living for nearly two thousand years."[20]

The doctrines of social utility, societal evolution, and the inevitability of progress brought greater understanding of Indian social problems, but they also produced discouragement. When educated Indians examined the record of social advance since Rammohun Roy they usually found it barren of substantial signs of advancement. Clinging to the idea that the course of European progress

[16] Ranade, *Miscellaneous Writings*, pp. 124-25.
[17] *ibid.*, p. 196.
[18] Telang, *Selected Writings and Speeches*, II, 549.
[19] Bhandarkar, *Collected Works*, I, 479.
[20] Chandavarkar, *Speeches and Writings*, p. 97.

must also apply to India—the categories of social analysis laid down in the West were accepted as universal—Indians sought some explanation for the apparently halting pace of social progress in India. Some turned immediately to India's political subservience to explain its social backwardness, and when that explanation blinded a man to all other factors which might account for India's condition, then the social reform movement lost a supporter and political agitation (usually the extremist variety) gained one. Most leaders of the reform movement, however, had the courage not to resort to self-deception; instead they probed relentlessly into the causes of India's social plight.

The reasons for India's alleged decline had been set down by Rammohun Roy and Keshub Chandra Sen as false religion and by Dayananda Saraswati as the hypnotic control over society of corrupt Brahmins. The western Indian reformers, with fuller awareness of social processes, cited a variety of causes. "Now what have been the inward forms or ideas which have been hastening our decline during the past three thousand [sic] years?" asked Ranade. He replied: "These ideas may be briefly set forth as isolation, submission to outward force or power more than to the voice of inward conscience, perception of fictitious differences between men and men due to heredity and birth, passive acquiescence in civil wrongdoing, and a general indifference to secular well-being, almost bordering on fatalism."[21] Bhandarkar made constant reference to the caste system as the root of all India's ills, and Chandavarkar was inclined to agree. For the latter, caste, even in its Vedic, or "purified" form, was a formula for social disruption, weakness, and immorality. "It is not in discouraging union alone," he wrote, referring to India's perennial problem of unity, "that the baneful influence of caste morality has been felt. Even if a man be a liar, a forger, or a thief, or has been guilty of some offense affecting his moral character, or leads a life of vice, he remains a member of his caste provided he conforms to caste rules. His society has no punishment to mete to him, and he is as good for its purposes as the best of men. There is in fact no moral indignation felt when a man has been guilty of sin . . . so long as his act does

[21] *Miscellaneous Writings, op.cit.*, p. 192.

19

not come within the idea countenanced by society of sin. . . .
Public opinion has never been strong in cases where it ought to
be strong for the healthy growth of society; and the hypocrite
and the rake are tolerated, whereas however pure and moral a
man may be, he is done in the eyes of his caste, if he ventures to
break through one of its rules."[22] Thorough and reasoned denunciations of the caste system and appeals for the uplift of low
castes and outcastes were added to the enumerations of India's
social ills by most reformers toward the end of the century.

Acknowledgment of social ills, reformers realized, was only
half of the battle. What was urgently required to solve them was
a courageous determination to persist in great enterprises, a
quality that many saw lacking in Indian culture. Dr. Mahendra
Lal Sircar pointed to the audience at the 1890 Social Conference
in Calcutta and said, ". . . there you are—a race, degenerated, paralysed in all your energies."[23] G. Subramania Iyer, editor of the
Madras *Hindu*, cited the "law of life" which was "ceaseless activity,
perpetual struggle, rivalry, defeat or success," in an address in 1897.
But, he argued, Hindu sages have recommended "a condition of absolute quietude for individuals. Starvation of the external as well
as the internal senses, their severance from their respective objective relations, self-contemplation, quietude, and nirvana. . . ."
Whatever value that condition may have for individuals, "no community has yet reached that higher plane where nirvana is the goal.
Nor do we, Hindus of modern days, aspire for it. We cherish an
aspiration to rise to the same level of material and moral condition
as other nations. We feel humiliated at our poverty, at our helpless-
ness, at our defeats. . . ."[24] Bhandarkar, who was never optimistic
about the success of reform in his own day, concluded in 1893
that "The half-hearted and lethargic manner in which all our
movements, political, social, religious and economical or industrial,
are conducted and the fact that we do not find a succession of
resolute or zealous workers in connection with them show that
the new civilization with which we have come into contact has
not, except in very rare cases, produced more than a skin-deep

[22] *Speeches and Writings, op.cit.*, pp. 208-09.
[23] Chintamani, *Indian Social Reform*, III, 141.
[24] *ibid.*, IV, 344-45.

improvement in us."[25] And C.Y. Chintamani, a Madras reformer and editor, criticized his countrymen's desire for repose and willingness to let others do the work. He tried to stir some activity into his readers by placing before them the example of Teddy Roosevelt and his "strenuous life."[26]

There was no doubt in the minds of the social rebels and reformers of the 19th century, with the notable exception of Dayananda Saraswati, that their dissatisfaction and their ideals of progress were the direct result of India's contacts with the West, especially with Britain. That contact, it must be emphasized, was not with a civilization which merely excelled in material prosperity, physical resources, and human vigor; but one which itself was experiencing in the 19th century a far-reaching social reformation, based on political reforms and economic changes, which excited Europeans and Americans with its revolutionary implications no less than it did Indians. Among the early reformers, the fact that they placed heavy reliance on the inspiration of the West presented no serious obstacle to their social criticisms or their advocacy of alien ethical and social doctrines. Like Rammohun Roy, Keshub Chandra Sen regarded India's contact with Christian civilization as the surest means of its moral regeneration. British rule, the agency of that contact, Sen felt, should thus be considered a chapter "of ecclesiastical history." "The book which treats of the moral, social, and religious advancement of our great country with the help of Western science, under the paternal rule of the British nation, is indeed a sacred book. . . . Who can deny that Victoria is an instrument in the hands of Providence to elevate this degraded country in the scale of nations. . . ." He advised his educated countrymen "to be loyal to the British Government, that came to your rescue, as God's ambassador, when your country was sunk in ignorance and superstition and hopeless jejuneness, and has since lifted you to your present high position."[27]

Ranade looked with favor on the "disciplining process" which he found characteristic of British rule and which he hoped would create in Indians "love of order and regulated authority," love of

---

[25] *Collected Works, op.cit.,* I, 468.
[26] "The Strenuous Life," in *The Voice of Progress,* I, 7, 3-7.
[27] Speech of March 3, 1877. K. C. Sen, *Lectures in India,* I, 323-24.

"municipal freedom, science and research, adventurous discovery," as well as "aptitudes for mechanical skills, and chivalrous respect for womankind." He concluded that "Neither the old Hindu nor the old Mahomedan civilisation was in a condition to train these virtues in a way to bring up the races of India on a level with those of Western Europe, and so the work of education had to be renewed, and it has been going on for the past century and more under the *pax brittanica* with results—which all of us are witness to in ourselves."[28] Chandavarkar was equally frank in stating his preferences for the Western social order: "The progress of the Western nations, more especially of the Anglo-Saxon race, marks the lines on which the progress of our own country should be directed. The Hindu civilisation based on the ancient Aryan institutions is doomed."[29]

In an illuminating analysis of the impact of British rule on Indian society Dewan Narendra Nath, President of the Lahore Social Conference in 1893, cited the almost unprecedented confrontation of two great civilizations, in a relationship of ruler and ruled, one he called "progressive" and the other "defunct and stationary." He observed the immense difficulties in the transferring of ideas and institutions from the one to the other. India was "not a barbarous nation" and therefore could not easily give up its rich and complex culture: "we have not only to put on a new garb but to take off the old one as well." With assurance that Western ideas and customs would ultimately prevail in India, Narendra Nath proceeded to explain that intellectual acceptance of Western ideas did not imply ease in adopting them in practice. "A foreigner is astounded, when an intelligent Hindu who is able to talk with sense and ability on all the topics of the day, declines to accept a cup of tea from him. . . . The Hindu understands that abstinence from eating and drinking with foreigners is a practice which should be abandoned. . . . [But] the foreigner has no idea of the fate which awaits his friend for breaking his caste rules. To the Hindu it means excommunication or social death—nothing short of a kind of martyrdom. . . . Excommunication or cessation of commensality and intermarriage is a punishment quite unknown

[28] *Miscellaneous Writings, op.cit.*, p. 226.
[29] *Indian Social Reform, op.cit.*, I, 112.

22

in the West, and the European has no idea of the moral courage which a Hindu requires in order to break his caste rules."[30]

The struggle required to adopt "reformed" customs, much more difficult than the intellectual acceptance of new ideas, was a persistent theme in the literature and speeches on social reform. The south Indian, Professor M. Rangachariar of the Madras Hindu Association, wrote in the early 20th century, "It must be within the every-day experience of every man, who has to any appreciable extent received Western education in India, that moment after moment he is slowly building up his own life as the result of a continuous struggle going on within him between the old and the new."[31] Vamanrao Madhav Kolhatkar, a social reformer in the Central Provinces, contrasted the popularity and support given to those who worked for political reform to the "jeer and ridicule" directed at the social reformers, "which frightens away many a man who would otherwise willingly work for the cause we have at heart." Whereas, he pointed out, most public figures must bear criticism from the outside, the reformers "have to meet and face . . . opposition proceeding from our own dear and near ones— parents, wives, daughters, sisters, brothers, neighbors, friends and countrymen—with whom we have to journey in this pilgrimage of life. . . ."[32] A British resident noted, "A Hindu reformer may preach anything he likes without necessarily incurring any censure, but no sooner he carries out his theories into practice, out he goes from his community. The Brahmo is more of an outcaste in the eyes of his neighbors than is the Christian in South India, who keeps caste."[33]

The sanction of active social disapproval of variations in established customs, often backed by religious censure from Brahmin priests, was so painful to experience or even to anticipate that many devoted reformers hesitated or back-tracked in the face of it. Gopal Hari Deshmukh, despite the vigor of his attacks against Brahmin priests, submitted to their demand that he go through a penance

[30] *ibid.*, III, 152-54.
[31] B. Subba Row Pantulu, *Hindu Social Progress*, p. 78.
[32] *Indian Social Reform, op.cit.*, III, 197-98.
[33] Alfred Nundy, "A Silent Revolution in India," *East and West*, II, 996-1,007.

ceremony, including taking *prāyaścitta*,[34] for having attended the remarriage of a Hindu widow. Deshmukh's reasons for doing penance illustrated the problem: his daughter's mother-in-law threatened to obtain a new wife for her son if the reformer did not submit to social and religious requirements.[35] Not only were the social reformers singled out for their violations of orthodox behavior, but anyone, notably an English-educated man, might be made to suffer for his infractions of caste regulations and established norms. When Surendranath Banerjea returned from England in 1871 the orthodox ban on overseas travel was still firm, and, in his words, "the whole attitude of Hindu society, of the rank and file, was one of unqualified disapproval. My family was practically outcasted. We were among the highest of Brahmins; but those who used to eat and drink with us on ceremonial occasions stopped all intercourse and refused to invite us."[36] Lokamanya Tilak, whose stated devotion to orthodoxy often conflicted with his reformed behavior, in 1891 attended a tea party given by Christian missionaries and was forced thereafter to take *prāyaścitta*.

Toward the end of the century overt acknowledgments of the superiority of Western social customs, if not Western religious and ethical ideals, were decreasingly apparent in the speeches and writings of the reformers. Uncertainty about how much of the Western example should be followed had plagued many Indians for nearly a century, causing in some of them psychological dilemmas which could not be resolved. Trying to hold on to domestic values and foreign ways of life simultaneously could be a discomfiting and unsettling experience. The ideas of nationalism forced most Indians around the turn of the century to modify their receptivity to Western ideas, at least on the surface, because excessive Westernization began to be ridiculed and condemned as unpatriotic. The return to native intellectual resources—never more than a partial return for most nationalists—stimulated the reformers' efforts to find traditional shastric, scriptural, justifications for their doctrines. Indeed, discovery of sacred literary authorizations for

[34] A penance for having offended against religious customs, involving imbibing (sometimes symbolically) five products of the cow.

[35] *Indian Social Reform, op.cit.*, I, 306.

[36] Banerjea, *A Nation in the Making*, p. 25.

reformed customs, though never free from challenge, gave some relief to those who had regarded the conflict between Indian and Western values as irreconcilable.

But in no sense did a transfer of allegiance from Western to Indian social and ethical ideals result in increased satisfaction or complacency among reformers. The cultural and religious revival which began in the late 19th century did not mark the end of the social revolt. In some ways—especially by the reintroduction of religious doctrines into the social reform movement, from which they had been virtually eliminated during the secular nationalist period of the 1880's and 1890's—revivalism added an urgency to the need for reform which rationalism had not instilled. India's essential spirit had been smothered by the centuries' accumulation of the refuse of degraded customs and untruths, and Indians must restore *it,* the reformers argued, not build afresh on alien foundations. Not an evolutionary progress toward a new society based on "social efficiency," but a regeneration of purified Hindu society based on a spiritual revival should occur at once.

The revered exponent of those ideas in their most forceful form was Swami Vivekananda, who felt wounded when he witnessed the malaise of his own society and would not remain mute in deference to his listeners' patriotic sensibilities. Personally above any suspicion of short-selling Indian culture in order to gain temporary advantages from an adherence to Western ways, Vivekananda wrote perhaps the most biting, articulate, and bitter condemnations in recent times of the physical misery and misguided beliefs of most Indians. Against images of the palaces of old India and the beauty of the natural environment, Vivekananda described the condition of his people: "Moving about here and there emaciated figures of young and old in tattered rags, whose faces bear deep-cut lines of the despair and poverty of hundreds of years; cows, bullocks, buffaloes common everywhere—aye, the same melancholy look in their eyes, the same feeble physique; on the wayside, refuse and dirt;—this is our present day India! Worn-out huts by the very side of palaces, piles of refuse in the near proximity of temples, the Sunnyasin clad with only a little loin cloth, walking by the gorgeously dressed, the pitiful gaze of lustreless eyes of the hunger-stricken at the well-fed and the amply-provided;—this is our native land! Devastation by violent plague and cholera; malaria eating into the very vitals of the nation; starvation and semi-starvation as second nature; death-like famine often dancing its tragic dance; . . . A conglomeration of three hundred million souls, resembling men only in appearance;—crushed out of life by being down-trodden by their own people and foreign nations . . . ;—without any hope, without any past, without any future;— . . . of a malicious nature befitting a slave, to whom the prosperity of their fellowman is unbearable;— . . . licking the dust of the feet of the strong, withal dealing a death-blow to those who are comparatively weak;—full of ugly, diabolical superstitions which come naturally to those who are weak, and hopeless of the future;—without any standard of morality as their backbone;—three hundred millions of souls such as these are swarming on the body of India, like so many worms on a rotten, stinking carcass;—this is the picture concerning us, which naturally presents itself to the English official!"[37]

Vivekananda attributed much of his country's tragedy to the hopeless quest of the Hindu for mukti, or release from worldly experience. With sarcasm he said to his people, "You cannot feed your own family, or dole out food to two of your fellowmen, you cannot do even an ordinary piece of work for the common good, in harmony with others, and you are running after *Mukti*."[38] He exhorted against inactivity and the doctrine of harmless passivity, which he said gave Europeans an advantage over Indians. "Always of active habits," he said of Europeans, "being possessed of a tremendous Rajasika [aggressive] nature, they are gathering with great enterprise and youthful ardour the comforts and luxuries of the different countries of the world, and enjoying them to their heart's content. And we are sitting in a corner, with our little bags and baggages, pondering on death day and night, and singing, 'Very tremulous and unsteady is the water on the lotus-leaf, so is the life of man frail and transient,' with the result that it is making our blood run cold and our flesh creep with the fear of Yama, the god of death. . . ."[39] For the Swami, the problem of

[37] Vivekananda, *The East and the West*, pp. 1-2. Vivekananda could see his country as an outsider might, but he also knew that such a view did not penetrate beneath the surface of Indian life.
[38] *ibid.*, p. 9.   [39] *ibid.*, p. 16.

India was too much religion and religion of the wrong kind. Referring to the reduction of religion to social regulations, he caustically observed, "There is a danger of our religion getting into the kitchen. We are neither Vedantists, most of us now, nor Pauranics, nor Tantrics. We are just 'don't touchists.' Our religion is in the kitchen. Our God is in the cooking-pot, and our religion is 'Don't touch me, I am holy.' If this goes on for another century, every one of us will be in a lunatic asylum."[40]

With the possible exception of Mahatma Gandhi no recent Indian leader has dared to voice as strongly as Vivekananda the depth of feeling aroused in many Indians by the ignorance and misery of millions of their countrymen. Political leaders and social reformers would have been classed as dangerous revolutionaries if their hatred of the status quo had been couched in such extreme terms. Indians regarded Vivekananda as one filled with superior spiritual power and sympathy with the distresses of mundane existence, and they thus expected that he would speak out as he did. But most of them could not accept him as a practical leader, partly because his constructive program for national regeneration was never fully formulated and partly because Vivekananda brought no political gospel, as Gandhi did later—with results in recruiting followers which have never been equalled in India.

Vivekananda's thought marked the culmination of the 19th century social revolt. Suitably for India it was a culmination expressed in religious terms, which carried the criticisms of judicious reformers and sensitive poets into a fulmination of ecstatic outrage that the power of man's soul should be debased by the wretchedness of his bodily existence. The challenge Vivekananda presented to Indians to reform totally their religious and social life was not accepted, because on the one hand it called for too great a self-sacrifice from the still complacent educated and privileged groups, and on the other hand demanded an uprooting of traditional customs and beliefs unacceptable to the general populace. But the authority of his criticisms of society and the spiritual inspiration of his reforming message gave many others increased courage to advocate social progress at a time when nationalism urged the priority of political agitation.

[40] Vivekananda, *India and Her Problems*, p. 23.

27

II

THE UNIQUENESS OF THE SOCIAL

REFORM MOVEMENT

THE practical ethical concern underlying Vivekananda's message to Indians to rebel against the evils of their society and establish a new life based on human freedom and the opportunity for individual fulfillment exemplified the unique character of the 19th and 20th century social reform movement. Vivekananda announced himself as an adherent of the advaita, non-dualist, philosophy of Vedanta, which directs men's attention to the essential oneness of all things and the desirability of release from sensed experience through mukti, or moksha, an escape from the bonds of maya.[1] Vedanta has often been criticized by Indians as a system of thought which denies the importance of mundane existence and hence of social morality, and the argument still continues over the question of whether or not that philosophical system does or does not admit of an ethical component.[2] But whatever position might be taken in that argument, the outstanding impression that Vivekananda made on his followers was not his adherence to a classical Hindu school of thought but his reinterpretation of ancient wisdom in order to meet actively the needs of contemporary Indian life. He argued that "Adwaita alone is morality," because it postulated the oneness of God and man; "Know through Adwaita that whom-

[1] Maya is the metaphysical principle understood as the delusion that the empirically perceived world, not pure-consciousness, Atman, is the true reality.

[2] See, e.g., the exhaustive treatment of that question in S. Radhakrishnan, *Eastern Religions and Western Thought*, Chap. III, "Mysticism and Ethics in Hindu Thought."

ever you hurt you hurt yourself" was for him an ethical imperative of prime importance in the mundane world. But he acknowledged that such a command and its positive counterpart, to immerse oneself in altruistic and socially constructive work, had not produced a society which could solve its basic social and material needs. Instead, "Adwaita has only been worked on the spiritual plane, and that was all; now the time has come when you have to make it practical," he told a Lahore audience in 1897. To make the novel point still clearer, Vivekananda informed his listeners that "as practical Vedantists the Europeans are better than we are."[3]

The Western example of a society embodying certain religious or spiritual ideals in its secular life, which Vivekananda observed during lengthy visits in the United States and England, stimulated his undertaking of practical reform in India. Other reformers from the time of Rammohun Roy responded in a similar manner to the West; most of them, unlike Vivekananda, acknowledged not only the inspiration they received from the observable operation of Western society but also the Western source of many of the ideals whose realization they desired for India. The common reaction of social reformers to Western society and Western ideals was responsible for the uniqueness of their movement in 19th and 20th century India, separated it from other movements for revision of Indian religious and social life, and established its place in the mainstream of modern Indian intellectual development.

Dissociated from that mainstream of development during the modern period notable men with missions of reform and inspiration for Hindus at large continued to appear from within the richly diverse popular Hindu tradition. As Nirmal Kumar Bose wrote about Bengal, "Behind all the changes which had affected Bengal's life in the eighteenth and nineteenth centuries, there was an undercurrent of religious tradition which had perhaps continued uninterrupted, as a living reality, in the hearts of a succession of poets and saints who belonged exclusively to the simple, and almost unlettered, majority of the rural population. This was true not only of Bengal but of India as a whole. . . ."[4] Whether in

---

[3] Vivekananda, *Speeches and Writings*, pp. 453, 455-56.

[4] Bose, "Modern Bengal" in *Man in India* (reprinted by Center for South Asian Studies, Berkeley, 1959), p. 49.

modern or in medieval times much of that tradition and most of those religious men formed the living testament to the spirit of bhakti, the devotional side of Hinduism which makes possible its religious, in contrast to its philosophical, appeal. "Bhakti consists in firm and overwhelming affection for God with a full sense of His greatness; through this alone can there be emancipation."[5]

It has been maintained that devotion to God is premised on the distinction between God and the worshipper, without which religion has no meaning.[6] Because Vedanta, the dominant philosophical school of Hinduism, postulated the essential oneness of God and man, it "offers to man no real object of religious affection, neither does it present to him any Being to whom he can pray."[7] Man's need for prayer and for the assurance that there is more than an impersonal, unreachable, and indescribable Force governing the universe inevitably produced the devotional, or bhakti, movements among Hindus, even as their philosophers surged onward into the ineffable areas of pure speculation where the existence of a personal divinity was vehemently denied or disdainfully ignored.[8] The theme of conflict and nonreconciliation between the nondualist and dualist positions in Hindu thought is ancient and ever-present in religious literature. An example is the following abhang (hymn) of Tukaram, the most popular and revered of the Maratha bhakti saints, whose abhangs provided many of the hymns used by the reformist Prarthana Samaj. Tukaram sang thus of the nondualist, advaita, doctrine and his own worship of God:

> Advait contents me not, but dear to me
> The service of thy feet.
> O grant me this reward! To sing of thee
> To me how sweet!

[5] Surendranath Dasgupta, *A History of Indian Philosophy*, 4, p. 347.
[6] Henry Haigh, *Leading Ideas of Hinduism*, p. 100.
[7] *ibid.*, p. 103.
[8] This is not to suggest that all schools of thought premised on bhakti conceived of the relationship of God to man in identical ways. Almost every gradation between pure monism and complete dualism can be found in the writings that supported devotional religious teachings. Even the advaita Vedanta philosophy had a religious manifestation with temple worship based on bhakti, but of course this involved some compromise in practice with the pure advaita (nondualistic) doctrine.

UNIQUENESS OF THE MOVEMENT

Setting us twain, lover and Lord, apart,
This joy to me display.
Grant it to Tuka—Lord of all thou art—
Some day, some day.[9]

Furthermore (Vivekananda's assertion of the morality inherent in the advaita doctrine notwithstanding), because the Vedanta philosophy designated ignorance, rather than sin, as the root of man's troubles, it failed to provide a meaningful moral guide for the majority of men, whose experience was with human will and emotion and not with intellect. Ethics, as Sarvepalli Radhakrishnan observed, "presuppose the separatist view of life. When we transcend it, we get beyond ethical laws."[10] If one holds the monistic view that transcendent Reality, or God, is all that exists, good and evil as understood in human society have no ultimate meaning. Although Radhakrishnan and others have pointed out that the advaita Vedanta philosophy and other monistic Hindu systems of thought left a place for mundane moral laws,[11] there is little doubt that religious beliefs upholding the dualistic view of the world provide a stronger support for ethics, based on a sense of ultimate good and evil, righteousness and sin. Thus, the so-called bhakti sects, or cults, really the religious substance of popular Hinduism in medieval and in modern times, provided

[9] "Advaiti to majhe nahi samadhana," translated by Nicol Macnicol in his *Psalms of Maratha Saints*, p. 68.

[10] *Eastern Religions . . . , op.cit.*, pp. 103-04.

[11] *ibid.*, p. 104. Dasgupta has taken a position on the Bhagavad Gita "diametrically opposite" to that of the Vedantist, Sankara, who argued that in the Gita earthly moral duties have no real significance for the wise man. Dasgupta, *op.cit.*, II, 438. Nevertheless, after an illuminating disquisition on the ethics of the Gita (*ibid.*, pp. 493-514), Dasgupta finally admits that the "Gita does not believe in the objective truth of virtue or vice. . . . There is nothing good or bad in the actions themselves." Therefore, only deference to established caste duties provide a Hindu who follows the Gita's teachings with a sense of moral obligation, *ibid.*, p. 522. In a brilliant exposé of the fundamental difference between Indian and Western philosophy in terms of the priorities of the ultimate values of freedom and morality, Karl H. Potter writes that "the ultimate value recognized by classical Hinduism in its most sophisticated sources is not morality but freedom, not rational self-control in the interests of the community's welfare but complete control over one's environment. . . ." Potter, *Presuppositions of India's Philosophies*, p. 3.

both a divine object for spiritual veneration and emotional devotion, and a religious sanction for morality.

In various ways and in differing degrees, the bhakti movements set forth in their scriptures ideas of religious and social reform. Among bhakti saints the reform in religious practices perhaps most generally subscribed to was a renunciation of idolatry, more accurately an assertion that God was not embodied in a material object. Along with that reform was often coupled the proclamation of man's direct access to the divine spirit, without any mediation by priests, who were supported in their claims to be venerated by their management of idols. The great north Indian poet-saint of the 15th century, Kabir, preached,

> There is nothing but water at the holy bathing places;
> And I know that they are useless, for I have bathed in them.
> The images are all lifeless, they cannot speak;
> I know, for I have cried aloud to them.[12]

The Bengali Vaishnava bhakta, Sankara Dev, in the same century also ridiculed idol worship; his most famous disciple, Madhava Dev, at one time proclaimed that, "To seek spiritual purgation in sacred waters, to believe divinity dwelling in idols, these ideas are never entertained by Vaishnavas. He who harbors these is worse than a cow, says Krishna."[13] A further doctrine of bhakti movements was a conception of the divinity as one, not many. Monotheism was the only premise compatible with the idea of salvation through a search for God.

The conviction that bhakti could provide personal salvation for anyone gave dignity and position to all classes of people who had been debarred from religious enlightenment and full participation in religious life under orthodox Brahmanism. As social reformers, the great bhakti saints preached fervently against caste exclusiveness and against the subjugation of women. Namdev, the 14th century Maharashtrian bhakta, sang,

> Or high or low my birth may be;
> Still, Hari, I would worship thee![14]

[12] *North Indian Saints*, p. 18.
[13] *Chaitanya to Vivekananda: Lives of the Saints of the Vaishnavism of Bengal*, p. 51.
[14] *Psalms of Maratha Saints*, op.cit., p. 44.

And Jnanesvar a century earlier in Maharashtra preached that God's grace could descend "alike upon the monarch and the thrall."[15] Ramananda, in the 14th century, and Kabir, his disciple, offered the possibility of direct spiritual contact between a devotee and his God, eliminating the mediation of a priest, and stressed the brotherhood of all worshippers. Ramananda urged, "Let no one ask a man's caste or with whom he eats. If a man is devoted to Hari, he becomes Hari's own."[16] Chaitanya, the late 15th century founder of a Vaishnava sect of major proportions in Bengal, also ignored caste distinctions, and his devotionalism was accessible even to the lowest classes.[17] On the matter of women's status, the great bhaktas were not as clear and consistent as on the question of caste. Women were sometimes placed in the degenerate category of temptresses against whom men should guard themselves. Women devotees, however, were generally admitted even to the inner ranks of disciples of most of the bhakti saints; in purely spiritual terms women were often acknowledged equal to men.[18] The use of vernaculars, rather than Sanskrit, in all the bhakti movements opened for the first time to women in general, as to low castes, the portals to the Hindu religious heritage.

But citing the bhakti movements' social messages does not answer the question posed by an Indian scholar, "How was it that, in spite of the great democratic Bhakti Movement which swept all over India during the pre-British period and which attacked the caste system and elevated the position of women, India's social life as well as the status of women, at the time of British advent, stood on a low level?"[19] Since Rammohun Roy thoughtful Indian writers have tried to provide answers to such queries, which arose from the discrepancies they observed between the lofty ideals in Hindu scriptures and the religious and social life among Hindus at large. To the question above three suggestive replies were offered by the questioner herself: 1. The

[15] *ibid.*, p. 45.
[16] *North Indian Saints*, p. 3.
[17] See M. T. Kennedy, *The Chaitanya Movement: A Study of the Vaishnavism of Bengal*, pp. 56-58, 82.
[18] See Neera Desai, *Woman in Modern India*, II, "Impact of Bhakti Movement on the Status of Indian Women," especially pp. 40-41.
[19] *ibid.*, p. 44.

bhakti movements fostered equality only in the religious sphere, not in secular life. 2. Although criticizing certain social practices the movements offered "no alternative program of social and economic reorganization of Indian society." And, she added, "In fact their appeal was emotional rather than rational. They felt the unreality of caste and they appealed to the people for equality in the emotional songs, but they could not argue it out on rational principles."[20] 3. The movements never built up organizations which could carry out any positive social program, even if they had had one; at best, they produced individual, not collective, opposition to the status quo.

A further explanation for the failure of the bhakti sects to effect any significant social changes was suggested by W. B. Patwardhan in reference to the movements in Maharashtra. It was their flexibility of doctrine and tolerance of opposition which prevented them from becoming practical instruments of revolt and change. "The fact is," wrote Patwardhan, "that the saints of the *bhakti* school were of a pacific turn of mind and did not love controversy or contest. I may go still further and say that is the frame of mind of Maharashtra. The people of Maharashtra are imbued with a spirit of conciliation, of quiet resignation and catholic toleration. ... We Marathas ... lack the conviction that we alone are in the right and all the rest of the world is in the wrong. Consequently we are very rarely fired with the fury of the fanatic. Being the eloquent embodiment of the peace-loving spirit of Maharashtra, the saints of the *bhakti* school have always been eager to reconcile the conflicting systems. ... Their principle was the principle of conciliation. ..." And further, "The *bhakti* school neither started as a revolt against nor aimed at the demolition of any established system. It has been the special feature of all Indian movements in the past—and especially Maratha movements—that they assimilated more than discarded. They disarmed opposition and contest by assimilation."[21]

[20] *ibid.*, p. 45.
[21] Patwardhan in *Fergusson College Magazine* (Poona) Feb. 1919, p. 142; and *ibid.*, July 1919, pp. 33-34. Quoted in J. Nelson Fraser and J. F. Edwardes, *The Life and Teaching of Tukaram*, p. 161. Patwardhan might be challenged for his generalized view of the Maharashtrian character as passive, if only by noting that

Evidence of the effects of bhakti movements on social relations has probably not been systematically collected. It appears certain that at festivals and pilgrimages where a bhakti saint's teachings were the focus of attention, social barriers against low castes and women were temporarily ignored. But were social customs regulating ordinary life permanently altered by attitudes transformed after occasional exposure to religious teachers or impressive ceremonies? M.G. Ranade thought that they were, at least in Maharashtra. He held that the effect of about fifty saints flourishing over a period of five hundred years in western India was one of loosening the grip of the caste system on Hindu society.[22] But many would disagree with his views. N.R. Phatak, a Bombay scholar and biographer of Gokhale, believes that the Maharashtrian saints preaching caste equality and other social messages had negligible effects on social customs; their influence was restricted to "devotional matters."[23] As for Bengali Vaishnavism, the social message of Chaitanya appeared to have produced no permanent liberalization of Hindu social organization. Bipin Chandra Pal, who was raised in a devout Vaishnava family, described the Vaishnava movement in Bengal in the 1870's and 1880's as "then under a cloud. Brahmanism had literally devoured the Vaishnavic cult and culture. People had little knowledge and less appreciation of the lofty social idealism and humanism of the message of the Mahaprabhu [great saint]."[24] Indeed, according to him, Vaishnavic literature "had reduced piety to erotic excitement and materially contributed to the physical and moral deterioration of the race."[25] Vaishnavas in Bengal even before the 19th century seemed to be either high caste Hindus who ignored

---

violence has been a feature of political agitation in that area at least since the nationalist attacks of the 1890's.

[22] Ranade, *Rise of the Maratha Power*, Chap. VIII, esp. p. 155.

[23] A view expressed in conversation with the author in Bombay, July 4, 1960.

[24] Pal, *Memories of My Life and Times*, I, 244.

[25] The Brahmo Samaj, according to Pal, had tried, but had "not clearly brought out the message of social uplift and emancipation of Shree Chaitanya and Bengal Vaishnavism." (*ibid.*, p. 245) Surendranath Banerjea did so in a famous lecture in which he showed Chaitanya as a prophet of social reform. A neo-Vaishnavic movement appeared among educated Bengalis in Pal's time, led by Sisirkumar Ghose and Kedar Nath Dutt Bhaktivinode and stressing Chaitanya's social message.

Chaitanya's social teachings, because they had no practical use for them, or lower caste men who upheld the social ideal of equality in an effort to improve their own status. Some of the more throroughgoing Vaishnavas who "adopted the rules of life promulgated by the early Vaishnava teachers who succeeded Chaitanya, came soon to be regarded as practically beyond the pale of respectable Hindu society. They became a class of Bohemians in the country, whose manners and customs necessarily had little or no influence upon the general community."[26] A somewhat similar characterization might be made of some of the followers of Kabir, the Kabirpanthis of northern India.[27]

Generalizing for the whole of India, B.B. Misra, the author of a recent work on the growth of the Indian middle classes, has observed that his study led him "to a conclusion that although popular forces like Jainism, Buddhism, or devotional cults tried to break the orthodoxy of the Karma-ordained and caste-ridden Hindu society, they could not leave a lasting impression. [Such forces for change] were in fact assimilated by the established Brahmanical order except in modern times when the growth of capitalism and English education created new classes . . . who brought their political influence and power to effect liberal reforms and changes. . . . Western education and modern economic development became the basis of change in India, not India's own tradition. . . ."[28]

Perhaps it is unfair to hold the bhakti movements accountable for not achieving results that were never a central part of their aims. Social reform was peripheral to the reconstitution of religious beliefs. Chaitanya, for example, was not concerned with the reform of Hindu society, and in certain of his preaching he reinforced the existing structure of authority when it did not conflict directly with his religious ideas. Like that of most other bhaktas, Chaitanya's "sole interest was religion, and it is only as his religious ex-

<hr>

[26] S. Tattvabhushan, *Social Reform in Bengal,* pp. 39-40. With this general analysis Pal also agreed, *op.cit.,* p. 357.

[27] See H. H. Wilson, *Religious Sects of The Hindus,* p. 39. Corroborating evidence showing the failure of bhakti sects in the Vaishnava tradition to effect social changes in Hindu society at large was made available in this work by Wilson, who wrote in the first half of the 19th century.

[28] In Selig Harrison, ed., *India and the United States,* p. 223.

perience, and that engendered by him among others, came into conflict with the Hindu social system that he can be called a social reformer. His social reform, so-called, was only a by-product of his bhakti."[29] But it was not the primacy of spiritual concerns alone that caused the bhakti movements to fail in the transformation of social life; religious movements have been known to overturn social structures. Most bhakti sects, like other Hindu religious movements, leaned toward mysticism, as a method of spiritual revelation, and thus often encouraged a drawing away from worldly concerns. Individual salvation, not the salvation of society or the group, was the reason for and the result of the religious quest through mysticism. N.G. Chandavarkar emphasized this point when he wrote, "The prophets and preachers of the Bhakti School have inspiration of the right sort in their teachings to fill us with healthy ideas of holiness; but they have somehow been interpreted by the people to have taught that man's mission on this Earth is to neglect the world, believe in fate and lead a life of asceticism."[30]

In discussing "the mystical outlook" as it affected Indian social life, D.P. Mukerji posed a question similar to the one cited earlier. Mukerji wrote of the mystic bhaktas: "Perhaps their democratic strength was over-estimated, otherwise why did their doctrines become esoteric and their sects merge into the Hindu fold?" His answer was that "The mystic revolution, in the absence of a fundamental change of the Indian social economy, was bound to be a mirror revolution." In India lasting social change had to be brought about by influences other than the traditional religion, because traditional religious spirit was predominantly mystic in its inspiration and in its continuing manifestations. Mukerji argued that such influences were secular ones which were brought into

[29] *The Chaitanya Movement . . .* , *op.cit.*, pp. 56-57. Further substantiation of this point is to be found in Thomas J. Hopkins, "Vaishnavism, Bhakti, and the Hindu Social System," an unpublished paper written at Yale in 1958. Hopkins, "The Vaishnava Bhakti Movement in the *Bhagavata Purana*" (Ph.D. thesis, Yale 1961), demonstrates that the scriptural source of the bhakti movement relegated social matters to a position secondary to religious experience. The *Bhagavata*, Hopkins concludes, makes no attempt to define a clear-cut social position comparable to its statement of religious doctrine (p. 15).
[30] Chandavarkar, *Speeches and Writings*, p. 42.

India by the British. "By the British rule the very basis of the Indian social economy has been changed." The British gave to India something which was never offered by Hindu religious leaders, an observable, functioning, and successful "alternative to her native systems."[31] Mukerji was only partly right in implying that the impact of the British was merely economic and social; for there were also the profound religious and intellectual alternatives which were presented to India by the West.

Traditional Reform in the 19th Century

Records exist for certain Hindu movements of protest of the traditional type flourishing in the 19th century which indicate the contrast in inspiration and influence between them and the Western-inspired religious and social reform movements. Initiated by diverse, yet typical, Hindu reformers manifesting the spirit of bhakti, their relationships to the mainstream of the modern social reform movement deserves at least a passing notice.

The Swami Narayana sect of Gujarat was a puritanical move-

[31] Dhurjati Prasad Mukerji, *Modern Indian Culture,* pp. 16, 23-24. Before judging the effectiveness of the "mystic revolution," Mukerji provided this summary of the mystic bhakti sects' attempts to change Hindu life: "They revolted against idolatry, the tyranny of caste and creed and the mechanics of ritualism. ... They were opposed—some practiced their opposition—to the barren asceticism of the Vedantist. They bridged the gulf between the communities, the Hindu and the Muslim, and made them one in faith, lives and deeds. Their acts and sayings are the final answer to the communalists and the Imperialists [in a religious sense] of today. They abolished the purdah among their disciples and recognized women's rights to illumination. ... Some of the mystic sects even permitted free selection of companions, separation and widow remarriage. Temples had no sanctity for them; the heart was the temple, and its keys were love and intuition. ... Priestcraft was sought to be avoided; it could have no place in a scheme of direct contact, unison, and intuitive comprehension. In the early stages, the head of the sect would often be selected by spiritual merit and rotation, irrespective of caste, creed and sex; later on, he would be hereditary. An important result was the modification of the rigidity of Brahmanical culture and aridness of its logomachy. The heyday of mysticism marked the beginning of the end of theological scholarship. From many points of view, the mystics' was an anti-intellectual movement. Positively, they released the Indian spirit for a fresh spurt of creative activity in the sphere of emotional disciplines." (*ibid.,* pp. 17-18). Yet Mukerji concluded his chapter on "The Mystical Outlook" with this judgment: "The present position of mysticism as an agency of social change is a hopeless one." (*ibid.,* p. 29)

ment founded by a famous bhakta who took that name—his original name was Gyanshyama. He was also known as Swami Sahajanand. A contemporary of Rammohun Roy, the Swami was born in 1781 and died about 1830. His departure from his Brahmin family at an early age, his wanderings and searches for a guru, or spiritual guide, his final success in locating an ascetic worthy of following (Swami Ramananda), his bodily and spiritual experimentations—all of this closely resembled the early career of Dayananda Saraswati, founder of the Arya Samaj.[32] The differences between the two men as religious leaders and reformers appeared only in their mature years when their respective teachings and organizational methods diverged widely. Swami Narayana never provided an exegetical exposition of theology in any way comparable to Dayananda's, and his influence rested therefore on personal example, parables and brief statements of faith, and the legendary luster of his personality. With a fervent faith in his special relationship to a theistic God, he encouraged his followers to regard him as an incarnation of the Divine, comparable to Krishna. Although typically tolerant of different faiths, Swami Narayana made two exceptions and attacked vigorously the monistic teaching of Sankara and the atheism of the Jain religion, whose stronghold was in Gujarat. His conception of God was simple in the extreme: "He is the Creator, Preserver and Sustainer of the Universe. He is the one who gives the reward for good as well as evil deeds, and He is also the Savior of those who trust themselves to His care. He incarnates Himself out of His infinite mercy again and again in history, and faith in the Incarnate One brings grace and salvation."[33]

The Swami offered a moral code which sought to rid the Vaishnavism of his day of many of its lax or vicious practices[34] and guide the faithful into righteous personal lives. Instead of

[32] See the full account of Swami Narayana's life in Manilal C. Parekh, *Sri Swami Narayana*. See Chapter v of this study for a discussion of Dayananda Saraswati.

[33] *Sri Swami Narayana*, op.cit., p. 230.

[34] All reforming sects in India have been concerned with similar religious malpractices: sexual license under the guise of religious ceremonies, fraudulent religious mendicancy, gross superstition and faith in magic, self-torture in order to gain religious merit, and excessive ritualism.

laying down universal moral prescriptions, however, Swami Narayana limited his code to his own followers, gathered into a Satsang, or Holy Fellowship, led by a disciplined group of sadhus, religious ascetics. The first duty of a Satsangi was to follow the com-
mands of the leader of the movement; then followed belief in God
and the requirements of pure community life, which included
strict observance of caste exclusiveness and rules of personal conduct and diet. Like other bhakti movements, the Swami Narayana
sect welcomed Shudras and untouchables, although it excluded
them from contacts with higher caste followers—except at yearly
conventions of the Satsang, where lower castes and untouchables
were temporarily accepted as equals. The Swami was "in no sense
a social revolutionary";[35] he did not set out to subvert the Hindu
social order. But he led campaigns against infanticide and against
suttee, and he urged better treatment for widows.[36] He was not
content to ignore lower castes, untouchables, and tribals and did his
part in the historic process of aryanization[37] by propagating among
them Brahmanic rules of diet (abstention from meat and alcohol)
and conduct (a "pure life" in place of lawlessness, adultery, tolerance of physical uncleanliness, and so forth). Swami Narayana's
social reform doctrine was based on humanitarianism and the religious premise of the equal accessibility of salvation to all, through
bhakti.

It is convenient to contrast the Swami Narayana sect with the
Arya Samaj because Dayananda Saraswati himself challenged
the teachings and practices of the Swami Narayanas, which he
found flourishing in Gujarat in the 1870's. He condemned the
idolatry, temple worship, pilgrimages and other religious practices of the sect and wrote a refutation of its beliefs.[38] In broad
terms, the differences between the Swami Narayana sect and the

[35] *ibid.*, p. 282.
[36] See Appendix 1 of this study which gives his regulations for widows, in
order to judge what "better treatment" meant.
[37] Or Sanskritization, the indoctrination of Indians outside the main Brahmanic
tradition with the ideas and practices associated with the Sanskrit scriptures.
[38] Dayananda's tract, "Swami Narayana Matkhandan," published in 1875, was
noted in Sarda, *Life of Dayanand Saraswati*, pp. 128, 491-92. In 1877 Monier-
Williams estimated the numbers of Swami Narayanas at between 150,000 and
200,000. See his *Hinduism*, p. 101.

Arya Samaj represented the sharp contrasts between traditional and modern Hindu religious and social reform movements. One sought to purge Hinduism of its degenerate forms by a rededication to God in the bhakti spirit; the other sought purification of beliefs as well as practices by establishing virtually a new religion, the Vedic Faith, based on a reasoned interpretation of the Vedas. One ignored the challenges to Hindu faith embodied in Christianity, Islam and Western knowledge; the other met all those challenges and set up a systematic creed that could accommodate scientific knowledge and thus appealed to English-educated men and women. Swami Narayana wanted to establish a regional cult limited to the scope of his personal contacts; Dayananda had a universal religion in mind but concentrated first on unifying and strengthening the entire Aryan nation. The former organized his following under the leadership of sadhus; the latter organized the Arya Samaj using Western-educated secular leadership and set up a legal body to administer his estate and carry out his program. In social reform the Swami Narayanas made few amendments in social practices, and those were based on a mild humanitarianism; the Arya Samaj replaced the existing Hindu dharma with a completely renovated Vedic dharma, which incorporated all the major reforms upheld in Western-educated circles.

Another religious reformer in the 19th century was Mahatma Ramalingam (1823-1874) of the Tamil country.[39] Born into a Shaivite family, Ramalingam gained recognition for his religious poetry in the bhakti mode when he was young. From a deep compassion for all human beings, he sung of the miseries of the world and preached against the injustices of the caste system and the unequal treatment of women. At one time he wrote, "Master of the Spirit, thou hast taught me thus: 'All the treatises upon the four-fold castes and orders of life are but child's play. They know naught that regard the caste superiority and the colour of the skin.' . . . O King of cosmic dance that is manifest to raise to the higher place those that have risen above the confusion of

[39] The following summary is taken from Shuddhananda Bharati, *Mahatma Ramalingam and His Revelations* and an article, "The Message of Ramalingaswami," in *The Hindu* (Madras), May 1, 1960.

caste and colour, be pleased to wear my garland!"[40] And again, more vehemently, "After manuring the dry fields, at the opportune hour, with the book-rubbish of ignorant caste-principles, after throwing into the pit and burying under earth all the confusing customs of the sectarian creeds, faiths, religions and orders, Thou has made me play [sic] . . . on the way of Thy Beatific Light."[41]

Ramalingam did not organize a sect, although he had a small body of disciples, the Sanmarga Sangha. After his death, allegedly by miraculous disappearance, his preachings continued to be taught at several institutions which he founded in Vadalur, in the South Arcot district of Madras: a school, a charity house, and a meeting house. Some of the luster surrounding Ramalingam was transferred to the Theosophical Society after Madame Blavatsky, one of its founders, claimed that the Swami had prophesied her coming to India with a message of Universal Brotherhood. The Swami's social influence, if any, was typically transient. His bitter outbursts against social injustices and malpractices were followed by no systematic efforts to alter men's behavior, much less the institutions of society which determined that behavior.

In contrast to the meek and nonascetic figure of Ramalingam in the south was a mystic of dynamic force in Bengal, Sri Ramakrishna Paramahansa (1833-1886). The details of his life have been recorded so often[42] that one need stress here merely his relationship to the social reform movement. His fame as a mystic was spread abroad by Keshub Chandra Sen, who met him in 1866, ten years after Ramakrishna had become a priest at the Kali temple in Dakshineswar, near Calcutta. Ramakrishna's worship of Kali quickly took on yogic form, and the worshipper frequently fell into trances which alarmed those about him by their duration and intensity. He claimed to have had visions of the Divine Mother, Kali, as well as of Christ; he himself took on the forms of worshippers of various faiths. At one time he seemed to be a normal, reasoning man, at another a being whose "spirit was a furnace whose leaping flames were the Gods."[43] Apparently, he could

---

[40] *Mahatma Ramalingam, op.cit.*, pp. 80-81.   [41] *ibid.*, pp. 81-82.

[42] See, e.g., Romain Rolland, *The Life of Ramakrishna*; F. Max Müller, *Ramakrishna: His Life and Sayings*.

[43] *The Life of Ramakrishna, op.cit.*, p. 41.

never completely reconcile his intellectual conviction of the truth of the advaita philosophy, bolstered by his experiences of oneness with the divine in the state of samadhi (mystic ecstasy), with the sincerity of his worldly devotion, bhakti, to God.[44] The impact of his life on his followers in later generations was that of one devoted to God and to the salvation of men. "Jiva is Shiva," he said; all living beings are God. "Who then dare talk of showing mercy to them? not mercy, but service, service, for man must be regarded as God!"[45] His compassion for suffering humanity, as much as his spiritual excesses, inspired those who listened to him and followed his teachings.

But compassion, rooted in the mystic revelation of the oneness of all men in the divine spirit, was the closest that Ramakrishna came to what was a recognized motive for social reform in the 19th century. Of practical measures for social amelioration he apparently had nothing to recommend, though he instructed his followers to care for their families' physical needs before attempting to renounce the material world—a definite break with the Hindu tradition of renunciation without thought of family duties. His example was clear proof of the shallowness and deception of rituals and customs, but he thought little of purifying Hinduism in the manner of Rammohun or Dayananda.[46] A natural extension of his beliefs and teachings would have been some efforts to lead

[44] His experience was that "one instant's contact with the Infinite is sufficient to make the Illusion of all 'differentiated' egos, our own and other men's, disappear immediately. But Ramakrishna expressly maintains that it is absurd to pretend that the world is unreal so long as we form part of it. . . ." Rolland, *op.cit.*, p. 70. The religious example that he set for his followers was that of a bhakta, and F. Max Müller considered him "much more" of a worshipper, or lover of the deity than a jnanin or knower of God. See Müller's *Rammohun to Ramakrishna*, p. 158.

[45] *The Life of Ramakrishna, op.cit.*, p. 92.

[46] On meeting Dayananda, Ramakrishna recognized in him some divine inspiration, but in Rolland's apt words, "the tortured and torturing character [of Dayananda], the bellicose athleticism of the champion of the Vedas, his feverish insistence that he alone was in the right, and therefore had the right to impose his will, were all blots on his mission in Ramakrishna's eyes. He saw him day and night disputing concerning the Scriptures, twisting their meaning, and striving at all costs to found a new sect. But such preoccupation with personal and worldly success sullied the true love of God, and so he turned away from Dayananda." *The Life of Ramakrishna, op.cit.*, p. 164.

others away from the popular beliefs and customs which kept them from the spiritual realization that Ramakrishna knew was possible. But for him devotion to God had become full knowledge of God, and the consuming effect of that experience—which he did not recommend to his followers in general—focused his concentration upon himself and the small group surrounding him and away from affairs outside. Such has often been the outcome of the greatest religious experiences of Hindus.[47] Furthermore, the direct knowledge of God's immanence in the world as well as in man denied to Ramakrishna that awareness of evil which, in varying degrees, gripped many bhaktas and pervaded their social messages. The practical moralist, Dayananda, might have cried, "O ye false Vedantism!", as he often did in criticism of the mystic, world-denying aspects of Hinduism. Nevertheless, through Ramakrishna's alter ego, Swami Vivekananda, and other lesser followers, the spirit of Ramakrishna, which was not ego-centered out of selfish need but out of uncontrollable religious passion, was carried into the sphere of deeds and good works, as a later chapter will show.

Ramakrishna's impact on Bengali thought has been immeasurable, and he has been credited with assisting in large part the growth of national (in this sense, Hindu) self-consciousness. His influence on social reform after his death in 1886, was a curious mixture of traditional and modern ideas. The great majority of his close followers were liberal, middle-class, educated men[48] who transformed the compassion of a mystic bhakta into programs of social betterment organized on modern lines. The Ramakrishna Math and Mission fully established by 1897 and legally registered in 1909, has the dual purpose of contemplation and social action.

[47] In an interview with Kristodas Pal, editor of the *Hindu Patriot*, who argued that social service and education, not renunciation, were India's greatest present needs, Ramakrishna stated, "How do you dare to talk of *helping* the world? The Lord will look to it . . . [feeding the poor, treating the sick, etc.]. These are good deeds, no doubt, but how trifling in comparison with the vastness of the universe! . . . God alone can look after the world. Let a man first realize Him." *Life of Sri Ramakrishna*, pp. 313-14.

[48] Rolland lists and describes twenty-five of them, many of whom were Brahmos. See also H. and U. Mukherjee, *The Growth of Nationalism in India*, p. 71.

In its first aspect it was inspired by the tradition of mysticism and devotion, in the second by Western philanthropy and social welfare work. The amalgam has worked, a tribute to the Indian ability to combine diverse inheritances with undogmatic ease, to the intellectual comfort and practical benefit of everyone involved.

But what of those who have not been directly involved? A contemporary scholar has made this estimate (perhaps unsympathetically, but not inaccurately) of Ramakrishna's effect on Indian society: "No petulant aversion from Western materialism, no sophisticated defense on rationalistic grounds, no intellectual pride of heritage ever dictated his spirituality. In him no snobbish attempts at equality with the powerful nations of the West by fictitious claims for religious superiority, no dissent, *qua* dissent, no rehash of Comte, Mill and Hamilton, no loss of breath in trying to keep pace with the progress of the world, but just the undefiled source and the clear vision of an illiterate priest, crude, raw, unmodern and the commonest of the common. He came from the people, he smelt of the earth, and he talked like the peasant. . . . He respected women, in the only way open to Indians, by calling them 'mother,' and avoiding them. He would not perform the daily rituals. He would allow non-Brahmins to be initiated. . . . Yet, and this is the tragedy of the situation, with all the help of the dynamic personality of Swami Vivekananda, Paramahansa Deb's [Ramakrishna's] influence has not succeeded in shaking our social foundations. A number of people have been inspired, no doubt, but the masses have not trembled in their sleep."[49]

Ignoring for the present the later developments of the movement begun by Ramakrishna, the immediate effect that his ideas had on his followers in terms of social reform were in essence synonymous with those of Swami Narayana and Mahatma Ramalingam. These three recent Hindu bhaktas were much closer in inspiration, character, and message to the traditional saints of the pre-modern period than to any of the religious leaders of the modern Westernized reform movements.[50]

[49] *Modern Indian Culture, op.cit.,* p. 28.

[50] In 1915 Farquhar cited evidence that certain modern, i.e. Western, procedures were being adopted by some traditional Hindu religious sects. Such nontraditional methods as holding conferences and discussions, producing religious litera-

The Stimulation for Modern Social Reform

The inspiration and the human compassion of Hindu bhaktas on occasions enriched 19th century social reform movements, but those movements were in no sense the products of the bhakti spirit, nor did they function primarily in the spirit of religious devotion. The social reform movements began with individual revolts against existing customs, took shape under the influence of Western methods of organization and propagation, and recruited their supporters from men who were English-educated or who had imbibed Western ideas indirectly. Some of the social doctrines underlying the movements were not unlike the ideals to be found in the multifarious living body of Hindu thought—the spiritual equality of men and women and people of different castes, the injustices arising from economic exploitation, the cruelty of suttee and infanticide, and the absurdities of many religious rituals. The premises upon which the modern social reform movements rested their doctrines, however, included not only humanitarianism and the spiritual equality of all people, but also the Western ideas of individualism, natural rights, the ethical duties of an individual to society at large, the possibility of human progress, "social efficiency," and the religious doctrine of acquiring merit through good works. Although a few reformers accepted some of those ideas on faith, most of them used reason as their standard of judgment, a Western approach to ethical principles. Some or all of those Western-inspired ideas, coupled with organizational devices derived from European and American patterns, were the distinguishing features of the modern social reform movements, observable in their methods of operation and in the writings and speeches of their leaders.

Of those aspects of the Western impact on India which had prominent effects in stimulating the social reform movement,

---

ture for general distribution, and raising educational foundations, were indications of Western influences on already established sects, such as the Madhvas, Chaitanyas, Sri Vaishnavas, and Lingayats. But adoption of these techniques of strengthening organizations did not necessarily imply a Westernized approach to religious or social problems or an involvement in social reform activities. See Farquhar, *Modern Religious Movements in India*, pp. 291-308.

two stood out with remarkable consistency during the period up to the First World War; they were the main vehicles which transmitted to Indians the ideas and procedures characterizing the movement. The first was English education, which Chandavarkar once noted was "accomplishing silently what no law could have accomplished—unsettling people's minds, raising controversies ... and thus forwarding the cause of social progress."[51] The social reform movement was uniquely a result of English education; its leadership was almost entirely drawn from men formally or informally exposed to it.

Western ideas, transmitted through English education or by other means, cannot be ranked in any order by their effectiveness in stimulating Indian dissatisfaction with their traditions or attachment to the doctrines of reform. Several ideas achieved such prestige among the intellectual group of reformers, however, that there should be no doubt about their influence. Rammohun Roy was one of the first Indians to expound the idea of a rationally ordered society along lines suggested by Jeremy Bentham and James Mill.[52] Utilitarianism, as such, never received support from Roy or the later reformers, but the Utilitarian arguments for increasing social contentment, for purging society of unnecessary customs and traditions, and for human rights based on a reasoned inquiry into the nature of man, appeared in Indian writings for the rest of the century.[53] The works of John Stuart Mill, James' son, were particularly impressive to Indians. His political writings, *On Liberty* (1859), an essay in which he showed that social tyranny

[51] *Speeches and Writings, op.cit.*, p. 17. See also R. C. Majumdar, *Glimpses of Bengal in the Nineteenth Century*, p. 21, for an acknowledgment of English education as the main source of the "remarkable transformation" which took place in Bengal in the 19th century.

[52] Roy met Bentham in London in 1831 but was acquainted earlier with his works and those of James Mill, which included the compendious *History of India* (1817).

[53] The effect of Utilitarianism on British administrators in India has been shown in Eric Stokes, *English Utilitarians and India*. Educated Indians and the British in India, it must be remembered, were molded in much the same intellectual tradition by having gone through similar educational systems. Much of the intellectual interplay between them, at least until the First World War, was governed by the mental rules and the philosophical assumptions that they shared.

might be more oppressive even than political subjugation, and *Considerations on Representative Government* (1861), were as influential among educated Indians as they were among Europeans. Of special importance to social reformers was Mill's *Subjection of Women* (1869) from which arguments in favor of female equality were often taken almost verbatim. It was perhaps through Mill also that Indians became aware of the philosophy of Comte; Mill's *Aug. Comte and Positivism* was published in 1865. Comte's ideas received great attention in Indian circles, in particular his "scientific" approach to the problems of critical social changes brought about by the disorganization of traditional ways of life, and his effort to discover "the laws of progress." In Comte's analysis of progress the key was said to be moral development, leading to altruism and thus social endeavor for common ends; in turn, moral development had to depend upon religion. Such an analysis, with references to Comte, frequently appeared in the writings and speeches of Indian reformers. Comte, furthermore, was as insistent as was Mill on the absolute necessity of women's equality, which was the keystone of all social reformers' creeds.

Underlying the substance of those philosophies was the principle that reason, rather than tradition or authority, should determine ethical norms and define human relations. As in Europe during the Enlightenment, so in India in the 19th century, acceptance of that principle released men's minds for an objective look at society and aroused excited speculation and inquiry into possible new ways of organizing social life. In intellectual terms, that new freedom to evaluate the foundations of social institutions marked the beginning of India's modern development. The contrast between traditional Hindu thought on the origin and nature of ethics and Western ideas on that subject was vividly presented by Sir P.S. Sivaswamy Aiyer: "The one great difference . . . between Greek and modern thought on the one hand and Hindu thought on the other is that the Hindu is satisfied with tracing the origin of rules to some text of scripture or some authoritative tradition and does not press home the question as to the rational basis of the rule. He is satisfied with an appeal to authority and does not believe that mere unfettered intellectual reasoning can furnish guidance in matters of morality."[54] The modern spirit of inquiry into ethics has never reached the bulk of the Indian population. Nevertheless, the acceptance of reason as a guide to individual conduct and social policies was acknowledged by the educated leaders of India in the early decades of the 19th century. Western rationalism had found a new home.

The Western writers just mentioned and many others of lesser fame provided inspiration to Indians by their idealism and their arguments in support of human rights and the good society. As 19th century thought began to face the realities of India's condition, idealism waned, discouragement set in, and impatiently some men turned away from their modest efforts to reform society through education, and toward political activity. It has often been noted that Indian political agitators were frequently men frustrated in their hopes for success in the civil service; it should be added that some of them were frustrated social reformers who turned to politics because the rate of advance there appeared more likely to be swift. Those Indians who remained true to the ideals of the reformer found inspiration in the writings of Herbert Spencer, who was concerned more with the process than with the ends of social change. Spencer's ideas of evolution as applied to human society showed that change in social institutions was a "natural" process, that it could be guided by men, that no violent breaks with the past were called for, and that ultimate progress was a certainty. However microscopic, India's advance in the 19th century was under way, according to Spencerian analysis, and the evolution toward a more individualistic, freer society was progressing despite all set-backs. Spencer's thought assumed an important place in late 19th century social reformers' estimates of the course of change that Indian society was then experiencing. The earlier expectations or hopes that change might occur all at once and with the suddenness of a religious conversion gave way to the more encouraging (in view of the slowness of visible prog-

[54] Aiyer, *Evolution of Hindu Moral Ideas*, pp. 7-8. Ethical discussions, in the Hindu tradition, wrote Aiyer, ceased with the texts of the Dharmashastras, which, in any case, were not philosophical works. "There have been no systematic treatises on the theory of ethics in Sanskrit literature," according to this author (p. 16).

49

ress) and perhaps less frightening picture of evolutionary development working along the lines of least resistance.

A close associate of many 19th century Indian intellectuals,
S.K. Ratcliffe, testified to Spencer's immense influence on Indians,
as well as on British civil servants in India.[55] Another British
resident in India recalled his surprise, when he first settled in the
country, at finding "how entirely the minds of educated Indians
had become obsessed by Herbert Spencer's doctrines, and what
implicit faith they placed in them, as though they were quite infallible." Spencer's exposition of the doctrine of evolution "appeared to sum up, for English-educated Indians at the time, the
whole trend of modern science, and to explain both the origin
of the universe and the history of mankind."[56] The "scientific"
approach to social change appeared to 19th century Indians as
a plausible doctrine, which explained how changes which they
regarded as necessary were also inevitable, if Indian society was to
survive. Reformers often warned their listeners that Indian society
had to meet the standards of "social efficiency" in order to be fit
for survival.[57] Spencer's writings were translated into the major
Indian languages, so that they reached an audience larger than
the English-educated class. The *Indian Social Reformer* wrote, "In
the history of Indian social reform—when it comes to be written—
the pages that will be devoted to the influence of Mr. Spencer cannot be pages of indiscriminate panegyric . . . his picture of the
social organism—first the blade, then the ear, then the full corn in
the ear—had the greatest charm to the Indian mind, prone to take
delight in contemplating consequences detached and isolated beyond the mind and vision from their actual and natural causes."[58]
The typical text of a major address on social reform questions in
the last decades of the 19th century included references to Spencer
or his school of thought; quotations from his writings began to
supplant citations from the Hindu scriptures in support of reform

[55] Ratcliffe, "Herbert Spencer and Asia," *Hindustan Review*, XIX, 209-14.

[56] Andrews, *Zaka Ullah of Delhi*, pp. 82-83.

[57] See, e.g. R.G. Bhandarkar in C.Y. Chintamani, *Indian Social Reform*, III,
188-89.

[58] Editorial, Dec. 13, 1903, p. 171. See also article by "Artaxerxes" on "Herbert
Spencer" in *East and West*, III, pp. 1-13, also showing his influence on contemporary Indian thinking.

measures. Spencer, however, proved to be a two-edged blade. Anti-reformers could quote Spencer's admonitions against overly rapid changes, which might bring social chaos, while advocates of only moderate reform measures could rely on "flowing with the tide," assured of the inevitability of progress.

The second, and it might be successfully argued the major, stimulus to social reform in India during the 19th century was the work and the ideas of Christian missionaries, a fact acknowledged by many reformers and sometimes cited by their opponents in order to weaken the case for reform. Western writers, missionaries in particular, have often made this point, with appropriate evidence gathered from their personal experiences. A recent student of Indian reform movements, Ronald W. Scott, carefully concluded that modern Indian religious and social reform has been, in large part, a response to the ethical challenges of Christian doctrine and to the "conception of human personality as expressed primarily in the Christian religion."[59] Some Indian writers of the present century, particularly those under the influence of certain nationalist ideas, do not fully subscribe to any position giving preeminent place to Christianity as a force in India for moral advancement. But Indians who were immersed in the social and intellectual reform movements of the 19th century, or who have studied their origins, provided a convincing record of the positive effects of the Christian missionary enterprises.

Nirmal Kumar Bose wrote recently of his bewilderment when he studied late 18th century Bengal, where "abuses and degradation . . . choked the life of the individual from all directions, unless he secured an escape in religious retirement from the burden and temptations of life." He indicated his surprise that "the moral poverty and cultural degeneration were not adequately felt," and concluded that "It required the challenge of Christian missionary activity to rouse Bengal from her slumber. . . ."[60] Rammohun Roy, caught in the milieu which Bose described, wrote in his *Precepts of Jesus*: "This simple code of religion and of morality is so admirably calculated to elevate man's ideas to high and liberal notion of one God, . . . and is so well fitted to regulate the conduct of the

[59] Scott, *Social Ethics in Modern Hinduism*, p. 18.
[60] Bose, *op.cit.*, p. 27.

human race in the discharge of their various duties to God, to themselves and to society, that I cannot but hope for the best effects from its promulgation in its present form."[61] Many social reformers of succeeding generations gave comparable acknowledgments of the effects on their thinking of Christian ideas. Debendranath Tagore of the Brahmo Samaj gave particular tribute to the missionaries for their example in educational work. They were founding schools "in every town and every village," he wrote, "whereas we [Brahmo Samajists] have not got a single good school of our own where our children can be taught."[62] N.G. Chandavarkar in the 1890's spoke as follows: "It is, I know, the fashion in some quarters to cry down the Missionary. . . . If today there is an awakening among us on the subject of religion and society, that is a great deal due to the light brought by him. . . . To the Christian Missionary . . . is due to a great extent the credit of the religious and social awakening of which the school of 'Hindoo Protestantism' of the present day is the fruit. . . . Christ, too, was a Bhakta, and the law of love which he preached has been the cardinal principle of the Bhakti School. . . ."[63] On another occasion Chandavarkar reported that he and his associates in the National Social Conference, K.T. Telang and M.G. Ranade, all read the Bible.[64]

Accounting for the origins of social reform work in Maharashtra, J.G. Joglekar gave major credit to the example of the missionaries. "The missions suggested collective compassion instead of individual charity," he wrote.[65] And Anjilvel V. Matthew, an Indian Christian, discussing the origins of social work in the same region, reported that "Missionary institutions, though their number has not been large in comparison with the total requirements of the country, have always been looked upon as models even by those who do not approve of the religious motive that lies behind their social service activities."[66] Missionary influences in the south Indian Telegu country were of equally great importance.

[61] *Raja Ram Mohun Roy*, pp. 15-16.
[62] *Autobiography of Maharshi Devendranath Tagore*, p. 99.
[63] *Speeches and Writings*, op.cit., pp. 43-45.
[64] *ibid.*, p. 331.
[65] Joglekar, "Evolution of Social Life and Ideals in Maharashtra During the 19th century and After" (M.A. thesis, Bombay Univ.), pp. 97-98.
[66] Matthew, *Bhaurao Patil*, p. 27.

One late 19th century observer wrote: "It is a noted fact that the bulk of the educated Telegu men who were inclined to take part in the progressive movements within the last forty years or so, mostly came from mission institutions as students. . . . It was Christianity that almost for the first time in the history of the country brought the people to a consciousness of their own backwardness and degeneration. . . ."[67] In the Punjab, Lajpat Rai (the Arya Samaj leader) took pride in the social work of the Samaj and noted that "there is now a network of social service agencies throughout India, due mainly to the contact of the East with the West, and to the example of Christian missionary enterprise. Ancient India had no use for these organizations, as social life was differently constituted; but modern India cannot do without them. . . ."[68]

The constructive social impact of missionaries was not always the result of their ability to convince Indians of the value of Christian labors. The Arya Samaj, for example, went forth consciously to compete with missionaries in reform and educational activities in order to cut down what it considered a dangerous rate of conversions to Christianity. Many lesser known religious and social reform associations were formed in part to counteract the influence of Christianity. K. Natarajan, the famous editor of the *Indian Social Reformer*, was reported as admitting that "The fear of the Christian missionary has been the beginning of much social wisdom among us."[69]

The activities of Christian missionaries and their supporters in England had another, though only indirect, impact on Indian reformers. The insistent prodding of the missionaries on the Indian Government to enact social legislation established precedents and a pattern of agitation which reformers, beginning with Roy's campaign against suttee, used to good advantage. The missionary enterprises in India were centers of vigorous social reform propaganda and often prepared documented cases of the need for reform through legislation that the Indian reformers later adopted

[67] Gurunadhan, *Viresalingam Pantulu: The Founder of Telegu Public Life*, p. 128.
[68] Rai, *The Arya Samaj*, p. 247.
[69] Fred B. Fisher, *India's Silent Revolution*, p. 85.

for their own uses. "They collected authoritative information relating to the evils they wished to counter. They presented it to the British public, both at home and in India, in a forceful yet scholarly fashion, and thus prepared the setting in which government action became inevitable."[70]

The influence of Christian missionary work through example in education, welfare work, and uplift of the backward classes was possibly of greater importance than the direct effects of Christian ideas. Missionaries were the first to open schools for girls and to urge equal treatment in the home for women. Their orphanages, medical dispensaries, and famine relief programs were examples that the social reformers followed, often because of genuine admiration for the novel humanitarianism, sometimes in competition for popular praise. Missionaries also led the way in agricultural education (technical assistance), savings bank schemes, and similar efforts to infuse economic life with new vigor. Above all, their spirit of unselfish service and the physical energy devoted to their work made the missionaries exemplars of the social welfare and social reform tradition of modern India.

In summary, Indian social reform movements in the 19th century and the religious reform movements on which they frequently based their creeds, differed in inspiration, in aims, and in methods from the bhakti movements of previous centuries and from contemporary religious reform sects based on the bhakti spirit. The differences can be accounted for by the influence on 19th century Indian thought of Western ideas and the examples of reforming endeavors provided by Christian missionaries; to a lesser extent British and Indian officials also provided stimulation to the movements. The motive behind the transmission of Western ideas into India and the means of their transmission concerned Indians but little. Notions of political liberty might come from missionaries, judges, or from reading Locke; ideas of Christian morality might be found in the Bible or in the decisions of district magistrates; scientific conceptions of the world could be learned through a public works department or a medical college.

[70] K. Ingham, *Reformers in India*, p. 33.

The results amounted to what Keshub Chandra Sen once called "the stupendous and lasting monuments of intellectual and moral conquest which England has raised here."[71] The results also included, as Macaulay foresaw, the downfall of British rule.[72]

The "conquest" which Sen so readily acknowledged should not be classified as a physical victory of one society over another. The ideas and institutions which have flourished in modern times in the West have been scrutinized by non-Westerners and accepted, modified, or rejected by them not as the result of the physical power of Western civilization, but oftentimes despite that power, or without any significant reference to it. The acknowledgment by Indians of the influence of the West in matters of social policy no more detracts from the value or the importance of the social reform movement, nor from the credit due to Indians who led it, than does the recognition of Western inspiration in India's modern political tradition reduce the value of India's political life. The originators of ideas establish their substance and sometimes determine the manner of their transmission; they are not, however, the custodians of those ideas.

[71] From a speech delivered in 1870, quoted in J. K. Majumdar, *Indian Speeches and Documents on British Rule*, p. 87.

[72] In a speech to Commons, July, 1833, Thomas Babington Macaulay speculated "that the public mind of India may expand under our system till it has outgrown that system; that by good government we may educate our subjects into a capacity for better government; that, having become instructed in European knowledge, they may in some future age, demand European institutions. . . ." Quoted in George Bennett, ed., *The Concept of Empire*, p. 74.

III

THE PROVINCIAL POLITICAL

REFORM MOVEMENTS

DISSATISFACTION with the social and religious life of their country, or even outright rebellion against it, prepared Indians for an intellectual acceptance of Western ideas—an acceptance, however, which did not lead to a passive reliance on the British to introduce alterations in Indian life or to an obedient acquiescence in the Government's policies. The main initiative for applying ideas of religious, social, and political reform in practical ways for the betterment and advancement of Indian life came not from the British governors, but from Indians themselves. Although the Government's support was often available and was even crucial for the success of many reform endeavors, the nature of specific reforms, their priorities, the manner of their introduction and spread, and ultimately their success or failure depended upon the desires and decisions of Indians and their willingness to devote thought and energy to the reforms that they sponsored.

Religious and social reform movements represented two of the main areas of intellectual and practical endeavor for educated Indians during the century preceding the First World War. For the first half of that century these movements were preoccupied with revolts against existing religious and social institutions and efforts to reform them according to the needs of individuals and small, local groups. A third area of activity during the same individualistic era was represented by political reform movements, which were separated from the religious and social reform endeavors though equally concerned with the needs of limited circles of educated people. These three distinguishable traditions of reform constituted a large part of the initiative that Indians displayed in their creative response to Western ideas, and together laid the intellectual foundations for the emergence of nationalism.

In the half century preceding the emergence of nationalism in an organized form, political reform movements occupied in the public and private lives of educated Indians positions of less importance than religious and social reform movements.[1] By the closing decades of the century the priorities had been reversed, and political ideas and goals were paramount. Nationalist political thought, in fact, came to exert a molding influence on religious and social ideals, and the methods of political organization and propagation for nationalist purposes set the pattern for other endeavors organized on an all-India basis.

Prior to British rule in India, politics and the publication of ideas about political affairs lay solely in the domain of the government; it was considered neither necessary nor proper for citizens to organize public criticism about matters over which the rulers asserted their authority. Under the administration of the East India Company, Indians who learned English discovered that the British were permitted to criticize their own rulers; this fact indeed was explicitly taught in many missionary schools. The results of that discovery were first the tentative, and then the forceful words of Indian petition and criticism heard from the 1820's onward.

In considering this phenomenon, Rammohun Roy's career is again of primary importance. He founded no political body but the beginnings of modern Indian political thought and the struggle for individual rights were marked by his pleas for political reforms: the inauguration of trial by jury; an end to racial discrim-

---

[1] A partial enumeration of public organizations in 19th century Bengal by N. S. Bose shows their overwhelming concern with social reform, cultural life, and education. "In most cases religion and politics were kept out of these organizations. . . ," according to Bose. See *The Indian Awakening and Bengal*, Appendix, p. 219f. Newspaper coverage up to the 1880's similarly stressed social, cultural, educational, and economic interests, with less attention given to politics. See, e.g., *ibid.* and R. R. Bhatnagar, *The Rise and Growth of Hindi Journalism*, esp. p. 129. It should be noted, further, that religious and social reform ideas had a profound impact on the private lives of Indians, whereas political ideas were almost exclusively matters for public concern.

ination in court procedures; consultation with Indians (aristocratic, wealthy, and educated) before enacting legislation; admission of Indians to higher civil service jobs; and, perhaps most
notably, freedom of the Indian press from arbitrary government
regulation. As in religious and social matters, Roy's political doctrines set the standards of liberalism and individualism in the 19th
century. Rising far above his specific grievances against the East
India Company's regime in India, however, was Roy's devotion
to the principles of British constitutional government; this became
his most significant political legacy to the generations of leaders
following him.

Rammohun Roy believed that political progress could be
achieved by operating within the British system, and later political
leaders, however much they declaimed against it, also found ample
opportunities for their activities without breaking out of this
system. One of the arresting features of Indian political activity
up to the First World War, distinguishing it from some revolutionary movements in other areas of Europe and Asia and
reminding one of the American experience, was the Indians' desire
not to terminate the system known as British rule but to increase
the advantages for themselves under that system.[2] Most educated
Indians in the 19th century believed that there was no alternative
system of administration that could possibly maintain the unity,
security, and social progress which the contemporary Government
had undertaken to provide. Furthermore, they recognized that
they themselves, trained in British schools and usually following
occupations directly or indirectly related to the British administration, depended for their survival as individuals and as a group on
the maintenance of the system. In the acceptance of this general
attitude toward the British Government, though not in complete
acceptance of specific Western political, social, and ethical values,
the Indian political leadership up to the First World War continued in the Roy tradition.

Flourishing as he did before the East India Company's rule was
extended throughout the subcontinent, Roy held ideas about In-

[2] Early in the 20th century, demands of an extreme nature were heard—not
for an end to the existing system of government, however, but for an end to
British rulers.

58

dian national unity that were embryonic and they had little effect on his political thought. He was sensitive to the political transformation along national lines then taking place in Europe, but he was equally aware of the extreme backwardness of India in just those areas which provided the basis for that transformation. He implied that the timetable for the emergence of a comparable transformation along democratic lines in India would be marked by the gradual acceptance of Western institutions. Roy felt that until that process had reached an advanced stage, India should be governed by the wisdom of the British monarch and his Parliament acting through the East India Company's officers. Roy did feel, however, that Indians' reactions to British rule must be taken into account, as expressed in their newspapers and by direct petition, in evidence before commissions, and in advice on pending legislation before Parliament. His reliance on the British Parliament for arbitration of political conflict, redress of popular grievances, and guidance in constitutional advancement was not widely challenged in India even at the end of the century. Roy's genius lay partly in his ability to use arguments which met Western intellectual standards, thereby appealing both to the British and to the newly influential group of educated Indians. His followers were, in one sense, all those who adopted the method of rational argument to promote the changes they were seeking; most of them did not accept wholeheartedly Roy's outlook on life, which would have logically led them to join the Brahmo Samaj or its affiliates.

A further legacy of Roy, quite as important as his confidence in the possibilities for advancement within the framework of British rule, was his high standard of political scholarship and writing. Firmly grounded in the educational system that Roy himself helped to found, it became the intellectual basis of later political activity. The standard was Western, not Indian. Inspiration for succeeding generations of Indian students of politics came from the West, and when they evaluated their own political tradition the criteria used were Western ideas of political liberty, effective administration and democracy.

Societies and debating clubs for discussion of political subjects were started in the early 19th century, usually in connection with college life. Indian newspapers and journals, in English and in vernaculars, were founded to propagate the political, social and sometimes religious views of their editors. Indian writers on political subjects, even in Bengal during Roy's lifetime, by no means accepted all of Roy's views on politics; in keeping with the individualism of the age, schools of political thought grew up representing the important European trends in political theory and agitational propaganda.[3] The results of the years of free inquiry into political matters by Indian intellectuals were felt when organizations for political purposes were first established to formulate demands on the government. These organizations issued petitions which were as knowledgeable about the processes of administration as they were mild and conservative; generally the government welcomed them.

Within its small intellectual sector, 19th century British India was a comparatively free society in terms of governmental controls, and advancement under an organized administration seemed inevitable. In such a setting revolutionary politics were uncalled for and impractical.[4] Indian political leaders were not hidden men whose ideas had been twisted and distorted by their need to protect themselves from oppression and by the absence of easy contacts with their fellows. They were instead gentlemen—after 1858, British subjects—whose thinking and aspirations had matured in the comparatively open intellectual life of metropolitan India. A further result of the open arena for the assertion of political ideas was that energies which might have been channeled into plots to overthrow British rule or hamper effective government were instead exerted to propagate ideas and then to organize public bodies and demonstrations. Competence in the verbal and written exposition of ideas, as opposed to expressing them by physical acts, may be a characteristic of many Indians; in any case that type of exer-

[3] e.g., see B. Majumdar, *History of Political Thought*, Chap. II, which describes "The Philosophical Radicals," a group variously influenced by Bentham, Hume, Thomas Paine, and the ideas of the French Revolution. Their acceptance of the existing system of government, however, was evident among other things by their fervent advocacy of Indianization of administrative services, which of course would provide them with jobs. See also N.S. Bose on the radical influence of Derozio, the Portuguese-Indian teacher at Hindu College, *op.cit.*, p. 37.

[4] cf. Bose, *ibid.*, p. 52f.

tion provided fairly generous personal rewards, as the careers of most Indian political leaders demonstrated.

When organized political groups were formed, first in Bengal and later in Bombay and Madras, their goals and methods were the practical corollaries of the more abstract political thought of the times. Probably the first organization formed for political purposes was the Zamindary Association of Bengal, founded in 1837 with obvious special interests to promote; its name was later changed to the Landholders' Society. In 1843 George Thompson, a prominent member of the British India Society of London, pointed out to his Indian listeners in a Calcutta lecture series the weakness of relying on written protests to influence the government, a procedure characteristic of the intellectual politics of the day. Like later British sympathizers with Indian problems, Thompson suggested to Indians, who were familiar only with disorganized, individual beseechings, the use of the Western organizational approach to political protest. He was the founder of the Bengal British India Society in 1843—an organization composed mainly of aristocratic Indians and Europeans that "failed to rouse political consciousness even amongst the limited circle of educated men in Bengal."[5]

An amalgamation of the Zamindary Association and the Bengal British India Society took place in 1851 partly to protest against the exclusion of European residents from the jurisdiction of mofussil (rural) courts—an issue which was to cause serious consequences later during the Ilbert Bill agitation. The united body was called the British Indian Association. Although this organization was dominated by the wealthy and aristocratic, its resolutions and petitions sometimes reflected not only their vested interests but in addition showed some real concern for the prosperity of the country (Bengal) and the rights of the Indian people under East India Company rule.

The first political organization in the Bombay Presidency was the Bombay Association, formed in 1852 to memorialize, from time to time, the "authorities in India, or in England, for the removal of existing evils, and for the prevention of proposed

<hr/>

[5] B. Majumdar, *op.cit.*, p. 174.

measures which may be deemed injurious, or for the introduction of enactments which may tend to promote the general interests of all connected with this country." It was an Association made up of the "principal inhabitants," and its first concern was to inform an otherwise poorly informed government of the true needs of the people, to protest against secrecy in official proceedings, and to urge that Indians be appointed to responsible positions in the administration.[6] The association initiated correspondence with similar groups in Bengal and Madras. In the Madras Presidency the Native Association was launched in the early 1850's and issued a strong protest to the British Parliament against various administrative evils. But the group soon lost its initial vigor.

It does not do serious injustice to the early political efforts of English-educated Indians to conclude, with A.C. Majumdar, that they were principally aimed at representing the particular and narrow interests of small groups, that they lacked any over-all program for the political advancement of India as a whole, and that they were not motivated by an "idea of a united nationality and of national interests."[7]

The uprising of 1857 and its aftermath of constitutional reorganization seemed to overshadow and even temporarily eliminate the weak beginnings of Indian political life.[8] But by the late 1860's a

[6] Govt. of Bombay, *Source Material for a History of the Freedom Movement in India*, I, 133-49.

[7] A. C. Majumdar, *Indian National Evolution*, p. 7.

[8] No study is available of the effects of the 1857 uprising on Indian political thought or activity, but from the general studies one gains the impression that a hiatus in organized political activity existed from about 1855 to the end of the 1860's. It is clear that many of the Indian members of political societies and writers on political subjects were entirely favorable toward the Company's suppression of the rebellion. See, e.g., messages of sympathy to the government from the British Indian Association, the Mahomedan Association, and leading Bengalis, in J.K. Majumdar, *Indian Speeches and Documents on British Rule*, pp. 56-73; and the corroborating view of Nirmal Kumar Bose, in "Modern Bengal," p. 45. See also N.S. Bose, *op.cit.*, pp. 163-65. But in any case, an emergency government regulation aimed at controlling irresponsible and malicious newspaper articles brought political sniping temporarily to an end during the outbreak. Haridas and Uma Mukherjee suggest, in their *Growth of Nationalism in India* (pp. 37-39), that the Bengal indigo workers' agitation in 1860 was a significant political issue stimulating "our patriotic and national self-consciousness." The available evidence seems to indicate, however, that the agitation in its vivid

new group of political spokesmen with new ideas and tactics was beginning to appear thus making the 1857 uprising a noncausal demarcation between old and new style Indian politics. The possibilities for new political activity lay in the growing number of middle-class men in all the provinces, many of whom had been educated in the recently founded universities. Their interests were not the same as those of the well-placed few who founded the earlier political bodies. Their political aims focused more on personal achievement and advancement than on protecting their property rights or providing constructive advice to a slow-moving administration. The middle classes were mainly composed of thousands of newly English-educated business and professional men, including civil servants,[9] in contrast to the hundreds of business and land-holding men who made up the earlier groups. The middle classes were increasing in all the urban centers, and their political strength and the extent of their demands grew accordingly.[10]

A fair foretaste of what could be expected from the more extreme representatives of that rapidly expanding group appeared in the activities of Sisirkumar Ghose, the Bengali founder of the newspaper, *Amrita Bazar Patrika*, in 1868, whom Tilak later acknowledged as his political guru. Ghose was a vehement advocate of political demands against both the government and the established upper classes, whose control of the British Indian Association was strengthened by the annual dues to the organization of Rupees 50. Although lacking a university edu-

---

portrayal of certain painful results of British rule had only local political significance and was certainly not a national issue.

[9] The term, middle class, designates a fairly well recognizable group in any country where Western institutions have been established. Professor B. B. Misra's definition of the Indian middle classes includes more groups than appear necessary, at least for the 19th century, i.e., middle-grade land holders, accountants, hotel keepers, clerks, and shopkeepers. See Misra, *The Indian Middle Classes*, pp. 12-13. A definition acceptable to the present writer would include those latter categories of people only if their personal lives or their jobs had been molded noticeably by Western influences.

[10] See B. T. McCully, *English Education and the Origin of Indian Nationalism*, chap. IV, esp. p. 184f. McCully pointed out that from 1857 to 1885, 48,251 candidates passed university entrance examinations; they thus had received a secondary education and were competent in English. Of these, 5,108 received the B.A. degree.

cation, Ghose gave voice to the frustration of some educated Indians whose advancement either in government or in the professions was increasingly hindered by obstacles associated with the nature of British rule. "By the 'eighties unemployment had become chronic among the educated class,"[11] and the forced leisure of a large body of talented and ambitious men generated new political grievances. The foremost complaint was the failure of the administration to open the civil service ranks to qualified Indians, clearly the self-interested view of an educated group without hereditary sources of wealth or position. But Ghose levied a broader attack against all forms of governmental restrictions on civil liberties and against economic exploitation, and he demanded that "the Indian nation" be given democratic, representative government, specifically a parliament along the lines of the British Parliament. Ghose's great contribution to political activity in Bengal lay in his organizational as well as in his intellectual ability, for he and his brother managed to create district political associations in the province based on communities of professional men who recognized the need for joint action to make their interests felt. Ghose founded the Indian League in 1875 as a focal point for the district bodies, after failing to persuade the British Indian Association to lower its dues; the new League's dues were fixed at Rupees 5, well within the means of the educated middle-class Bengali.

The Indian League was the first political body in India to seek more than casual ties with political groups outside its own province, and thus it antedated Surendranath Banerjea's Indian Association in this all-India purpose. Ghose traveled to Bombay in order to create unity between the political organizations of the two Presidencies and found, to his surprise, that constructive work was in certain ways more advanced there than in Bengal.[12] The Poona Sarvajanik Sabha had been in operation since 1870, when

[11] ibid., p. 196. "Educated" refers here to suitability for positions in the administration, Western businesses, or the professions.

[12] B. Majumdar recounted that Ghose, with characteristic Bengali "self-conscious superiority," was amazed to find political life in western India far advanced and altered his earlier impression of the backwardness of Bombay. Majumdar concluded that "the beginning of the superiority of Bombay in political progress is to be traced from the 'seventies of the last century." op.cit., pp. 347-48.

Ganesh Vasudeo Joshi founded it; later the better known Ranade, Gokhale, and Tilak dominated its proceedings. Similar to other political societies in purpose, it was unique in organization. The Sabha was representative since the members were elected by interest and caste groups; thus it could mold, as well as reflect, public opinion by spreading ideas among a wider group than actually attended the meetings of the Sabha. Although it was a major center of western Indian political activity for over two decades, the Sarvajanik Sabha never assumed a significant all-India role.

A year after Ghose founded the Indian League, the Indian Association was established in Calcutta. Chiefly because of a personal rivalry the two organizations could not merge, and the Association quickly become the dominant political body in Bengal. This was due primarily to Surendranath Banerjea's hard work and exceptional political talents—a fact attested to by many outside observers, as well as by Banerjea himself. The Indian Association "soon focused the public spirit of the middle class, and became the centre of the leading representations of the educated community of Bengal."[13] With Banerjea, if not with Sisirkumar Ghose, the Western-educated middle-class Bengalis were introduced to a new kind of political activity. Political organizations before the 1870's made little or no effort to organize public opinion generally, thereby creating an interest group larger than their own memberships for whom they could act as representatives. The petitions to government issued on behalf of small groups of "respectable Native Gentlemen" might provide some outlet for frustrated minds, but they could do little for frustrated careers. An organized public opinion expressed on a question of vital concern to all educated people, Banerjea felt, would produce two results. It would create unity among Indians, where none had existed before; and, because of the influence that unified demands could exert, it would ultimately achieve formal concessions from the British.

The approach to the government used by both the Indian Association and a decade later by the Indian National Congress to bring about desired concessions was, formally, the same as that used by

[13] Banerjea, *A Nation in Making*, p. 42.

earlier political groups: petitions, resolutions, and press campaigns, directed mainly at British officials in India or in England. But Banerjea and those who worked with him made this approach much more effective by assuring that political demands were understood and supported by a rapidly increasing body of educated Indians, most of whom had never before joined political societies. That body of Indians, whose emergence had been promoted by certain British representatives,[14] then began to turn against its promoters, demanding fairer treatment and opportunities to make full use of their newly acquired knowledge and to live a full life according to their newly adopted standards. Many of the British found themselves having to agree.

But the struggle for concessions in the 1870's and 1880's could hardly be called bitter, or even vigorous. Bipin Chandra Pal gave this description of the somewhat less than deadly serious attitudes of the thousands of followers of Banerjea in the 1870's: "Politics did not involve in those days any sufferings or sacrifices. The political authorities in the country did not take our infant political movement seriously. They saw no menace to their authority in it. The whole thing was, more or less, as a pastime, though certainly the more serious minded of our youthful intellectuals did not consciously pursue it as such."[15]

The Indian Association came to life a year after its founding by taking issue with the lowering from twenty-one to nineteen of the maximum age at which the competitive examination for the Indian Civil Service could be taken; the Indians assumed this measure was a direct British move to discourage Indians from the competition. The measure was bound to create a stir, and Banerjea

[14] Most famous of those representatives was Thomas Babington Macaulay whose aim, like that of earlier administrators, such as William Wilberforce and Charles Grant, was to liberate Indians from the "thraldom" of superstition and outworn customs by means of English education. A complementary object to be achieved by the government's support of English education was the creation of "a class who may be interpreters between us and the millions whom we govern— a class of persons Indian in colour and blood, but English in tastes, in opinions, in morals, and in intellect." Macaulay's "Minute on Education," Feb. 2, 1835, quoted in E. Stokes, *The English Utilitarians and India*, p. 46. See Stokes also for a perceptive account of the introduction of Western learning into India in the early 19th century.

[15] Pal, *Memories of My Life and Times*, I, 234-35.

exploited the Indian objection to it by making two tours through the major urban centers—from Rawalpindi to Madras and Benaras to Bombay—collecting resolutions on the civil service question to submit to the House of Commons. As he progressed across the country a sense of the unity of the English-educated class throughout India was created, as Banerjea had hoped it would be. He mistakenly believed, however, that this unity of a class somehow stood for, or perhaps at least presaged, the unity of "the people of India" along political lines.[16] The civil service competition between Indian and British aspirants for admission and advancement, according to Pal, "was really the beginning of our political conflict under British rule, which was the parent of our new political freedom movement."[17] Sir Henry Cotton wrote in 1885, "At the present moment the name of Surendro Nath Banerjea excites as much enthusiasm among the rising generation of Mooltan as in Dacca."[18] The far-reaching excitement stemmed partly from the fact that Banerjea had earlier been dismissed, probably unjustly, from the civil service and thus stood as a martyr to the cause of professional advancement within the British system which all educated Indians supported. The unified response from the English-educated class could hardly have been aroused by any religious or social reformer.

Banerjea's campaign showed how educated Indians from all provinces could unite on a political issue; in one sense it demonstrated too that they could unite on little else—since they had not done so previously. His appeal, wrote Bipin Chandra Pal, "was predominantly political. He did, no doubt, specially in the earlier years of his political leadership, combine social with political idealism and sought to draw the inspiration of both from religion. But the emphasis of his teaching was, all the same, far more on political freedom than on personal and social freedom. . . . Surendranath's political propaganda gathered a much larger following than that of the religious and social revolt of Keshub Chandra Sen and the Brahmo Samaj."[19]

According to Banerjea, the purposes of the Indian Association

[16] See Banerjea, *op.cit.*, p. 51. [17] Pal, *op.cit.*, II, xxi.
[18] Cotton, *New India*, p. 16.
[19] Pal, *op.cit.*, I, 234-35.

were: to create a strong body of public opinion in the country; to unify the "Indian races and peoples" on the basis of common political interests and aspirations; to promote "friendly feeling" between Hindus and Muslims; and to involve the masses "in the great public movements of the day."[20] Those aims were too ambitious for the Association. Nevertheless the task of bringing to the attention of the literate public the issues at stake in the Vernacular Press Act and the Arms Act of 1878, the Afghan War, and the Ilbert Bill was well within its competence. Banerjea's hope of making the Indian Association an all-India organization failed, probably because the organizational technique employed was one of spawning branch associations and linking up with already organized bodies in other provinces; this method could not create an all-India leadership primarily loyal to the Indian Association. After 1885 its leadership and most of its following went over to the National Congress, and the Association became a kind of provincial sub-Congress body.[21]

In the 1880's political organizations in Bombay and Madras were also enlarging the base of their memberships and reaching out into the small towns to strengthen their claim to represent popular opinion. G. Subramania Iyer was the co-founder of the Madras *Hindu* in 1878, a paper which subsequently became the outstanding nationalist organ in peninsular India. Six years later he was the moving spirit behind the creation of the Madras Mahajana Sabha; this Sabha adopted the task of arousing public opinion and sponsoring unity throughout the Presidency in addition to submitting memorials. Within a year fifty associations in the province had associated themselves with the new Sabha.

In Bombay, Budrudin Tyebji, Pherozeshah Mehta, and Kashinath Trimbak Telang also saw the chance of organizing on the basis of the new spirit among educated groups, and they joined to sponsor a new Bombay Association with a large membership and an ample treasury. The Association was founded in January 1885, the month following the spectacular and unprecedented

[20] Banerjea, *op.cit.*, p. 42.

[21] It followed Congress policy on national issues until 1920, while also working for special reforms related to Bengal. See Jogesh Chandra Bagal, *History of the Indian Association, 1876-1951*, esp. pp. 117, 139, 221.

send-off given by appreciative Indians to the retiring Viceroy, Lord Ripon. The unity of applause from all sections of the country, culminating in a mammoth demonstration in Bombay, was regarded by amazed Indians and British alike as evidence not only of a successful viceroyalty but of a new national identity, focused, for a time, significantly, on a British statesman.

The few Indians who were concerned with arousing public opinion had mastered fairly well certain techniques of propaganda and demonstration by the early 1880's; in the press and on the platform they were the equals of any Europeans in India. It was made clear to them again in 1883, however, that propaganda and displays alone were no substitute for organized political pressure. In that year Lord Ripon instructed his Law Member, Courtney Ilbert, to introduce in the Council a bill giving Indian judges outside of the Presidency towns jurisdiction to try European British subjects. The European response against the so-called Ilbert Bill was so intense that Ripon was forced to capitulate and offer an innocuous alternative to the measure. The racial bitterness that the Bill caused dismayed the Indian leaders and troubled moderate British officials. But one constructive purpose was nevertheless served: Indians witnessed the strength of the united, vociferous, European minority and saw their own weakness in the face of it. Segments of the Indian press were active in rebutting Anglo-Indian abuse and in supporting the Viceroy; but Indian opinion was disorganized, and in Madras, the United Provinces, and the Punjab no strong views were expressed. On an issue which struck directly at the newly developing racial and national sensitivities of educated Indians, they were unable to muster an effective defense. Indian leaders long remembered the bitter affair and from it derived the lesson that their failure "was largely owing to the want of adequate, vigorous and united support throughout the country to counter-balance the spirited and well-organized opposition of the Anglo-Indian [European] community ... it was further felt that if political advancement were to be achieved it could only be by the organization of a national assembly wholly devoted to wider politics than hitherto pursued in the different provinces independently of each other."[22]

[22] Mazumdar, *Indian National Evolution*, p. 39.

The Ilbert Bill fiasco added to the momentum building up behind aspirations for an all-India political movement. The "new spirit," as Henry Cotton called it, demanded the creation of a nation in India, along lines popularized by the writings of Mazzini and other European nationalists, and this in turn stimulated thoughts about an all-India political body to represent the nation's aims to the government. A political organization limited to Bengal or Bombay could hardly speak in behalf of the Indian nation.

India was united under a single government, and hence only from a united people, or nation, could pressure on that government be made effective. At the same time, the central government was recognized by the more acute writers as a crucial factor in building effective nationhood. A further reason for a strengthening of political organization was the rising horizon of political ambitions among educated Indians. To the demand for higher posts in the bureaucracy was added, by the end of the 1870's, a somewhat novel demand for a voice in legislation. That, noted Banerjea, "was a new departure ... fraught with immense potentialities. . . . The demand for representative government was now definitely formulated. . . ."[23] The demand was aimed at gaining influence in the top levels of policy-making—the Governor-General's Council and even the British Parliament—although Lord Ripon had sought to channel the new political enthusiasm into participation in local government on the grounds that solid preparation for self-rule should be made first.

The Calcutta National Conferences of 1883 and 1885 and the National Fund campaign[24] demonstrated Bengal's more rapid advance toward the all-India ideal than was evident elsewhere,

[23] *A Nation in Making*, p. 67. Banerjea, however, was in error. In 1852 the British Indian Association had sent to Parliament a petition asking for an Indian legislature, "placed on the footing of those enjoyed by most of the colonies of Her Majesty," to include Indian representatives. See B. Majumdar, *op.cit.*, Appendix 1, p. 479.

[24] A campaign to raise a large sum to defray the costs of presenting Indian views to the British public and Parliament, which never succeeded in its main object but which stimulated a great deal of comment from all provinces on the subject of national unity. See R. C. Majumdar, *Glimpses of Bengal in the 19th Century*, pp. 91-104, for a revised interpretation of the importance of the National Conference in the development of political nationalism.

but on the other hand, the dominant role of Bengalis in those programs hindered their countrywide appeal. What was needed was an entirely new organization without links to previous bodies to represent the recently evolved all-India outlook among the educated classes. Such an organization was the National Congress, brought into existence in 1885 through the idealistic challenge and organizational skill of Allan Octavian Hume, but prepared for and anticipated for nearly a decade by farsighted Indians.

THE PROVINCIAL SOCIAL

REFORM MOVEMENTS IN BENGAL,

BOMBAY, AND MADRAS

DURING the greater part of the 19th century, political reform was a public preoccupation separate from the private lives of Indians involved in it. Stimulating a kind of pseudo-professional activity, it had no relationship to family or personal life. Religious and social reform, on the other hand, were closely related to the private lives of educated Indians. For those men political matters occasionally aroused their concern—a tax assessment, a court procedure, or perhaps an election to a municipal board—but scarcely any of them could ignore the ever-present example of Europeans thinking and living in a manner which they regarded as in many ways superior to their own. Consequently, within the limited circle of partly Westernized Indians, ideas about the deplorable condition of society and the restrictions which customs imposed upon their own lives were for many decades more effective incentives to action than were thoughts about India's inferior political status.[1] Nothing like the personal dedication to religious, and, to a lesser

[1] Writing about the 1870's, B. C. Pal recalled that "Our youthful intellectuals were not only anxious to acquire political freedom, but also equally, if not more, anxious to break through every shackle that interfered with their freedom of thought and action. Social reform was even more popular than political reform . . . in those early days consciousness of sacerdotal and social bondage was far keener than the consciousness of political bondage." Pal, *Memories of My Life and Times*, I, 252.

extent, social reform which characterized Rammohun Roy's Brahmo followers was to be seen in any political organization until the last quarter of the century.

In the period before the emergence of nationalist organizations, religious and social reform were often inseparable phenomena, both outcomes largely of individual revolt against the restrictions of the religious and social order. That the revolt should immediately take the form of a national or even large-scale repudiation of the traditional Indian way of life in favor of any of the reformist creeds was not part of the early reformers' practical programs. Although the reform movements had a generally unsettling effect on Hindu society, religious and social reform meant the reorganization of individual lives, scarcely at all reorganization of the religious and social environment at large. Enlightenment was for the English-educated group, and reform doctrines and the literature supporting them were not geared for popular consumption. From the time of Rammohun Roy (who held a vision of an Indian society ultimately renovated by centuries of exposure to Western science and Christian morality) to that of Dayananda Saraswati (who urged a more immediate regeneration of Hindus through adherence to a purified "Vedic faith"), the reformers presented creeds suited to their own personal need for individual opposition to existing society and to the intellectual needs of a limited following of educated men. A resolute determination to achieve personal integrity in the face of demoralizing social pressures made many of them refuse to compromise with the popular mentality in order to obtain a wider following. As was the case with the writers on political subjects, the early religious and social reformers were more involved in preaching than in organizing, and were concerned more with ideas than with how they themselves might become effective leaders.

The Reform Movement in Bengal

A satisfying formula for introducing certain Western ideas and ways of life into their personal lives could attract educated Bengalis in the 19th century. Such a formula was presented in the teachings of Rammohun Roy. He gave it institutional form by founding in 1828 the Brahmo Sabha, a monotheistic religious body "to teach and to practice the worship of the one, supreme, undivided eternal God." Many of the Samaj's teachings and particularly its ethical tenets resembled Christian doctrines. The Samaj rejected the Brahmin priesthood's intermediation between man and God (although the leaders of the Samaj were mostly Brahmins themselves); repudiated idolatry and sacrifices for its public services; ignored caste distinctions (in theory, not in practice); and adopted a congregational form of worship similar to that of the Unitarians. At various times, particularly in educational endeavors, Roy worked closely with Christian missionaries in Bengal. Nevertheless, he believed that all fundamental religious truths could be found in Hindu scriptures, particularly in the Upanishads; that conviction, in addition to the dogmatism he found among many Christians, kept him from conversion to Christianity. His announced purpose was to restore the Hindu faith to its original purity.

Like nearly every Hindu religious reformer of the century, Roy was attracted by the ethics of Christianity. In the Introduction to his *Precepts of Jesus* (extracts from the New Testament, chiefly of ethical passages), Roy wrote, "a due estimation of that law which teaches that man should do unto others as he would wish to be done by . . . although . . . partially taught also in every system of religion with which I am acquainted, is principally inculcated by Christianity."[2] In a private letter he was more specific: "I have found the doctrines of Christ more conducive to moral principles, and better adapted for the use of rational beings, than any other which have come to my knowledge."[3]

A decade before establishing the Brahmo Sabha, Roy undertook the social reform crusade for which he is well known, the cam-

[2] Roy, *English Works* (J. C. Ghose, ed.), p. 483.

[3] To John Digby, *ibid.*, pp. 928-29. The similarity of thoughts and language between Roy and the English Evangelicals was frequently apparent. Wilberforce, for example, during the Charter debates of 1813 claimed that "Christianity, independently of its effects on a future state of existence, has been acknowledged even by avowed sceptics, to be, beyond all other institutions that ever existed, favourable to the temporal interest and happiness of man; and never was there a country where there is a greater need than in India for the diffusion of its genial influence." Quoted in E. Stokes, *The English Utilitarians in India*, p. 33.

paign against suttee. The government had been under pressure for years from missionaries to use its authority to put down a custom which appeared to be growing in popularity, at least in lower Bengal. Roy's vigorous attacks on the rite, based on Hindu shastras as well as on appeals to humanitarian and natural rights doctrines, began to appear in 1818, and he was not alone among Indians in his condemnation. In that year a petition was sent to the Governor-General "signed by a great number of the most respectable inhabitants of Calcutta"[4] asking for official measures to end the burning of widows. The government under Lord Hastings (1813-1822) and Lord Amherst (1823-1828) took various measures to try to discourage the extraordinary practice, which was never followed by the majority even of high-caste Hindu families. For years the government discussed suttee, which was regarded by the British as a blot on the administration's record of spreading civilization. The government hesitated to take the full step of outright prohibition for fear that such a move would create distrust of the announced British policy of not interfering with Indian religious practices. When Lord Bentinck in 1829 again took up the question of legally suppressing suttee, he called upon Roy for advice. Following an interview, Bentinck wrote that Roy presented the weak suggestion "that the practice might be suppressed quietly and unobservedly by increasing the difficulties and by the indirect agency of the police."[5]

Nevertheless, after the historic regulation prohibiting suttee was issued in December 1829,[6] Roy and three hundred others supported the government against a much larger group of protesters. The orthodox opposition formed the Dharma Sabha, in obvious retort to Roy's Brahmo Sabha, to seek repeal of the measure by a memorial to the British Government; it was hoped, too, that the Dharma Sabha, by appealing to popular suspicion of Roy's religious and social views, might bring an end to the Brahmo Sabha. Although such an appeal by Hindu pundits and their supporters

---

[4] According to a contemporary source, cited in Collet, *Life and Letters of Raja Rammohun Roy*, p. 48. Miss Collet stated that Roy's first tract against suttee appeared in 1818. *ibid.*, p. 40.

[5] Cited by Collet, *op.cit.*, p. 147.

[6] The regulation applied only to Bengal. Similar regulations affecting Bombay and Madras were issued in 1830.

over the head of the Governor-General was not likely to succeed, Roy was determined to make certain that it would not and undertook a voyage to England, unprecedented for a high-caste Hindu, armed with written arguments that suttee was not a religious duty. He had other important political business in England as well and left India for what was to be his last journey in November 1830. He died in Bristol in 1833.

It was Roy in his own capacity, not as leader of the Brahmo Sabha, who generated this first Indian agitation for social reform, and his death left no one who could continue that aspect of his work. The Sabha was a religious body, and the involvement of its adherents in the tasks of social reform was a secondary preoccupation. Roy was able, through the largeness of his vision of men and society, to combine in his thought and in his public career the advocacy of religious, social, and political reforms. India's political advancement, Roy believed, could rest only on prior social advancement, and that in turn depended upon reformation of religious beliefs and practices. Roy's almost simultaneous involvement in the three major areas of reform was simplified by the fact that in his day movements for reform had no institutional structure. In the decades to follow a leader who sought to fuse the reform movements was faced with the difficult task of bringing together for common purposes separate groups of men each having special commitments.

After Roy's death the leadership of the Brahmo Sabha, or Samaj, as it was soon referred to, fell to the hands of Pundit Ramchandra Vidyavagish, one of his devout followers. The weak and unpopular Samaj barely managed to survive and did so physically because of the generous patronage of the wealthy Dwarkanath Tagore, a close friend of Roy. In a decade, however, the fortunes of the Brahmo Samaj began to rise, because of the new spiritual leadership given to it by Dwarkanath's son, Debendranath Tagore (1817-1905). The young Tagore had established in 1839 a society of youthful intellectuals in search of spiritual truth, the Tattvabodhini Sabha, whose informal association with the Brahmo Samaj gave the latter new strength in membership and purpose. The religious growth of Debendranath, whose creative leadership assured the Samaj of a prominent place in 19th century Bengali intellectual life, testified to the vitality of Hindu thought even at a time when it was besieged, so to speak, by Western rationalism and the attraction of scientific knowledge. For Debendranath's thought developed through the rationalistic, deistic phase typical of a follower of Rammohun Roy to a final realization that the essence of the religious spirit is devotion, bhakti, the forms of which would determine its thoroughly Indian character. In his remarkable *Autobiography*[7] he described the development of his religious life, a critical point in which was a repudiation of the Upanishads, which Rammohun regarded as the purest source of religious truth. Already he had found the advaita Vedanta philosophy of Sankara unsatisfactory, because, as he wrote, Sankara "seeks to prove therein that Brahma [God] and all created beings are one and the same. What we want is to worship God. If the worshipper and the object of worship become one, how can there be any worship?"[8] At that stage he had developed the declaration of faith for the Samaj; ultimately its scripture, known as the Brahma Dharma, was to emerge to conform to Debendranath's interpretation of the Upanishads. But Debendranath's curiosity induced him to collect the authentic scriptural sources of Hinduism, in that day unavailable in Bengal and requiring the despatch of scholars to Benaras to gather the material together. The result was his disillusionment with many of the Upanishads as well. As a whole, he concluded, the Upanishads constituted a foundation "shaky and built upon sand; even here I did not touch firm ground. . . . Our relation with God is that of worshipper and worshipped—this is the very essence of Brahmaism. . . . But when in the Upanishads I came across 'I am he' and 'Thou are That,' then I became disappointed in them also."[9]

The outcome of Debendranath's search for religious truth was in essence the religion of bhakti; or, as he expressed it, "The pure, unsophisticated heart was the seat of Brahmaism."[10] As a devotee, and one who asserted the objective existence of the mundane

[7] Written in Bengali; the translation referred to here is by Satyendranath Tagore and Indira Devi.
[8] D. Tagore, *Autobiography*, p. 72.
[9] *ibid.*, pp. 160-61.
[10] *ibid.*, p. 161.

world,[11] Debendranath's compassion towards men was a real force in his life, and he searched for a proper formulation of a moral code to parallel the religious principles of his Brahma Dharma. The outcome was a sincere statement of ethical duties which recognized the need for changes in Hindu social life, particularly in matters regarding the treatment of women. But it did not lend great moral urgency to the Samaj's mission, which remained predominantly religious, and to a lesser extent educational. Debendranath's intense devotionalism and his ability to convey his feelings to others and organize a service of worship though drawing membership to the Samaj, had little social reform impact on Brahmos, much less on Hindu society in general. Above all, the Samaj under Debendranath did not desire a separation from Hindu society and wished to steer a middle course between popular religion and a total reform.

A group within the Samaj, however, urged more radical measures for the Samaj and Hinduism generally. Led by Akshay Kumar Dutt (1820-1886), it urged a more rational approach to religious ideas and greater efforts for social reform. As Debendranath summed up the difference between himself and Dutt, "I was seeking to know my relations with God, he was seeking to know the relations of man with the outer world."[12] Dutt's major literary contributions to the intellectual development of Bengal, including his editorship of the *Tattvabodhini Patrika*, have often been noted,[13] but his social reform endeavors have been given less recognition, probably because they resulted in no organized movement or in legislation. Stating views that many of the members of the Tattvabodhini Sabha accepted, Dutt argued in favor of marriage reform, which should include widow remarriage, inter-caste marriage, and even courtship before marriage; he viewed marriage of girls before puberty and polygamy with abhorrence and advocated divorce under certain circumstances.[14] Debendranath did not

[11] He wrote with a firmness comparable to Dayananda Saraswati's in denying the doctrine of maya, or Illusion: "This universe is not dream-stuff, neither is it a mental illusion, but it exists in reality." *ibid.*, pp. 175-76.

[12] Quoted in M. C. Parekh, *The Brahma Samaj*, p. 41.

[13] See, e.g., N. S. Bose, *The Indian Awakening and Bengal*, p. 203f; also B. Majumdar, *History of Political Thought*, p. 124f.

[14] See Majumdar, *op.cit.*, pp. 128, 137-39.

vocally take issue with the views of Dutt and the radical groups in the Brahmo Samaj, but neither did he support them warmly.[15] In 1855 Dutt proposed that the government pass legislation to raise the age of marriage, citing the disastrous physical effects on the population of the custom of early marriage. That was possibly the first well-publicized appeal for government interference in marriage age customs, and it was three-quarters of a century before the desired law was finally enacted. Shortly after Dutt proposed the enactment he became ill and was forced to withdraw from his energetic public activities.

The most famous social reform movement which emerged from the numerous reform societies, discussion groups, and literary activities of mid-century Bengal was the crusade for widow remarriage, rightly linked to its chief promoter, Ishwar Chandra Vidyasagar (1820-1891).[16] Often referred to as the "father of the Bengali prose style," and noted for a vast output of scholarly books and educational materials, Vidyasagar was not a member of the early Brahmo Samaj, though he collaborated with members of the Samaj and the Tattvabodhini Sabha, in particular Akshay Kumar Dutt and Raj Narain Bose. After he became principal of the Sanskrit College in 1851, Vidyasagar immersed himself in written pleas for marriage reform, which included not only widow remarriage but also the abolition of polygamy. On the latter question considerable support was forthcoming from liberal Indians, who condemned the specific privileges of the Kulin Brahmins. The latter were customarily permitted to "marry" an indefinite number of wives in order to satisfy the desires of the brides' families (who often paid large sums for the contracts) to have daughters wedded to men of one of the highest of Brahmin castes. The much-married groom frequently never saw his wife after the ceremony.[17] In 1855 the Maharaja of Burdwan petitioned the Legislative Council for an act against polygamy, and the government took the matter under serious consideration, but the uprising

---

[15] His views on social reform presented a somewhat confusing picture, as N. S. Bose indicated, *op.cit.*, pp. 90 and 150.

[16] Vidyasagar is not a surname, but a title, meaning "ocean of knowledge," conferred upon Ishwar Chandra upon his graduation in 1841 from the Sanskrit College, Calcutta.

[17] See Chintamani, *Indian Social Reform*, I, 186.

intervened, and no action was taken.[18] On widow remarriage, however, Vidyasagar and his many Bengali supporters had more success.

Vidyasagar's agitation in favor of widow remarriage started in the early 1850's and culminated in the publication of his major work on the subject, *Marriage of Hindu Widows*, in 1856. In that book he sought to prove shastric sanctions for the remarriage of widows and stated his unwillingness to rest the case on reason alone. In a statement typical of 19th century social reform appeals he argued that "A total disregard of the Sastras and a careful observance of mere usages and external forms is the source of the irresistible stream of vice which overflows the country." After cataloguing the miseries of widows he concluded with the rebuke, "Countrymen! . . . You are not willing to follow the dictates of your Sastras, to give them in marriage again, and thus relieve them from their intolerable sufferings, and yourselves from miseries, crimes and vices."[19] Vidyasagar proposed that the government pass legislation which would legalize marriages of which the bride was classed as a widow, that is, a woman whose husband had died, even if her marriage to him had never been consummated and she had never left her parental home. Under existing legal prescriptions the courts, guided by the opinions of Hindu pundits on customary law among the higher castes, would declare illegal marriages involving a widow. Unlike the suttee legislation, which created a prohibition affecting everyone, the measure proposed would have no universal applicability. It was intended simply to provide government backing for widows who wished to remarry and the men who consented to marry them, and, of the greatest psychological importance, support for the advocates of widow remarriage. Those advocates were to be found among English-educated groups in many parts of India, including Bengal, and

[18] See C. E. Buckland, *Bengal Under the Lieutenant-Governors*, I, 324-25. New petitions were submitted in 1863, but the government and the Secretary of State in London decided against any such measure during the existing state of public opinion. In any case, such an act would have had to provide for polygamy under certain conditions prescribed by Hindu law, as when a wife was barren or sickly, and the government felt that it was undesirable to give official sanction to such conditions by codifying them.

[19] *Marriage of Hindu Widows*, p. 93.

thus the remarriage issue could bring forth a sense of unity among all social reformers.

The widow remarriage movement forms a unique part of the history of Indian social reform. It was preeminently associated with the first stage of the social reform movement, when the individual, not the community or nation, was the central focus of concern. Agitation for widow remarriage never was aimed at creating general adoption by Hindus of that practice. Such a revision of attitude by the Hindu public at large was less feasible even than breaking down sentiments against inter-caste association, including inter-dining and inter-marriage. The reformers knew this, and history has borne them out.[20] The real purpose of the widow remarriage movement for the bulk of its participants was to gain social acceptance or at least tolerance for an individual deviation, of an extreme and socially significant kind, from the normal pattern of behavior. However brought about, such acceptance would confirm individual rights, as against religious and customary law, to an outstanding degree. Prohibition of widow remarriage affected only the higher castes,[21] and a more nearly absolute and universal regulation among those castes could scarcely have been singled out. Thus, non-remarriage of widows could be taken as the epitome and symbol of orthodoxy.

Advocacy of remarriage by the middle of the century became one of the surest signs of being a reformer. It also was perhaps the easiest way for someone to identify himself with social reform, because advocacy involved no work or personal sacrifice. Few

[20] While caste restrictions on social intercourse have been steadily wearing away, and many social abuses have been virtually eliminated, non-remarriage of widows remains today a general practice among high caste Hindus. Because of a marked advance in the age of marriage for girls and a generally increased life span for men and women, widowhood is less common, however, and because of female education less of a problem.

[21] See W. Macnaghten, *Principles of Hindu Law*, as quoted in N. K. Vaidya, *A Collection Containing the Proceedings which led to the passing of Act XV of 1856 . . .*, p. 12: "It is well known that women are betrothed at a very early period of life, and it is this betrothment, in fact, which constitutes marriage. One contract is then valid and binding to all intents and purposes. It is complete and irrevocable immediately on the performance of certain ceremonies, without consummation. Second marriages after the death of the husband first espoused, are wholly unknown to the Hindu law; though in practice, among the inferior castes, nothing is so common."

reformers married widows, even when they could have done so, and mere assertion of unorthodox ideas scarcely ever led to excommunication; it was behavior that counted. Furthermore, actual widow remarriages were so few in number that only an occasional gesture of support to the cause of reform was needed to be recognized as holding unorthodox ideas. The widow remarriage movement attracted to its banner more transient reformers, curiosity-seekers, and chronic infringers of the law than any other social reform cause. For those directly involved in arranging a widow remarriage, which was certain to cause a popular stir, the rewards were not only public recognition but frequently too the clandestine excitement of concealing a young widow from her familial pursuers until she could be married to a willing spouse. Most of the existing accounts of such episodes are from Bengal, where undercover activities in modern times have been more common than elsewhere in India. Brahmo Samajists made a kind of profession of arranging widow remarriages.[22]

Vidyasagar and other remarriage champions might have singled out some other custom to oppose which would have provided equal scope for individual revolt against society. But distress over the treatment of widows was one of the earliest preoccupations of Indian critics of the moral condition of Hindu society. Rammohun Roy's attack on the most notorious practice connected with widowhood became an almost legendary crusade, which marked the Hindu widow for special attention thereafter. Vidyasagar thus sought the government's official sanction for a reform which seemed a natural development from the Act prohibiting suttee: after protecting widows from self-immolation, the government might be disposed toward removing restrictions on their remarriage.

Apart from the shastric arguments used by Rammohun Roy and Vidyasagar, social reformers condemned the Hindu treatment of widows on grounds of humanitarianism and the more specific doctrine of the equal rights of individuals. No one, they argued, echoing the highest ideals of Western liberalism, had the right

[22] See, e.g., the accounts in B. N. Motiwala, *The Life and Career of Mr. Sasipada Banerji*. Banerji was a reformer who carried on welfare and reform work for widows with constancy and at great cost to himself, and proved his sincerity by marrying a widow.

to deprive another person of his chances to live the fullest possible life. The misery of widows was ordinarily due not to their own choosing, but to society's—their families' and the priests'—demands that they remain unmarried and chaste, give up participation in festivities, undergo periodic penances, and even suffer the humiliation of tonsure and forced wearing of unattractive clothing.[23] The condition of young girl widows was particularly distressing, because they scarcely understood why they were being mistreated. Older widows created a social problem of some proportions because of the possibilities of their contracting illicit relationships or becoming prostitutes.

Following the publication of Vidyasagar's book on widow remarriage, petitions were submitted to the Legislative Council signed by 5,191 prominent Bengalis who sought passage of the proposed legislation. Vidyasagar's petition stated in part that the custom prohibiting remarriage of widows was "cruel and unnatural in itself, is highly prejudicial to the interests of morality, and is otherwise fraught with the most mischievous consequences to society." It noted that widow remarriages "are neither contrary to nature nor prohibited by law or custom in any other country or by any other people in the world." And further, to provide the government with the argument that it needed most, "in the opinion and firm belief of your Petitioners, this custom [of prohibiting remarriage] is not in accordance with the Shastras, or with a true interpretation of Hindu law."[24] A friend of Vidyasagar and member of the Legislative Council, J.P. Grant, submitted to the Council the draft bill and presented the case for its enactment, laying greatest stress upon the immorality which, he claimed, enforced widowhood produced in society.

The main opposition to the Bill came from petitions signed by 55,746 persons. One such petition cited previous government regulations dating from 1772 which proclaimed that in matters such as

[23] Unwilling to tolerate their daughters' miseries, fathers were occasionally known to have sought special exemptions from religious authorities so that their daughters could remarry. See, e.g., Tattvabhushan, *Social Reform in Bengal*, p. 73; Chintamani, *op.cit.*, I, 291; K. Datta, *Survey of India's Social Life . . .* , p. 36.

[24] Vaidya, *op.cit.*, p. I.

marriage and all other religious usages and institutions due regard for Hindu law should be taken in formulating the Civil Code. Another struck out at Vidyasagar's efforts to disprove the alleged shastric prohibitions on remarriage and began its argument with "One Ishwarchandar Vidiasagar, *Modern* Pandit . . . in conjunction with a few young men of the rising class. . . ."[25] In fact, orthodoxy had little difficulty at the time in proving its own case for interpretation of the shastras and existing Hindu law. (More substantial arguments against the orthodox interpretation appeared several decades later from Poona.) However, the Select Committee of the Council concluded that the orthodox objections to the Bill did not apply because the proposed act would not affect the religious or social customs of those who opposed widow re-marriage. In recommending enactment of the legislation, the entirely British Committee reinforced the human rights argument raised first by the Bill's Indian supporters: a Hindu widow who wished to repudiate Hindu law by the dictates of her own conscience should not be denied the right to marry and raise legitimate children. Under existing law the government interfered with religious practices of at least some Hindus by invalidating marriages of widows, the Committee's argument ran; the Bill would reinstate the traditional British policy of noninterference. Mr. Grant took note of the great majority of petitioners who opposed the Bill and discounted it, saying that the minority's interest was a personal one directly involving the happiness and honor of individual families. Minority rights against any possible oppression by the majority were enunciated firmly and were to remain a settled British policy in India until the end. The humanitarian motive was urged by Grant in just as forceful a manner. "If he knew certainly," it was recorded, "that but one little girl would be saved from the horrors of *Brahmacharia* [celibacy] by the passing of this Act, he would pass it for her sake." And finally, just before the voting: "If he believed, as firmly as he believed the contrary, that the Act would be wholly a dead letter, he would pass it for the sake of the English name."[26]

[25] *ibid.*, pp. 33, 37-38.
[26] Govt. of India, Legislative Council, *Proceedings, from January to December, 1856*, vol. II, 438.

The English name was indeed ennobled by the Hindu Widows' Remarriage Act XV, passed in July 1856, but for Hindu society generally the Act was ineffectual. For on the matter of prohibiting widow remarriage, unlike that of suttee, infanticide, and slavery, Hindus were governed not merely by habitual custom or religious prescription, but by deep convictions about the sacrament of marriage and relations between the sexes generally. In the 19th century literature on widow remarriage, which is as extensive as the writings on any other social reform topic, even proponents of the reform recognized the strong attachment among the upper castes to the notion that a marriage, a profound sacrament, should be eternally binding on a woman. Consummation of the marriage was incidental. Once given to her husband, even if he was only a young child at the time, a woman must not subsequently be passed on to another man. An even stronger repugnance was felt against remarriage if the husband had lived with his wife before his death;[27] this feeling was so strong in fact that reformers concentrated their attention almost exclusively on child widows, arguing that for practical purposes the latter had not really been married.

Of all social reforms for which major campaigns were undertaken, widow remarriage reform actually produced the most meager results.[28] Yet because agitation for the reform continued to provide a forum for personal revolt against the injustices of society and because exposures of the miseries of widows continued to arouse sympathy, the movement persisted, nourished periodically by reports that one Hindu or another had married a widow. Pundit Vidyasagar himself, it was reported, became disappointed not only in the relatively small number of widow remarriages but

[27] A frank, and possibly typical, statement of the prevailing attitude on widow remarriage was provided by a Bombay pundit in the 1880's: "The thing called woman is the crowning piece of all the objects of enjoyment in this world, and being subject to the special power of the husband, is not like a house, etc., capable of being enjoyed by the husband's relations. How much more incapable must she then be of being fit for remarriage and enjoyment by a stranger. Like a dining leaf [a leaf used to hold food, in the manner of a plate] used previously by another person, she is unfit to be enjoyed by another person." Cited in D. Gidumal, *The Status of Women in India* . . . , pp. 216-17.

[28] In his Bombay Social Conference speech, at Satara in 1900, Ranade estimated that 300 remarriages had taken place throughout India "in the higher castes" since Vidyasagar initiated the movement. Chintamani, *op.cit.*, II, 133.

in the exploitation of him and other supporters of the cause by men willing to marry widows only for the monetary rewards involved.[29] S. Tattvabhushan viewed the whole movement of Vidyasagar as "morally very weak, for most of the persons who married under his auspices received ample pecuniary assistance from him, and not a few of them were even tempted to marry widows for the settlement which that large-hearted Pandit made upon those who married under his auspices, a circumstance which . . . contributed very largely to sow the seeds of a fatal weakness in the very heart of his reform work. Instances have not been rare when the men who married a widow [sic] under Pandit Vidyasagar's auspices, actually threatened to desert their wives and children if their most unreasonable demands for money were not met by him." Tattvabhushan concluded that it was because of this "fatal weakness" that the widow remarriage movement "practically died out, at least in Bengal, long before the death [in 1891] of the illustrious reformer who first set it on foot."[30] In 1866 a Widow Remarriage Association was started in Calcutta, but it "failed to achieve any tangible results, because the public did not evince any active or practical interest in the matter."[31]

In other parts of the country hopes were somewhat brighter. In 1866 the Bombay Widow Marriage Association was started by the translator of Vidyasagar's book into Marathi, Vishnu Shastri Pundit (1827-1876), with the active backing of young reformers like Ranade, K.T. Telang, and Gopal Hari Deshmukh, who were soon to lead a movement which in aims and in public recognition far outreached the social reform efforts in Bengal. Isolated cases of widow remarriage were known in the Presidency before 1866; the first one brought about by the new Association, in 1869, led to the excommunication of Vishnu Shastri, Ranade, and five other supporters. Vishnu Shastri's leadership in the Bombay remarriage agitation was comparable to Vidyasagar's in Bengal. But the methods of the two reformers differed significantly and reflected an important difference in approach between Bombay and Bengal reformers. While Vidyasagar sought government sanction for

[29] *ISR* (*Indian Social Reformer*), Sept. 16, 1906, p. 32.
[30] Tattvabhushan, *Social Reform in Bengal*, p. 77.
[31] *ISR*, Sept. 16, 1906, p. 32.

widow remarriage, Vishnu Shastri Pundit desired the sanction of the highest religious authority with jurisdiction in western India, the Shankaracharya of Karver and Sankeshwar.[32] Widow remarriages had been legalized by an Act of the State, but the Bombay reformers sought their validation also by the seat of orthodoxy: social reform should be made acceptable to all, not just technically valid by laws imposed from the outside. In accordance with ancient Hindu tradition a great debate between the reformers and their opponents was staged in Poona under the Shankaracharya's auspices on the subject of the legality under Hindu law of widow remarriage.[33] For nine days from March 20, 1870, the debate went on in Poona. The final decision reached by ten arbitrators was against the reformers, but not without charges of unfair dealings.[34]

The defeat did not deter the reformers in Bombay, and because of the publicity and the strength of their arguments may in fact have gained them some popular favor. In any case, the widow remarriage movement had been vigorously launched in western India, and it soon spread to other places. In Ahmedabad, Gujarati reformers, with a long literary reform tradition already established, formed a Remarriage Association. In Madras Presidency, Viresalingam Pantulu (1848-1919), the "Vidyasagar of South India," founded the Rajahmundry Social Reform Association in 1878 and began his crusade against enforced widowhood. Soon thereafter in northern India, Dayananda Saraswati and the newly founded Arya Samaj advocated the remarriage of child widows.

The remarriage movement, though never organized on an all-India basis, thus became the first social reform cause to be taken up throughout the country. Despite its meager showing in terms of general public acceptance or high-caste widows actually remarried, the movement retained a surprising vigor well into the 20th

---

[32] See Chintamani, op.cit., I, 301.

[33] It was later recorded that the Shankaracharya offered to support a compromise instead of the debate, namely, the validation of remarriages of child widows but continued prohibition of adult remarriages. But the reformers, overly confident of their strength, declined the offer. loc.cit.

[34] Conflicting evidence exists on the exact vote. M. B. Kolaskar in his Introduction to the Ranade collection, Religious and Social Reform, p. xviii, reported the division at 7 to 3. W. M. Kolhatkar in his essay in Chintamani, op.cit., I, 303, provided a fuller account and gave the vote at 6 to 4.

century. Many of the original remarriage bodies ultimately expired, often for the same reasons that led to Vidyasagar's disillusionment.[35] But while the older remarriage enthusiasts turned to movements of broader scope or lost interest altogether, new remarriage associations continued to appear in parts of the country which had hitherto not enjoyed (or been embarrassed by) much reform activity. In any locality, widow remarriage agitation often marked the beginnings of concern with social reform, because of its uniquely individualistic and humanitarian appeal. In supporting widow remarriage, an individual could combine social revolt with what appeared to be constructive humanitarianism; as in religious devotion, the benefits accrued to the devotee of widow remarriage in greater abundance than to the object of his concern, who up to the present generally remains unmarried.[36] Some benefits to widows who did not marry, however, resulted from the movement. As a result of publicity given to their condition, homes for their care and education, and for the maintenance of their illegitimate children, were founded in many places.

In Bengal the enthusiasm among Brahmos for widow remarriage and other social reforms was greatly strengthened in the years following the outbreak of the 1857 uprising[37] by the addition

[35] Viresalingam's Association in the Northern Circars, with N. Subba Row Pantulu as secretary, broke up in 1891. A major reason for the failure was that "remarried men mostly joined the reform movement not out of any love for social reform, but because they expected large sums of money and greater social recognition. . . ." Yet despite the attraction of money, the Association could claim only three marriages after almost a decade of work. J. Gurunadham, *Viresalingam; The Founder of Telegu Public Life*, p. 116.

[36] This is true in the higher castes toward which the widow remarriage movement was directed. Recent figures on the ratio of widows to married women in the Hindu community vary widely according to caste position and family occupation, with over 23 widows per 100 married women typical of Brahmins and other high castes, such as Kayastha and Bania. See Kingsley Davis, *The Population of India and Pakistan*, pp. 36, 74-75. Davis indicates that figures on non-remarriage of widows are incomplete, but he observes that "authorities agree that the taboo on widow marriage is not being broken down in India very fast" (p. 36).

[37] The 1857 uprising has been regarded by some scholars as partly the result of Indian fears that British rule would undermine their traditional way of life. See, e.g., Surendra Nath Sen, *Eighteen Fifty-Seven*, p. 5f. But it appeared to have no appreciable effects on the activities of social reformers, at least in Bengal and Bombay.

to their ranks of Keshub Chandra Sen. A non-Brahmin then in his twenties, Sen developed an affectionate respect for Debendranath Tagore, and the older man found in Sen's devotion and energy the qualities needed for leadership of the Brahmo Samaj. In 1862, therefore, Debendranath appointed Sen the leading minister and later the secretary of the Samaj, next in rank to himself. Keshub Chandra Sen's views on social reform were considerably in advance of Debendranath's. In contrast to the older Brahmos, Sen, along with a young following that he had acquired even before joining the Samaj, opposed any form of idolatry, even in domestic worship services; denied the significance of caste; urged adult wives to appear in public and receive education; and condemned in an outspoken way certain semi-religious practices (such as nautch dancing) which his conservative colleagues had never repudiated. Debendranath for a time acquiesced in the younger leader's desire to reform the Samaj, gave up wearing his sacred thread, a symbol of caste status, and consented to have his second daughter married in 1861 according to a new set of nonidolatrous rites which progressive Brahmos had devised.[38]

Nevertheless a split inevitably developed within the Samaj between the conservative and the liberal or radical members, with Debendranath vacillating between loyalty to his old colleagues and affection for Sen. The latter's vociferous attacks against caste, his support for various social reform causes, and finally his acknowledgment of the truth of Christ's teachings became intolerable to Debendranath, who felt it necessary therefore to divest Sen of his official positions in the Samaj. For a few years the liberal Brahmos remained nominally loyal to the society, while Sen undertook several missionary tours of southern and western India creating a notable following for himself and establishing the image of the Brahmo Samaj as a liberal force outside Bengal and the Ganges valley region.

While Debendranath's religious aims concerned only the Hindu community, and in fact only the high castes within it, Sen's vision encompassed the world, and he sought a universal faith. Unlike Rammohun Roy, however, that faith was not to be based on reason

---

[38] The text of the reformed marriage ceremony was reproduced, in translation, in Collet, ed., *Brahmo Year-Book for 1879*, p. 7f.

but on devotion, a common realization of the one God, and a common sense of sin. His frequent lectures, which often extolled the virtues of Christ, resembled an evangelical revival more than they did the sober meetinghouse atmosphere of the Calcutta Brahmo Samaj.[39] Typical of his oratory was the following exhortation combining religious and social reform ideas: "Brethren! As worshippers of the God of love, it is your duty to love all men as your brethren, and to make charity the ruling principle of your heart. Fling away arrogance and pride, and be humble and meek. Prayerfully rely upon the Lord of Salvation, for without His aid your strength will be but as weakness and the light of your knowledge as darkness. Pray to Him that He may be your light and life and strength. . . . Reform yourselves, your families and your neighbors; train up your children in the knowledge of God, and educate your wives and sisters. Manfully direct your energies against caste, and pull down the strongholds of idolatry. . . . There is before you a wide field for reformation, and you who desire to live as the servants of God, go forth and conscientiously fight the battle till the last day of life."[40]

At another time Sen explained that all social reforms "are involved in this grand radical reformation—religious reformation . . . through faith, the sense of duty of each individual will have been awakened to this work—to the urgency and momentousness of attending practically to the social interests of India." Religious and moral conviction, he held, would overcome caste and idolatry, would call forth widow remarriages, female education, the end of purdah, and even economic improvements. "I do not undervalue social reformation," he declared, "but make religion the center of all your reform movements—make religion the basis on which reorganized, reformed, and regenerated India will stand in future."[41] The message was powerful, and it reached a far wider audience than any reformer had previously known. Like Vivekananda's similar proclamations three decades later, however, it did not bring forth immediate practical results.

[39] See *Keshub Chandra Sen's Lectures in India*, 2 vols., which cover the period, 1866 to 1881.

[40] *ibid.*, II, 202-03.

[41] *ibid.*, II, 401-05.

In 1866 Debendranath Tagore and Keshub Chandra Sen could no longer maintain the façade of Brahmo unity, and the Calcutta Samaj formally split into two separate bodies, the conservative Adi (Original) Brahmo Samaj and the Brahmo Samaj of India. The Adi Samaj rapidly lost most of its adherents and became almost solely the responsibility of the Tagore family. The Brahmo Samaj of India, under Sen's influence, was identified in the popular mind with true Brahmoism and rapidly moved ahead along two lines: a further development of public devotionalism using elements from the traditional Bengal Vaishnava bhakti sects in order to reach Hindus beyond the confines of the Western-educated groups; and an active leadership of social service and reform causes. Sen's visit to England in 1870 crystallized his thinking on the means for social advancement, and on his return he founded the Indian Reform Association, the only general social reform body with significant influence that existed in 19th century Bengal. Previous Brahmo social service work—for famine relief, support of orphanages, uplift of laboring classes—and the support of widow remarriages were incorporated into the larger scope of the new English-inspired Association, whose membership was not limited to Brahmos. The Association sponsored new educational endeavors for women and working people, founded an Industrial School, worked for charity and temperance movements, and started inexpensive journals.

The Brahmo Samaj movement as a whole, beginning with Rammohun Roy, can be credited with establishing a major objective of all Indian social reform movements, the social freedom and cultural advancement of Hindu women. The Indian Reform Association was not notably successful as an agency sponsoring crusades in behalf of specific social reform doctrines, in the manner of reform bodies in other parts of the country. But the Association's work for the advancement of Bengali women, within the sphere of influence of the Brahmo Samaj, was for a time impressive.

Keshub Chandra Sen's first personal preoccupation was with religious, not social, reformation. Yet on one reform issue he moved vigorously for practical results; that was marriage reform. In 1871 through the Indian Reform Association, Sen circularized Indian and European medical men to elicit from them a scientific opinion on the proper age for marriage of girls. Writing to the doctors, he expressed "no doubt that the custom of premature marriage, as it prevails in this country, is injurious to the moral, social and physical interests of the people, and is one of the main obstacles in the way of their advancement."[42] The replies reinforced Sen's convictions; overwhelmingly they specified sixteen as the proper minimum marriage age for Indian girls. At about the same time Sen took a deep interest in the revised marriage ceremony of the Brahmo Samaj, which he wished to establish as the standard form for all Brahmos and popularize among other Hindus as well. The legal standing of the revised Brahmo rites was in question because they did not conform to established Hindu religious laws; a petition in 1867 from the Brahmo Samaj of India to the Advocate-General of India brought forth the opinion that Brahmo marriages were illegal. Accordingly, in the following year Sen appealed to Sir Henry Maine, the law member of the Governor-General's Council, to introduce a bill which would legalize them.

Sir Henry sympathetically moved a bill to provide for civil marriages, because Brahmoism was so ill-defined and internally divided that no one pattern of Brahmo marriage could be specified. In response to Maine's proposal the orthodox uproar, which included a petition from the foremost native political body, the British Indian Association, was considered so serious that the government shelved the measure. When it was again brought under review, after the customary collection of official opinions on the matter from the provinces, the bill was so drafted that it would apply to almost no one but a Brahmo, in other words one who acknowledged that he was not a Hindu, Muslim, Sikh, Parsi, Christian, Jain, Buddhist, or Jew. It was passed into law in March 1872, an entirely permissive piece of legislation, anyone benefiting from which, however, had to abide by its quite radical provisions: a prohibition against polygamy, a legal allowance for divorce, no reference to the castes of the marriage partners, and an age limit for marriage of fourteen for girls and eighteen for men. Sen felt satisfied with the Act, despite its many revisions before passage, and he himself had suggested the age minimum for girls, a revision

[42] See text of the letter in Chintamani, *op.cit.*, IV, 261.

of the doctors' recommendations, as a practical compromise with custom.

The orthodox had little reason to complain that this Native Marriage Act III of 1872 was a serious challenge to their views, because it necessarily would apply only to hopeless renegades. Nevertheless, petitions came to the government challenging its wisdom and right to tamper with marriage customs. One memorial asked the Secretary of State for India to seek disallowance of the Act by the Queen. It was sent by a group of prominent Madras Hindus after a public meeting held to consider the question in June 1872. The Madras memorialists, though taking note of the religious disclaimer provision of the Act, insisted that "every young Native of the country who, knowing little of other religions, and less of that of his forefathers, but primed with a certain amount of English Education, and predisposed to indulge in great libertinism of thought and action, required only the bidding of such a law to break off from his family, and those wholesome social restraints, which at present keep Native Society together." In candid fashion the petition continued, "Your Memorialists are perfectly aware that the progress of education in the country must eventually subvert Native Institutions, and bring about a complete revolution in Native Society. Nothing, they are persuaded, will stay this which must follow the progress of Western Ideas and Western Civilization as surely as the night follows the day. It is not of this that your Memorialists complain . . . but what they do complain of is of the Legislature, such as it is in this country, going out of its way to hasten and force on such changes by, as it were, directly inviting the rising generation of the country to set at defiance and break with the religion, the usages, and the traditions of their forefathers."[43] Young men, it was feared, would marry when, where, and whom they chose, and thus the social fabric would be torn apart.

Brahmos themselves were split over the Act, the Adi section opposing it on grounds that it would cast all Brahmos "out of the pale of Hindu society,"[44] and in the decades following its passage,

[43] From "A Memorial to His Grace The Duke of Argyll . . . from the Hindu Inhabitants of Madras . . ."

[44] From the Adi Memorial on the Act, quoted in Collet, op.cit., p. 21. Collet's Brahmo Year-Book provided a full account of the origin and passage of the Act.

Adi Brahmos refused to marry under its provisions. The government was aware of the possible impact of the Act on the Brahmo community; Fitzjames Stephen, Maine's successor on the council, had expressed impatience with the variety of Brahmo opinions on the bill before it became law. "I think," he told the Council, "that it is hardly possible for us to hold other language on the subject than this—'Be a Hindu or not as you please; but be one thing or the other, and do not ask us to undertake the impossible task of constructing some compromise between Hinduism and not Hinduism which will enable you to evade the necessity of knowing your own minds.' The present Bill is framed upon these principles."[45] Sen's Brahmo Samaj of India, by its adherence to the provisions of the Act, announced itself as a religious sect that was "not Hinduism."

Because marriage relations form the meaningful links binding a caste group together, and the absence of marriage relations separates one caste from another, the Brahmo Marriage Act, as it was called, silhouetted the Brahmo Samajists against the background of the rest of Hindu society. Virtually all Brahmos were married under its provisions after 1872.[46] As the historian of the Brahmo Samaj, Siva Nath Sastri, wrote, the Act "was hailed with a shout of joy by the progressives; but ever since it has been one of the principal causes that have alienated the Brahmos from the sympathies of their orthodox countrymen."[47] The Brahmos' separation from the Hindu community was not unintentional. Many Brahmos, beginning with Debendranath, were unable to remain Hindus and be true to their reformed faith. As Sen's close friend, Pratap Chunder Mozoomdar, expressed it, they felt pain at living "a life of public unfaithfulness" while remaining a discontented part of an unsympathetic and ridiculing orthodox community.[48] Sen's newspaper, the *Indian Mirror*, wrote approvingly of the Act

[45] *ibid.*, p. 32.

[46] Contemporary Hindu marriages are regulated by the new Hindu Marriage Act passed in 1955, which incorporates all the advanced provisions of the 1872 Act, except that the age limits are now set at 15 and 18; of course there is no religious disclaimer. In their marriage customs the Brahmos were about 75 years ahead of their times.

[47] As quoted by Farquhar, *Modern Religious Movements in India*, p. 249.

[48] Mozoomdar, *Faith and Progress of Brahmo Samaj*, pp. 272-73.

which effectively established the Brahmos as a separate caste: "We verily believe that the Brahma Samaj has thereby been saved, just in time, from falling into that vast and all-absorbing vortex of Hinduism, which by its treacherous tolerance has swallowed up almost all the reform movements in the country, . . . Such absorption is inevitable, unless our people guard their Church carefully against the danger. The clause in . . . the Marriage Act [providing for renunciation of established faiths] will serve as an effective safeguard."[49]

At the time of the Marriage Act's passage Sen held the position of the most vigorous religious and social reformer in the land. Despite differences over methods, all liberals in matters of reform found inspiration in his preaching and writing and in his fearless espousal of the causes he undertook. The end of his career as a social reformer, however, was close at hand. The devout Bengali's tendency to seek truth from intuitive and mystical sources, to the detriment of rational and practical concerns, produced the setting for his downfall. About 1875 he began to have sessions with a generally unknown ascetic worshipper of Kali, Ramakrishna Paramahansa, and within a few years Sen's teachings had lost most of their logical and practical content in favor of an eclectic, mystic, and universal message not unlike that of Ramakrishna *in spirit*. God should be worshipped as Mother; Christ was held to be God; Sen himself was to be regarded as the combined spokesman of Christ, Socrates, and the Bengali saint, Chaitanya.[50] Sen's new mystic spiritual life, identified simultaneously with Christianity and with Hindu Mother-worship, served to separate him from many of his followers but could not, on the other hand, create new adherents among the orthodox. The decline in his following was also the result of his religious austerities and unpredictable behavior. The more fervently that he asserted his newly found spiritual revelation, the less authoritatively was he able to voice the religious ideas of others. Furthermore, according to Siva Nath Sastri, the enrichment of Sen's devotional practices turned his

[49] Quoted in M. C. Parekh, *op.cit.*, p. 110.
[50] An excellent account of Sen's mysticism and his doctrine of the New Dispensation can be found in R. Rolland, *Life of Ramakrishna*, p. 113f. and Appendix II.

attention and that of the Samaj away from social welfare and reform.[51] On the ramifications of that issue a second split in the Brahmo Samaj occurred in 1878, though probably such a schism would have taken place anyway.

Never did the community of social reformers in India experience a shock so profound as when Sen, on the basis of his special revelation, decided to allow his daughter to be married to the young Maharaja of Kutch-Behar. The girl was thirteen and the Maharaja not yet sixteen, both below the minimum that Sen himself had publicly advocated, and the marriage ceremony was a flourish of almost unmitigated orthodoxy; his reasons for consenting to the union did nothing to allay the outrage that reformers thought he had committed. The government, wishing to liberalize the regime in Kutch-Behar through the offices of the young Maharaja, asked Sen to provide his educated daughter as a potentially modernized Maharani; he consented, trusting the assurances of Kutch-Behar that the girl would be brought up in an enlightened environment. The alliance with a royal house for a man not of the highest caste was appealing; and consideration for the government's wishes seemed to Sen only a fair acknowledgment of the advantages that he had received from the state. Above all, the marriage symbolized Sen's reliance on his personal judgment instead of consideration for the integrity of the reform movement of which he was the leader.[52] Those Brahmos, the majority, who already were restive under Sen's self-acknowledged preeminence

[51] As cited by Farquhar, *op.cit.*, p. 52. Sastri, it should be noted, led the criticism at the time of Sen's declining interest in social reform. P. C. Mozoomdar, Sen's chief disciple and successor, denied Sen's loss of interest in social reform in his *Faith and Progress of the Brahmo Samaj*, pp. 325-26.

[52] Sen agreed with the government that a marriage alliance might well keep the young prince on the path of reform for himself and his state. Sen wrote that he "felt that the Lord had himself brought before me, in the strange ways characteristic of His providence, the young Maharaja of Cooch Behar for alliance with my daughter." He realized the risk he was taking but relied on the Maharaja's word that he was a Brahmo in faith and would take only one wife. Sen implied that his daughter at the time of her marriage had reached puberty, in a letter to Frances Power Cobbe of April 26, 1878. Cited in *East and West*, II, 23 (Sept. 1903), pp. 1008-24. Apparently the young Maharani was indeed brought up in an enlightened environment. By her early twenties she had visited England, met the Queen, and was living an active social life in Calcutta. See E. F. Chapman, *Sketches of Some Distinguished Indian Women*.

and his mystic leanings, broke away in 1878 to form the Sadharan (General) Brahmo Samaj, which incorporated into its constitution checks against future personality cults. Only temporarily discouraged, Sen began a new "revival," as he called it in Christian terminology, and a previously announced message—The New Dispensation—was proclaimed more vigorously.

The New Dispensation was not an organizational success. It was too intimately linked with the "constant mental oscillation" and spiritual torture of "a being exhausting itself in searching after God"[53] to have any general appeal. Though Sen's new Church, in doctrine at least, insisted upon social service as a prerequisite to salvation, his alleged neglect of his own daughter's welfare eliminated him from any future leadership of the social reform movement. The Sadharan Brahmo Samaj persisted, especially strong in provincial areas of Bengal, and carried on the educational and philanthropic work already begun. But Brahmoism and Bengal, its homeland, had lost its claim to propagate social reform for the whole country. Henceforth other agencies in other provinces would have to point the way.

Sen's ultimate failure to organize a lasting social and religious reform movement that could penetrate with increasing effect into the popular conscience and consciousness illustrated the futility of the individualistic approach to reform. The search for personal truth or for a new mode of life among a limited number of enlightened men had no effect at all on the ideas and customs of the multitudes, who continued to look to priests and men of orthodox demeanor for their guidance. Sen's fervent appeal was an inspired and courageous cry, and the wilderness responded with a deafening silence. He and many lesser men never really reached the people with their message to lead a new life *as individuals*. All the reformers faced what finally subdued Sen, against whom "were the three hundred million gods of India and three hundred million living beings in whom they were incarnate—the whole vast jungle of human dreams wherein his Western outlook made him miss the track and the scent. He invited them to lose themselves in his Indian Christ, but his invitation remained unanswered. They did not even seem to have heard it."[54]

[53] Rolland, *op.cit.*, p. 137.   [54] *ibid.*, p. 139.

97

The Reform Movements in Bombay and Madras

The difference between the Bengal and Bombay social reformers was illustrated by their attitudes toward the ceremony of marriage. The traditional Hindu ceremony brought together, symbolically if not in fact, nearly all the characteristic features of Hindu society which were the subjects of criticism and discussion: the rights of women, the age of marriage, the family system, inter-caste relations, the role of the priests, and idolatrous rites. The Bombay reformers, no less than the Bengal group, were aware that the ceremony and the pre-marriage dealings between the families could not be reconciled with advanced liberal ideas. But customs, as Ranade once put it, should not be changed "with the facility of fashions."[55] In Bombay Presidency, there were modifications in marriage ceremonies, particularly when widows were being married, but no definite break with the old forms, which were not only tolerated but revered for the sanctity they provided to a ceremony which was a sacrament of the highest order for Hindus. Thus, Bombay social reformers made little use of the Brahmo Marriage Act.[56]

The fundamental reason for the divergence between Bengali and western Indian social reformers was the difference in their views on religious reform. To most educated Bengalis social reform required some adjustment in religious beliefs and outward religious behavior. Religion was felt to be the prime motive of behavior, and any questioning of social customs had to involve a religious inquiry as well. The reverse was also the case: a serious alteration of religious beliefs was thought to lead necessarily to changes in individual and family customs. Western ideas had proved very unsettling to Bengalis, and most of them felt driven either to reject them outright and revert to a more extreme orthodoxy, or to revise wholly their ways of thinking and acting in accordance with the sudden new insights which Western knowledge provided—insights of a spiritual, not just of a practical, kind. Other Indians might adopt a judicious curiosity about the West and its ways; for Bengalis of the 19th century, the West was an

[55] Ranade, *Miscellaneous Writings*, p. 127.
[56] Murdoch, *Papers on Indian Religious Reform*, IV, 75-76.

obsession, leading to extreme reactions, *pro* or *contra*. Bengalis who found their beliefs and habits transformed by Western influences often became members of the Brahmo Samaj. Their social reforming spirit was thus often exhausted by the heavy demands which excessive nonconformism created. Merely to survive with one's family in reasonable peace and dignity required for Brahmos great fortitude, and not all of them appeared anxious to undertake public crusades which would increase their difficulties.

A western Indian could characterize the different impacts that religious reform had on social reform in Bengal and in Bombay by the following analysis: "The religious movement in Bengal was far more successful than that in the Bombay Presidency. The result has been that in Bengal religious reform has kept pace with social reform, while in the Bombay Presidency it has given place to scepticism and atheism. On the other hand, in Bengal social reform has been in a degree impeded by the tacit requirement of conformity with the principles of Brahmoism, which is the religion of the reformers, while in Bombay the reformers, apparently continuing as they do in the religion of their ancestors, are not estranged from popular sympathy to the degree they have been in Bengal. In Bengal, social reform has assumed the shape of a caste question, while in Bombay the refusal of the reformers to claim a separate caste for themselves has set the whole society in a ferment. Reform is bound to live an isolated life in Bengal, and to be general in Bombay."[57]

During the period of Debendranath Tagore's leadership of the Brahmo Samaj in Bengal, Bombay Presidency was developing a religious and social reform tradition whose influence on later generations in western India equalled the influence of the more publicized Brahmo Samaj in Bengal. Perhaps because of the lesser notoriety of the religious and social abuses in western India, but also possibly due to the more practical and less revolutionary temperament of Indians in the western Presidency (if one accepts M.G. Ranade's explanation), the religious and social revolts there were less extreme than in Bengal. The earliest religious and social reform group on record in Bombay Presidency was the Paramahans Mandali (The Divine Society), founded in 1840 with the

[57] W.M. Kolhatkar, in Chintamani, *op.cit.*, I, 311.

object of working for the abolition of caste, the introduction of widow remarriage, and the renunciation of idolatry. Typical of the Bombay reformers, who were not seeking dramatic personal breaks with society, the society's meetings were held in secrecy.[58] In 1848 the Students' Literary and Scientific Society was established to discuss social questions and undertake education of girls. Among Gujaratis in the city of Bombay, the Buddhi-Vardhak Hindu Sabha (Society for Advancement of Knowledge), founded in 1851, served as a center for discussion of the new ideas penetrating from the West. The Dnyan Prasarak Mandali (Society for the Diffusion of Knowledge), one of whose organizers was the Parsi, Dadabhai Naoroji, met for similar purposes. Both religious and social reform societies recruited their memberships largely from students and graduates of the Elphinstone Institution, founded in 1827, and from John Wilson's English School, later Wilson College, organized in 1835.

One of the first students and subsequently the first Indian Professor at the Elphinstone Institution, Bal Gangadhar Shastri Jambhekar (1812-1846), provided powerful intellectual incentives for the young generation of the mid-19th century in Bombay, the generation which was to produce some of India's greatest leaders in the 1880's. Bal Shastri urged widow remarriage, a liberalization of caste formalities, and the readmission to Hindu society of persons who had been baptized Christians. His weekly journal, *The Bombay Durpan*, was the first in western India to espouse social reform causes—in the late 1830's. Bal Shastri was not, however, a revolutionary; he observed orthodox patterns of behavior and pressed for social reform that did not entail giving up religious beliefs.[59]

In Gujarat, too, the earliest social reform activity did not lag far behind that of the intellectually more advanced Bengal. One of the first social reformers in western India was Mehtaji Durgaram Mancharam (1809-1876), a product of the new elementary education system set up under Elphinstone's administration. A government teacher in Surat from 1828, Mehtaji never knew

---

[58] Kellock, *Ranade*, pp. 18-19. Incidentally, R.G. Bhandarkar placed the time of the founding of the Paramahans Mandali in the early 1850's.

[59] See *Memoirs and Writings of Acharya Bal Shastri Jambhekar*.

English, but despite that handicap he held views on the ideal position of women which evidenced Western inspiration and composed attacks on idolatry and witchcraft which were similar in essence to Rammohun Roy's. In 1838 he began a public protest against the treatment of widows, and in 1844 he organized the Manay Dharma Sabha (Universal Religious Society) to discuss social problems, including those arising from the caste system. Narmada Shankar (1833-1886), another Gujarati, took up the cause of women's education, urged widow remarriage, attacked caste barriers and advocated travel to England in order to acquire Western scientific knowledge. The careers of other Gujarati reformers—Dalpatram of the Gujarat Vernacular Society; Mahipatram Rupram, the first modern-day Gujarati to travel abroad; and Karsondas Mulji, of Maharaja Libel Case fame—provide convincing evidence that many western Indians were by the 1840's as aroused to the issues of social change and reform as were Bengali Brahmos. Most of the Gujarati reformers were associated with the Gujarat Vernacular Society in Ahmedabad, similar in purposes to the Literary and Scientific Society of Bombay. The Ahmedabad Society was founded in 1848 under the inspiration of Alexander Forbes and the following year began a coeducational school, possibly the first in India. The Society's main work was in female education and improvement of the position of women.[60]

Gujarati and Marathi reformers placed major reliance on vernacular literary media, poetry, dramas and novels, and their opponents retaliated in like fashion. Great public debates on social issues became standard fare for readers of the vernacular press in western India. A foremost literary advocate of social reform was Gopal Hari Deshmukh, known as Lokahitwadi, a product of the government English School at Poona, who ultimately became a judge in Ahmedabad. His critical writings on social matters began to appear in the 1840's and provide a classic example of the early

[60] Discussions of the Gujarati reformers appear in Neera Desai, *Woman in Modern India* and in her M.A. thesis, Bombay Univ., "The Impact of the British Rule on the Position of Indian Women"; H.T. Parekh's history of the Gujarat Vernacular Society, cited by Miss Desai; J.G. Joglekar, "Evolution of Social Life and Ideals in Maharashtra," M.A. thesis, Bombay Univ.; Uttamlal K. Trivedi, "Social Reform in Gujarat: A Retrospect," in *The Indian Review*, VI, 12 (Dec. 1905), pp. 840-45.

Maharashtrian response to the West. He knew English well, but he wrote in the vernacular. His words were often bitter outbursts against almost everything in traditional Indian life—the caste system, child marriage, the treatment of widows were his particular targets. But in his personal life he did not break with customary ways or even take an active part in social reform bodies. The following excerpt from his *Shatapatre* (*Hundred Letters*) illustrates Deshmukh's mode of attack: "I think that the misery of women is so great that when I remember it my hair stands on end. These Brahmins, instead of killing their daughters, put them into greater misery. . . . And still there are some who speak against this reform [widow remarriage]. . . . Doesn't the heart stir when the throats of girls of twelve, fifteen, twenty, and thirty years are being cut? . . . You yourselves unprotestingly become the butchers of your own daughters. There is no comparison on earth to a nation like yours. . . ."[61] Deshmukh's major message took the form of attacks upon the intellectual monopoly exercised by the Brahmins over Hindu life. Struck by the idea of a freedom which only knowledge could provide, he condemned the popular veneration of Sanskrit because it hindered the spread of new ideas to all classes of people. Like Rammohun Roy he supported English education, and he urged that education be based on English-language texts, or translations of them, and that it be used for the transmission of scientific, not Brahmanic, learning.

Many early western Indian reformers appeared more concerned with public crusades that offered the possibilities of immediate, observable improvements than with inner spiritual debates that might bring new insights into the meaning of modern life. A contemporary of Deshmukh, and supported by him, was Jotiba Govind Phule (1827-1890), one of the few social reformers whose practical efforts matched his announced convictions. While most of the crusaders against unreasonable orthodoxy confined their activities to individual protests in journals or private groups, Phule started a girls' school at Poona, about 1850, two schools for untouchables, and in 1863 a foundling home to care for the unwanted children of widows—Home for the Prevention of Infanti-

[61] *Shatapatre*, No. 99; quoted in S.A. Wolpert, "Tilak and Gokhale" (Ph.D. dissertation), p. 40.

cide. Central to his scheme for rebuilding Hindu society was the liberation and education of women, whom he felt had been kept unenlightened by men who wanted to preserve their own superiority. Consequently he favored widow remarriage and opposed polygamy and child marriage.[62] In 1873 he began his greatest life work by organizing the Satyashodhak (Search for Truth) Samaj, whose aim was to save the "lower castes from the hypocritical Brahmins and their opportunistic scriptures."[63] The Samaj later became the nucleus of a movement in Maharashtra which was to have profound reverberations on social and political life in the 20th century, the awakening of the non-Brahmin castes and their struggle for influence and even dominance. Phule was a prolific writer, and though he knew English he published in Marathi, like Deshmukh, in order to reach the non-Westernized but educated reader. His most famous work was *Gulamgiri* (Slavery), published in 1872. A member of the Poona Municipal Council from 1874 to 1883, he regarded Western influence in the country not only as conducive to individual liberation from restrictive ideas and customs, but as the basis of a massive social upheaval. Of low caste birth himself, he wrote that "The Creator has purposely sent the English people to this country to liberate the disabled Shudras from the slavery of the crafty Aryas."[64]

A rare example of reforming methods was a crusade in Bombay undertaken by the Gujarati reformer, Karsondas Mulji (1832-1871). Proceeding beyond many of the usual reform advocacies—widow remarriage, foreign travel, simplification of marriage ceremonies, and female education—Karsondas worked his way gradually toward an uncompromising exposure, in his newspaper, *Satya Prakash*, of the nonreligious, immoral practices of the Maharajas, hereditary priests of the Vallabhacharya sect.[65] His exposure of

[62] A.K. Ghorpade, *Mahatma Phule* (in Marathi), p. 29. Phule once asked if there was any husband who would become a "sutta" (comparable to a suttee) because of devotion to his deceased wife. *ibid.*, p. 30.

[63] Quoted in Wolpert, *op.cit.*, p. 43.

[64] Phule, *Everybody's Book of Religion and Truth* (in Marathi, 1891), quoted, *loc.cit.*

[65] The Maharajas received personal devotion, as incarnations of Krishna, which, when the devotees were women, sometimes led to sexual intercourse. See the brief account of this sect in J.M. Farquhar, *An Outline of the Religious Literature of India*, p. 312f.

the conduct of the Maharajas brought him, at the age of thirty, into the famous libel suit of 1861-2 in which testimony in court on hitherto concealed facts about temple practices of the Maharajas was publicized, with considerable educative detail, throughout western India. Karsondas won his case and was awarded costs. Sir Joseph Arnould, the judge in the case, proclaimed from the bench axioms of Anglo-Saxon jurisprudence which undermined orthodox Hindu customs one year and a half after the concluding battles of the 1857 uprising. Sir Joseph easily discounted the argument that the Maharajas should have immunity because religious matters were involved, "It is not a question of theology that has been before us," he said, "it is a question of morality. The principle for which the defendant [Karsondas] and his witnesses have been contending is simply this, that what is morally wrong cannot be theologically right, that when practices which sap the very foundations of morality, which involve a violation of the eternal and immutable laws of Right, are established in the name and under the sanction of Religion, they ought, for the common welfare of society, and in the interests of Humanity itself, to be publicly denounced and exposed."[66] Indeed, this was the principle being followed by Karsondas, the basic credo of the entire Indian social reform movement, and a doctrine whose enunciation set the reformer outside of and in opposition to orthodox Hinduism.

Karsondas Mulji, though a great admirer of Anglo-Saxon morality after his visit to England, apparently did not repudiate the essentials of the Hindu tradition.[67] Corruption of that tradition, however, aroused in him more vigorous protests than were common even among reformers in western India. His attacks on individuals rather than on customs, the use he made of the British courts, and the single-mindedness of his crusade, lasting for many years, marked him as a unique figure in the Bombay Presidency.

The social and religious rebels of western India were more anxious to infect public opinion with their rationalism and new

[66] Quoted in Motivala, *Karsondas Mulji; A Short Sketch* . . . , p. 36.

[67] N.G. Chandavarkar reported that Karsondas opposed radical changes in society, worshipped idols, and accepted the system of caste. Later reformers admired his courage but regarded him as only partially reformed in his personal life. Chandavarkar, *Speeches and Writings*, p. 32.

proposals for reform than they were concerned with working out a new and integrated philosophy of life for themselves. They did not, therefore, separate themselves from society, as the Brahmos of Bengal did, by adopting a novel religious creed and assuming unconventional manners. They maintained confidence in the existing social structure and its formalities, and they urged the introduction of Western ideas and institutions as crucial amendments to the Indian tradition but not as determinants of a wholly transformed way of life. Refusing to break completely with traditional society the Bombay reformers tried to develop practical ways of adjusting their convictions and behavior to the minimal demands of the orthodox leaders. Some Bombay reformers were outcasted because of breaches of caste rules, but most of them carefully avoided spectacular affronts to leaders of caste communities, though they vigorously condemned many caste practices in their writings and speeches. Thus, their reform ideas found somewhat readier public acceptance, or at least tolerance, than those of the advanced groups of Bengal. Propaganda, practical social work, and education were their main tools, while religious reform and individual iconoclasm, as well as education, were the major weapons in Bengal.

The stress by the western Indian reformers on vernacular education for widespread public enlightenment can be considered a continuation of Lord Elphinstone's policy of trying to provide secondary school education in vernaculars to a broad segment of the population. Elphinstone's policy reflected his sympathy for the virtues of the conservative tradition of Bombay Presidency and his belief that change should be gradual. Its wisdom was recognized by the social reformers.

In 1867 the special genius of the Bombay school of reform brought forth its original contribution to modern Indian theism, the Prarthana (Prayer) Samaj. Its origin was due to the missionary enthusiasm of Brahmo Samajists led by Keshub Chandra Sen, who first visited Bombay in 1864 and returned in 1868 to give the new Samaj his personal encouragement.[68] In doctrine the Prarthana

[68] The expansion of the Samaj movement under the aegis of Sen was one of his greatest accomplishments. When Sen joined the Brahmo Samaj there were 14 Samajes, all in Bengal. During the next twenty years 72 units were added;

Samaj closely resembled Sen's branch of the Brahmo Samaj—belief in a single, all-powerful, all-loving God; salvation through worship of God; denial of the ideas of karma and transmigration; opposition to the authority of priests and idolatry.[69] Like the Brahmo Samaj of India the Prarthana Samaj revered the Upanishads but stressed the idea of devotion to a personal God, through bhakti. Theism was for many social reformers the only acceptable conception of God, because God as a personal divinity with moral purposes provided the necessary link between religious devotion and worldly righteousness. It was consistently preached by the Prarthana Samajists to produce in the minds of their audiences an inseparable connection between reverence for God and reverence for man. The leaders of the Prarthana Samaj, according to Chandavarkar, showed "how the holy truths of religion should be applied to the practical duties of life, and how religion was meant by our prophets as by the prophets of Israel to be 'the practice of civic virtues—truth-telling, honesty between citizens, tenderness to the poor, inflexible justice in high places.'"[70] The Hindu Protestants[71]—a convenient term for the religious reformers—had a wider choice of texts than did the Christian missionaries, because they could cite passages from the Upanishads and Bhagavad-Gita and rely also on the voluminous devotional literature of the bhakti sects. While in Bengal, Vaishnava bhakti

---

Sen and his followers travelled from Baluchistan to Travancore and from Assam to Sind. The Sadharan Brahmo Samaj, under Siva Nath Sastri and Ananda Mohan Bose, maintained the missionary enterprise and added 125 units, not all of which bore the name, Brahmo Samaj. See A. Gupta, *Studies in the Bengal Renaissance*, pp. 479-80.

[69] On the use of idols in worship the Prarthana Samaj did not adopt as strict a prohibition as did the Brahmo Samaj of India. It was noted by Fraser and Edwardes in 1920 that the Bombay Prarthana Samaj defeated a motion to drop from membership anyone engaging in an idolatrous rite. Fraser and Edwardes, *Life and Teaching of Tukaram*, pp. 153-54.

[70] Chandavarkar, *op.cit.*, p. 45.

[71] See the discussion by Chandavarkar, "Hindoo Protestantism," *ibid.*, pp. 38-46. Also Manohar Lal Zutshi's series, "Hindu Protestantism," in the *Hindustan Review*, 1906-7, esp. iv, March 1907. One of the first Hindus to use this term was Ranade, who meant by it a continuing liberal protest against orthodoxy, based on direct revelation of God. See his "Hindu Protestantism," in *Religious and Social Reform*, p. 198f.

literature furnished inspiration for Sen's Brahmo movement, in Bombay the poems and stories of Marathi and Gujarati saints supplied texts and inspiration for the Prarthana Samaj.

In social practices, however, the Prarthana Samaj deviated from the precedents laid down in Bengal, and by this deviation accentuated the unique course of the western (and to some extent peninsular) Indian tradition of reform. Despite Sen's efforts to broaden the base of popular acceptance of the Brahmo faith by the use of traditional references in his teaching, his movement could not bridge the firmly established social gap between Brahmos and the general population. The Prarthana Samaj, on the other hand, did not set itself apart from Hindu society, though many Samajists broke away from popular Hindu religion almost as completely as Brahmos did. The predominant attitude among Bombay Samajists was that religious reform and social reform could proceed along different courses and at varying rates, and that neither reform need involve a sharp break with the past. They regarded most social institutions as subject to alteration without affecting the essential character of Hinduism as a religion, and although as individuals they found spiritual satisfaction through the Protestantism of their Samaj, they did not set out as missionaries to revolutionize Hinduism along the same lines. They were "men paying allegiance to Hinduism and to Hindu society with a protest," one observer wrote, and he continued, "The members observe the ceremonies of routine, destitute of all religious significance. This much sacrifice they make to existing prejudices. Their principle, however, is not to deceive anyone as to their religious opinions, even should an honest expression of views entail unpopularity."[72] Toward the end of the century a notable Christian missionary, M. Murdoch, similarly noted that "The theism of western India has never detached itself so far from the Hindu elements of Brahmoism as the progressive Brahmos of Bengal have done, and both in religious observances and social customs, it clings far more closely to the old models." Murdoch referred to the "learned, sober-minded, and wealthy Marathi and Gujarati theists of the Bombay Presidency," and with obvious bias wrote that they "resemble in type English

[72] From *ISR*, as quoted in S. Natarajan, *A Century of Social Reform in India*, p. 61.

Unitarians, respectable and philanthropic, but without any strong sense of sin or depth of piety."[73]

Kashinath Trimbak Telang, one of the first to join the Prarthana Samaj, stated his position directly when he asserted, "I am first and last a Hindu."[74] Most of the Prarthana Samajists tried to retain at least a semblance of their caste position and for census purposes gave their hereditary caste, unlike their Bengali counterparts who were always known as Brahmos. From that fact J.A. Baines concluded that there was "a wide difference" between the new theism of Bengal and Bombay, and that in the latter case, "it is desired to restrict its operation to the spiritual or moral side of the Vedic religion, not to interfere with the more important element of social interests."[75] Ranade, another early member of the Prarthana Samaj, defended more vigorously than anyone else the special Bombay approach to social reform: "The peculiar feature of the movement in [this] Presidency is that we want to work on no single line, but to work on all lines together and above all not to break with the past and cease all connection with our society. We do not proceed on the religious basis exclusively as in Bengal. We have the different Samajes, but somehow or other there is something in our nature which prevents us from bodily moving into another camp. We do not desire to give up our hold on the old established institutions."[76] Ranade himself had "passed without crisis and without conflict into a new outlook," wrote one of his biographers,[77] but he knew that such a fundamental alteration of beliefs by the uneducated general public would have meant social chaos. For him, therefore, and for most of the Bombay group, social reform, though urgently required, had to come about gradually and without radical breaks with the past. To be genuine, reform should proceed from inner motives. But reform by any legitimate means was preferable to none at all, and several of the

[73] Murdoch, op.cit., iv, 75-76.
[74] Quoted in N.V. Naik, "Telang as a Social Reformer," *Social Reform Annual*, *1951*, p. 33.
[75] Govt. of India, *Imperial Census of 1881: Operations and Results in the Presidency of Bombay*, i, 47.
[76] Ranade, *Miscellaneous Writings*, p. 159.
[77] James Kellock, *Ranade*, p. 22.

eminent Maharashtrian reformers, Phule, Agarkar, and D.K. Karve, had no connection with the Prarthana Samaj.

Such were the reform activities in the two Presidencies most advanced in education[78] and in public communication when comparable intellectual developments first attracted attention in Madras. Sen's missionary activity in Madras in 1864 bore fruit when the Ved Samaj was established in that year. After a visit to Calcutta Shridharulu Naidu in 1871 reorganized the body and renamed it the Brahmo Samaj of South India.[79] After the 1878 split in the Bengal Samaj, Siva Nath Sastri, the leader of the Sadharan Brahmo Samaj and its chief missionary, visited Madras and recruited new strength for the movement. M. Butchiah Pantulu and R. Venkata Ratnam were leaders of the Samaj, the former establishing its permanent headquarters in Madras City in 1885, and the latter subsequently becoming president of the body. The Brahmo Samaj movement, however, spread very slowly, and a Brahmo community of influential families and a unique social status never emerged as it did in Bengal. M.C. Parekh observed the weakness of Brahmoism in Madras: "In the people of Madras there is excellent material whether from the point of view of subtlety of intellect or tenderness of heart, but whether it be due to the extreme orthodoxy of the people or to the very strict caste system prevailing there, the message of the Brahma Dharma has fallen more or less on deaf ears."[80]

The Prarthana Samaj had a greater missionary impact than the Brahmo Samaj in Madras, and ultimately about two-thirds of the

[78] Govt. of India, Home Dept., Selection from Records: "Note on the State of Education in India, 1865-66," by A.M. Monteath, and "Note on the State of Education in India During 1866-67," by A.P. Howell gave a reasonably accurate impression of the relative positions of the major provinces in English and vernacular education in the 1860's. Both agreed that Bengal was far ahead in English education at all levels. Bombay's quality of English education was about equal to Bengal's, and it was far ahead in spreading vernacular education. Madras could be said generally to rank third; missionary education, however, mainly elementary and in English, was most advanced there. In the North-Western Provinces higher education was least well developed, but elementary vernacular education and high school English education was being stressed and was judged successful by Monteath. The Punjab was behind the others in all areas.

[79] See Parekh, *op.cit.*, pp. 229-230; and Murdoch, *op.cit.*, p. 70.

[80] Parekh, *op.cit.*, p. 230.

theistic churches in peninsular India were called Prarthana Sa-majes.[81] Viresalingam Pantulu, mentioned earlier as the leading advocate of widow remarriage in the Telegu-speaking area, stood out as the most energetic and vocal Prarthana Samajist in the southern Presidency. In 1878 he began the theistic movement in the Telegu country and the same year founded the Rajahmundry Social Reform Association. Probably the most renowned Telegu scholar of his time Viresalingam aided the revival of that language through his original dramas, his journalism, and his translations of English and Sanskrit works into the native tongue. In religious and social reform his concern was of the broadest kind, at one time analyzing the disintegrating effects of British rule on traditional beliefs, at another sarcastically exposing caste and idolatry.

Like the other reformers of his day, Viresalingam made his mark as an individual in protest against society, as well as in private work for social change. In Madras in the 1870's and 1880's he was a rare type, and if a movement for reform could be said to have existed in the southern Presidency in his time, that movement was largely the personal career of Viresalingam. Unlike Bombay, Madras then had no group of social reformers who gave fairly consistent and influential support to the established causes. The religious reforms exemplified by the Madras Samaj meant little more than the quiet expression of certain preferences in forms of personal worship. Many of its members were students, most of whom tended to terminate their membership when they grew older.[82] The Samaj in Madras, as in Bombay, had the effect of modifying, not revolutionizing, the views of its adherents, who were not required or expected to make complete their revolt against society by adopting an unorthodox way of life.

To explain the relative backwardness of Madras in religious and social reform one must go to factors more significant than the Prarthana Samaj in the life of southern Hindus. Even by the late 19th century the social rebellion, which was the most effective stimulus to social reform on individualistic lines, was not as pronounced in Madras as elsewhere in India. It would be too facile

[81] Farquhar, *op.cit.*, p. 78.
[82] According to J. Gurunadham, *Viresalingam: The Founder of Telegu Public Life*, pp. 138-39.

an explanation for this lack of a strong reform movement merely to cite figures on English education in the Presidency, because there has never been an absolute correlation in India between the numbers of English-educated men and the intensity of social dissatisfaction, intellectual stimulation, or political agitation. Madras, it is true, was markedly behind Bengal and Bombay in education in the early 19th century, and although it was rapidly catching up in higher education by the 1870's, the number of college graduates in Madras still remained lower than in Bombay or Bengal. In the following decade the census showed that Madras had the largest number, and the highest proportion to the general population, of Indians with a knowledge of English,[83] but most of those had left school long before the university stage and knew little more about the West than one of its languages.

More suggestive of the true reasons for less social rebellion in Madras was the caste structure in peninsular India, which provided for the distinct social dominance of the Brahmin castes over the low castes composing the bulk of the population. That structure, less affected by the disrupting Muslim and Maratha influences that had been an outstanding feature of northern India, Bengal, and the Deccan, showed no signs then of breaking apart because of pressures from the non-Brahmin groups. The Brahmins, who constituted the "overwhelming preponderance" of university graduates,[84] could scarcely afford to advocate any fundamental social changes without at the same time seeming to undermine their unchallenged dominance. Though Brahmins anywhere, whether social reformers or not, were generally unwilling to see all their social advantages as members of the highest caste undermined, the threat of losing caste was a more terrifying outlook in Madras than in Bengal or Bombay, where a cosmopolitan intermingling of Brahmins with the substantial intermediate and high caste groups just below them in the hierarchy was going on, notably in the Westernized urban centers. To say that Madras Brahmins were socially conservative, of course, begs the question. More meaningfully, social innovation by Madras Brahmins could mean more even than ostracism by caste brethren; it could mean the

[83] McCully, *English Education and the Origins of Indian Nationalism*, p. 178.
[84] *ibid.*, p. 190.

extinction of the privileges which separated them, and their entire families, from the benighted lower orders. Conservatism was based on necessity, if not on preference.

Although Madras in that period did produce a vigorous propagandist like Viresalingam and constructive supporters of reform like T. Madhava Rao and Raghunatha Rau, there came from the southern Presidency no man of a stature comparable to Rammohun Roy, Keshub Chandra Sen, or Ranade. No Madrasi formulated the kind of intellectual and spiritual responses to Western thought which were occupying the attention of certain Bengalis, Gujaratis, and Maharashtrians. Intellectual life in Madras either was a reflection of Indian thought originating elsewhere or, for a small group centered about the missionary schools and colleges, was Christian in inspiration and content. After the establishment of the university system in Madras there was a rapid spread of Western ideas through the ranks of the higher educated, and Madrasis soon became noted throughout India as capable administrators and professional men. The new ideas, however, seemed to affect their thinking without changing to any great extent their religious observances and modes of social behavior. When the social reform movement did get fully under way in Madras, in later decades, it stressed peripheral issues, such as nautch dancing, alcoholism, and income distribution in the joint family. Social welfare work, along lines laid down by the missionaries, was always a more popular form of organized endeavor than social reform.

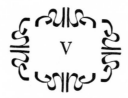

V

DAYANANDA SARASWATI AND

THE SOCIAL REFORM MOVEMENT IN

NORTHERN INDIA

"The Arya Samaj may quite logically be pronounced an outcome of the conditions imported into India by the West. . . ."

LAJPAT RAI[1]

"Western civilization had not the slightest influence in making him [Dayananda] what he was. He did not know English and was in no way influenced by European culture or European thought."

HAR BILAS SARDA[2]

THESE two observations illustrate the present lack of clarity in historical writing about the most significant religious and social reform movement of the latter half of the 19th century in northern India (here meant to include the North-Western Provinces, Oudh, and Punjab, or pre-1947 United Provinces and Punjab). The Arya Samaj was founded by Dayananda Saraswati in 1875, and some of its cardinal features place the movement in the category of an individualistic rebellion against society and an espousal of a creed which satisfied personal needs in an era of intellectual and social revolt. Other features of the Arya Samaj,

[1] Lajpat Rai, *The Arya Samaj*, p. 293.
[2] H.B. Sarda, *Dayanand Commemoration Volume*, p. xxxiv.

113

notably its organization and its message of invigorating unity for all Hindus, carried its influence into the later nationalist periods. Not easy to define is its relationship to Western ideas; Dayananda, the founder, was very different from the typical Westernized Indian. It is equally difficult to classify Dayananda among other modern Indian religious and social thinkers. But whatever may be the problems facing an historian in understanding Dayananda's work, it is clear that the Arya Samaj, in terms of its continuity and the depth of its influence, was the most popularly acceptable single movement for religious and social reform in late 19th and early 20th century India.

In nearly every particular the early career of Dayananda Saraswati differed but little from those of the hundreds of mystics and regional saints for which India was still noted in the 19th century. Born Mool Shankar,[3] 1824, in Morvi, an obscure princely state in Kathiawar, he grew up in a well-to-do orthodox Shaivite family, without, his biographers stress, any exposure to Western intellectual influences. At an early age he began to question the worship of idols[4] and pondered the significance of death, and hence of life. His main object was to devote himself to study, and when that seemed threatened by his family's efforts to have him married, he escaped from home at the age of twenty-one. After a few years he established himself as one of the thousands of anonymous sannyasis wandering from place to place, and until the age of thirty-six Dayananda's life was one of nearly constant travel, on foot, from one holy place to another. Crisscrossing the northern part of the continent, wandering up and down the Ganges, fighting his way through jungles and into the glacier-bound passes of

[3] Dayananda's origins and even his family name are still subjects of dispute. The most critical discussion of Dayananda's early life, which drew on all published sources and on interviews with persons in the locale of Dayananda's birth, is found in J. Reid Graham, "The Arya Samaj as a Reformation in Hinduism with Special Reference to Caste" (Ph.D. thesis, Yale, 1942), 2 vols. The name, Mool Shankar, Graham pointed out, was never acknowledged by Dayananda. (pp. 37-38.)

[4] The story of Dayananda's early incredulity about idol worship arising from the sight of mice clambering over a temple figure representing Shiva is to be found in his autobiographical fragment written for *The Theosophist*, journal of the Theosophical Society. See Sarda, *Life of Dayanand Saraswati*, and Graham, *op.cit.*, p. 57f.

the Himalayas, walking across the plains of Hindustan, resting occasionally for a month or so at temples or ashrams, the man eschewed the relative comfort and prestige which he could have had as a settled priest or guru in favor of a rigorous physical life and an unsatisfied quest for spiritual truth.

It is, perhaps, a sad commentary on the religious and intellectual life in Dayananda's day that until 1860 he could find no teacher well enough versed in the Vedas and with a critical enough approach to popular religious beliefs to satisfy his exacting standards. And then, in that year, when he finally became a disciple of a blind guru, Virjananda, he received probably a greater measure of iconoclastic fervor and arbitrary interpretations of the Vedas than was the ideal of Sanskrit learning. But Virjananda's teachings apparently bridged the torturing gap which for Dayananda existed between the essential truth and nobility of Hindu philosophy and the degraded superstition and venality of popular religious practices. The gap could be understood by recognizing that the revealed excellence of the Vedas had been obscured by the accumulated untruth of the bulk of post-Vedic smriti[5] literature. More important for the genius of Dayananda's life, the gap could be bridged by a reformation of the Hindu faith, by causing the "light of truth" to remove the "darkness of ignorance from the land." The latter injunction was given to Dayananda by Virjananda, and the pupil became the teacher, instructing where he had previously searched, throughout Hindustan, and as far south as Bombay and Calcutta. The year 1868 marked the end of his seclusion and spiritual searchings and the start of his active career of religious and social reform.

His method of propagating the Vedic faith, as he called it, was at first only by word of mouth, in the historic tradition of all

[5] There are disagreements as to what the smriti literature is composed of, in relation to the shruti literature. The distinction between these classifications stems from the meaning of shruti as "recalled" or "heard" and smriti as "remembered" scriptures. The former may be referred to as knowledge from divine sources and the latter as knowledge from human sources, supposedly derived from the original shruti revelation. Although Dayananda particularly criticized the Upanishads, which some consider part of shruti literature, he strongly supported the *Manusmriti* and derived from it most of his ethical teachings. He thus used non-Vedic scriptures in his teaching but did so only if he felt they were in accord with Vedic truth. See Sarda, *op.cit.*, p. 407.

115

Indian holy men, and only in the sacred language, Sanskrit. Teaching in such a manner, and indeed with such a message—to purify old beliefs and eliminate "un-Aryan" social customs— Dayananda was no more, nor less, than any other of the true sannyasis who brought new light into Hinduism and injected human values into ossified social customs and then passed on, revered and even worshipped by many of those who heard and saw them. He was far more vigorous and ambitious than most of the contemporary Hindu sannyasis, however. Besides engaging in public debates on the shastras with established pundits, lecturing in temples and at melas (large gatherings), and collecting disciples, Dayananda ventured to engage the leading Brahmins of Benaras in a Shastrarth, a debate on the shastras, and thus, if possible, nominally to overthrow the entire order of popular Hinduism in a single, magnificent stroke. However effective such a procedure of robbing orthodoxy of its unchallengeable reference point at Benaras might have been, it was never tried by any one of the 19th or 20th century reformers except Dayananda. Of course, the Benaras pundits, patronized and venerated for their wisdom, would never admit defeat. The Shastrarth, which took place late in 1869 under the auspices of the Maharaja of Benaras, was doomed to failure. Dayananda challenged his opponents to prove that the Vedas sanctioned idol worship, and according to despatches in the *Hindu Patriot*, the *Tattvabodhini Patrika*, and the *Pioneer*,[6] their response was evasive, and Dayananda's position against idol worship was upheld. However, the pundits claimed victory and refused to acknowledge the rebel's right to interpret the sacred writings.

In the early 1870's Dayananda began to formulate a systematic presentation of his religious beliefs, and in 1874 he dictated the most important of his many works, the *Satyarth Prakash* (*Light of Truth*), written in Hindi in order to obtain wide circulation and published at Benaras in 1875.[7] It is probably significant that

[6] For excerpts from those contemporary sources, see Sarda, *op.cit.*, pp. 71-73.

[7] This first edition was not supervised by Dayananda through the printing process and hence contained many misstatements of his views, which he later acknowledged. A new and entirely revised edition came out in sections beginning in 1882 and is considered a true rendering of the Swami's beliefs. The English

116

the written rendition of his thinking appeared following a lengthy visit to Calcutta, where he entered into intimate intellectual contacts with Brahmos, notably Keshub Chandra Sen.

Central to Dayananda's religious thought were his beliefs in a dualistic universe, of mind and matter, and in the absolute separation of God and the human soul. Those two ideas ran counter to the dominant Hindu philosophy, advaita Vedanta, which held that the only reality is pure spirit or consciousness, that the physical world is an illusion (created by maya negating consciousness), and that man's soul is a part of God, temporarily separated from God by its embodiment in the illusory mask of the body. The neo-Vedantists of Dayananda's day found little difficulty in maintaining their nondualist doctrine, and against their teachings Dayananda launched the most erudite of his philosophical crusades. The motive for his attack, similar to that of the bhaktas, on the neo-Vedantist position was his conviction that the concept of the oneness of all reality precluded the existence of evil. According to the Vedantists neither good nor evil could exist at all because God was the only true reality, and the world, where good and evil seemed to exist, was an illusion. Man's object, therefore, was to escape the world, where evil appeared to exist, and seek union with God. By the 1870's Dayananda was attacking this neo-Vedantist viewpoint from all sides.

His main thrust was directed toward disproving the notion that the world that we know by sense perception is unreal. That he did by epistemological inquiries, in dialogue form, which are reminiscent of Plato, though by no means as exhaustive. The common-sense view of the physical world was the one Dayananda supported. He argued that objects existed independent of our perception of them, and they had a reality of their own. Attempts to prove the contrary were, for him, denials of reason. God created the world, separate from Himself, because "had He not created this world, how could He have been able to award souls their deserts, and how could they have reaped the fruits of their deeds—good and evil—done in the previous cycle of Creation? If you were asked, what is the function of the eyes, you could only say,

translation referred to here is by Chiranjiva Bharadwaja, 2nd edn., Allahabad, 1915.

'sight, of course.' In the same way, of what use could the knowledge, activity, and power of creating the world be in God other than that of creating? Nothing else. The attributes of God, such as justice, mercy, the power of sustaining the world, can have significance only when He makes the world."[8] Dayananda believed God to be an active, creative agency involved in the world, not a passive spectator. The contrary view, he felt, had helped to rob Hindu life of vigor and purposefulness. "What object had God in creating the world," asked an Imaginary Objector (O). Dayananda (A) answered, "A.—What object could He have in not creating it? O.—Had He not created it, He would have lived in happiness. Besides, the souls would have remained free from pleasure and pain and the like. A.—These are the ideas of the lazy and the indolent, but not of men of energetic and active habits."[9] God and the world, thus, were two separate entities and in essence they had always been so. According to Dayananda, God created the universe, but matter existed before the creation in an elementary and eternal form. Worldly existence, therefore, could have in it elements which were unGodly or evil.

Besides God and the world, there were souls which took on physical form when they were born as human beings. Souls were not parts of God but had separate existences and their own unique histories according to their good and bad deeds. "God can never become the soul, nor can the soul become God. They can never be one. They are always distinct from each other."[10] Nor was man's soul a mere observer of bodily life, remaining apart from it and untainted by it. In the *Satyarth Prakash* this forthright assertion of man's involvement in the moral world appeared: "It is the soul that thinks, knows, remembers and feels its individuality through the organs of thought, discernment, memory and individuality. It is, therefore, the soul that enjoys or suffers. . . . it is the soul that . . . does acts—good or evil—and consequently it is the soul alone that reaps the fruits thereof—joy or sorrow. The soul is not a witness of acts. It is the actual doer that reaps the fruits of deeds done. The One Incomparable Supreme Spirit alone

[8] *ibid.*, p. 250.
[9] *ibid.*, pp. 249-50.
[10] *ibid.*, p. 278.

118

is the Witness. It is the soul that does acts and is, therefore, naturally engrossed by them. The soul is not God and, consequently, it is not the seer of acts (but the actual doer)."[11] Thus man could not escape from the reality of good and evil either by saying that good and evil were nonexistent or that they had no effect on man's essential nature.

Dayananda further held that no one could avoid responsibility for his actions by claiming that human deeds were predetermined. Nevertheless, he accepted the doctrines of transmigration and karma, according to which a soul may be reborn in bodies of men or beasts an indefinite number of times before achieving mukti, or emancipation. The ideas of transmigration and karma appeared to be the only important traditional Hindu doctrines with which Dayananda found no serious fault.[12] The method of achieving emancipation was not the casting off of bodily concerns and existing in a state of pure consciousness, nor was that the desired end. Emancipation resulted only from "obedience to the will of God, dissociation from sin, ignorance, bad company, . . . the promotion of public good, even-handed justice, righteousness. . . ."[13]

With the moral stature of man's soul established firmly, so as to meet any objections based on neo-Vedantism, Dayananda could develop his ethical doctrines and make them the central feature of his new creed. Because there are practically no Vedic references to right conduct, Dayananda took the *Manusmriti*[14] as his main authority for Chapter x of the *Satyarth Prakash*, which dealt with conduct and diet.[15] Mastery over the senses was the dominant theme of Dayananda's ethical teachings. Beyond that, the standard personal virtues were enjoined, and the doing of good works was emphasized. Basic to Dayananda's social reform creed was his belief that social customs having to do with marriage, food, dress,

[11] *ibid.*, p. 275.

[12] For a discussion of Dayananda's views on transmigration and karma see Upadhyaya, *Philosophy of Dayanand*, pp. 384-93.

[13] *Satyarth Prakash*, p. 279.

[14] The *Code of Manu*, a work of 2,685 verses dealing with law, politics, religion, and custom, probably written in the 2nd to the 1st century, B.C.

[15] In a sub-tropical country such as India, where the safety and palatability of food has always posed a critical problem, religious teachers have often incorporated dietary advice in their spiritual messages. Many of the food regulations associated with Hinduism are the results of this understandable practice.

and the multitude of petty practices related to caste, had no religious significance. As he wrote, "Let all good men remember that good conduct consists only in the avoidance of untruthfulness, injustice, inordinate affection or hatred and other evil habits, and in the practice of love and kindness towards all, in the cultivation of gentle disposition and in the promotion of public good, etc. Let them also understand that religion has reference to one's soul and good life."[16] Customs, he insisted, should be based on reason applied to the social condition of each country. In India the main problem was strengthening men's bodies and creating social unity and harmony. Ethical codes had to meet that need, a standard of judgment approximating utilitarianism and the notion of social efficiency.

Dayananda stated that he opposed the current basis of caste and all the injustice and human wastage it produced, but he held fast to the Vedic notion of the four varnas, or classes. In the eyes of God, a person was not born into any varna, but he was identified as a Brahmin, Kshatriya, Vaishya, or Shudra according to the kind of life he led. Women were equal to men in their ability to achieve emancipation, and they should be accorded rights commensurate with their abilities. They should be educated and not allowed to marry before they reached eighteen—later revisd to sixteen; Dayananda called Hindus the "children of children" because of the customarily early age of their marriages. Widows, he said, should be allowed to take other husbands and thus fulfill their role as mothers. It is not unlikely that Dayananda's ethical ideas were derived, to some extent at least, from the English-educated reformers whom he met in Bombay and Bengal.

A burning issue in the 1870's was the controversy over foreign travel, the social reformers taking the view that a journey to England would do more to liberate a man from the grip of absurd customs than any amount of English education in India could accomplish. The upholders of orthodoxy disagreed, and caste leaders frequently excommunicated men returned from England in order to diminish enthusiasm for overseas journeys. Dayananda ridiculed the practice, citing the records of Indians in the past who

[16] *Satyarth Prakash,* p. 317.

pursued trade and even empire-building (as he thought) abroad.[17] "Those who do not hesitate to go abroad," he wrote, ". . . become fearless and bold, and attain great power and prosperity by studiously imbibing the good qualities and adopting the good customs and manners of the foreigners and rejecting their faults and evil habits and bad manners. O ye foolish people! Your character and faith are not lost by having sexual intercourse with a low, despicable prostitute, but you consider it harmful and debasing to associate with good men of other countries!" The ban on foreign travel, like the other customs which he attacked, originated, Dayananda charged, with the priests. "These hypocrites, the so-called priests and other religious teachers, perfectly understand that if they educated the people and let them travel abroad they would get enlightened, and consequently would no longer be ensnared in the net of fraud and hypocrisy spread by them. They would thus lose their livelihood and respect." Echoing European mercantilists, Dayananda asked, "Can a country ever make any progress unless its people trade with or extend their rule over other countries? What can you expect but misery and poverty, when the people of a country trade only among themselves, whilst the foreigners control their trade and rule over them."[18]

For Dayananda, India's degradation was a personal humiliation. He attributed it chiefly to the Hindus' preoccupation with superfluous rituals, sponsored by Brahmin priests. Referring to his fellow Hindus he wrote that by observing "absurd" rituals in connection with eating and preparing of food "and other foolish practices, these stupid people have lost all independence, happiness, wealth, political power, learning and activity, in short, everything. Now they are sitting idle with empty hands, praying for someone to come and relieve their distress and give them something in charity. . . . But that help is never forthcoming. They have completely ruined *Aryavarta* [India]."[19] Like Vivekananda in the succeeding generation, Dayananda was struck by the need in Hindu culture for vigor, self-assertion, and physical courage. He

[17] One of his more doubtful examples, taken by free translation from the *Mahabharata*, was the journey to America made by Krishna and Arjuna in an electric boat. *ibid*. pp. 315-16.
[18] *ibid.*, p. 317.   [19] *ibid.*, p. 318.

admired European civilization for producing men and women whose character he could respect, and he attributed the West's advancement to its liberal and rational social practices, its energetic people, and their steadfast adherence to their own religious principles.[20] Hindus and their culture would disappear, he argued, overcome by the aggressive civilization of the West if they continued to lack those European characteristics, which in turn could be developed only by overhauling Hindu religious life. A rugged and sometimes aggressive man himself, Dayananda set about that overhauling, urging Hindus to cultivate their bodily powers while returning spiritually to the true "Vedic Faith."

Dayananda's intellectual aggressiveness was particularly evident in the belligerent tone of his criticisms of Christianity and Islam. Contrary to the tendencies of most Hindu religious reformers, who sought universality for their beliefs by defining them in the broadest possible terms, Dayananda was conscious of the struggle between contending religions, particularly in India. "As night and day are opposed to each other," he once wrote to Madame Blavatsky, "so are all religions opposed to one another."[21] Though Madame Blavatsky disagreed with such an approach, *The Theosophist*, the journal of her Theosophical Society, wrote admiringly of Dayananda that "he never attempted the folly of forcing down the throats of his followers the hybrid compound of the *Durga-Moses, Christ and Koran,* and *Buddha-Chaitanya* mixture of the modern reformers. The Arya Samaj rites certainly make the nearest approach to the real Vedic national religion."[22] The last chapters of the *Satyarth Prakash* are vigorous condemnations of the Bible and the Koran in language which was certain to produce hostility toward Dayananda and the Arya Samaj from the followers of those two faiths. Scoffing at the pretensions of the Bible and Koran, he held up the Vedas as timeless, revealed truth, divine in origin.[23]

[20] See Dayananda's analysis of the causes of European advancement, as quoted in de Bary, ed., *Sources of Indian Tradition*, pp. 634-35.

[21] Letter of Nov. 23, 1880, quoted in Sarda, *op.cit.,* p. 544.

[22] Quoted in Rai, *op.cit.,* p. 70.

[23] European scholars, such as Max Müller, considered the Vedas as the simple, natural, even commonplace, religious ideas of a primitive people and as such a valuable source for the study of religion, and also linguistics. See Müller, *Indian*

Apart from his intolerant and dogmatic view of non-Hindu faiths, Dayananda approached religion and society from a rational standpoint, giving greater weight to empirical evidence than to transcendental prescriptions and tolerating no inconsistencies in his program for the practical regeneration of the Hindus. He eschewed revelation, except that of the Vedas, which could be interpreted as he saw fit. He did not rely on special insights of a spiritual or mystic sort, as have most Hindu religious leaders.[24] He never set himself up as an avatar (divine incarnation) and was more interested in the spread of his teaching than in the extension of his personal influence as a teacher.

The Founding of the Arya Samaj

Though without the pretensions of Western learning and lacking the organized approach to shaping public opinion, Dayananda found himself in the mid-1870's engaged in enterprises that soon made him appear in the role of a modern Indian religious and social reformer, rather than a traditional Hindu sannyasi. On his visit to Calcutta in 1873 he met the creative minds of Bengal, and the techniques of his mission were deeply affected by the encounter. Keshub Chandra Sen, who sought out Dayananda and organized meetings at which the latter spoke, advised the Swami to speak in a vernacular (Hindi) rather than in Sanskrit, in order to gain a wider audience and avoid misunderstandings through faulty translations. He and Vidyasagar successfully convinced Dayananda that he should put on a reasonable amount of clothing for public appearances. The reformers of Bengal benefited by the support that Dayananda could give them, in particular that sup-

---

Philosophy, chap. 11. Dayananda, who had Müller's writings translated for him, countered that generally accepted interpretation by making the Vedas the holy books of Hinduism and by raising them to a status even higher than the sacred writings of Christianity or Islam.

[24] Graham wrote that "A careful reading of Dayananda's works and of his *Autobiography* fails to reveal any great positive and illuminating experience of God . . . he nowhere speaks of any great illumination of his own spirit . . . though he sought long for some mystic experience, it was not forthcoming and . . . he therefore threw himself into the way of strenuous activity." *op.cit.*, p. 237. In this respect Gandhi resembled Dayananda.

port which his knowledge of the Vedas provided. (Sen could not read the Vedas in Sanskrit.) But their doctrines were not acceptable to Dayananda; Debendranath's denial of the Vedic revelation and Sen's reverence for Christianity made any identification with the Brahmo Samaj impossible. Later he referred to the influence of the Samaj as denationalizing.[25]

Dayananda's idea of forming a samaj for the propagation of the Vedic religion, instead of relying solely upon the magnetism of his personality and the impact of his message, came from the example of the Brahmo Samaj in Calcutta and the Prarthana Samaj in Bombay. The organizational approach to religious and social reform was an innovation derived from the West and was first used by the Bengal and Bombay Samajes. Dayananda had functioned until 1873 in the world of temples, melas, ashrams, pilgrimages, and in the company of yogis and pundits; his largest audiences were attracted by his skillful and courageous use of the traditional Shastrarth. The Westernized methods of organization and communication, in the absence of which the social reform movement could never have been launched, he unhesitatingly adopted, and his work thereafter had to be recognized as a part of modern India's intellectual and social history.

In the cool months of 1874-1875 Dayananda was in Bombay Presidency and received there much the same respect and guidance from at least some of the modern reformers as he had in Bengal. Vishnu Shastri Pundit and Bhandarkar, both Sanskrit scholars, were taken aback by the vehemence of Dayananda's often arbitrary interpretation of the Vedas, but Ranade gave him strong support in Poona in his nearly violent encounter with the local orthodox faction and later edited a Marathi translation of some of the nearly fifty lectures which Dayananda delivered in Bombay. Gopal Hari Deshmukh, the Marathi publicist, was possibly his strongest supporter and at one time was President of the Bombay Arya Samaj.[26] Support from recognized reformers gratified Dayananda but at the same time provided him with an excuse to lock horns with still other exponents of "untrue" or only "partially

[25] See *Satyarth Prakash*, chap. 11, for his criticism of the Brahmo Samaj.
[26] Graham, *op.cit.*, pp. 157n, 159n, 160n.

true" sets of beliefs. It was soon clear that the Prarthana Samaj was no more acceptable to this strongheaded arbiter of the scriptures than was the Brahmo Samaj. More vigorously in Bombay Presidency than in Bengal, perhaps because he spoke in one of the languages of the region, Dayananda charged into the strongholds of local sects, such as the Vallabhacharis (who tried to murder him) and the Swami Narayanas, to debate against their chief exponents. His work by 1875 was a formidable exorcism of superstitions and religious impurities. Christianity, Islam, Buddhism, Jainism, the modern eclectic theisms, and the popular Hindu sects, as well as the advaita Vedanta school of philosophy—all of them appeared to merit attacks of varying intensity.[27] Dayananda passed exuberantly, yet devotedly, from one challenge to another, clearing the way for his own exposition of the "only true and universal faith."

He established the first Arya Samaj at Rajkot in Saurashtra in 1875, the new group being composed of local Prarthana Samajists who found that their major beliefs corresponded with Dayananda's and were willing to accept the authority of the Vedas. The Samaj dissolved within a short time, but Dayananda with foresight had framed a set of printed rules for the organization which was used as a model for organizing other Samajes. An Ahmedabad Arya Samaj was formed in the same year, and shortly thereafter another was begun in Bombay City with about one hundred members.

Although Dayananda's social reform ideas found general acceptance among educated Indians throughout the country, his program for religious reform faced insurmountable obstacles in most provinces. A few Bombay intellectuals were impressed by Dayananda's teaching, and the Arya Samaj first took shape among them, but the emancipated rationality and scholarly sobriety of the educated groups in Bombay limited the appeal of a doctrine which was based chiefly on the Vedas and which sought to derive all modern learning from that source. Dayananda's attacks on popular Hinduism and against the religious teachings of Brahmins marked him as overly radical in the eyes of Bombay reformers. He never visited Madras Presidency, where, in any case, there was

---

[27] See Sarda, *op.cit.*, chaps. xxx-xxxi for summaries of Dayananda's attacks on established faiths.

no fear of Islam, one of the Arya Samaj's paramount concerns. In Bengal the religious reform tradition was dominated by the Brahmo Samaj, and a competing faith with similar aims had little chance of success. Although Arya Samaj branches were established in Patna, Ranchi, and Calcutta, Hindus in the lower Ganges valley did not appear satisfied with Dayananda's creed, barren of mystic revelation and noticeably weak in the spirit of bhakti.

In the Punjab, however, and in areas adjacent to it, the religious, intellectual, and social conditions among Hindus made Dayananda's work eminently fruitful. Surrounded and infiltrated by the Sikh religion and Islam, Hinduism was not as inflexible in creed as it was elsewhere, and the caste system was less rigid than in other parts of the country.[28] Brahmins were unable to dominate large and powerful groups like the Jats, who, as it developed, were to make up a large segment of the Arya Samaj's membership. Religious and social reform in that part of the country in the pre-British period had been not just passing phenomena dependent upon fleeting enthusiasms for popular saints, but were established features of Hindu society. Islamic ideas, which stressed monotheism, a personal God upholding a determinate moral code for all men, and the equality of believers, permeated the thinking and behavior of many non-Muslims. The religious reforming tradition in Hinduism, from Ramananda through Kabir and Nanak, had been embodied in the Sikh community and the small sect of Kabirpanthis.[29] Those non-Muslim groups, and also the orthodox Hindu communities who had come to tolerate and even respect them, might not be expected to welcome Swami Dayananda as a new leader. But living in an environment where liberating ideas had found an established footing they might not be expected, on the other hand, to mobilize an outraged orthodox reaction, as had happened in Benaras and Poona.

[28] Citing evidence from the 1911 Census Report and M.L. Darling's studies on the Punjab, L.S.S. O'Malley succinctly described the looseness of the Punjab caste structure in *Modern India and the West*, pp. 371-72. Vidyavachaspati attributed Arya Samaj successes in the Punjab directly to the Islamic impact, which weakened conventional Hinduism; see his *Aryasamaj ka Itihas*, I, 267.

[29] For a vivid description of Hindu religious reform in north India, which, however, does not give proper attention to the influence of Islamic thought on Kabir and Nanak, see *North Indian Saints*.

The Punjab had been the last major region to fall under British rule, in 1849. The English educational system there and in the North-Western Provinces and Oudh to the south was in its early stages. Nevertheless it was the English-educated group which, though small in numbers, gave Dayananda an encouraging reception in the cities and towns of the upper Ganges valley and the Punjab during his tours there during the years, 1877 through 1881. Arya Samajes emerged in almost every place in which Dayananda presented his challenge to popular Hinduism—Lahore, Amritsar, Gurdaspur, Rawalpindi, Multan, Meerut, Delhi, Roorki, Cawnpore, Lucknow. The greater attractions that the Arya Samaj had over the Brahmo Samaj, which was active in the same region, were its proud assertion of the superiority of a faith which was entirely free, at least on the surface, from alien influences; the fact that it did not require of its adherents a break with Hindu society; and its aggressive program to halt Hindu conversions to Christianity and Islam. A later British observer noted that the Arya Samaj "allows the educated man to regard himself as still a Hindu, while freeing him from the burden of much of the superstition, against the absurdity and depravity of which his education has led him to rebel. He welcomes this new version of Hinduism with a sigh of relief."[30]

At the establishment of the Lahore Samaj in 1877 Dayananda, in collaboration with three associates, revised the principles of the organization as they had first appeared in Bombay. The effects of that revision were of two kinds: great simplification of the required procedures to be followed by any Arya Samaj, leaving each local body free to determine its own rules and omitting references to a general controlling organization; and an elevation of the social purpose of the Samaj above all other aims. The sixth principle of the revised statement declared that "The primary aim of the Arya Samaj is to do good to mankind, i.e. to ameliorate the physical, spiritual and social condition of all men."[31] In the decades to fol-

[30] W.G.S. Holland, quoted in the *Indian Review*, viii, 7 (July 1907), 535.
[31] The other nine principles enunciated the attributes of God as infinite, almighty, incorporeal, just, merciful, the maker of the universe and the source of all truth; claimed the Vedas as the worldly source of true knowledge; insisted upon righteous conduct of all Arya Samajists; demanded that members

low, the deep social and political involvement of most Arya Samajists was to validate many times over the sincerity of that "primary aim." By the century's end the Samaj led all other religious bodies in India, except the Christian churches and missionaries, in temporal endeavors.

The exclusive concerns of the Arya Samaj were religious and social reform. Dayananda instructed his followers to avoid political involvement, and the Samaj was prohibited from taking any active political role. In principle Dayananda favored indigenous rule. "A foreign government," he wrote, "perfectly free from religious prejudices, impartial towards all—the natives and the foreigners—kind, beneficent and just to natives, like their parents though it may be, can never make the people perfectly happy."[32] But he never took a stand against British rule, both because he respected the existing government and its officials and because he recognized that an open attack on the British was not feasible, or even right, while Indians were disunited and weakened from degenerate customs. In his view, foreign rule had been brought upon the Indians by their own failings. In a rare reference to contemporary political conditions Dayananda wrote, "The causes of foreign rule in India are: mutual feud, child-marriage, marriage in which the contracting parties have no will in the selection of their life-partners, indulgence in carnal gratification, untruthfulness and other evil habits, the neglect of study of the Veda, and other malpractices. It is only when brothers fight among themselves that an outsider poses as an arbiter."[33]

In the 1870's and 1880's such a sharply defined analysis of the reasons for India's political degradation did not elicit resentment among Indians, but gave hope and encouragement. The optimistic view of human progress which many English-educated Indians had imbibed from their studies could be applied to Indian society, and Dayananda's diagnosis of India's ills and prescription for their cure appeared more reasonable than other proffered advice. The

work for the good of society ahead of their own personal ambitions. Sarda, op.cit., p. 180.

[32] As quoted in Suraj Bhan, *Dayanand: His Life and Work*, pp. 145-46.

[33] *Satyarth Prakash*, p. 320.

Arya Samaj, however, was to outlive that passing age of naive optimism, and it did so because its founder offered to Indians more than an example of self-assured pride in the Hindu heritage and a liberating social gospel. Though often discounted by professional philosophers because of his unconvincing attempts to reduce modern knowledge to Vedic antecedents and his failure to produce a complete systematic philosophy, Dayananda did provide substantial and persuasive intellectual and ethical teachings which continued to attract thoughtful men and women long after his death. A noted Western authority, H.D. Griswold, wrote that Dayananda "succeeded in founding an indigenous Indian theism, non-polytheistic and non-idolatrous, right in the very home of pantheism, polytheism and idolatry. This was certainly a notable achievement."[34]

Before he achieved his first important successes in the Punjab, Dayananda had been drawn to Delhi in 1877 by the prospect of gaining recognition for the Vedic religion among high personages attending Lord Lytton's Imperial Assemblage in January. Fragmentary records show that one of his plans was that of unifying various reform groups into a single body, and with that in mind he met with Indian leaders, including Keshub Chandra Sen and the Muslim leader, Sayyid Ahmad Khan. His proposal to join together for the reform of Indian society was rejected, among other reasons, because Dayananda insisted that everyone accept the authority of the Vedas as a basis for common belief and action.[35] Muslim leaders soon discovered that the Arya Samaj was not only doctrinally unacceptable but presented a militant challenge to their community. Progressive Hindu reform bodies were apprehensive because a new Samaj had appeared to compete in a very limited field for recruitment of membership. The Brahmo Samaj, though weakened by the split within its ranks, had not yet been replaced as the premier religious and social reform body, and Brahmos were particularly upset to find some of their colleagues shifting allegiance to the Arya Samaj. Dayananda's religious beliefs were regarded as backward-looking by most

[34] Griswold, *The Religious Quest of India,* pp. 369-70.
[35] See accounts of the episode in Sarda, *op.cit.,* p. 162; Suraj Bhan, *op.cit.,* p. 81; and the *Indian Mirror,* Jan. 14, 1877.

Brahmos.[36] In an all-India sense the Arya Samaj's impact was unobtrusive, particularly in the main centers of modern Indian life, during the 19th century. The groundwork was being laid, however, for the most successful unification of religious and social reform with nationalism that was to be found in pre-Gandhian India.

Despite his lack of conformity with the influential intellectual groups of his day and his hostility toward education through the medium of English, Dayananda was caught up in the excitement of the individualistic spirit, the common feature of the enlightened schools of Indian thought at that time. Though he claimed to speak in behalf of Hindu tradition, his message was in fact one of revolt against customary law and its upholders and of complete reformation of Hindu society. More radical than most of the Western-oriented reformers, his revolt and reformation were based on the principle of the primacy of the individual's needs over the demands of society.[37] But Dayananda's individualism was not that of a man seeking personal salvation by isolating himself from society.[38] He demanded that Indians participate more fully in social endeavors, the object of which was to liberate society from poverty and ignorance. The assertion of the soul's uniqueness coupled with the injunction to work for social amelioration and liberation were ideas—and, more strikingly, a conjunction of ideas—that were intended to revolutionize Hindu life. The fact that Dayananda could present those ideas acceptably in the context of Vedic truth was a remarkable accomplishment.

[36] See e.g., "The Arya Samaj and a Refutation of Its Tenets," by "A Punjabi Brahmo."

[37] See discussion of this point by Upadhyaya, *op.cit.*, p. 404f.

[38] Dayananda once replied to an aged Mahatma, who advised him to give up an active life and seek mukti, as follows: "I am not anxious about my salvation. I am particularly anxious about those lakhs of people who are poor, weak and suffering. I do not mind if I may have to take birth several times. I will attain salvation when these people attain it." Sarda, *op.cit.*, p. 110.

VI

THE EMERGENCE OF NATIONALISM

A SECOND STAGE in the modern development of Indian intellectual life was emerging in the 1870's and 1880's, as the local efforts to achieve religious, social, and political reform began to combine into organized movements with adherents scattered throughout several provinces. Physically this was made possible by the rapidly growing communications systems, the increased number[1] and circulation of newspapers, and the expansion in the numbers of literate and educated graduates of secondary schools and universities. More important, however, was the desire of Indians to identify themselves with large groups with which they had something in common. The larger community might be based on a commonly held status in society, a common cultural and linguistic heritage, similar religious views or customs, as well as shared ideals for social reform or aspirations for political advancement. Because the unifying ideas were varied, so also were their appeals: Bengali or Maharashtrian nationality, the non-Brahmin status, and the Kayastha community were ideas of obviously limited appeal. Indian nationality, or Hindu or Muslim nationality, could call forth wider participation. The earlier individualistic ideas of religious, social, and political reform were swept into the ever-widening currents of consciously extended group loyalties; the

[1] Estimates of the number of newspapers, English-language and vernacular, vary, but all historians agree that their influence in the last three decades of the 19th century was immense among educated Indians. McCully cites evidence that between 300 and 400 newspapers were being published throughout the country in the mid-1870's. Bruce T. McCully, *English Education and the Origins of Indian Nationalism*, p. 234.

goals and programs for reform were adjusted or renovated to suit the new contexts.[2]

It is hazardous to assume that Indian nationalism was a logical historical outgrowth of 19th century political reform activities. As Indian political figures of the late 19th century realized, the earlier political activities in various parts of the country were concerned chiefly with local or provincial issues. They represented the interests of groups which had little sense of identification with the entire nation. Probably the explanation of why Indian nationalism has often been interpreted as an enlargement to the all-India[3] level of political activities originating earlier in the century is that the National Congress was a movement which grew out of the earlier, local political activities and, in a way fortuitously, became the major propagating agency for nationalism. While it is correct to say that late 19th century all-India nationalism found expression through the National Congress, it is inaccurate to identify as nationalist the early 19th century political associations which were precursors to the Congress; they expressed only the feelings and ideas of limited groups of people.[4]

A further hazard—a greater one because it long went unrecognized by Indian nationalists of all descriptions—is to assume that Indian nationalism was a single or unified movement with perhaps local manifestations which were related to an over-all conception

[2] While consciousness of mutually held interests was expanding, so also were assertions of individualistic views; individualism among Indians was not in decline as a result of the spread of collective sentiments. We are concerned here with the ideas underlying the public movements for reform, and the distinction to be drawn is between ideas formulated solely to meet the needs of individuals and small communities who found that their interests temporarily coincided, and those formulated to express the unifying sentiments of large societies whose members, organized or not, continued also to find outlets for their individualistic needs.

[3] "All-India" is used throughout to distinguish those movements with participation from all regions and from diverse cultural and religious groups from those with participation only from certain local regions or groups. The usage is common in India, as in All-India Labor Conference, All-India Handloom Weavers' Association, and so forth.

[4] Haridas and Uma Mukherjee have made a similar observation, dating the "birth of Indian nationalism" no earlier than the Ilbert Bill episode in 1883. See their *Growth of Nationalism in India*, pp. 32-34. The Mukherjees' and the present writer's assessments of Congress nationalism should be compared with

making for unity or homogeneity. India in fact experienced many "nationalisms," as many as there were generally accepted ideas of the nation. As developments in the 20th century proved, some of those "nationalisms" worked in opposition to others.[5]

There has never been agreement on a clearcut, yet all-embracing, definition of nationalism, even when the conditions which indicate its presence are examined in the case of a single country. But for the present purposes it may be defined as an attitude of mind, or set of beliefs, that is shared by a group of people large enough to be influential, and that embodies ideas of the nation and the nation's goals, elevates those ideas to a prime position over other public values, and compels the assertion of the identity and the aims of the nation.[6]

The crucial component of the phenomenon, in India as elsewhere, was the definition of the nation. Perhaps because the bulk of Indian accounts of the nationalist movement were written by the nationalists themselves, an impression was created that nationalism, at least in the late 19th century, represented an irresistible momentum and drive toward unity, as well as liberation, when in fact several competing nationalisms were emerging, which were ultimately to split the country apart. Each of those nationalisms was based on a distinct, although not always explicitly defined, conception of the nation.

---

that of the eminent Professor R.C. Majumdar in his *History of the Freedom Movement in India*, I, 423f. and 439f. Majumdar's distinction between the "Congress School" and the "Nationalist School" centers on the dissimilarity in methods and in definitions of the kind of Indian nation desired which existed between these two movements. In the present analysis Majumdar's "Nationalist School" becomes Reconstructed Nationalism (Chapter XII) which, as a nation-wide movement, is dated from the early 20th century.

[5] Not to be discussed in this book, for reasons noted in the Preface, is Muslim nationalism which was historically of a significance equal to any nationalist movement dealt with here.

[6] cf. "Nationalism is first and foremost a state of mind, an act of consciousness. . . ." Hans Kohn, *The Idea of Nationalism*, p. 10. Carleton Hayes noted four different meanings of nationalism: 1) the name of an historic process, 2) the ideas embodied in that process, 3) the activities of a particular party, and 4) a condition of mind among members of a nation. Indian nationalism meant all of these things, and the definition proposed seems broad enough to encompass them, yet more precise than Hayes' catalogue. Hayes, *Essays on Nationalism*.

A reason for the emergence of more than one nationalism in India was that the subcontinent as a whole had few, if any, of the preconditions which might bring a single nation into being.[7] India, to be sure, had long been recognized as a distinct civilization, but that civilization was more nearly comparable to European civilization, with its varieties of national groups, than it was to any one homogeneous European nation.[8] In the absence of conditions obviously conducive to the development of a sense of national unity—for example, commonly held ideas and symbols, a common culture which permitted easy intercommunication and self-conscious participation in mutually held aims—Indian nationalists could and did conceive of a national identity which was sometimes more nearly the product of their own preferences than it was an enunciation of social realities. On the other hand, in those cases in which nationalists sought to build their movement on social realities and root their ideas of the nation in the soil of living myths and symbols, the sentiments thereby aroused turned out to be meaningful only to those who shared common religious, linguistic, or geographical identifications. Bengali nationalism could produce a popular response that all-India nationalism could not produce; *Hindu* Bengali nationalism evoked more intensely unifying sentiments than did conceptions of the Bengal nation as a whole.

There was nothing spontaneous about the appearance in India

[7] Although efforts were made by Indians to overlook or to deny this fact during the struggle for independence, since 1947 and the partition of India brought about by Muslim nationalism, it has now been acknowledged, even by the Indian Government. The *Report of the States Reorganization Commission* stated: "The culture-based regionalism, centering round the idea of linguistic homogeneity represents to the average Indian values easily intelligible to him. Indian nationalism, on the other hand, has still to develop into a positive concept." (p. 43) Two recent studies of regional nationalism are: Selig Harrison, *India: The Most Dangerous Decades*; J.V. Bondurant, *Regionalism versus Provincialism: A Study in Problems of Indian National Unity* (U. of Calif. Monog. Series). An earlier exposition of a similar theme was R.N. Gilchrist, *Indian Nationality*. For a more general analysis of the disintegrating effect of the spread of the idea of nationalism in any society, see Hans J. Morgenthau, "The Paradoxes of Nationalism," *Yale Review*, XLVI, 4 (June 1957).

[8] The literature on the Indian "nation" or "nations" is extensive. British historians of the 19th century, such as Elphinstone, regarded India as many nations forming a unified political entity under British rule. See Mountstuart Elphinstone,

of nationalism in the 19th century. Unlike patriotism, which appears to be universal and exists among all groups of people, nationalism results from consciously propagated ideas.[9] In India, as in almost every nation, the propagandists, that is, the original nationalists, were "an eminent company of intellectuals."[10] Nationalists, whose thoughts and activities constituted the fabric of nationalism, were individuals who asserted that an Indian nation, however defined, existed or ought to exist, and that the nation had unique characteristics and unique goals, such as a reformed or a revived religious life, a purified or renovated social system, economic well-being for all, or an independent and democratic political structure. Whether or not their ideas were conceived of as means of promoting personal ends or as poetic symbols stimulated by religious involvement, or as genuine efforts to establish a single, unified Indian society, the nationalists must be given credit for the spread and acceptance of a concept which never existed in India before the 19th century. Their ideas began to appear in printed, and hence widely communicable, form after the 1857 uprising, but not until the 1880's was all-India nationalism well established.

Nationalists were religious and social reformers, political agitators, poets, saints, and statesmen; they were British-born as well as Indian-born. Some had programs for change, others merely criticized conditions around them, and still others were content to express devotion to an India which existed only in religious and mythological symbols. The absence of an observable nation and a sense of common nationality among the people in general was not an impediment to the development of nationalism among

---

History of India (2nd edn.), vol. I, book II, chap. XI. Later writers on Indian nationalism, both Western and Indian, sought to show the basic cultural unity present in India: e.g. Radhakamal Mookerji, *The Unity of India*. Present scholars are more inclined to regard India as a culture area with many subcultures and avoid using the word, nation, which has political overtones that make it an "unscientific" concept. See the paper by Bernard S. Cohn, "India as a Racial, Linguistic, and Cultural Area," in *Introducing India in Liberal Education*.

[9] "Nationalism is not a natural, instinctive thing, it is artificial, and its growth and spread are traceable to artificial stimulation, in a word to propaganda." Hayes, *op.cit.*, p. 62.

[10] *loc.cit.*

that educated and often well-travelled group. A nation could not be discovered; it had to be created. Addressing delegates to the National Congress of 1886, Dr. Rajendralal Mitter said: "For long, our fathers lived and we have lived as individuals only or as families, but henceforward I hope that we shall be living as a nation, united one and all to promote our welfare and the welfare of our mother-country. . . . It has been the dream of my life that the scattered units of my race may some day coalesce and come together; that instead of living merely as individuals, we may some day so combine as to be able to live as a nation."[11] Reporting on the same Congress session for a Bombay newspaper, N.G. Chandavarkar wrote, "I care not whether the array of resolutions we have passed in the past and may pass in the future are attended to or not by the Government as long as these Congress meetings develop the bond of union among the people."[12]

Before the view of a united Indian nation, such as Dr. Mitter expressed, had gained much support there had been several decades during which nationalist ideas were proclaimed in regional or communal contexts. Speeches and writings on political, as well as on social and religious, subjects were sometimes made in behalf of the Indian "nation," although the "nation" was in fact only Maharashtra, Bengal, or at most the Hindu community. For example, Raj Narain Bose's Jatiya Gaurav Sampadini Sabha, founded in Bengal in the 1860's, aimed its program toward the stimulation of "national feeling," which in fact meant the sense of community among Bengali Hindus. Bose's nationalism, perhaps better termed patriotism, was aroused by Western culture's inroads into local traditions and the moral laxity among young Bengalis which he attributed to that development. Bose put his case into a manifesto, which read in part: "Now that European ideas have penetrated Bengal, the Bengalee mind has been moved from the sleep of ages. . . . People discontented with old customs and institutions are panting for reform. Already a band of young men [Brahmos] have expressed a desire to sever themselves at once

[11] Quoted by the Mukherjees, *op.cit.*, p. 32.
[12] Quoted in Govt. of Bombay, *Source Material for A History of the Freedom Movement in India*, II, 35.

from Hindu society and to renounce even the Hindu name. . . ."[13]

To check this movement away from Hindu culture, Bose proposed stimulating "national feeling," which in turn should promote social reform. In 1867 Nabagopal Mitra organized the Chaitra Mela in Bengal, popularly known as the Hindu Mela, on the pattern of Bose's Sabha. It never developed ties with other provinces and, by definition, sponsored national sentiment only among Hindus. "The Hindus are destined to become a religious nation," Mitra wrote in 1872,[14] and apparently he felt that no tie other than religion could unite Indians. Mitra's political speculation was antiliberal; he advocated a benevolent native autocracy as the form of government best suited to India, and thus he fell out of line with the predominant political thought of his day, which conceived of political progress as the development of liberal constitutionalism along Western lines. The Mela expired after 1880, but the emotional overtones of Mitra's idea of the nation were echoed by other Bengalis in literature and song, as well as in the increasingly influential Indian-owned press.

Of the early national sentiments among Bengalis, those which incorporated the richest historic, cultural, and linguistic references were expressed in reference not to India as a whole, but to the province of Bengal. Bankim Chandra Chatterjee, whose patriotic poem, "Bande Mataram" (Hail to the Mother), later found acceptance by Indians from other provinces, limited the patriotism in his stirring writings to Bengal, where unifying traditional references could be found. To be accurate, Bankim Chandra's melodious yet fervent proclamations of patriotic spirit might stand as the beginning of Bengali, not Indian, nationalism.[15] The "Mother," the spiritual embodiment of the country whose worship Bankim Chandra urged on his listeners, was Bengal, not India. "As a poet and a stylist," wrote Aurobindo Ghose in 1907, "Bankim did a work of supreme national importance, not for the whole of

[13] H. and U. Mukherjee, op.cit., p. 40.

[14] B. Majumdar, *History of Political Thought*, p. 294.

[15] The uniquely Bengali character of Bankim Chandra's nationalism needs stressing, in view of the often implied all-India meaning attached to it by such authors as H. and U. Mukherjee, op.cit., pp. 54-57.

India, . . . but for Bengal which was destined to lead India and be in the vanguard of national development."[16] Bankim Chandra's Bengali nationalism, indeed, gave the rest of India the prototype of the state of mind which inspired many subsequent nationalist endeavors. Aurobindo sympathetically described that state of mind as Bankim Chandra would have done: "It is not till the Motherland reveals herself to the eye of the mind as something more than a stretch of earth or a mass of individuals, it is not till she takes shape as a great Divine and Maternal Power in a form of beauty that can dominate the mind and seize the heart that these petty fears and hopes vanish in the all-absorbing passion for the Mother and her service, and the patriotism that works miracles and saves a doomed nation is born."[17]

Bankim Chandra understood that essential to nationalism was "the close identification of the individual with a particular community" and "the differentiation of the interest of the particular community from other communities." He realized that "the basic problem of Indian politics was the lack of social solidarity."[18] Anticipating the position later taken by Tilak, who also sought solidarity by appeals to regional sentiments, Bankim Chandra opposed government help in effecting social reforms and ridiculed the petitioning political strategy of the Western-educated middle class.[19] Social and political progress, he argued, should not rest on Western procedures, if the purpose was to strengthen the nation.

A few years before Bankim Chandra's death in 1894 a clear split could be observed among Indian nationalists. It resulted from the tendencies, on the one hand, to work for the creation of a nation which resembled European nations in its social and political structure and aims; and, on the other hand, to root nationalism in already existing or latent native institutions and ideas. The methods of propagating nationalist ideas and, as it soon devel-

---

[16] Aurobindo Ghose, *Bankim-Tilak-Dayananda*, p. 9. cf. B. Majumdar: Bankim Chandra "was intensely provincial in character. He always thought in terms of Bengal alone, and seldom took into consideration the larger problem of promoting Indian nationalism," *op.cit.*, p. 433.

[17] Ghose, *op.cit.*, pp. 12-13.

[18] In the words of B. Majumdar, *op.cit.*, pp. 413-14, 460.

[19] *ibid.*, pp. 403-06, 470.

oped, the very nature of nationalism itself, were influenced by those tendencies.[20]

The dominant nationalist group, which was responsible for founding the Indian National Congress, supported the creation of conditions that they felt, from their knowledge of the West, should exist before a nation embodying all of India's people could make its identity felt. Those were mass education, economic advancement, social reform, and a unity of a kind that Western nations enjoyed. Having at its base an antitraditional, liberal-democratic, secular, and politically oriented concept of the nation, the nationalism of the early Congress could properly encompass all Indian cultures and religions. Apart from its failure to incorporate middle-class Muslim aspirations, it ultimately succeeded in its 20th century objective of winning independence for a unified state and in maintaining a Westernized democratic political structure in the face of numerous pleas for a return to pre-modern Indian traditions and for a disengagement of the Indian educated groups from their Western cultural and political acquisitions.

Challenging the established moderate Congress leadership in the 1890's and thereafter were nationalists who believed that unity could rapidly be achieved, or in fact already existed in a latent form, among Indians who recognized their common heritage as a single religious community. If, as Bankim Chandra Chatterjee had indicated, unity could be achieved on a provincial level by stimulating religious and cultural loyalties, a grander coalescence of the Indian people would be possible on the basis of a national revival of the ideas of Hinduism. The so-called extremist political leaders began to expound on their national heritage as Hindus, and to distinguish that heritage from traditions associated with

[20] The author is in general agreement with a short, perceptive study of Indian nationalism by D.F. Pocock of Oxford which states, in part: "There are, basically, two patterns of nationalism in India of the 19th century which we may characterize respectively as liberal and, following [A.R.] Desai, 'national chauvinistic.' It should be noted that we are dealing here with two ideal types, not with historical action. The actions and motives of any one individual or group show, when analyzed, a mixture of both types." "Notes on the Interaction of English and Indian Thought in the 19th Century," in *Cahiers d'Histoire Mondiale*, IV, 4 (1958), 832-47. A fuller account of the same split in the nationalist movement is available in McCully, *op.cit.*, chapter v, "Nationalist Doctrines."

Muslim or British rule. The nation, then, would be the embodiment of the unity among Hindus.[21]

While the Indian National Congress and prominent nationalists of both moderate and extremist temper urged cooperation between Hindus and Muslims, Hinduism's ancient ideals and traditions were being extolled and popularized throughout the country.[22] Men such as Bankim Chandra had made the fateful conjunction of religion and nationalism an almost irresistible doctrine for many Hindus. The nation conceived as a religious community seemed bound to deny participation to those who were not members of the community, notably Muslims, who constituted one-fourth of the population of India. But such an exclusion was not the conscious, or at least stated, intention of most 19th century exponents of the Hindu revival. Rather, in their intensified search for an Indian cultural integrity many nationalists considered that a reinvigorated Hinduism was the surest way to a strengthened India; it was sometimes suggested that Muslims should stop pretending that they were not Indians and should join the predominantly Hindu national culture which was catholic enough to encompass many diverse beliefs and practices.[23] Nationalism, if it was to be elevated above the legalistic substance of the annual resolutions of the National Congress, must penetrate deeply into the consciousness of everyone. Once established, according to Bipin Chandra Pal, "It is something that touches every department of our collective life and activity. It is organised in our domestic, our communal, our social, and our socio-economic institutions. In fact politics form . . . the least important factor of this nation-idea among us. The so-called free political institutions of Europe might, indeed, hinder, instead of helping the growth of our real national life . . ."[24]

[21] Unity among Muslims, too, was beginning to be felt in the closing decades of the century, after Sir Sayyid Ahmad Khan's founding of the Aligarh Movement in 1875. But not until the 20th century were Muslim leaders, such as Muhammad Iqbal, able to arouse much popular following with appeals for unity on the basis of common Islamic faith.

[22] The nature of the Hindu revival as it appeared in two parts of India was discussed in earlier sections on Dayananda and Ramakrishna.

[23] See, e.g., Bipin Chandra Pal's exposition of this theme in his *Nationality and Empire*, pp. 371-72.

[24] A portion of Bipin Chandra Pal's analysis of nationalism, *ibid.*, p. 6.

The leaders of the Hindu nationalist movement based on a revival of Hindu culture openly acknowledged their identification of nationalism with Hinduism. Tilak at one time put the matter this way: "The common factor in Indian Society is the feeling of *hindutva* [devotion to Hinduism]. I do not speak of Muslims and Christians at present because everywhere the majority of our society consists of Hindus. We say that Hindus of the Punjab, Bengal, Maharashtra, Telangan, and Dravid [Madras] are one, and the reason for this is only *Hindu Dharma*. There may be different doctrines in the Hindu religion but certain principles can be found in common, and because of this alone a sort of feeling that we belong to one religion has remained among people speaking different languages in such a vast country. And this feeling of being one is still alive because in different provinces there are different institutions of the Hindu religion like temple, etc., or famous places of pilgrimage."[25]

In place of English, the language of the all-India nationalist movement promulgated by the Congress, the vernacular languages were the vehicles for spreading Hindu nationalism.[26] Bankim Chandra in Bengal had warned that "We . . . are strangely apt to forget that it is only through Bengali that the people can be moved. We preach in English and harangue in English and write in English, perfectly forgetful that the great masses, whom it is absolutely necessary to move in order to carry out any great project of social reform, remain stone-deaf to all our eloquence."[27] As a recent author described the move to spread nationalism through

[25] B.G. Tilak, *Journey to Madras, Ceylon and Burma* (in Marathi), p. 3. Quoted in S.A. Wolpert, "Tilak and Gokhale," *op.cit.*, pp. 201-02. Similar ideas were expressed by B.C. Pal, *op.cit.*, chapter II, "Hindu Nationalism."

[26] R.C. Majumdar, unself-consciously uses the term, Hindu nationalism, to describe that phenomenon. Along with its development he notes that "there was slowly evolving a broad political nationalism on an all-India basis embracing all castes and creeds," whose most successful embodiment was in the Congress. Majumdar, *Glimpses of Bengal in the Nineteenth Century*, p. 77.

[27] Quoted in B. Majumdar, *op.cit.*, p. 431n. Bankim Chandra, though unwilling to depend on British-sponsored legislation, favored social reform, which he thought should come about through education and a new sense of cultural vitality. Influenced by Mill's *Subjection of Women*, he pled for equal treatment of Hindu women and also exposed and protested against social inequalities imposed by caste and the economic system. B. Majumdar, *op.cit.*, pp. 403-04, 453-58.

vernacular literature, "The regional languages were links to a past that the new generation wished to recapture, and there began to be those, even among the English-speaking leadership, who consciously attempted to use the regional languages for modern cultural expression. Beneath the surface of the Western-oriented elite culture a literary renaissance was beginning in the regional languages, some of its early products crude and imitative of English models but others, as in the Bengali historical novels of Bankim Chandra Chatterjee or the Telegu classics of Guruzada Apparas, authentic expressions of a deep cultural ferment. Moreover, as the languages of everyday speech, these were the only possible vehicles for any mass independence movement."[28]

The results of the stress which revivalist nationalists placed upon the vernaculars were not immediately apparent. Only in contemporary India, where linguistic nationalism has grown to serious proportions, have those results come to be fully recognized.[29] But even in the latter part of the 19th century the indications were present that many so-called Indian nationalists were, in fact, expressing their own primary loyalties to their linguistically and culturally defined regions. Tilak, for example, was not clear on the question of whether India was a single nation or several nations until after the Bengal partition, according to one scholar;[30] the Lokamanya expressed his nationalist feelings often in terms peculiarly suitable to Maharashtra. Chitta Ranjan Das, the Congress leader, wrote of his participation in the early 20th century Bengali nationalist movement that "our idea of nationalism was centered in Bengal. We never looked beyond Bengal." Das' writings were replete with references to the "Bengalee nation," and he urged nationalists to support "provincial individuality" first and Indian nationality following that.[31]

[28] S. Harrison, op.cit., p. 53.

[29] e.g., the Report of the States Reorganization Commission acknowledged that "The national movement which achieved India's independence was built up by harnessing the forces of regionalism." op.cit., p. 38.

[30] S.A. Wolpert, op.cit., pp. 240-41.

[31] Das, India for Indians, pp. 60, 56-66. As late as 1918 Das wrote: "I look forward to the time when the Bengalee nation will rise and stand in all its glory. . . . Bengalees as a nation will make themselves felt and will stand in all

Most of the moderate leaders of Congress, and particularly those from western India, appeared to grasp the need for a truly all-India nationalism which would rise above regional and communal loyalties. Within the existing Indian educational and cultural framework such nationalism had to be based on liberal constitutional ideas derived from the West and aimed at unifying Indians around commonly held political and economic aspirations, rather than on cultural and religious sentiments. The propagation of those ideas throughout India could best be carried forth in the English language among the small English-educated groups in the major towns and cities. Allan Octavian Hume's challenge to Indians to create a new national political movement came in the form of an "Open Letter" to Calcutta University graduates and was directed specifically toward the "elite," as Hume identified them.[32] When the challenge was accepted, the new "elite" naturally turned out to be "leading politicians well acquainted with the English language," as the invitation to the first Indian National Congress session in 1885 was phrased.

In an analytical sense, the all-India nationalism promulgated by those English-educated men, completely committed to Anglo-Saxon political institutions in India and holding a Western-style image of the Indian nation, was a British-European phenomenon in an Indian setting.[33] The fact that Europeans were a part of the movement underscores this point. The instigators of the all-India nationalist movement—men such as Naoroji, Ranade, Telang, Pherozeshah Mehta, Budruddin Tyebji, G. Subramania Iyer, W.C. Bonnerjee, Surendranath Banerjea, and Ananda Mohan Bose, along with British associates, Hume, Wedderburn, and Cotton—drew their political ideas from the West, including their idea of an Indian nation and its proper means of advancement.

---

their strength and face the world." *ibid.*, pp. 122-23. cf. R.L. Park, "The Rise of Militant Nationalism in Bengal . . . ," Ph.D. dissertation, Harvard, p. 3: "Indian nationalism was expressed through the agency of Bengali patriotism."

[32] W. Wedderburn, *Allan Octavian Hume*, pp. 51-53.

[33] Lest this strongly worded case for the dependence of Indian nationalism on Western ideas be regarded as biased, it should be understood by those unfamiliar with the nationalist literature that the case rests entirely on the testimony of Indians themselves. See one of its most recent formulations by the Mukherjees, *op.cit.*, esp. pp. 109-110.

And they carried on their public crusade in India along lines essentially the same as those prescribed for politicians in England. Indeed, several of them expounded Indian nationalist ideas in England, as well as in India, and the phrasings and content of their speeches to English audiences were identical to those presented to Indian listeners.

For at least two decades following its foundation in 1885 the Indian National Congress was the movement best representing nationalism on the all-India level, despite the fact that it "was more a general movement, an idea, and an attitude of mind than a concrete political party."[34] Its annual sessions were the focal points of the increasingly vocal "loyal opposition" to British rule in India. Speeches and resolutions criticizing the restrictions on Indians' entrance into the higher ranks of the Civil Service, the government's revenue policies, the slow progress toward representative government, official military policies and expenditures, and others urging a variety of economic, administrative and constitutional reforms issued from the Congress platform and echoed throughout the year in the press and in local meeting places. All the complaints and suggestions that emerged were made in behalf of the nation conceived by minds filled with images of Western nations and the course of liberal advance defined in the West. Superimposed above the expanding so-called renaissance of Indian cultural life and isolated from the popular culture by the education and sophistication of its leaders, the Congress movement nevertheless rapidly evolved a working definition of Indian nationalism, which found its ultimate expression in independent India's 1950 Constitution.

The original leaders of the Congress were not so much unaware of the superficiality of their movement, in terms of the living culture of India, as they were determined to impose at least a semblance of structural unity and intercommunal and inter-caste harmony on Indian society for the purpose of winning British and world recognition of India's national existence. Once recognized as a nation, India would be assured, by the workings of the histori-

[34] J.R. McLane, "The Development of Nationalist Ideas and Tactics . . . ," Ph.D. dissertation, Univ. of London, p. 7.

cal forces that they observed elsewhere, advancement to a status of modern independent statehood. By working within the framework of British rule, as a "loyal opposition," the Congress leaders were confident not only of the ultimate success of their political aims but also of the continued progress of their country in economic and social terms, because that progress was, again, to be judged by norms established by Western civilization.

After their annual passing of political resolutions, which emphasized the Congress leaders' demands for their own advancement within the existing dispensation as well as their claim to speak in behalf of the people of India on political and economic matters, some of the delegates devoted themselves during the rest of the year to the work of building a modern nation.

That work was represented best by the efforts of nationalists of all descriptions in behalf of social reform. No one denied that social progress of some kind was an aspect of national advancement. However, the specific doctrines of the social reformers appeared to collide, toward the end of the century, with those of the extremist groups among the nationalists. Henceforth, for nearly two decades, those two groups were in bitter opposition, despite the concern of both to achieve a rehabilitated, strengthened national society. The crux of the conflict could be described in various ways. Religious differences represented a phase of the disagreement: social reformers had been nurtured in the earlier 19th century reformed theistic movements, while some nationalists were finding in religious traditions not personal spiritual benefits but a reservoir of popular beliefs which could promote social solidarity. Another aspect of the disagreement bore upon the methods and goals of social reform: reformers, recognizing that their aspirations for India's social advancement were shared by the British, sought the government's support in effecting social changes; a growing body of nationalists, however, dissociated themselves from the government for political reasons and regarded social reformers as lacking in patriotism because of their open acceptance of Western values and their attachment to reform through legislation. Furthermore, as the nationalist movement reached out for popular participation, the social reform movement was seen as a hindrance and a suspect adjunct to nationalism.

The basic issue dividing the extremists from the social reformers, however, was that of the proper source from which the nation should derive its ideals. Whether Western standards or Indian standards should define the goals of reform was the question underlying the Age of Consent Bill controversy—the most serious single dispute between social reformers and their opponents to erupt in the modern period.

VII

THE ORIGIN AND ENACTMENT OF

THE AGE OF CONSENT BILL

THE Indian social reform movements in the 19th century, like the political reform movements, remained unorganized on an all-India basis until the 1880's. Local groups functioned throughout the country in many cases along similar lines, but without regular and specific knowledge of each other. Virtually the only effort for social reform well publicized throughout the country had been Vidyasagar's widow remarriage movement, which however was never nationally organized and which found local support only when a reformer felt inclined to press for it; the founder himself lost interest in the cause long before his death in 1891. Unlike the political reformers, the social reformers gave little evidence of concern about the absence of a national organization to direct and stimulate their activities. If it had any strength, such an organization would, in fact, embarrass them into a unity of principles and methods for which, before 1880, they were quite unprepared.

Whereas the 19th century political reform movement sought a further development of the Western constitutional ideas already embodied in the unified administrative framework of British India, the social reform movement had to relate itself to existing social institutions which took a great variety of forms throughout the country. While, for example, unity between political reformers of the Indian Association of Bengal and the Bombay Association meant little more than establishing communications—the fundamental aims of the two bodies and the political environments in which each operated were nearly the same—unity between Bengali and Maharashtrian social reformers posed great problems. Each local social reform body attacked social evils present in its own environment, and while one group determined that polygamy (for example, Kulinism in Bengal) was its major concern, another, in a region where polygamy among Hindus was an insignificant problem, centered on undesirable temple practices (for example, in the Vaishnava Vallabha sect of Bombay), or the restrictions on education of girls, inter-caste marriage, and widow remarriage. Caste and religious practices varied throughout India, and the social reform movement accordingly found varying expressions. Differences between social reform bodies existed also because of a growing divergence of opinion on social ideals (for example, between Arya and Brahmo Samajists) and methods of reform (for example, through caste bodies or through general societies), so that in one area several groups often pursued different programs.

In short, the unity among virtually all English-educated Indians on political questions, such as demands for more openings in the Civil Service and expansion of the legislative councils to include Indians, was not easily matched when social questions were broached. What national issues were there upon which social reformers in all regions could agree? In 1884 a Bombay Parsi, Behramji Malabari (1853-1912), discovered one such issue: the need for legislation controlling the age of marriage of Hindu girls.

The Parsi community had emigrated to Gujarat from Persia on the conquest of that country by the Arabs in the 8th century, and in the 17th century a Parsi colony arose in Bombay city. On public matters of political and social concern, as in commerce and industry, the Bombay Parsis provided singular leadership for western India in the 19th and 20th centuries, while they maintained their separate identity as a religious group. One of the first Indian groups to take advantage of Western education and the liberalization of social customs stimulated by association with Europeans, the Parsi community substantially advanced the cause of social reform first, by carrying out reforms and welfare schemes for itself, and next, by providing leadership for reform movements in the general population. Parsi girls' schools were opened in the 1850's by Sir Jamsetjee Jejeebhoy's Parsi Benevolent Institution; Naoroji Ferdoonji formed a Parsi religious reform sabha in 1851, which was influential in breaking the hold of narrow orthodoxy over the community; beginning in the 1860's Sir Dinshaw Manockjee Petit added to the growing number of Parsi charities and dispensaries. Dadabhai Naoroji, noted mainly for his political activity, exercised influence for social reform through his newspaper, *Rast Goftar*, begun in 1851, and with Sorabji Shapurji Bengalli he joined the pioneers in Parsi girls' education and helped to found the Widow Marriage Association. The crowning achievement of the Parsi reformers came in 1865 in the form of the special Parsi Marriage and Divorce Act. For decades an internal controversy among Parsis on marriage customs had been going on, and there was confusion in the courts about what domestic laws to apply to Parsis. In 1855 the Parsi Law Association was founded, and led by Naoroji Ferdoonji, S.S. Bengalli, and Framjee Nusserwanjee Patel, it succeeded in obtaining passage of the Act, which was partly based on the English Divorce Act of 1858. As a result of this Bengalli could claim in 1868 that "the Parsis may, with proper pride, point to the fact that, of all purely Asiatic communities, they were the first . . . who have voluntarily imposed on themselves a law declaring bigamy a criminal offense. . . ."[1] The Act promoted the emancipation of Parsi women which, with the encouragement of their husbands, was already under way.

Accustomed to the advanced reform of his own community, Malabari pressed more fervently than other Parsis to extend the social advantages enjoyed by a distinguished minority group to the general population. His motive was that of a nationalist convinced that social reform must precede political advancement. A Gujarati born in 1853, Malabari was educated in a missionary school and never attended college, but he was profoundly influenced by Dr. Wilson, the Scotch missionary and first Vice Chancellor of the University of Bombay, who patronized Malabari's early writings, which included pieces on social reform. Malabari credited "the spirit of Christianity" for inspiring him and other reformers to an active humanitarianism.[2] He was accepted and admired in English circles in Bombay, chiefly for his brilliance in English poetry and prose, but he remained a strict Parsi in religious matters.

[1] *Famous Parsis; Biographical and Critical Sketches*, p. 88.
[2] D. Gidumal, *The Life and Life Work of Behramji M. Malabari*, p. lix.

Malabari's contribution to the social reform movement was his courage and skill as a propagandist. Lacking the scholarly attainments of a Bhandarkar, the personal following and organizational skill of a Ranade, and the religious enthusiasm of a Keshub Chandra Sen, Malabari nevertheless knew what publicity and public opinion in behalf of reform could accomplish in India and in England. Indeed, after reviewing Malabari's journalistic crusades one is inclined to the view that Malabari's methods of urging reform on the apathetic literate public were more successful than those of the scholars, organizers, or prophets. Most Indians lacked information about the injustices committed in the name of social and religious usages; Malabari gave them the details. Indians, even many reformers, hesitated to act boldly and relied on the gentle pressure of new ideas introduced gradually through education. Malabari did not rely only on considered arguments to support his cases but allowed his pen to flow freely, sometimes into exaggeration, painting a graphic picture of social evils which few could ignore. Some action had to follow.

An individualist, holding aloof from organizations,[3] not counted as anyone's follower, and as a Parsi separated from the dominant social order, Malabari was free to pursue a lone course which was sometimes offensive to other reformers. He wondered how reforms could ever come about as long as reformers were not in touch with the common people. He criticized the gulf which English education and official position had placed between the intellectuals and the masses: "We are raising an intellectual aristocracy," he wrote, "which owns to no concern in the fortunes of the vulgar herd . . . unless college education quickens sympathy with the mass, is it worth imparting . . . ?"[4] He saw in Ranade and Bhandarkar the true spirit of reform, but he was critical of the slight impact that their intellectual approach had. "Could they do no more for the people than at present?" he asked.[5] In the heat of the controversy

[3] He once wrote: "I cannot join a combination, cannot work in a ring. For instance, the Congress movement in the abstract is one of the dreams of my life—indicating the first awakening of national life for India. But if you ask me to fall down and worship its outward symbols—its huge pavilion and annual show, its camp-hotels and unions, its resolutions made to order, and its unanimous votes—I must decline the honour. . . . In a word, I am unfitted by nature to use the Congress. . . ." Quoted in *Famous Parsis*, p. 436.

[4] Gidumal, *op.cit.*, p. xcix.   [5] *ibid.*, p. c.

aroused by his marriage reform campaign he ridiculed reformers who withheld their full support: "Reformers have their clients to please, and their plaudits to win. Can they afford to say anything unpleasant to the mob?"[6]

Malabari seemed more sensitive to the nation's ills than most western Indian reformers, perhaps because as a journalist he was closer to the people than were high court judges and scholars. Enforced widowhood, for example, aroused more than just the humanitarianism of one set apart from human suffering. The sights of mistreated widows, he said, "burnt themselves into my brains. It is not merely that I know the miseries of widowhood, not merely that I feel them, feel for and with the widow; I am the widow for the time being."[7] With fervor matching that of the great social reform publicists of the West, Malabari spread widely his descriptions of personal tragedies due to infant marriage and enforced widowhood. His appeal was to the sentiments of all Indians, not merely to the minds of the educated classes.

His newspaper, *Indian Spectator*, was probably the outstanding Bombay paper in the 1880's and a major organ for the spread of social reform ideas. (Later, in 1901, Malabari founded the journal, *East and West*; it and K. Natarajan's *Indian Social Reformer* were the major literary vehicles for the all-India social reform movement in the first decade of the 20th century.) Early in his career Malabari began issuing tracts and delivering lectures on reform, and when his "Notes" on "Infant Marriage in India," and "Enforced Widowhood" were published on August 15, 1884, they were the product of years of training in the effectiveness of the printed word. These "Notes," which were circulated among officials and private persons, British and Indian, marked the beginning of the all-India social reform movement.

The two documents could hardly be considered well-reasoned. The cases they made were based not on substantial facts, available in the Census Report and in court records, but on journalistic appeals for sympathy and action. Even some of Malabari's friends among the reformers rejected many of his overstatements, although

[6] *ibid.*, p. 56.
[7] Quoted in *Famous Parsis*, p. 438.

they acknowledged the purity of his motives and the skill with which he conducted his crusade. His chief proposals to check infant marriages were: that, after five years, universities prohibit married students from taking examinations; that heads of government departments give preference in hiring to unmarried men; and that education departments insert material in school books describing the evils of early marriage. To improve the conditions of life for widows, he asked the government to assure that all widows learn of their rights to remarry under the Widow Remarriage Act of 1856; to use its authority to protect widows from involuntary seclusion and "social ill-usage"; and to prohibit priests from excommunicating anyone who assisted in a widow remarriage. Finally Malabari urged the creation of "a national association for social reform with the existing societies as branches" to include "most of the prominent members of Government . . . from the Viceroy and the Governors downward."[8]

The substance of the "Notes" was insignificant as compared with the replies they elicited—from virtually every social reformer in the country, supporters of orthodoxy of all descriptions, medical men, lawyers, princes, government servants, British administrators in their private capacities, scholars; and from public bodies, some long established and some created for the purpose of supporting or attacking the proposals. There were at least two hundred formal replies, ranging from remarks to short treatises. In addition, a voluminous body of official opinions, data, Council debates, and resolutions was printed over the seven-year period preceding the culmination of the Malabari crusade in 1891.[9] The crusader himself made an extensive tour speaking in behalf of his proposals, reminiscent of Banerjea's tour on the civil service question.[10]

Facts until then unknown or unpublicized claimed public

[8] The "Notes" were reproduced in Govt. of India, Home Dept., *Selections from the Records*, No. ccxxiii, Serial No. 3.

[9] Many official and nonofficial opinions and much of the data may be found in the Home Dept. *Records, op.cit.* The replies sent to Malabari were reproduced in Dayaram Gidumal, *The Status of Women in India, or A Hand-Book for Hindu Social Reformers* and, in a shorter form, in *Infant Marriage and Enforced Widowhood in India* . . . (Bombay, 1887). See also Govt. of India, Home Dept., *Public Proceedings*, Nov., 1886, Nos. 131-138E.

[10] He spoke to social reform bodies or specially organized meetings in Agra, Aligarh, Lucknow, Barielly, Allahabad, Benaras, and Muthura, according to a

attention, and the India-wide problems of widowhood and child marriage had to be admitted. The census of 1881 was used to emphasize the seriousness of the problems. It revealed a high proportion of widows (approaching one-fifth in certain areas)[11] in the total female population. As for early marriages, the customs varied throughout the country and according to caste. Among higher castes in Bengal, marriage before age ten was not uncommon, and the general custom among Brahmins was to marry girls before they reached puberty. In Bengal 14 per cent of all Hindu girls under the age of ten were either married or widowed; in Bombay the comparable figure was 10 per cent; in Madras it was only 4.5 per cent.[12] Widowhood was enforced through sentiments and sanctions against remarriage chiefly among high caste Hindus. Early marriage, too, was more general among high castes, where the competition for suitable marriage partners for their children forced parents to arrange alliances while their children were young—the longer the delay in concluding a marriage, the fewer the suitable partners still available. Other reasons strengthened the custom of child marriage for females: the desire of the groom's family to have a daughter-in-law young enough to adjust easily to her new domestic surroundings; occasional "sale" of brides to old men or unsuitable men who demanded a very young girl and were willing to pay a large "bride price"; and the shastric injunction, especially highly regarded in Bengal, that girls must be married so that intercourse might take place with the first signs of puberty.[13] Clearly, the younger the girl when she mar-

description of the tour by Baijnath, in his "Social Reform for the N.W. Provinces."

[11] As late as 1931 in Bengal 21 per cent of all women between the ages of 15 and 40 were widows. Benoy Kumar Sarkar, *Villages and Towns As Social Patterns*, p. 157.

[12] Cited, from the 1881 Census, in Gidumal, *op.cit.*, p. 18.

[13] To re-enforce the injunction about prepuberty marriage, the shastras held that a father whose daughter menstruated before being married was guilty of procuring an abortion, worse than certain kinds of murder. Reasons underlying the encouragement in the sacred literature given to early marriage of females are suggested in A.L. Basham, *The Wonder That Was India*, pp. 166-67. Perhaps the most understandable reason for early marriages was to assure that a girl had every possible chance of bearing a child.

ried, the greater her chances of becoming a widow; so early marriage and widowhood were related. Most reformers considered that limitations on early marriages might be more easily obtained than removal of the sanctions against widow remarriage.

On several important factual questions raised by Malabari, opinions varied. No agreement was apparent on whether or not child marriages were followed by premature consummation; some respondents to the "Notes" held that marriages were not generally consummated until the girl reached full puberty, while others disagreed. Of course customs in that matter, as in all matters, differed between regions. Views were also in conflict on the average age of puberty among Hindu girls, and that disagreement led to differences over the suitable marriage age for girls. One of Malabari's arguments was that early marriage was sapping the vigor of the Hindu "race." Many reformers agreed with him and argued that national progress rested in part on a biological strengthening which should include prohibitions on child marriage.[14] Others felt that spiritual welfare, achieved by adhering to the shastras, was more important than biological fitness. Although two reformers, Bhandarkar and Ranade, felt that Malabari exaggerated the extent and ill-effects of infant marriage and enforced widowhood, others sent Malabari their vigorous condemnations of those practices. Pundit Badri Dutt Joshi of Almora, for example, and many others who had never been heard from before on social reform matters, expressed outrage at the failure of government and society to take action against clearly injurious social customs. Joshi went on to char-

---

[14] For example, the Jessore Indian Association (Bengal) wrote: "We hold that early marriage weakens the physical strength of the nation; it stunts its full growth and development, it affects the courage and energy of the individuals, and brings forth a race of people weak in strength and wanting in hardihood." Gidumal, *op.cit.*, p. 35. That view, widely accepted among reformers, was supported by evidence of the weakening effects of child-bearing on young mothers and by the observation that young mothers were more likely than fully mature women to produce and rear sickly children. The beneficial effects of increased vigor which the reformers felt would accrue to the male population whose marriages were postponed may well have been associated with the traditional notion that asceticism brings rewards of greater physical endurance and mental keenness. Vivekananda, Gandhi, and many modern Indian leaders have also held that view.

acterize some reformers: "I am very sorry to see and hear of many men who don't hesitate to dine at hotels, use English hats and pantaloons, English soap, biscuits, and brandy, and thereby lose religion, nationality, money and respect, and call this reform. . . . But what would be a real reform, they have thrown into the background, and quite neglected."[15] Though a Parsi, Malabari held that the Hindu shastras did not prescribe enforced widowhood, and some Hindu scholars agreed. But the shastras were many and could be interpreted in different ways. The notable Sanskrit scholar of Deccan College, Bhandarkar, reviewed the question and concluded that "the general spirit of the Hindu Shastras is in favour of perpetual widowhood."[16]

The calls for action from those who responded directly to Malabari's "Notes" must have heartened the reformer, but no consensus arose on what steps, if any, the government should be asked to take. Some pointed to the ineffectiveness of Malabari's proposal to restrict college education to unmarried boys, others to the injustices of penalizing a boy for what his parents had arranged. Some reformers wanted to make early marriages illegal; others urged a law against premature consummation of the marriage. Many respondents took up related issues, such as ill-assorted marriages (of old men and young girls) and polygamy, and urged legislation in those areas. A logical suggestion was made to encourage inter-marriage among castes of equal social standing and thus remove some of the pressures for early marriages by making more partners available. Scarcely anyone thought that the government could pass legislation which would materially assist widow remarriages.

Official British opinions given to Malabari, with few exceptions, opposed immediate passage of laws on social reform, generally on grounds that Indian opinion must first develop and that governmental powers should be used only as a capping stone for successful private efforts. Sir William Wedderburn and A.O. Hume, for example, urged moderation and postponement of

[15] Gidumal, op.cit., p. 55.
[16] ibid., p. 188.

legislation.[17] Wedderburn told Malabari, "You have plied the whip and spur with much vigour, and the steed is fairly aroused; but there is danger of its getting out of hand altogether and going off the right track." He suggested approaching the people through their "natural leaders" and avoiding attacking them from the "outside."[18] Most British observers were skeptical that any real social amelioration could come from the reformer's propaganda. H.H. Risley, for example, in an official note (March 22, 1886) responding to the government's inquiry on Malabari's proposals, pointed out that most Hindus took their standards from the Brahmins, through a process he called "Hinduizing." He went on to write that "at one end of Hindu society Mr. Malabari and a small handful of reformers brought up on a foreign system of education [are] proposing to Government to legislate for the purpose of carrying out domestic reforms of a most searching character, while at the other end thousands of people are every year abandoning the very practices which Mr. Malabari wishes to introduce. For one convert that Mr. Malabari may make, at the cost of much social obloquy, among the highly educated classes, Hinduism sweeps whole tribes into its net."[19]

The majority of Indians who replied to the "Notes" favored legislation or other government action of some sort to restrict infant marriages; only a few thought that the desired results could be accomplished through voluntary action. Indians also produced a wealth of ideas on how the government might cope with the problems of enforced widowhood. Laws permitting prosecution by those who disfigured widows (by tonsure) or who excommunicated remarried widows, establishment of foundling hospitals for the offspring of widows (to discourage infanticide), education of girls, preferences in government service for

[17] When the Bill was finally under active consideration, in 1891, however, Hume took a vigorous part in the campaign for its passage and urged Indians to do likewise if they were to prove themselves worthy of political privileges. See the *Statesman and Friend of India*, a European-run Calcutta newspaper, for Hume's letters on the Bill (esp. Jan. and Feb., 1891), as well as for a running account of the last stages of the controversy.

[18] Gidumal, *op.cit.*, pp. 136-37.

[19] Govt. of India, Home Dept., *Public Proc.*, Nov., 1886, Nos. 131-138E, p. 28.

men who married widows, the founding of widows' homes—those and other programs of action were suggested. The most thoughtful replies pointed to connections between widowhood and child marriage and thus urged the priority of the latter problem. For achieving reform along all lines the most generally acceptable proposal was also the vaguest, that of forming an all-India social reform organization, a suggestion which may have originated in the "Notes." That idea found its concrete form in the National Social Conference founded in 1887.

The direct replies to Malabari constituted only a fraction of the total serious published considerations given to the problems. Newspapers ran frequent editorials and articles on marriage age and widowhood; it is likely that there were more case histories of social injustices to individuals being published in the Indian press in the late 1880's than there are today. Most existing social reform bodies backed Malabari, and several new societies were formed partly for that purpose, some by Dayaram Gidumal, an assistant judge at Ahmedabad and the author of a substantial biography of Malabari published in 1888. The reports and resolutions of those groups, which showed how progress might be achieved within particular local conditions, inspired action elsewhere. Such publicity expanded public awareness of the activities of the reformers, so that not only educated Indians responded but ordinary people as well—widows from Surat sent an appeal to the leaders of their community, widows of Nansari petitioned the Gaekwar of Baroda, to gain some improvement in their status. For the first time the social reform movement attracted truly national attention, probably much more of it in the 1880's than did the restricted, one-a-year meetings of the National Congress; political reform in general, however, was still given the fullest consideration in the press.

The Indian Government regarded the public pressure for social legislation in the 1880's with more interest and concern than it did the spasmodic demands for political reform. Its nominal policy of not interfering in Indian religious and social life had been compromised often enough so that it could not ignore the invitation to intervene again, especially in view of Malabari's suggestion that the Governor-General lend his own prestige to a national organization for reform.

Before his retirement at the end of 1884, Lord Ripon had written to Malabari that the government would have to proceed very slowly in response to his appeal; but he added, "I shall rejoice if the results of your inquiries should show that there exists an opening for the Government to mark in some public manner the view which it entertains of the great importance of reform in these matters. . . ."[20] The official inquiry under Lord Dufferin's administration to determine whether legislation should be introduced led to publication in 1886 of the official replies to the "Notes," and an attendant Resolution of His Excellency in Council on the matter. The Resolution stated the government's view that no administrative or legislative action should then be taken. The reasoning behind the decision not to act was that the "evils" which Malabari described did not fall under existing civil or criminal law, nor were the courts being asked to enforce the social customs productive of those "evils." Therefore, nothing could be done within the "ordinary machinery" at the government's disposal. Nor should the Legislature enact new laws and thereby "place itself in direct antagonism to social opinion." Instead, Malabari's reforms "must be left to the improving influences of time, and to the gradual operation of the mental and moral development of the people by the spread of education." The government was willing to consider 1) amendment of the Widows' Remarriage Act of 1856 to allow the remarried widow to keep property inherited from her first husband, and 2) a provision that a "widow, who fails to obtain the consent of her caste-fellows to her remarriage, may nevertheless marry without renouncing her religion."[21] But such consideration was to take place only when the demands by the Hindu community itself for such action became stronger. Clearly, the government did not wish to raise new problems of opposition by any substantial groups of Indians at

[20] Quoted in Gidumal, op.cit., p. cxii.
[21] Home Dept., Public Proc., op.cit. The reference to renunciation of religion suggested that many widow remarriages took place after the bridal couple had become Brahmos so that they could be married under the terms of the Brahmo Marriage Act.

158

that time. It may have reasoned that the reformers' demands were virtually unlimited and that giving effect to their proposals on certain issues would logically require further and continuing involvement in social reform matters. In any case, to satisfy the demands of the social reformers would, in effect, free those same Indians to pursue more vigorously the agitation for political reforms.

An insight into another facet of the government's reaction to Malabari's proposals came in the form of Finance Minister Sir Auckland Colvin's reply to Malabari on July 15, 1884. Stating the position that he later elaborated upon in the famous "Audi Alteram Partem" correspondence with A.O. Hume in 1888, Colvin observed that "the natives are calling on Government (in the intervals of abusing it for its want of appreciation of their efforts) to save them the effort of themselves showing their appreciation of their most elementary duties," that is, social reform. Here was a task which Indians themselves were the most fit to undertake, Sir Auckland argued, and it logically followed that unless Indians worked for their own advancement the government surely could not be expected to do so. The Indian press, he added, might be of greater assistance by supporting social reform, "the merits of which it thoroughly understands, than in wasting itself in barren philippics against English rule and English character." But Sir Auckland despaired of seeing many Indians working for social reform; "so that you, and I, and the widow, and the five-years-old bride must possess ourselves in patience, until a humbler and truer conception of its needs and duties at length breaks in upon the native mind. . . ."[22] Sir Auckland's reply to Malabari was published in the press and brought forth rejoinders from Kashinath Trimbak Telang in the press and on the platform.[23] The general question, which Telang raised to a major debate, was Should Social Reform Precede Political Reform," henceforth one of the classic issues facing Indian nationalists.

After the seemingly irreversible rebuffs from official India, Malabari undertook his most significant effort to obtain legisla-

[22] *Infant Marriage and Enforced Widowhood in India,* p. 17.
[23] See Telang, *Selected Writings and Speeches,* I, 269-99.

tion. In the tradition of political reformers such as Dadabhai Naoroji, who saw the possibilities of influencing the Indian Government by appealing to the British voter, Malabari took his crusade to England.[24] There, by speeches and writings, he reinforced the concern about Indian society already present in circles such as the National Indian Association in Aid of Social Progress and Female Education in India. That Association had been founded in 1871 by Mary Carpenter, and its major activity was the support it gave to primary and secondary education in India. When Malabari reached England, the Association arranged for his appearances, and its journal, *The Indian Magazine and Review*, publicized the debate that the reformer had begun, which by then had many English participants. Malabari published an *Appeal on Behalf of the Daughters of India* in 1890, which was answered by the formation, under the auspices of the Association, of a permanent committee which "shall give any practical help that the course of legislation and the progress of public opinion may appear to render desirable."[25] The composition of that committee left nothing to be desired if influencing the British or Indian Government was its aim: "Viceroys distinguished for their habits of caution, like Lord Northbrook and Lord Dufferin [no longer Viceroy]; Governors of Indian provinces like Sir Rivers Thompson, Sir Charles Aitchison, Sir William Muir, and Lord Reay; the great aristocratic houses of England and Scotland, headed by the Duke of Westminster, the Duke of Argyll, and the Duke of Fife; leaders of national thought and sentiment like Lord Tennyson, Mr. Herbert Spencer, Professor Max Muller, and Mr. James Bryce—have given to that committee the powerful support of their names. The Bench of Bishops, the Roman Catholic Episcopacy, the Scottish Churches, the Nonconformist communities, and the Universities and superior Law Courts, both in England and India, contribute the authority of some of their

[24] The famous Sanskrit scholar, Max Müller, had earlier written to Malabari to suggest that he appeal to the women of England to offset the government's decision not to intervene with legislation. Gidumal, *The Life . . . of Malabari*, p. 204.

[25] *Indian Magazine and Review*, XXI, 237, 441.

ablest and most representative men."[26] Malabari had made his point; some kind of legislation would have to be passed.

The Age of Consent Bill Debate

While Malabari was in England, other reformers in India sought to translate the growing national interest in social legislation into proposals more realistic than those of the "Notes." K.T. Telang, the reformer and later Bombay high court judge, in his reply to the "Notes" in 1884 had argued that "reform is most urgently called for in regard to the time of consummation and not so much in regard to the time of marriage."[27] Admittedly, Telang was trying to appease the opposition, and he urged that delayed consummation of marriage be a "reform from within" Hindu society and not imposed from without. It was Dayaram Gidumal, Malabari's chief propagandist, who carried the Telang prescription to its logical conclusion with the suggestion that ultimately became the Age of Consent Bill. Gidumal published a pamphlet which concentrated attention on the Indian Penal Code instead of on caste and family customs. The Code incorporated an earlier Age of Consent Act, passed without much opposition in 1860 at the urging of Vidyasagar, which established ten as the age of a girl below which sexual intercourse with her was regarded as rape. Gidumal proposed simply that there be enacted an amendment to the Penal Code raising the age of consent to twelve, for married and unmarried girls. Reformers saw the value of such a proposal; it had the obvious advantage of not seeking new government interference but rather working within existing statutes. Opposition might thus be curtailed.

But opposition, nevertheless, was fierce and rose to a level never before seen in India on a social reform issue when, in 1889, the government appeared to be considering legislation to raise the age of consent. Bengali newspapers were the first to sound alarms at the government's renewed interest in Hindu marriage customs. To defend "Mother India" from calculating, alien attacks, such as the Age of Consent Bill, appeared to many editors as a first

[26] From a "Correspondent," the *Times* (London), Sept. 13, 1890.
[27] Telang, *op.cit.*, p. 242.

step toward rehabilitation of the nation. The bulk of vernacular newspapers in Bengal opposed the measure, concentrating on the religious injunction to perform the *garbhādhāna*[28] ceremony at the proper time. Government interference, it was held, would cause great spiritual suffering, possible misuse of police investigating powers, and a breakdown in the moral fiber of Hindu women.[29] There were even veiled references to revolts if the measure was passed. Several authors seemed genuinely afraid that postponement of marriage consummation—it was generally assumed that puberty was reached before twelve—would lead Hindu girls into the allegedly loose life of European women. Numerous public meetings were held against the measure, and the British Indian Association opposed it. Limited support for it came from the Indian Association and the Central Mahomedan Association. Among non-political organizations, the Brahmo Samaj provided the only significant unqualified support that the measure received in Bengal.[30]

In contrast to Bengal, the public interest over the Age of Consent Bill expressed in northern India appeared mild. The educated groups, increasingly alert to public issues, were split on the question, and no powerful organized bodies were moved to defend or attack the proposed measure. The Arya Samaj, suffering from the loss of its founder in 1883, had not yet developed the momentum for social reform that later characterized it. Nevertheless, a contemporary observer wrote that "The Age of Consent Bill forms a topic of general conversation at Lahore and heated con-

[28] Literally, "impregnation," performed ceremonially as the consummation of a marriage. Its value lay solely in the ceremonialism surrounding the act, which, like other ceremonies required of Hindus, had psychological value in "impressing on the mind of the person that he has assumed a new role and must strive to observe its rules." Pandurang Vaman Kane, *History of Dharmasastra*, ii, Pt. i, 193. For a description of the ceremony, see *ibid.*, pp. 201-06.

[29] *Dainik-o-Samachar Chandrika*, a substantial Calcutta daily, charged that the government, by passing the Bill, would be "plunging Hindu girls into sin." The paper further maintained that the government was going to force Hindus to produce healthy children (by postponing childbirth) and protect the health of girl brides, without any concern over the Hindus' welfare in the next life—which, for the orthodox, was held to be more important. Issue of Jan. 11, 1891, cited in Govt. of India, Imperial Record Dept., *Reports on Bengal Native Press, 1891*.

[30] See the *Times* (London), Dec. 8, 1890; Feb. 12 and 16, 1891.

troversies take place daily outside the Lohari Gate among the native preachers and always end in the discomfiture of the supporters of the measure."[31]

In southern India supporters and attackers of the Bill seemed evenly matched. Sir T. Madhava Rao, the noted administrator of Indian states who had, years before, urged the government to raise the age of marriage to ten for girls, unaccountably decided to lead the opposition and organize protest meetings. Dewan Bahadur R. Raghunatha Rao, General Secretary of the National Social Conference, led the supporters of the Bill and on one occasion succeeded in breaking up an opposition gathering by publicly challenging Madhava Rao, who led the meeting.[32] Considerable strength was added to the Bill's supporters in south India by the founding in Madras in 1890 of the journal, *Indian Social Reformer*, by a group of young reformers; that publication soon became the organ of the radical social reformers and something like a conscience for the reform movement. Reformers in Madras, however, at that time and in later years, were prone to expend their energies in bringing about limited reforms; early in 1891 they were engrossed in supporting passage in the Madras legislature of the controversial Hindu Gains of Learning Bill, which received as much press attention as did the Age of Consent Bill.

It was in Bombay Presidency that the Consent Bill received its elevation to a major national issue, thanks to the use made by Lokamanya Tilak of the issues it raised. As progressive in his personal life as most of the western Indian reformers, Tilak nevertheless saw in the Age of Consent question a religious issue which, though it chiefly concerned Bengal, could be aggravated into a major weapon for use against his personal enemies, the social reformers (and political moderates) in Maharashtra. Though the Bill's alleged offense against religion was a focal point of attack, Tilak's underlying concern was to increase the political strength of the forces at that time moving in the direction of extremist opposition to British rule. As the vigorous editor of *Kesari* and

[31] From *Khair Khwaik-i-Kashmir* (Lahore), Mar. 1, 1891, cited in Govt. of India, Imperial Record Dept., *Selections from the Vernacular Newspapers Published in the Punjab, 1891.*
[32] The *Times*, Dec. 15, 1890.

Mahratta in Poona, Tilak began his notable crusade against social reformers on the age of consent issue and led the western Indian opposition to the proposed legislation. He produced a pamphlet in answer to Dayaram Gidumal's suggestion of amending the Code, and his newspapers set the tone of orthodoxy outraged and nationalism insulted by the threats of government intervention in Hindu social practices.

As early as January 1885, Tilak had organized the first of a long series of meetings opposing government interference in marriage customs. When the Age of Consent Bill was finally introduced, "all over Bombay Presidency Tilak set to work energetically to organize the orthodox Hindu opposition. Public meetings were held to condemn the Bill and were attended by thousands ... the agitation grew in size and momentum. It spread from Maharashtra to Bengal, Madras, and other provinces of India."[33] The *Kesari* and *Mahratta* writings on the consent question seemed sober in contrast to some Bengali journalism. Their targets were Bhandarkar, Telang, and Agarkar, the Age of Consent Bill's major proponents after Ranade's withdrawal from the struggle, and their arguments rested chiefly on religious grounds, that is, the requirement of the *garbhādhāna* ceremony. The *Mahratta* regarded the Bill as the "thin edge of the wedge" of increasing government interference with religion. Its editorial of February 15, 1891, gave voice to Tilak's position: "We have often pointed out that we are not against the particular reform advocated. Individually, we would be prepared to go even further than what the Government proposes to do, but we are certainly not prepared to force our views upon the large mass of orthodox people. . . . We have every confidence that in time most of the reforms now preached would be gradually accepted. . . ."

The Hinduism-in-danger cry formed the backbone of most opposition arguments, including Tilak's. But Tilak's case also brought out a point which was more difficult for the reformers to face: a people prepared and anxious to liberate themselves from foreign domination should refrain from seeking help from the alien rulers, above all, in solving their private domestic problems.

[33] D.V. Tahmankar, *Lokamanya Tilak*, pp. 46-47.

It was humiliating, Tilak kept urging, morally wrong, and socially weakening to ask for legislation to curb a domestic social evil. He admitted the need to control consummation of marriages below the age of puberty (which, he felt, could not arbitrarily be set at twelve), but he contended that "education and not legislation is the proper method for eradicating the evil."[34]

The issue Tilak raised was a valid one, and protagonists on both sides wrote and spoke on it with arguments which rested on political, as well as social, philosophies. To argue in favor of legislation in behalf of social reform seemed to require acknowledgment that India's advancement was dependent upon the British, who could see the need for reform and act effectively to bring it about. Yet the moderate political leaders, many of whom were also social reformers, were also arguing that British rule was a kind of holding operation in the context of which Indians themselves should assume increasingly greater responsibilities for their own advancement. The contradiction here implied went to the heart of the political nationalist movement, and Tilak recognized that it did—hence the strength and popularity of the case he made not only against social reform legislation but against all forms of continuing cooperation with the government. Tilak wanted a new movement, in his terms truly nationalist because it would rest on independence of spirit and deny reliance on Western guidance and example.

Few social reformers dared meet Tilak's challenge to the consistency of their nationalist principles. Most of them took the easier course of debating with him on interpretations of the shastras or on the alleged ill-effects of government interference in social life. Ranade, who toward the finale of the Age of Consent campaign weakened in the face of the heated controversy, in the early days had defined the only convincing answer to Tilak. In 1885 he expounded the case for legislative action with arguments which thereafter became standard among social reformers.[35] Ranade answered first the argument that state interference in social and religious customs was wrong in principle by referring

[34] ibid., p. 46.
[35] Ranade, Miscellaneous Writings, pp. 70-86.

to the precedents of government action against the rites of suttee, hook-swinging, and the like, and in behalf of compulsory education, vaccination, and sanitation—actions to which few took serious exception. Similarly, he held that regulation of the age of marriage was in every country "a part of its national jurisprudence"; in India remedies for the widows' condition were also within the State's proper function. Secondly, the argument that the State could not interfere when the victimized party, that is, widows or infant brides, failed to complain did not hold, because there was no way for them to complain. "Perhaps the worst effect of injustice," he wrote, "is that it depresses the down-trodden victims to such an extent that they lick the hand of the oppressor."

Ranade's main case was against the proposition that help from a "foreign government" could not be trusted or was demoralizing. Initiation of social reform measures, he wrote, was not foreign but came from native sources. In the cases at hand, "the foreign rulers have no interest to move of their own accord. If they consulted their selfish interests only," he contended, "they would rather let us remain as we are, disorganized and demoralized, stunted and deformed, and with the curse of folly and wickedness paralyzing all the healthy activities and vital energies of our social body." If Hindus abjured government help in social reform they would shut out this very useful agency and fall behind other Indian communities which had received official assistance, that is, Parsis and Christians. Finally, Ranade astutely claimed that legislation would not constitute an imposition of alien rules on Hindu society but in fact would reinstate the ancient social regulations which had disappeared because of "the predominance of barbarous influences and by the intolerance of ruthless conquerors."

As the dominant figure in the National Social Conference, created in 1887 as an adjunct to the National Congress, Ranade secured the support of that new body for a resolution supporting Dayaram Gidumal's proposal to amend the Age of Consent section of the Penal Code. At the third Social Conference (Bombay, 1889) he moved that "in the opinion of this Conference . . . cohabitation before the wife is twelve years old should be punishable as a criminal offense," and that public opinion should be aroused to demand postponement of consummation of marriages until the wife was "fourteen at least."[36] The Conference passed the resolution, but not without debate. Tilak was present, and a few members supported his stand against legislation. But the dominant view was stated by N.S. Kale, among others, who urged legislation, saying, "our people as a body, I am sorry to confess, are an inert mass, which requires some external force or agency to stir them up and set them a-going."[37] Dr. Mahendra Lal Sircar, the president-elect, provided the kind of language typical of some social reformers of the day, which must have impelled many Indians into the opposing camp. Few outside the small group of reformers could listen without some resentment to words such as these on infant marriage: "The Hindu race consists at the present day . . . by virtue of this very blessed [sic] custom, of abortions and premature births. . . . every man and woman born of parents of such tender years as 10 or 12 years for a girl and 15 or 16 for a boy must be pronounced to be either an abortion or a premature birth (hear, hear). And are you surprised that the people of a nation so constituted should have fallen easy victims under every blessed tyrant that ever chose to trample upon them?"[38]

At the next year's Conference in Calcutta the chief preoccupation of the members was with the Consent Bill, then under official consideration, but Ranade's firmness of purpose the year before was no longer apparent. The almost fanatical sentiment aroused against the Bill, notably in Bengal, the Conference site, moved the cautious Ranade to seek conciliation. Against the wishes of the Madras delegation headed by Raghunatha Rao, he refrained from including in the Conference business agenda any reference to the Age of Consent Bill, and instead Resolution II simply called for pledges from members of all social reform associations to postpone marriages. Tilak's presence at the Conference may have affected Ranade's decision to avoid an open struggle. Seeking to embarrass the reformers Tilak proposed an amendment to tighten

[36] C.Y. Chintamani, *Indian Social Reform*, ii, 6.
[37] *Report of the Third National Social Conference*, 1889.
[38] Chintamani, *op.cit.*, iii, 140-01.

up Resolution II by omitting the phrase, "as far as possible," after the injunction to reformers to postpone marriages; it had to be accepted.[39]

The Age of Consent Bill debate reached furious proportions toward the end of the year 1890. Fifty-five women doctors practicing in India appealed to the viceroy to enact a law prohibiting consummation of marriages with girls under fourteen.[40] A petition to Queen Victoria along similar lines came from two thousand Indian women.[41] Malabari and Gidumal and their secular approaches to the problem were forgotten, and the controversy raged not over the question of government interference so much as over the religious injunctions to marry Hindu girls before puberty. Delicacy was not the order of the day as shastric passages on characteristic signs of puberty, the virtues or evils of early consummation of marriage, the controversial *garbhādhāna* ceremony, and similar matters, were cited by both sides in efforts to substantiate their positions. One Calcutta newspaper, the *Bangavasi*, was prosecuted for seditious writing in connection with the Bill. Brahmos attacked Bengali pundits; Arya Samajists quarrelled with the Benaras orthodoxy; scholar fought scholar in western India; Bhandarkar and Tilak were at the heads of the opposing camps in Poona. The Bhandarkar-Tilak debate was carried on partly through the columns of *Mahratta* (whose articles and letters on the Bill were reprinted in newspapers as far distant as Calcutta) and sometimes hinged on such fine points of Sanskrit syntax as the use of "a" or "the" preceding a noun in translation.[42] Bhandarkar and the reformers took the position that the bulk of the shastras sanctioned or even urged delaying marriages, or at least their consummation, until girls reached full womanhood, some time after attainment of puberty. A great many citations from scriptural authorities, including Manu, and

[39] *Report of the Fourth National Social Conference*, 1890.
[40] The *Times*, Oct. 8, Nov. 7, 1890.
[41] *ibid.*, Nov. 29, 1890.
[42] See Bhandarkar, "A Note on the Age of Marriage and Its Consummation; According to Hindu Religious Law." The author noted, "I have been carrying on literary controversies since 1864; but never did I hitherto meet with an opponent who treated me with such studied discourtesy as Mr. Tilak has been doing." (p. 49).

from literary accounts of Hindu heroes were brought out in support of their stand.[43]

The pertinence of the debate to the impending legislation was brought out by those who opposed the measure. The shastras, opponents claimed, required "that certain ceremonies constituting the consummation of marriage must be performed immediately after a young woman attains puberty."[44] Because puberty was often attained before the age of twelve, it followed that a girl might have sexual intercourse with her husband before she became twelve. The new amendment would make this a crime for the husband, punishable as rape.

Neither the reformers nor the government contemplated any systematic probing into Hindu family affairs under the terms of the new amendment. The threat to the integrity of the garbhādhāna ceremony was artificially posed, but it was capable of producing sentimental and irrational ideas of a kind that few other topics could have aroused. Tilak's efforts, therefore, to insert religious and nationalistic passion into the Age of Consent Bill controversy was a recognized success. He extended to the entire country the western Indian breach between reformers and anti-reformers and did so on an issue which only Bengalis really understood. Tilak's campaign, however, produced no real unity among those who opposed the social reformers; it was passionate, but uncoordinated. Even when political issues were raised as the basis for opposition to social reform through legislation, Tilak could not align a solid anti-reform bloc in the country.[45] It was

[43] Authorities have long differed on the subject of the proper age for marriage, especially for girls. Even Manu's work suggests various ages for female marriage, depending on the circumstances. There seems to be no passage in Manu itself which states clearly that a girl must be married before puberty, or, for that matter, at any specific age. However, various commentators on Manu and other writers insist on specific ages, usually below twelve. See *The Ordinances of Manu*, transl. by Arthur Coke Burnell (London, 1884), lect. ix, sec. 88-94, and notes. For a full discussion of marriage age in the dharmashastras, see Kane, *op.cit.*, ii, Pt. i, 438-47.

[44] In the words of R.N. Mudholkar, Chintamani, *op.cit.*, i, 173.

[45] e.g. Bipin Chandra Pal, in whom Tilak later discovered a kindred soul on political matters, supported the Age of Consent Bill. Pal, *Memories of My Life and Times*, ii, 113f.

169

instead the reformers who had the superior organization and the necessary unity of purpose.[46]

At the time that the Age of Consent Bill came up for consideration in the Viceroy's Legislative Council in 1891, several factors were present which had not existed five years before, when the government rejected Malabari's proposals. Of greatest importance was the attitude of the London government, which took a decidedly pro-reform stand, under pressure from British societies and newspapers interested in the welfare of Indians. Next, the fact that the Bill was not a major innovation in the law but was an amendment to the existing Code made the official stand easier to defend. Finally, Indian opinion favoring the legislation had gained strength since 1886, and those Indian leaders supporting the legislation were the moderates whose backing the government was glad to have. Opponents failed to agree on the basis for their opposition, even in Bengal where the religious issue was most strongly felt. Emphasizing the government's estimate of the quality of the Indian opposition, Sir Andrew Scoble, who introduced the Bill in the Council, observed that "were I a Hindu, I would prefer to be wrong with Professor Bhandarkar, Mr. Justice Telang and Dewan Bahadur Raghunath Rao than to be right with Pundit Sasadhur Turkachuramani and Mr. Tilak."[47]

In the Council deliberations the government explained that only the minimum in legislative reform of marriage customs was being contemplated, out of deference to orthodox sentiments. Several proposals for more sweeping marriage reforms had been made. One such proposal arose out of the famous restitution of conjugal rights case raised by the husband of a Hindu girl, Rukhmabai. The consumptive husband brought suit to force his young wife to live with him; when she adamantly refused, the Court (following British precedents) ordered her imprisoned.[48]

[46] The *Times* correspondent wrote: "The progressive party, though much smaller numerically, is better able to make itself heard." Dec. 1, 1890.

[47] Govt. of India, Council of the Gov.-Gen., *Proceedings, 1891*, p. 83. Turkachuramani was a notable Hindu revivalist in Bengal, recognized for his speaking ability.

[48] The Rukhmabai case (Dadaji v. Rukhmabai [1886], 10 Bom 301) is covered in Govt. of India, Home Dept., *Proceedings (Judicial), June 1887*, Nos. 189-192.

The English permanent committee supporting Hindu marriage reform had urged the Secretary of State to include in the legislation a prohibition of imprisonment in cases like that of Rukhmabai; but the government decided against that step. Another proposal which the government preferred not to act upon would have allowed a remarried widow to retain an inheritance received from her first husband's estate, which was not permitted under the 1856 Widows' Remarriage Act. The Viceroy, Lord Lansdowne, in presenting his administration's views, argued that the Penal Code amendment affecting age of consent was a trifling matter, as compared with the far-reaching measures that he had been urged to take.

Sir Andrew Scoble, on the other hand, presented an urgent appeal, citing the highly publicized Hari Maiti case,[49] and referred to the mass of evidence that had been collected, some of it by a select committee, showing the prevalence of the practice of marriage consummation with immature girls. Scoble urged the need to tighten up the law in such cases and admitted favoring tampering with accepted customs.

The hero of the anti-reformers was Sir Romesh Chunder Mitter of Bengal, one of two Hindus (and four Indians) in the Legislative Council. "The proposed amendment," he warned, "is likely to cause widespread discontent in the country"—by which he meant Bengal.[50] It would be unwarranted interference in religious practices of orthodox Hindus, Sir Romesh alleged, comparable to the effects of requiring Englishmen to burn instead of

---

Ranade and the principal of Elphinstone College, W. Wadsworth, formed a Rukhmabai Defense Committee, which publicized widely the novel case and the contemporary treatment of women. Tilak found that cause unworthy and in defiance of the shastras. Rukhmabai, incidentally, ultimately became an English-trained physician, practiced in India, and lived until 1955.

[49] Hari Maiti, aged 35, caused the death of his wife, Phulmoni, aged 10, by forceable intercourse. A judge ruled that the law of rape was inapplicable because the girl had reached her tenth birthday and was married to the defendant. See the *Times*, July 28, 1890.

[50] Govt. of India, Council of the Gov.-Gen., *Proceedings, 1891*, p. 14. Sir Romesh, it is interesting to note, had previously supported social reforms in overseas travel and marriage expenditures.

bury their corpses. Krishnaji Lakshman Nulkar, from his Council seat, denied the threat of trespass on Hindu customs and asserted that the proposed Act was not a measure of social reform but merely "seeks to remove a glaring defect in the criminal law."[51] Disgusted and embarrassed by his official position, Sir Romesh Chunder absented himself from the Council deliberations on the second reading of the Bill in March 1891, on complaint of illness. He did not return during subsequent consideration of the measure and was hailed by the anti-reform groups throughout the country, and particularly in Bengal, where no local opponent of the Bill could be found with as much popular following as Tilak could muster in Maharashtra. Expressing the reformers' views of Sir Romesh's stand, the Bombay weekly *Subodh Patrika* of January 18, 1891, wrote: "Mr. Nulkar has, in fact, to some extent tried to repair the mischief done by Sir Romesh, and to save the credit of educated Natives on this side of India at least."

The major argument that the government was forced to answer entailed a partial reversal of the 1886 declaration, which had registered unwillingness to place the Legislature "in direct antagonism to social opinion."[52] Scoble announced in Council that the Queen's Proclamation of 1858—a bulwark for India's orthodox and aristocratic groups—while enjoining the government to abstain from interfering "with the religious beliefs or worship of any of our subjects," also gave all citizens (including wives) equal protection of the laws. Further, while the Queen had promised that "generally" in legislation due regard was to be paid to "ancient rights, usages and customs," there was no undertaking of absolute noninterference. Concluding the Council discussions, Lord Lansdowne candidly summed up the official position with a notable statement of Anglo-Saxon reformist doctrine: ". . . in all cases where demands preferred in the name of religion would lead to practices inconsistent with individual safety and the public peace, and condemned by every system of law and morality in the world, it is religion, and not morality, which must give

[51] *ibid.*, p. 18.
[52] On the other hand, the 1886 declaration asserted the state's right to enforce "the ordinary criminal law" if it went against customary practices.

way."[53] Of course everyone realized that the amendment would scarcely affect either religion or morality. Answering the objection that the law would be largely unenforceable—it was noncognizable with respect to husbands and wives—Scoble said that he would settle for it as an "educative" measure, "if it strengthens the hands of fathers of families for protection of their daughters. . . ."[54] The supporters of the measure realized that most social reform legislation had little more than educative effect.

After the Bill was passed on March 19, 1891, Tilak, through the *Mahratta*, called for "a grand central organization" based on "self-preservation, self-protection, and self-support," whose main purpose would be to counteract the reformers' propaganda in England. The *Mahratta* charged that "we have been mischievously and shamelessly represented as a nation of savages and the *sudharaks* [reformers] have shamelessly testified to it. Let these *sudharaks* therefore form themselves into a separate nationality. . . . We ought no longer to allow to be amongst us those of our fellow-countrymen who are really our enemies but who pose as our friends. The time has come when we should divide."[55] However, Tilak's call by then aroused no public response.

By means of the Age of Consent Bill controversy the social reform movement achieved national recognition, and henceforth the social reform question was inescapably a part of nationalist ideologies. But the agitation on that issue had its sobering side: while it unified and "nationalized" the social reform movement, it also publicized the anti-reformers and the revivalist nationalists and aroused great public support for orthodoxy. Opponents of the Bill, though unable to sway the official position had at least attained a major secondary purpose. They had registered an effective protest against any kind of government interference in social and religious life and had made that protest a great public concern. They had stimulated popular distrust and ridicule of the social reformers, who were thereafter regarded by many In-

[53] *ibid.*, p. 146. Note the similarity to Sir Joseph Arnould's decision in the Karsondas Mulji case, described in Chapter iv.

[54] *ibid.*, p. 14.

[55] Quoted from *Mahratta*, March 22, 1891, in Govt. of India, Imperial Records Dept., *Report on Bombay Native Papers, 1891.*

dians as meddlesome, intolerant, insincere, and unpatriotic. Finally, many of the Bill's opponents had temporarily satisfied their desire to attack the government for something, it scarcely mattered what.

Tilak's reasons for opposing the Bill included all of those purposes, and his was the last dissident voice to be heard in the Age of Consent controversy. In resigned bitterness, nearly a month after the Bill was passed, Tilak registered through the *Mahratta* sentiments which were soon to spread even into the reformers' camp and alter the philosophy of the social reform movement. On April 12 this appeared in *Mahratta*: "We are very sensitive and we feel nothing so much as an attack on our national character. That the Age of Consent Act will write in the statute book the character of the Indian nation in the blackest letters is our grievance. . . ." Tilak proposed to carry the agitation against the Act to England; "so long as this certificate of bad character remains on the statute book we can enjoy no rest," he wrote in the same article. There is no evidence, however, that he took any steps toward that end. Tilak's antagonism against the Bombay Presidency reformers crystallized during the Consent controversy, and henceforth his efforts to undermine them were unceasing. His most potent weapon, ridicule, was wielded as much because of his sincere concern that enlightened men were prone to hypocrisy as because he wished his enemies lowered in public estimation.

Perhaps the opponents of the Age of Consent Bill could be held responsible for the fact that no major social reform legislation was passed between 1891 and 1929,[56] when minimum ages for marriage were established by the Sarda Act. But if this was the case, it was probably not so much due to their direct opposition to social reform as to the political activities of at least some of them, which made the government increasingly wary of furthering popular unrest by again raising issues for social legislation.

The Age of Consent Bill controversy tested the strengths of two contending factions for leadership of the nationalist move-

[56] In 1925 a minor bill was passed, which raised the age of consent to 13.

ment in the late 1880's and early 1890's by causing an open split on the issue of acceptance or rejection of Western standards and methods of political and social reform as essential parts of Indian nationalism. The narrow question of the government's right to amend the Penal Code was, for nationalists of either persuasion, not the real issue at stake. Nor was the desirability of raising the age of consent or the age of marriage a matter of widespread controversy. Both sides to the controversy desired social reform to at least some degree, and neither side was wholly content with having to accept an alien bureaucracy's often insensitive attempts to manipulate the Indian way of life. Only reluctantly for the most part were social reformers willing to defend government interference for the sake of the rightness of the measure in dispute. Except for Malabari and for some orthodox Bengali leaders who were sensitive to the decline of their authority, the chief antagonists were not single-minded in their support or their opposition to the measure. Just as there was a mixture of Western liberalism and cultural chauvinism in every Indian nationalist, so there were often unresolved doubts in the mind of every social reformer about supporting legislative action rather than trusting to spontaneous social amelioration. Thus, an assessment of the Age of Consent Bill controversy leads one to conclude that the real issue brought into focus by the controversy was the confidence of the Indians in Western-inspired political and social change and, to a lesser extent, their faith in the British Government. In 1891 that confidence and that faith outweighed the desire to define and manage the course of India's advancement along traditional, non-Western lines. Accordingly, the nationalist leadership which stood for that dominant view was given at least half-hearted encouragement.

MAHADEV GOVIND RANADE AND THE

NATIONAL SOCIAL CONFERENCE

MAHADEV GOVIND RANADE represented in his thinking and action the complexity of ideas and motives incorporated in late 19th century Indian nationalism. His withdrawal from the Age of Consent controversy toward its finale is evidence that he perceived the real problem for nationalism raised by that social reform issue, although it was generally held that the rancor of the dispute was what bothered him most. Simply stated, the problem was: how could a national unity and purpose be defined and promoted which would assure genuine advancement in all aspects of Indian life but at the same time would not constitute a break with India's unique and valuable heritage and an uncritical adoption of alien ways. The problem was, in fact, a dilemma, as 20th century Indian culture demonstrates, but Ranade worked strenuously and occasionally brilliantly to resolve it.

Mahadev Govind Ranade

Nationalism and social reform, as ideologies and as public movements, were united in the person of Ranade: a leader of the political activities of the Poona Sarvajanik Sabha; a vigorous lecturer and writer on economic and political subjects; a participant in the founding of the Indian National Congress and a "power behind the throne"[1] in that body until his death; and an organizer and the mainstay of the all-India social reform move-

[1] Surendranath Banerjea, *A Nation in Making*, p. 50.

176

ment during the last two decades of the 19th century. In politics, economics, and in social reform his conception of Indian problems and their solution was truly national. Ranade's nationalism was grounded in his acceptance of the administrative unity of the country, achieved under British rule, and the new opportunities which that presented for advancement in all lines of endeavor through both private and governmental efforts. The British connection with India, Ranade thought, would last until India, inspired by long association with the civilization of the West, should have regenerated herself and prepared herself to "take her proper rank among the nations of the world."[2] For him the forces making for Indian unity were those associated with British rule—the civil service, the judicial system, modern communications, the English language and the new secular knowledge transmitted by it, and the economic structure.

But nationalism for him was more than the workings of these functional elements. Ranade's nationalism had its intellectual and emotional appeal in the belief that India was the home of a "chosen race,"[3] which not by mere chance had survived, preserved from extinction "as though they were a people with a special mission entrusted to them."[4] Indians, he said, "represent a continuity of creed, of traditions, of literature, of philosophy, of modes of life and forms of thought, which are particular to this land"; thus, Indians "are under the severe discipline of a high Purpose." In modern times "vast energies" have been "set in motion, by the guiding hand it is our privilege to recognize at every step (British rule)," which after decades, perhaps centuries, will fulfill the mission of Indian civilization.[5]

Ranade's leadership of the social reform movement and his simultaneously immense influence in the National Congress offered a model of integrated nationalist activity which was not typical of the age. Although he understood the inevitable conflicts between certain social reform doctrines and those of nationalism, in his own practical philosophy those two doctrines were

[2] M.G. Ranade, *Religious and Social Reform*, p. 107.
[3] Ranade, *Miscellaneous Writings*, p. 125.
[4] Ranade, *Religious and Social Reform*, p. 145.
[5] *ibid.*, p. 149.

fused. Many of the Indian leaders of his day were prone to taking strong, uncompromising stands on political or on social questions, ignoring their complexity and interrelationships. Such rashness, or, if one likes, momentary courage, was usually followed by embarrassing recognition of errors and temporary let-downs in enthusiastic leadership. Ranade was rightly accused of a compromising nature, which may, in a time of growing self-assurance, be considered a weakness. Nevertheless, in his personal life and in his recorded achievements were brought together all the intellectual forces of the day, in a logical and harmonious blend which the more single-minded of his countrymen, then and later, were unable to achieve.

Around him flowed the most influential all-India movements of the century, as well as the peculiarly Maharashtrian intellectual ferment which was always centered in Poona. Among his acquaintances in the earlier generation were: the educationists, Dadoba Pandurang and Bal Shastri Jambhekar; the social reformers, Karsondas Mulji and Vishnu Shastri Pundit; and the missionary from Bengal, Keshub Chandra Sen. He was closely in touch with the contemporary Maharashtrians: Agarkar, Bhandarkar, Gokhale, and Tilak, and in addition met the leaders of north India, Bengal, and south India at the yearly Congresses. His influence on the succeeding generation was felt most strongly through Gokhale and the moderate wing of the Congress before the First World War. Reacting sensitively to all of that display of talent and ideas, yet able to rise above it and assert his own spiritual and moral integrity, Ranade set a unique standard for all who knew him and provides historians with an enticing glimpse of what modern India *might* have been. As it turned out, Ranade founded no lasting school of thought; the integration of his ideas and his approach to life were suited to few apart from himself. Yet in each endeavor and in each enunciation of his convictions he made his impact, and contemporary nationalist thought was undeniably affected.

Born a Chitpavan Brahmin at Nasik in 1842, educated at Kolhapur English School and Elphinstone High School in Bombay, Ranade passed the first matriculation examination of the new

Bombay University in 1859. Receiving his B.A. in 1862 he began a teaching and journalism career which lasted nearly all his life. A few years later, he took a government position as a reporter on Marathi literature, which sent him to Poona and into the study of his region's literature and history, for which he later became famous. In 1871, after several years preparation in judicial offices, he was appointed judge in Poona by the Bombay Government. Passing through various judicial and administrative positions and three terms as law member on the Bombay Legislative Council, Ranade's official career culminated in his appointment to fill K.T. Telang's seat on the Bombay High Court Bench in 1893, a position he held until his death in 1901. His associations with public bodies, many of which he founded, were diverse in scope but, with few exceptions, limited to the geographical area of Bombay Presidency.[6] His greatest individual achievement was his almost single-handed creation of the National Social Conference in 1887.

Ranade's early involvement in social reform was limited to local efforts in the Widow Marriage Association, founded by Vishnu Shastri Pundit, which resulted in his public excommunication[7] in 1869 by the Shankaracharya of western India, more as a warning than as a permanent disability. He was branded as a young rebel. But for Ranade, as for the bulk of his Maharashtrian Brahmin colleagues, rebelliousness was not a repudiation of the fundamentals of Indian life. It was rather an intellectual protest against superficial dogmas untenable for a rational mind, and a moral protest against human indignities sanctioned by Hindu society. Ranade believed that an intellectual and moral purification could come about without destroying traditional virtues. His

[6] James Kellock's list of Ranade's affiliations includes the Sarvajanik Sabha, the Industrial Conferences and Exhibitions, several small manufacturing firms and a bank, Fergusson College, the Female High School, the Prarthana Samaj, and the Marathi Literature Encouragement Society. These were not merely nominal affiliations. Kellock, *Mahadev Govind Ranade*, p. 80.

[7] Excommunication as a practice within a caste group meant the exclusion of a member (and usually his family) from ritual social intercourse and intermarriage with other caste members. Appendix II reproduces a typical proclamation of excommunication; this was proclaimed by the leaders of the Kapole Banya caste of Bombay in 1871.

aim of purifying without destroying Hinduism led him into the Prarthana Samaj, and he soon became its dominant spokesman. Yet Ranade did not conceive of social reform as necessarily a product of religious reform along the lines of Hindu Protestantism. In his own life, religion and social reform were conjoined, as his moving testament, "A Theist's Confession of Faith,"[8] demonstrated. But in the modern western Indian tradition, he denied the necessity of conversion to a particular set of religious beliefs in order to achieve a transformed social life. He acknowledged his respect for the Brahmo and Arya Samajes and assumed some responsibility for the reception tendered to Dayananda Saraswati when the latter visited Poona to deliver fifteen lectures in 1875.[9] But the rebelliousness followed by the social exclusiveness of the other Samajes found no acceptable place in Ranade's thinking or behavior.

In his frequent discussions of the techniques of social reform Ranade explained his objections to what he called "the method of rebellion," by which he meant "separating from the [Hindu] community," forming "another camp on a religious basis" and thereby a new social group with the characteristics of a caste. Though respectful of those who followed that course and sympathetic toward their impatience with slow, evolutionary changes, Ranade urged his followers not to forsake the Hindu tradition with the attitude that Hindu society is a "festering mass of decay and corruption" and that one's "highest duty is to separate oneself from the decaying mass and look to our own safety."[10] The social condition of Bengal, where the Brahmo Samaj had been in existence for half a century, excited him to one of his few barbed criticisms of those he did not agree with: "So far as the orthodox community is concerned, Bengal is more orthodox than any other part of India. So far as the reformed community is concerned,

[8] In *Religious and Social Reform*, p. 250f.

[9] On the final day of the Swami's visit there was a serious riot during which Ranade gave full support to Dayananda; typically, he refused later to testify against the orthodox instigators, whom he knew personally. See Kellock, *op.cit.*, pp. 63-65; and D.G. Karve, *Ranade: Prophet of Liberated India*, p. xxiv.

[10] From Ranade's address at Hislop College and his Seventh Social Conference speech, *Miscellaneous Writings*, pp. 113, 127.

Bengal is more reformed than any other part of India. They form in fact two separate camps. Kulinism and Kali worship thrive in all their extravagance on one side, and puritanical theism on the other." Brahmos, he charged, were so absorbed in their personal religious life that they forgot about the general community. The "true test of progress," he insisted, "must be seen in signs which show that this vast mass of humanity is being vivified"—not that a small, favored group has managed, with the support of English education and wealth, to elevate itself.[11]

Ranade's singular contribution to the social reform movement, apart from his organizing efforts, was his broadly conceived philosophy of cultural change in India. That philosophy expounded the evolutionary nature of change in Indian thought and social institutions, which meant preservation as well as advancement, which linked the past to the future without a revolutionary interim, and which, though stimulated often by outside forces, was governed by the inner resources of the society itself. Such ideas helped to form the basis of the necessary compromise that social reform made with cultural revival at the turn of the century.

Ranade's philosophy was met by two groups of challengers: the single-minded, uncompromising reformers whose behavior perplexed and annoyed ordinary people and who were typically forced into talking with each other, for lack of public interest in their ideas; and the upholders of orthodoxy, sincere or not, who warned of sin and chaos if social reform were pressed. To the former group Ranade pointed to India's history, which showed "change for the better by slow absorption—assimilation not by sudden conversion and revolution,"[12] as a result of which India had outlived all other civilizations. The varna/caste system, he perceived, was never a static order: Shudras lost their slave status and became Vaishyas, Brahmins became warriors and statesmen, Kshatriyas became philosophers, and Vaishyas became saints. Religious life advanced over the centuries, and tribal organizations gave way to civilized communities. "All these changes have been brought about consciously without any violent struggle, and with-

[11] ibid., pp. 156, 127.
[12] ibid., p. 126.

out breaking up the continuity of the old life."[13] Herbert Spencer's influence was apparent in Ranade's warnings to avoid the temptation of trying "to achieve the work of a century in a decade. This temptation has to be resisted, and in this respect the teachings of the evolution doctrine have great force, because they teach that growth is structural and organic, and must take effect in all parts of the organism." Reformers must "seek to turn the stream with a gentle bend here, and a gentle bend there, to fructify the land; we cannot afford to dam it up altogether, or force it into a new channel. . . . The society to which we belong has shown wonderful elasticity in the past, and there is no reason for apprehending that it has ceased to be tractable. . . ."[14]

Even further he pursued this line of thought, almost seeming to repeat the arguments of those attacking reforms: "The Hindu community . . . is no doubt conservative to a degree, but that conservatism is its strength. No nation has any destined place in history which changes its creed and its morals, its customs and its social polity, with the facility of fashions."[15] Reformers, he announced, seek "not to revolutionize, but to lop off the diseased over-growth and excrescences, and to restore vitality and energy to the social organism."[16]

The fullest exposition of Ranade's philosophy of Indian social change appeared in his discussions of the historical movement for theistic Protestantism within Hinduism.[17] While holding the view that the theistic movement in the India of his day was the embodiment of the modern spirit working within Hinduism, Ranade pointed out that in fact theism had an early origin in India, and was for centuries enriched by the teachings of the bhakti saints. "The movement is older than modern India," he said, "and it is not confined to the English educated classes in the towns. Its roots lie deep in our history. . . ."[18] In the evolution of the Hindu religion, as in other faiths, according to Ranade, the process al-

[13] loc.cit.
[14] ibid., p. 118.
[15] ibid., p. 127.
[16] Religious and Social Reform, p. 50.
[17] In particular, his addresses, "The Philosophy of Indian Theism," "Raja Rama Mohana Roy," and "Hindu Protestantism," in Religious and Social Reform.
[18] ibid., p. 205.

ways worked towards higher forms, of which worship of a monotheistic personal God was the highest. In that development Hinduism freely assimilated ideas from other faiths; yet despite the
"convergence of historical faiths actively at work," it never lost
its uniqueness. Historical precedent thus confirmed the value of
accepting new ideas into the body of Hindu thought. Buddhism
and Islam had introduced worthy amendments and additions
to the catholic conceptions of Hindus, and Christianity was beginning to do so. "The power of organization, active hatred of sin,
and indignation against wrong-doing in place of indifference, a
correct sense of the dignity of man and woman, active philanthropy and a feeling of fraternity, freedom of thought and action,
these are Christian virtues which have to be incorporated into
the national character, and this work is actively going on in all
parts of the country."[19]

The continuity of religious growth and progress, with their
social counterparts, was Ranade's most important message. For
him, Rammohun Roy was not a revolutionary, but a recent exponent of the historical forces always at work in Hindu religion
and society. "The members of the Brahma Samaja," he said,
"can claim a long ancestry, as old as any of the sects prevailing
in the country. The Brahma movement was not first brought into
existence in 1828. ..."[20] The "Samaj movement" was "only a faint
reflection and a humble off-shoot" of the two-thousand years of
progress in religious thought brought about by a series of protestant movements within Hinduism,[21] the last of which, before modern times, was the bhakti movement. Roy's rationalism,
his Westernized approach to religious, social, and political questions Ranade regarded as manifestations of the true national spirit,
and Roy's followers—religious and social reformers—could not
rightly be charged with propounding a "de-nationalizing" creed.

As in religious thought, so in social practices, for Ranade the
genius of Hindu culture was its continuity, tolerance, and ability
to assimilate. But tolerance often went too far, and hence there
had to be periodic purifications. The 19th century reform move-

[19] *ibid.*, p. 23.
[20] *ibid.*, p. 116.
[21] *ibid.*, p. 199.

ment, Ranade believed, was in the great Hindu tradition of re-form—reform which always sought out the ancient principles in order to restate them. In many places he documented his conviction that ancient Indian society was free of the trammels and iniquities of contemporary life. Vedic society, as presented in the grihyasutra, recognized woman's liberty and dignity and a mature age for marriage. Later in the period of the *Ramayana* even a woman's freedom of choice in marriage was acknowledged. Also, widow remarriage was permitted in Vedic times, although subsequent smriti writers disagreed on that matter.[22] On the one hand Ranade sincerely paid his debt to the alien influences which stimulated the 19th century reform movement,[23] but on the other argued that reform "is sought not as an innovation, but as a return and restoration to the days of our past history."[24]

Recognizing that it was by deeds, not by words, that orthodoxy was most offended, the leader of the western Indian social reformers submitted to orthodox restrictions on his behavior in order to increase the acceptability of his unorthodox message. These episodes illustrate the point: In 1873 his wife died in Poona, and influential friends from Bombay anticipated that Ranade would remarry a widow in order to lend needed support to the cause and prove his sincerity as a reformer. His father, in haste to prevent a family catastrophe, arranged with an orthodox family to marry his son to their eleven-year old daughter, Ramabai. Arguments failed, the respect of two families and the happiness of his father were at stake, and Ranade consented. His child wife became his pupil, and later in life she organized a woman's welfare society, the Seva Sedan of Poona. Another such episode occurred when Vishnu Shastri Pundit married a widow and after

[22] See "The Sutra and Smriti Texts on the Age of Hindu Marriage" and "Vedic Authorities for Widow Marriage," *ibid.*

[23] viz. the influence of the Western treatment of women: "Fortunately, the causes which brought on this degradation [of Indian women] have been counteracted by Providential guidance, and we have now, with a living example before us of how pure Aryan customs, unaffected by barbarous laws and patriarchal nations, resemble our own ancient usages, to take up the thread where we dropped it under foreign and barbarous pressure, and restore the old healthy practices . . . ;" *ibid.*, p. 101.

[24] *ibid.*, p. 107.

which was invited to Ranade's house for dinner. Again Ranade's father intervened with threats to leave his own home if his son persisted in entertaining such a person as Vishnu Shastri. The son apologized, and it was reported that an invitation for Vishnu Shastri to dine was never again presented.[25] An affair, ludicrous by present standards, provides still another example of Ranade's view that "There are some matters in which we must stand out, but there is no reason why we should stand out on all matters simply for the fun of the thing," as he put it in a letter to Telang.[26] In 1890 Ranade found himself with fifty-one other Brahmins, including Tilak, at a tea party given by Christian missionaries. It was later charged by a rabid antireformer that both Ranade and Tilak had taken food with the Christians, for which they should be ignored and refused religious rites. Ranade did penance for his unacceptable act, by taking *prāyaścitta*, as did Tilak. The former later explained, reasonably, that a stand taken against doing the required penance for a breach of caste rules would have created the public impression that the social reform movement chiefly aimed at abolishing inter-dining restrictions.[27]

Reformers were startled and even outraged by Ranade's conduct in the latter episode, and even his wife, by then a staunch reformer herself, expressed dismay. Many years later, after Ranade's death, Malabari recalled the disillusionment he felt at Ranade's remarriage and his taking of *prāyaścitta*. "It was an immense misery," he wrote in his journal, *East and West*, "to one who admired Ranade so much to find such a giant in intellect act like a child. . . . A lapse like this, on the part of a leader, cannot but prove disastrous to his party, try how you may to exaggerate its cause or explain away its effects."[28] These were harsh comments, but other reformers, too, with a sense of guilt about the backsliding of many of their number, accepted Malabari's judgment.[29]

[25] Kellock, *op.cit.*, p. 67.
[26] *ibid.*, p. 109.
[27] *ibid.*, p. 106.
[28] "Ranade and His Times," in *East and West*, II, 25, 1,302.
[29] In interviews with the older generation of social reformers and scholars in Maharashtra I found no one who defended Ranade's methods of compromise

Although public leaders in India have often retained or even increased their following while revealing their own doubts about their beliefs and making no effort to cover up their inconsistencies,[30] Ranade's close associates found it difficult to understand his two-sided approach to reform. In the same paper, for example, he could refer to social reform as "this gentle revolution" and then use the following harsh imagery: "The sharp surgical operation, and not the homoeopathic infinitesimally small pill, is the proper remedy [for diseased mal-formations of the body] . . . the analogy holds good in the diseases of the body politic."[31] But if his followers were sometimes confused by his attitude toward reform, his enemies knew that in Ranade they faced a powerful critic of the status quo, whose cautious behavior could not allay their suspicions and hatreds. Ranade's approach to those who defended traditional beliefs and customs from a devotion, even if naive, to religious principles was through education and persuasion. But he had no respect for those anti-reformers whose irresponsible words sometimes led to violence and crude displays. Those opponents, he felt, had to be challenged with vigor. Often educated men, they frequently appeared more anxious to advance their personal popularity and embarrass the reformers than to strengthen the resources of orthodoxy.

Throughout the Indian literature on social reform it is impossible to find a match for Ranade's astuteness in argument against the anti-reformers, until one reads Gandhi's equally keen and many-sided writing against those opposing his reforms. Ranade told the stubbornly orthodox and the uncritical revivalists that they were resisting a strong tide of social liberation and warned that they offered no possible alternative channel into which to

---

and gradualism. All of them admired the strength of purpose, if not the objectives, of men like Tilak. A typical comment was, "Ranade had no guts; Agarkar was the only full-bodied reformer." In his own day, however, Ranade was very popular and his views represented those of most of the educated groups in western India.

[30] The reason for this is probably that a leader is believed in and followed chiefly because of the kind of person he is—or the kind of personality he exhibits—rather than the persuasiveness of his program.

[31] *Religious and Social Reform*, pp. 101, 108.

direct the inevitable changes taking place in modern India. In human society, he argued,[32] there must be progress toward justice and equality, or there will be decay, and in the case of India, to stand still would mean extinction. Could the orthodox and revivalists ignore the changes taking place around them? Those changes, for Ranade, meant progress, and "All progress in social liberation tends to be a change from the law of status to the law of contract, from the restraints of family and caste customs to the self-imposed restraints of the free will of the individual."[33] Then, softening his approach to meet the psychological needs for security of his unconvinced listeners, Ranade tried to show that in fact all of his reform proposals substituted ancient ideals for the modern degeneration and corruption of those ideals.

Ranade's greatest legacy to the reformers following him was his integration of the social reform doctrines with the spirit, if not always the outward appearance, of national cultural revival. In the 20th century that integration made possible an almost unnoticed substitution of the doctrine of "reform along national lines" for the earlier doctrine of "social efficiency." Such a legacy assured that social reform would not lose its proper place in the nationalist attitude of mind. At the same time, and this was a remarkable accomplishment, Ranade laid the philosophical groundwork for movements of practical social reform and service in the 20th century by elevating individual conscience and humanistic ideals to a position of primacy—above the values of caste and community loyalties. That contribution was a product of Ranade's religious beliefs, but others benefited whose religion was devotion not to a theistic God, but to humanity.

The Congress and the Social Conference

The original intention of Ranade and his associates who founded the Indian National Congress, including A.O. Hume, was to provide a platform for the discussion of social, as well as political, issues which were on the minds of Indian nationalists.[34]

[32] *ibid.*, pp. 26-27; also *Miscellaneous Writings*, pp. 234-45.
[33] *Religious and Social Reform*, p. 109.
[34] Several accounts of the origin of the Congress cite the intentions of the

K.T. Telang, a secretary at the first Congress session, explained that because the representatives began to disperse by the third day of the sessions there was no time to discuss publicly and pass resolutions on matters of social reform, but that Raghunatha Rao and Ranade gave addresses to the Congress on social questions.[35] However, behind the scenes consultations apparently took place during the first session, in which Congress leaders firmly decided to eliminate social reform from future annual agenda.[36]

Dadabhai Naoroji's Presidential address at the second Congress in Calcutta provided the frank reasoning behind the Congress decision to omit discussions of social reform. Naoroji asked why a purely political body should be required to take up social problems; it would be just as appropriate to do so, as for the House of Commons to discuss the abstruser problems of metaphysics, he said. The Congress President then exposed the most serious objection that he had to social reform discussions. "How," he asked, "can this gathering of all classes discuss the Social Reforms in each individual class? What do any of us know of the internal home-life, of the traditions, customs, feelings, prejudices of any class but his own? . . . Only the members of that class can effectively deal with the reform therein needed. A National Congress must confine itself to questions in which the entire nation has a direct participation, and it must leave the adjustment of Social Reforms, and other class questions, to class Congresses." He then acknowledged that all the delegates present were as deeply—"nay, in many cases far more deeply"—interested in social as in political questions, and that they were doing what they could in their particular spheres to promote social reform.[37]

Naoroji was speaking for himself as well as for several of the

---

leaders to consider social questions, e.g. Annie Besant, *How India Wrought for Freedom*, p. 7.

[35] In a letter to the *Times* (London), March 9, 1886, cited in Govt. of Bombay, *Source Material for A History of the Freedom Movement in India*, II, 22-23.

[36] See W.C. Bonnerjee's presidential address at the eighth Congress (1892), in which he described those consultations and the decision reached, namely "that it would not do for the Congress to meddle itself, as a Congress, with questions of social reform." *The Indian National Congress*, p. 116.

[37] *Indian Politics*, 2nd Part, pp. 8-9.

other Congress leaders. One of the earliest of the Parsi social reformers, Naoroji had participated in the Bombay Students'
Literary and Scientific Society, fostered female education and
worked on two reform journals, the *Stri Bodh* and the *Rast Goftar*,
both of which appeared in the 1850's. But his name is not to be
found among the sponsors of the various reform crusades later
in the century, probably because of his preoccupation with political affairs and his long sojourns in England. Naoroji understood
the immense task of uniting even English-educated men by their
adherence to all-India ideals and programs, and he judged that
a unity on political issues was all that could be expected.[38] Before
the founding of the Congress, Naoroji might have taken a different view; it might well have appeared that English-educated men
could as easily agree on social as on political aims. But in 1885
and 1886 Malabari's campaign was already splitting Hindus into
pro- and anti-social reform factions, and Naoroji and others feared
the extension of that controversy into the Congress.[39]

Many of the representatives at the Calcutta session appeared to
disagree with their President and to urge discussion of social
reform, judging from the cheers initially heard when Naoroji
broached the subject. Later Congress sessions took up the question anew, and a debate continued well into the 1890's over the
wisdom of excluding social reform from the Congress resolutions. But the Naoroji position had its merits: apart from the
overriding concern for nationalist unity, discussions of social reform would have required considerable prolongation of the sessions and perhaps sharp debates over the question of priorities for
various social and political issues. This would have exposed weak-
nesses and inconclusiveness, when the main object of the Congress
in the early years was to present a front of united opinion to the
British Government and people.[40]

[38] Naoroji explained: "It may be seen that there is scarcely any union among
the different nationalities and races [of India] in any shape or ways of life,
except only in political associations. In these associations they go hand in hand
with all the fervour and sympathy of a common cause." In Naoroji, *Essays,
Speeches . . . of Dadabhai Naoroji*, p. 468.

[39] See N.G. Chandavarkar's report to the *Indu Prakash* from the Calcutta
Congress, Govt. of Bombay, *Source Material . . . , op.cit.*, II, 34-35.

[40] In its early years the Congress did discuss and pass resolutions on two

Naoroji's stand was clearly premised not on the incompatibility of social and political advancement, but on the infeasibility of working out a national social philosophy acceptable to all those who agreed on a national political philosophy. Other Congress supporters, notably Ranade and Raghunatha Rao, rejected that premise, but not by openly challenging Naoroji. Instead, at the third Congress session, in Madras in 1887, they formed an adjunct body to the Congress for social reform discussion, the National Social Conference. It is not unlikely that the platform provided by the Conference for pronouncements on public issues, separated from the proceedings of the Congress, constituted a special boon to Ranade and Rao, because both of them were government servants and were thereby inhibited from taking openly critical stands on official policies. Ranade was a member of the Bombay Legislative Council and a judge; Rao was Deputy Collector of Madras. However, a larger consideration influenced these two men and several others who wished to create a close alliance between the political and social reform movements. Ranade, the chief organizer and sustainer of the Conference, argued the case, at the second annual session: "We are in a sense as strictly national socially, as we are politically. Though the differences are great for purposes of immediate and practical reform, yet there is a background of common traditions, common religion, common laws and institutions and customs and perversions of such customs, which make it possible to deliberate together in spite of our differences."[41] Most reformers agreed that social issues were a legitimate, nay a vital, part of the nationalist program, and that the stature of the social reform movement should not be permitted to suffer in comparison with political activities.

From the earliest years when Indians were propounding the

issues, alcohol consumption and prostitution, that would have fallen within the compass of social reform in other countries. Indian social reform, however, was defined differently (see Introduction), and resolutions on those two issues were addressed not to Indians but to the government, which was held responsible for introducing both alcoholic beverages and metropolitan prostitution into India.

[41] Ranade, *Miscellaneous Writings*, p. 89.

new ideas of nationalism, many of the social reformers had been under attack and ridicule because of their seeming distaste for certain aspects of Indian social and religious life. However, in the 1880's the revivalist-nationalist position from which such criticisms originated had few adherents among the liberal, all-India nationalists. Within the confines of that English-educated group there were few serious objections to the designation of social reform activities as truly nationalist.[42] Social reformers were thought by most nationalists to be as devoted as anyone else—perhaps more so by virtue of their year-long activities—to the creation of India's national unity and strength. For a decade after the founding of the Congress, spokesmen for the National Social Conference could unselfconsciously ignore, at least from their national platform, the few Indian leaders who expressed doubts about the social reformers' adherence to nationalist principles. A political nationalism which was based on Western political ideals could also logically embody Western social ideals. Nevertheless, despite the almost unanimous acknowledgment by nationalists in the Congress of the propriety of social reform ideals, there was little agreement on the methods and the pace of social advancement. Naoroji's reference to the special problems which social progress faced in each community and region reflected an honest scepticism about reaching any national consensus on specific issues. With this scepticism in mind, Ranade carefully began his work of organizing the Social Conference.

Just as the Congress decided to exclude social reform from its annual agenda, in order to avoid unnecessary fissions among its supporters, so also the National Social Conference carefully excluded religious reform from its purview. Conference members included representatives of several reformed religious groups

[42] Apart from Tilak, an exception to this general pattern was M.V. Mandlik, an important Bombay political nationalist, who gave up a youthful enthusiasm for social reform—including support for Karsondas Mulji's crusade and for female education—to become a severe critic of Malabari and the social reformers of western India. D.G. Padhye wrote of Mandlik in 1896 that he "was almost as orthodox in social matters as he was one of the most advanced in political matters," *Writings and Speeches of the Late Hon'ble Rao Saheb Vishvanath Narayan Mandlik,* p. 22. See also N.G. Chandavarkar's speech on "The Mandlik School," *Speeches and Writings,* p. 32f.

(Prarthana, Brahmo, and Arya Samajes), and various caste associations, and for those men the Conference could create a common front on social questions, provided their religious differences remained in the background. At the time of its founding, therefore, the Conference could not be properly regarded as an outgrowth of the earlier social reform movements, most of which developed from religious reform movements, but was understood as a component of the nationalist movement, with intellectual roots identical with those of the Congress. Although religious and social reform retained their conjunction in the Samajes and in the minds of many Indians,[43] the all-India social reform movement was based on a secular ideology, nationalism. For Ranade, whose own ideas of social reform rested on personal religion and morality, the Social Conference was an organization which had an intellectual integrity only in so far as it stood for national regeneration.[44] Belief in national progress was, for him, the proper philosophical foundation of the Conference; it was a belief that could be shared by all reformers, with or without theistic religious convictions. The importance of the nonreligious approach to social reform was made particularly clear to the founders of the Conference by the outburst of religious revivalism in the Age of Consent Bill controversy, which had social reformers as its chief target. Revivalism's growing strength was a warning to any reformer to avoid linking his social program with religion, and in any case Malabari's crusade demonstrated that the case for social reform was stronger without the support of religion.

When the Conference held its first meeting at the time of the Madras Congress session in 1887, Ranade regarded the affair as a "scaffolding"; the real foundations he hoped to lay at the Allahabad session the following year.[45] Two eminent Madrasis, Sir

[43] The divergence of the religious and the social reform movements had already been apparent in western India, where several notable reformers were not members of a religious Samaj; the Prarthana Samaj took no official stand, as a body, on social reform.

[44] In their work for national regeneration the Conference and the Congress, Ranade said, "were two sisters. . . . The cause of the Conference [is] the cause of the well-being of the people, even as the cause of the Congress [is] the cause of [the] country's progress." *Miscellaneous Writings*, pp. 113-14.

[45] *ibid.*, p. 91.

T. Madhava Rao and Dewan Bahadur R. Raghunatha Rao, gave
Ranade the local support that he needed in 1887. Madhava Rao, a
former Dewan in Travancore and Baroda, was named the first
President and Raghunatha Rao General Secretary of the Conference; the latter retained his position for many years, although
age and illness kept him from assuming an active role. Neither
man, however, attended the Allahabad session the next year.
Ranade was Vice-President (later a Joint-General Secretary) and
henceforth assumed full charge. He defined for the assembled
reformers and delegates from local groups the purposes of the
Conference. It was not to supersede the local reform bodies by
undertaking action or propaganda of its own, nor was it to specify
particular goals and methods which would be binding locally.
In view of the diversity of the local associations, centralized planning was impossible to achieve; that was the chief way in which
the Conference differed from the Congress. Instead, the Conference was intended to encourage local reformers by giving to their
work its proper national recognition and by drawing them together annually for mutual inspiration. It appeared possible that
some common principles to guide a national reform movement
could be agreed upon, along with a general consensus on the
methods to be followed. But the discussions and resolutions of
the Conference were directed at providing no more than recommendations to local reform groups, "which these latter are to take
into their consideration and give effect to, within their own sphere,
in such directions as they deem convenient or necessary."[46]

As circumstances showed, such looseness of constitution and
lack of discipline among its adherents was a *sine qua non* of the
Conference's existence. For example, Sir T. Madhava Rao opposed
the Age of Consent Bill publicly at the 1891 Conference session,
and many delegates sided with him; the Conference had already
been forced to adopt a weak position on that issue. Again, K.
Subramanyam Aiyar, a speaker at the eighth Conference, announced that he could not personally sanction widow remarriage, one of the more generally accepted reforms. He went on to
voice the stand that most Conference delegates would accept: "I

[46] Ranade's speech at the second Social Conference, *ibid.*, p. 89.

heartily sympathize with every reform that has been urged from this platform today, but I am prepared to take action only with reference to a few of them; and you may rest assured that there are a good many like me."[47]

The Conference met for several days each year, with only one exception, after the Congress sessions had concluded. In the early years of the National Social Conference, at least, several hundred persons might be expected to attend, almost all of them delegates to the Congress as well as interested local inhabitants, including students. Most observers of the proceedings were not active social reformers, and not a few were present out of curiosity and sometimes even hostility. Ranade ordinarily took charge of the local arrangements and sent out the invitations to reform associations to send delegates. The choice of president, nearly always a prominent local figure, and decisions on the agenda and even the wording of resolutions were made by Ranade and a small group of supporters. That group, although varying in composition, was made up of leading reformers from the major regions, including the Conference officials. Although of great importance in the western Indian reform movement, the Parsis of Bombay took little part in the Social Conference, regarding it, sometimes with sympathetic interest, as a loosely organized beginning of a much-needed Hindu social reorganization. Malabari, the leading Parsi reformer, was often at odds with the compromising Ranade, who in turn resented Malabari's coolness toward Congress political agitation.[48] Muslim leaders generally avoided the Conference, which they, too, considered a Hindu organization. The participation in the Conference of Budrudin Tyebji, a Bombay Muslim reformer, provided the only exception to the important conclusion of S. Natarajan that the Hindu and Muslim social reform "streams" never came together at the Conference.[49]

As the Conference gained stature as the focal point of the social reform movement throughout the country, and as lines of cleavage between it and the Congress began to develop, participation in

[47] Report of the Eighth National Social Conference, Madras, 1894, p. 37.
[48] See S. Natarajan, A Century of Social Reform in India, p. 70.
[49] ibid., p. 81.

the annual sessions declined somewhat. But the participants were more likely, than in the early years, to be true representatives of local associations, whose numbers increased steadily in the decades following the Conference's founding, despite the simultaneous growth of antireform groups. In the *Reports* of the Conference sessions, published each year in Poona, were given lists of the local social reform associations which sent annual reports, and sometimes delegates, to the Conference.

From the local associations' reports and from his own knowledge of the movements, Ranade presented to the Conference yearly summaries of the progress being made throughout the country. Admittedly meager efforts in relation to the contemporary social condition of India's nearly 200 million Hindus, the progress reports illustrated, nevertheless, the range and intensity of the new ideas about society which were spreading through the large and small urban centers. Improvement in women's position in the Hindu family and in society was the most general concern among reform associations throughout the 19th century, as the response to Malabari's "Notes" had already established. Groups from Madras to Sind urging marriage reform, some of whose members were pledged not to marry their daughters below a certain age, found that they faced similar problems, despite their regional differences. The Conference discussed and passed resolutions favoring: raising marriage ages (to 12 and 18), prohibition of imprisonment for women in conjugal rights cases, discouragement of marriages in which differences in ages between the parties exceeded thirty years, reduction in marriage expenses, remarriage of child widows, prevention of disfigurement of child widows and other improvements in the condition of widows, inter-marriage between castes which inter-dined, discouragement of the custom of paying a bride-price, discouragement of polygamy and Kulinism, and support of female education.[50]

If the resolutions passed on female advancement and marriage reform are for the moment ignored, the remaining subjects on

[50] See Chintamani, *Indian Social Reform*, Appendix, for resolutions passed by the Conference through the year, 1900.

which the Conference took stands reflected the parochialism of the local reform groups and the limited areas for possible common efforts among them. Resolutions were frequently passed whose purpose was not to identify a nationwide social problem but to lend the encouragement of the national body to a small, struggling group of reformers. Madras reformers, for example, although surrounded by more basic hindrances to progress, undertook campaigns against alcohol consumption and nautch dancing, and their work received growing support in certain north Indian provinces; several resolutions were passed by the Conference on those matters. Other reformers who deplored the "Siapa system of loud mourning and beating of the chest which prevails in Sind, the Punjab, the North-West Provinces, and Guzerath,"[51] also found Conference support, as did those (Arya Samajists) who wanted recognition of their efforts to readmit to Hindu communities persons converted to other faiths. Some reformers worked for improvement in the management of Hindu temple endowments, others for introduction of religious and moral education in conjunction with the government schools; Madras groups supported the passing of the Hindu Gains of Learning Bill in the Provincial Legislature; the evils of prostitution and the desirability of inter-dining among sub-castes were matters of concern to still others. On all those subjects the Conference provided whatever support it could.

From Bengal the Conference received very little backing, due to the absence there of any "regularly-constituted social reform associations."[52] As Dr. Bhandarkar said in his Presidential address to the 1895 Conference, in Bengal "social reform is now confined to Brahmos. The great body of educated Bengalees, who are not Brahmos, are indifferent or hostile."[53] A few Bengalis, however, among them Romesh Chunder Mitter (who opposed the Age of Consent Bill) and Surendranath Banerjea, did arouse themselves to protest against the treatment by high castes of their members who had travelled overseas; Madrasi Brahmin and northern

[51] *ibid.*, p, 372.
[52] *Report of the Seventh Social Conference, Lahore, 1893*, p. 52.
[53] Chintamani, *op.cit.*, III, 186.

Indian Kayastha reformers joined in this protest. The Conference duly passed the proper resolution.

Toward the close of the century, which also marked the end of Ranade's leadership of the Conference, there were evidences that social reform leaders, increasingly concerned with the problem of general (as opposed to local and individual) progress, were willing to confront India's most fundamental and perplexing social phenomenon, caste. The inferior condition of women was an equally basic problem, and reformers had long been actively aware of it, but programs for female progress continued to be restricted to women of the upper castes. Non-remarriage of widows, child marriage, ill-assorted marriages, heavy bride prices, and polygamy were all customs associated chiefly with high-caste groups. Recognition of the caste system as probably the greatest obstacle to progress appeared in early social reform writings, but no public bodies had ventured to take a stand against the organization of Hindu society on caste lines. The Social Conference in 1895 made the first move directing national attention to the baneful effects of caste by passing a resolution (Number 10) favoring the uplift of pariahs and untouchables, and succeeding Conferences reaffirmed the motion.

It was probably not by chance that the first resolution on caste was passed when the Conference met in Poona, and R.G. Bhandarkar presided since he more fervently condemned the caste system than other Conference leaders. In his Presidential address he despaired of seeing India a united nation so long as caste distinctions prevailed; the rigid system of castes, he said, which has "corroded the vitals of this country," will ever act as a heavy drag on our race towards a brighter future."[54] The more cautious Ranade was critical of Bhandarkar's vehemence in condemning the basic structure of Hindu society as well as his candid observations on the shortcomings of the reformers; Ranade considered

[54] *ibid.*, III, 181-82, 187. Of further interest is Bhandarkar's prophetic vision of an India in the future where caste and regional sentiments would wrench the nation into hostile and warring factions. "Caste feeling," he observed, after the beginning of some caste conferences, "is of the same kind as national feeling, but its mischievousness consists in its being confined to a small community . . . ." From an article published in 1915, in *Collected Works of Sir R. G. Bhandarkar*, II, 484-85.

his Poona colleague an unwarranted pessimist.[55] Ranade was probably representing the sentiments, or fears, of the majority of the Conference by not taking a strong stand against the caste organization of society.[56] By 1900 the most that the Conference could agree upon regarding caste was to deplore the treatment given to low castes with no definite suggestions for advancing their interests.

Most Social Conference adherents tended to ignore or resent the candor and pessimism of Bhandarkar and instead adopted the reform doctrine of Kashinath Trimbak Telang, which was designated, "progress along the lines of least resistance." It became a Conference byword.[57] For most reformers, including Ranade, the "line of least resistance" doctrine defined the directions in which social change should proceed as well as its methods and pace, although Telang had no such clear purpose in mind when he first enunciated it.[58] The doctrine had the advantage of allowing a reformer himself to "flow with the tide" of social change while at the same time urging his countrymen to welcome and hasten the adoption of reforms, so as to make the tide more compelling. After succeeding to Telang's seat on the Bombay High Court upon the latter's death in 1893, Ranade identified himself with the "Telang School" on social reform matters, although he could not accept Telang's ultra-conservatism on polit-

[55] See Bhandarkar's letter to the *Bombay Gazette* (April 1894) in reply to Ranade's criticisms, *ibid.*, I, 453. Also Ranade's *Miscellaneous Writings*, pp. 297-315.

[56] On the other hand, Ranade never upheld the caste system as worthy of preservation. Indeed, he seemed to agree with Bhandarkar on one occasion, when he said, "this caste difficulty is the main blot on our social system. The great fight has to be maintained here. . . ." *Miscellaneous Writings*, p. 236. Unlike Bhandarkar, Ranade avoided the fight on the merits of the caste system as a whole, stressing only the need to break down inter-caste distinctions and to raise up the lower castes.

[57] It had one attraction, among others, of being a phrase taken from the writings of Herbert Spencer.

[58] In a famous address to the (Bombay) Students' Literary and Scientific Society in February 1886, made chiefly in answer to Sir Auckland Colvin's response to Malabari's "Notes" (see Chapter VII). The address argued, in the context of Colvin's criticism, that political reform should take priority over social, on the principle, "secure first the reforms which you can secure with the least difficulty." In different contexts Telang argued for the importance of simultaneous social and political reform. See his *Selected Writings and Speeches*, I, 259f.

ical questions.[59] Toward the end of his life Ranade went so far as to state that the "only" difference between anti-reformers and reformers was that the latter were accomplishing consciously what the former were yielding to unconsciously. In either case, reform was "inevitable."[60]

The sociologically inspired idea that profound changes in Indian society were under way in the late 19th century was perhaps the belief most generally shared by all social reformers. The Ranade-Telang "school" of reform appeared sometimes not in the role of fomenting dissatisfaction with existing conditions but of trying to direct the course of "inevitable" change into constructive channels, which would not undermine the foundations of Hindu society. The "least resistance" doctrine acknowledged the merits to be derived from the transforming impact on Indian life of the British. But it suggested, too, that changes must be gradual, so as not to substitute "anarchy for a regime which, however ill-suited may be its principles to our present requirements, still possesses the advantages of an organized system."[61] Furthermore, by encouraging changes which were relatively easy to effect, the orthodox leaders would not be so quickly provoked into open hostility. A Madras judge, Sir V. Bhashyam Iyengar stated the case in this advice to reformers: "Do not despise small reforms for which Society may be prepared, simply because they do not satisfy your ambition. On the other hand, reforms which are small in themselves, but are regarded as revolutionary by the people, are not worth your attempt."[62] Such an approach to reform, which constituted the minimum level of agreement that could be achieved, was in accord with the "least resistance" doc-

[59] See Ranade's address, "The Telang School of Thought," delivered at the Hindu Union Club, Bombay, in 1895, in *Religious and Social Reform*, p. 135f.
[60] Bombay Social Conference speech in 1900; *Miscellaneous Writings*, pp. 234-35. Ranade was more specific: "People will visit England whether their elders like it or not. . . . The education of women will similarly be encouraged as each year rolls on. The limits of age for marriage will be raised. Intermarriage restrictions will be dissolved. Caste exclusiveness must relax. . . . As prudent men, the question for us will be, shall we float with this current or resist it?"
[61] Dewan Narendra Nath's Presidential address to the Social Conference, 1893. Chintamani, *op.cit.*, III, 154.
[62] Subba Row Pantulu, *Hindu Social Progress*, Appendix, p. 15.

trine and explained the absence of much directive force in the Conference resolutions.

By the end of the century certain voices associated with the Conference were being raised in protest against the Ranade-Telang "school" because of its toleration of public inaction and private backsliding. Narayan G. Chandavarkar (1855-1923) challenged the "line of least resistance" principle which, "once made the keynote of social reform, was bound to wreck the cause and prove a plea for indolence and inaction."[63] And the *Indian Social Reformer*, the Madras journal for which Chandavarkar was the Bombay correspondent, maintained a steady line of criticism directed at Ranade. Within the Conference an alignment of interests and policies existed between Bombay and Madras reformers, who wished neither to break with society and form separate Samajes nor to rely on caste organizations as vehicles for reform. Western and southern Indian social reform leaders, virtually all of them Brahmins,[64] were united by common adherence to ethical-humanitarian and nationalist-utilitarian prescriptions for reform, sometimes overlaid by scholarly appeals for shastric reinterpretations. Nevertheless, when it came to questions of how rapidly reforms should proceed and with what consideration for sincere traditionalism, several Madras reformers toward the end of the century were pressing the more radical answer.

[63] Chandavarkar, *Speeches and Writings*, p. 30.

[64] No complete caste breakdown of participants in all the Social Conferences or in all local reform associations is available. From the many references in the literature, however, I venture to estimate that 80 per cent of the Hindu social reformers of Bengal, Bombay, and Madras in the 19th century were Brahmins. In the North-Western Provinces, Punjab, Sind, and Gujarat the percentage was much lower, because of the dominance of caste reform associations in several of these regions. The following information is provided in the *Reports*, respectively, of the fourth Social Conference and ninth Social Conference: The Poona Social Reform Association in 1890 had collected reform pledges from almost 1,500 persons, in the following proportions, by castes: 1,121 Brahmins; 110 Prahbus, Kayasthas and Kshatriyas; 22 Vaishyas; 54 Marathas; 11 Brahmos; 5 Aryas; 10 Sikhs; 12 Jains; 84 "Hindus"; 63 gave no caste. The Association collected some pledges outside of Maharashtra. Of those also listing their occupation, the largest number was of students. In 1895 the delegates attending the Social Conference numbered 797, of whom only 303 did *not* give their caste as Brahmin; of these latter a fair number listed themselves as "Theist," "Hindu," or "Vedic" and may have been Brahmin by family connection.

The rise of Madrasi influence in the national social reform movement in the 1890's was more the result of its English-language press than it was due to impressive leadership or to exemplary social reform associations in the southern Presidency. *The Hindu*, founded by G. Subramania Iyer in 1878, the *Madras Mail*, and the *Indian Social Reformer* provided reformers with major public support in south India. The *Social Reformer*, established in 1890, exhibited initial indecision on the proper basis for reform— whether it should be reliance on shastric reinterpretations or on reason and humanism. When the issue was settled, the shastric approach to reform was given up,[65] and that weekly journal assumed a position of loyal critic and sensitive conscience of the social reform movement at the national level. The *Social Reformer*'s self-appointed undertaking was to demand more radical and rationally motivated breaks with tradition than the Social Conference under Ranade was prepared to endorse, to debate with and ridicule all those who unquestioningly supported orthodoxy, and to draw public attention to failings of the reformers and the ineffectualities of their associations.

Its criticisms of the Ranade-Telang school and the Social Conference reflected the views of Chandavarkar, who was to assume the leadership of the Conference after Ranade's death in 1901. Ranade was well aware of the undercurrent of dissatisfaction with his leadership and at one time wrote, "I wish the *Reformer* did not bear witness against its best friends. . . ."[66] As radical reformers Chandavarkar and his supporters recommended not the replacement of the Social Conference, but its immediate growth into a permanently organized force, with funds and labor at its disposal. They urged that Raghunatha Rau, who had demonstrated his timidity by failing to attend a symbolic widow remarriage dinner, resign as General Secretary in favor of Dr. Bhandarkar.[67] If the reformers wanted effective propaganda, the *Reformer* advised, they would create full-time propagandists: "Every movement has its preachers and missionaries, but the social re-

[65] S. Natarajan, *op.cit.*, p. 86.
[66] At the time of the Poona controversy in 1895 (see Chapter IX). *ibid.*, p. 87.
[67] Natarajan, *op.cit.*, p. 89.

form movement in India has none . . . persons who are otherwise busy in the exercise of their various professions devote a portion of their time to deliver lectures now and then. . . ."[68] Furthermore, reformers were "ready enough . . . to lecture to English-knowing school boys on social reform. But how many of us are ready to stand up before an orthodox audience and lecture to it in a vernacular?"[69] The *Reformer* recognized that local bodies, such as the Arya Samaj and various caste organizations, were active instruments for reform. But it saw the further need of a national reform organization, at least as well equipped as the Congress.[70] When Chandavarkar assumed charge of the Conference a permanent national social reform organization was seriously proposed, but it was never founded.

In a spirit of loyal opposition the *Reformer* and Chandavarkar proffered more than criticism of Ranade and the Conference. In the revolutionary style of the early Brahmo reformers of Bengal, they demanded courageous self-sacrifice and nonconformity, individual reform as a precondition for general social reform, and an end to talk of "moving society along with the reformer," and of piece-meal change which would preserve the integrity of the "social organism." In his famous speech to the Mangalore Social Reform Association in 1900[71] Chandavarkar appealed for men and women who were unafraid to act from a free conscience and to stand against any form of social persecution. If reformers waited until society relaxed its opposition to change—the "least resistance" doctrine—then the task in India would be hopeless.

[68] Editorial, June 3, 1900.　　[69] *ISR*, June 17, 1900, p. 333.

[70] The *Reformer* provided the following description of a provincial social conference held at Coimbatore in May, 1899; the meeting with which it was contrasted was a provincial Congress session held the day before: "The Social Conference meets without any flourish of trumpets, as though it is half ashamed of itself. Most seats are empty, the platform looks so deserted, there are no committee men rushing to and fro, no volunteers about, no punkahs overhead, no gong on the President's table. Yesterday and the day before, everything was merry and gay, like a marriage ball; today it is all so dull and solemn and we seem to imagine we are attending a funeral. When people enter, there is no ovation, either deserved or desired. There are sensible speeches, but the men for whom they are intended have hardly recovered from the effects of the previous meeting's entertainments." *ISR*, May 28, 1899, p. 305.

[71] Chandavarkar, *Speeches and Writings*, pp. 77-91.

Social change, he admitted, involved pain for the individuals who showed the way to advancement in their own lives, and that pain must be expected and accepted as part of the assertion of the individual's conscience over the evils of society. "All progress"—he quoted the historian, Ranke—"is through conflict, and we must be prepared to suffer." Attacking Spencer with Carlyle, Chandavarkar called for men inspired by heroism who would denounce the shibboleth of "organic" social growth and stand forth as individual examples of moral growth. Certain individuals could mold society, he argued; it was not always the other way around. Reformers, complacent with their faith in inevitable progress, did not deserve the name unless they acted as they so willingly said they believed.

The *Reformer* adopted Chandavarkar's philosophy of change. K. Natarajan, its editor, always reacted vigorously against signs of weakness in the reformers' camp. "It is not along the line of least resistance," he asserted, "but rather along that of most resistance that mankind has progressed from savagery to civilization. Every secret wrung from Nature, every step in man's moral advancement, has been at the cost of persistence against difficulty and opposition."[72] For Chandavarkar and the radicals of the *Reformer* staff, Telang of course was "too soft for the fight—and succumbed."[73] Ranade, too, was "too gentle" for the struggle which those men saw in progress between opposing moral forces then at work in India. Comparing Ranade with Indian "heroes," such as Rammohun Roy, Dayananda, Vidyasagar, and Karsondas Mulji, Chandavarkar concluded that "Ranade's greatness was not of their height. He had not that strenuousness of convictions, that moral indignation, that active spirit of combat, which is so necessary to accomplish anything great."[74]

The breach between Ranade's and Chandavarkar's philosophies of life and their prescriptions for social reform signified more than a divergence in personalities. It marked the transition from the 19th century spirit of moderation and accommodation to the 20th century spirit of urgency and assertiveness in the Indian

[72] Natarajan's Introduction to *ibid.*, p. 2.   [73] *ibid.*, p. 29.
[74] Speech at Wilson College, quoted in the *ISR*, October 1, 1905, pp. 52-53.

nationalist movement, which could be observed in all areas of public life. The abrupt transfer of the leadership of the National Social Conference from Ranade to Chandavarkar, on the former's death in January 1901, symbolized the beginning of a new stage in the social reform movement. Ranade had prepared the way for the reformers' adjustments to a fundamental aspect of the new spirit, the increased veneration it insisted upon for ancient ideals, because Ranade had never urged a total rebellion against tradition. But there was little compatibility between Ranade's cautious personality, his adherence to moderate and gradual change and the vigorous determination of 20th century reformers to stake their personal position and the authority of their ideas on a rapid push toward a new society. Furthermore, Ranade's moderate political views found little favor in the generation succeeding him, and the National Congress, on which he had depended for future political advance, was in the process of momentous change by the time of his death. While Ranade had considered the National Social Conference as a child of the Congress, many later reformers ignored the ineffectual Congress and tried to establish a social reform movement without connections with a political organization whose future seemed uncertain.

Ranade's service to the social reform movement was in establishing its character as a national movement. But the Conference was scarcely an organized body; it had no permanent staff, no office, and no publications, other than the yearly report of Conference proceedings. It was, simply, a conference, whose influence in public life was largely a reflection of its leader's influence. People acted with Ranade and supported the Conference because of personal devotion to their chosen leader. Impressed with Ranade's spirit or soul—often referred to in such terms—men considered him as an ideal type who must be venerated. In deeds he was not steadfast, not heroic; he vacillated and urged others to be cautious. But despite this—or perhaps because of this—he provided a leadership, based chiefly on his personality, which all could recognize and many could revere. The organized national social reform movement was as strong as was Ranade, and several dozen lesser leaders; without them, the movement did not exist.

$$I X$$

SOCIAL VERSUS POLITICAL REFORM

ONE OF THE most urgent questions that the nationalist movement faced may be stated concisely: Should social reform precede political reform, or vice versa.[1] Among nationalists in the Congress and the Social Conference this question was secondary in importance only to the question of what were the proper methods for advancing political or social objectives. After the 1880's this issue of the proper priorities for social or political reform was an unavoidable subject of dispute; few leaders in fact failed to take a public stand on it, at least at some point in their careers. The moderate founders of the Indian National Congress resolved the issue, in effect, by assigning political reform to the national arena for public discussion and recommendation, and social reform to the local arena for private action. Both political and social reform, however, in their separate spheres, were understood to be components of nationalism, and to assure the social reform movement of the national recognition it deserved, Ranade was allowed to attach the National Social Conference to the Congress, in a subordinate relationship. For most Congress leaders, then and later, political reform attained a more important position in their thoughts and activities than did social reform, and when-

[1] In contemporary India the question persists in the new formulation of whether direct attempts to generate social reform should take precedence over other aspects of national development or whether society should be left to reform itself, as a byproduct of mass education and of progress and change in economic, political, and cultural spheres. See, e.g., K.M. Panikkar, *Hindu Society at the Crossroads*; Government of India Planning Commission, *Social Legislation; Its Role in Social Welfare; Democracy and Caste, a Topic to Think Over.*

ever a conflict arose between the two undertakings political interests became paramount. A small number of Congress participants, nevertheless, could always be found, in the decades preceding 1920, who gave social reform preference over political reform whenever an open conflict appeared.

An open conflict did, indeed, appear in 1895 at the Poona session of the Congress. There the convenient solution of the social versus political reform question by the Congress leadership was challenged by Tilak, whose personal fight with the social reformers had not ended with the passage of the Age of Consent Bill. Tilak attacked the compromise solution which permitted the Social Conference to operate in the Congress precincts and thus challenged the premise that social reform was a necessary or a proper part of nationalism. His argument could be reduced to his enunciation of an ideology of nationalism which differed from that of the majority in the Congress by its repudiation of Western ideas and its insistence on an uncritical manipulation of traditional Hindu values. His position was strengthened by the revivalist movements of the day, all of which, however, did not fully support his hostility to the social reformers.

The views of the government and of certain of the British spokesmen in India influenced the thinking of the nationalists on the relationship of social to political reform. An impression was created that the British favored the involvement of nationalists in social reform endeavors because, thereby, Indians might vent their dissatisfaction against social, rather than political, abuses. Antireformers were thus able to allege that social reformers had made themselves willing or unwilling abettors of British purposes. That political critique of the reform movement was a variation on the established theme that the objective of the social reformers was to alienate Hindus from their own national heritage with the help of foreign rulers. The Consent Bill and the possibility of future social legislation were revealed to some nationalists as conspiracies between the government and its agents—the reformers—to uproot Indian culture and replace it by Western culture.

Tilak and the National Social Conference

Tilak's insistence in 1891 that the Age of Consent Bill had blackened the honor of Hindu society did not move him into an unavailing crusade against the government to force repeal of the Act, as he indicated at one time that it would. Instead, Tilak's skill in organizing support and his convincing writing and rhetoric against the social reform movement were henceforth aimed chiefly at the social reform leaders found in the Social Conference.

The ostensible motive behind Tilak's hostility to the social reform movement was his overriding desire to advance the nationalist cause by recruiting mass support to its banner. The Indian—largely Hindu—public to which Tilak sought to address his appeals could not be enlisted, he believed, in a nationalist movement which embodied, or even tolerated, ideas of the degradation of Hindu religious and social life and of the superiority of alien institutions. At the time of his 1895 collision with the Social Conference leaders, Tilak revealed his thinking in a letter to the *Times of India*, which said in part: "One party [his own] wishes to draw to the Congress as large a portion of the public as it possibly can, irrespective of the question of Social Reform; the other does not wish to go much beyond the circle of friends of reform. The real point at issue is whether the Congress in Poona is to be a Congress of the people or of a particular section of it."[2] He thus shared the view held by Naoroji and other Congress leaders, that, in the words of Aurobindo Ghose, "the political movement could not afford to cut itself off from the great mass of the nation or split itself up into warring factions by a premature association of the social reform question with politics. . . ."[3]

But Tilak went much further than the Congress leadership by insisting not only that the Congress should ignore social reform in its official proceedings, but that, in the name of the nationalist movement, it should adopt open hostility to social reform. More

[2] Ram Gopal, *Lokamanya Tilak*, p. 112.
[3] Ghose's "Appreciation," in *Tilak: His Writings and Speeches*, pp. 14-15.

vigorously than any nationalist leader of his day Tilak argued the case for a total exclusion of social reform ideas from nationalism, on the grounds that political freedom must come before any real progress in nonpolitical spheres of life was possible.

Satisfactory reasons for Tilak's aggressive antipathy toward the social reform movement can scarcely be given by citing his farsighted and strong devotion to political nationalist ideals, although most of his biographers state his case in that way.[4] In one recent biography, the author expresses what may be a perplexity felt, but not often stated, by many admirers of Tilak. D.V. Tahmankar observes that Tilak was "at heart no less ardent a reformer than Ranade," but for some reason never came out openly in support of the reform movement. Perhaps, he suggests, this was partly due "to the narrow religious influences which prevailed in and around Poona."[5] A far more reasonable explanation is that Tilak's personal relations with the leading Poona reformers, in particular Agarkar, converted a politician's natural concern for the appeal of his platform into outspoken ridicule of the entire social reform movement.

Tilak, his LL.B. examination completed, entered public life in 1880 by assisting Vishnu Krishna Chiplunkar found the New English School in Poona; G.G. Agarkar and M.B. Namjoshi were also supporters of the unique venture in providing English education under solely Indian auspices. Chiplunkar, Tilak's senior and probably the single most important personal influence on his thinking, was a brilliant Marathi writer of political criticism who viewed the deterioration of Indian life as a direct result of foreign rule and sarcastically repudiated the social reform doctrines of the older Gopal Hari Deshmukh. The same small group of Poona intellectuals started the *Kesari* and *Mahratta* in 1881; the next year, two of the editors, Tilak and Agarkar, were jailed for four months on charges of defamation. In 1884, with expanded support which included Ranade's and Bhandarkar's, the New English School was augmented by the founding of the Deccan Education

[4] e.g., D.P. Karmarkar, N.C. Kelkar, Ram Gopal, Theodore Shay. Kelkar's study is of particular value because it deals at length with the social reform movement.

[5] Tahmankar, *Lokamanya Tilak*, pp. 320-22.

Society, which was responsible for establishing Fergusson College. By that time Chiplunkar had died (1882), and Gopal Krishna Gokhale had joined the group of young educators and publicists. During the ten years of Tilak's involvement in the Deccan Education Society he could easily have qualified as a social reformer by any standards then established. It is true that after Malabari's "Notes" were published in 1884, conflicting views on social reform began to appear in *Kesari*—Tilak and Agarkar apparently taking opposite editorial positions—[6] but many reformers were no less critical than Tilak of some of Malabari's ideas. In 1890 Tilak signed a social reform pledge, along with Ranade and thirteen other liberal-minded men. In the form of a "circular letter" it advocated reforms in marriage expenditures, the prohibition of polygamy, the use of liquor only for medicinal purposes, the promotion of female education, and a rise in the ages of marriage for girls and boys.[7] It is said that, despite his subsequent ridicule of such pledges, he permitted his daughters an English-language education, and he did not have them married until they were sixteen years old.[8]

By 1887 certain differences between Tilak and Agarkar had come to the surface in the Deccan Education Society and in the editorship of the two journals. In that year Agarkar left *Kesari* and *Mahratta* and Tilak became their sole proprietor; in 1888, Agarkar and Gokhale established *Sudharak* (*Reformer*), thus lending weight to the view that the major conflict between him and Tilak was over social reform. But, according to N.C. Kelkar, Tilak's most impressive biographer, the social reform issue was not the "real *casus belli*," and "the differences were far deeper."[9] Kelkar did not specify what they were, but appended to his biography is the full thirty-two-page text of Tilak's resignation from the Deccan Education Society in 1890, which reveals the deep bitterness that had grown up between the Tilak-Namjoshi

[6] D.P. Karmarkar, *Bal Gangadhar Tilak*, p. 39.

[7] Govt. of Bombay, *Source Material for a History of the Freedom Movement in India*, II, 201.

[8] Tahmankar, *op.cit.*, p. 49. But in Tilak's view woman's functions were to "look after the house." Wolpert, "Tilak and Gokhale," p. 50.

[9] Kelkar, *Life and Times of Lokamanya Tilak*, p. 157.

and the Agarkar-Gokhale factions. Tilak scarcely mentioned the question of social reform in his resignation, alluding to it once as Agarkar's "hobby,"[10] but he poured out in disillusioned anger his various major resentments, financial and administrative in nature, against his colleagues. By that time, the newspaper debates between Tilak's *Kesari* and Agarkar's *Sudharak* were reaching dramatic heights and, in the view of one witness, were "likely to remain enshrined in Marathi literature."[11]

Thus, the bitterness of Tilak's attack on the reformers during the Age of Consent Bill controversy, which reached its climax only a year after his resignation from the Deccan Education Society and his subsequent leadership of the antireform faction in the nationalist movement, must be explained by substantial reference to the personal effects upon him of his break with his colleagues, with whom he had worked closely in his youth. But the historical importance of Tilak's antisocial reform stand rests not in the explanation for it but in the fact that it provided a clear and logical assertion of the thesis that nationalism and social reform were incompatible, and that the movements supporting them were at essential cross-purposes. Vigorously propounded by a Western-educated man who himself adopted certain reformed practices, that thesis stimulated critical and constructive thought which ultimately benefited the nationalist cause.

The 1895 sessions of the Congress and the Social Conference at Poona provided an opportunity for Tilak to wage a direct fight against the social reformers' claims to participation in the nationalist movement. During the preceding decade continuing assurances had been offered by the liberal Congress leaders to those hostile or indifferent to social reform that the Congress would take no interest in social matters. In their Presidential addresses Budrudin Tyebji at the 1887 Madras Congress and W.C. Bonnerjee at the 1892 Allahabad session had officially reinforced Dadabhai Naoroji's earlier statement on social reform,[12] and Ranade

[10] *ibid.*, p. 540.
[11] *ibid.*, p. 159. Kelkar wrote unsympathetically about Agarkar, "he was nothing if not a root-and-branch social reformer ... he with his pen levelled to the ground all respect for traditions, all love of Indian culture, all pride in Hinduism, all regard for public sentiments ... ," *ibid.*, p. 158.
[12] *The Indian National Congress*, pp. 32, 118.

had acquiesced for the reformers without a struggle and accepted the judgment of his politically minded colleagues. But those assurances meant little to Tilak, since they issued from a moderate Congress leadership which was known to favor social reform and the continued loose association of the Social Conference with the Congress. By 1895, two years after he began his organizing of Ganapati[13] festivals to strengthen the solidarity of Hindus and their devotion to their cultural and religious heritage, Tilak was prepared to issue a direct challenge to the National Social Conference. The Congress was to meet in Poona, where both Tilak and Ranade could count on a substantial local following, and the issue presented was: Should the Social Conference be allowed to use the meeting facilities of the National Congress for the scheduled annual sessions of the Social Conference?

Tilak was on the local reception committee and used his position to urge the committee and Congress leaders from other provinces to prohibit the Social Conference from using the Congress pavilion, or pandal. *Kesari* and *Mahratta* publicized his views on the Social Conference, and unruly public meetings were held in Poona to debate the issue.[14] Ranade tried to meet Tilak's challenge fairly. In a letter to K. Subba Rao of October 16, 1895, he noted the struggle already in progress between antireformers and reformers and called it "a genuine struggle between earnest men and, though we may be out-numbered now, I have faith . . . that we must win in the end."[15] He requested Rao, then an editor of the *Social Reformer*, to ask Subramania Iyer of the Madras *Hindu* to send a reporter to Poona to cover the important affair. The reception committee, dominated by moderate Congressmen, resolved to be bound in its decision on the use of the Congress pavilion by the views of the majority of local Congress committees. Messages were then frantically sent forth by both sides to the local bodies to elicit their opinions. The response was poor; not all local committees answered the messages. But of forty-two

[13] Or Ganesh, the Hindu Elephant God, whose worship Tilak raised to the level of great Hindu festivals, some of which lasted ten days.

[14] Kelkar, *op.cit.*, p. 300. See also the excellent account of the Poona conflict in S.A. Wolpert, *Tilak and Gokhale*, p. 71f.

[15] Rao, *Revived Memories*, p. 249.

which replied within the three-week time limit, twenty-eight favored use of the pavilion by the Conference and fourteen were opposed.

Nevertheless, Ranade could not consider that a clear-cut victory had been achieved. He wrote to Rao: "The majority is thus decidedly for the Conference. But, as many of those who sent a favourable reply [including Bengal and Madras] advised me to see that the Congress did not suffer, and as many others [including Bombay] were quite indifferent either way, I did not think it proper to prolong the controversy; more especially, as many who voted against said that they did so reluctantly, and only asked me to make a concession this year." As it turned out, the reception committee agreed to permit the Social Conference the use of the pavilion, thus forcing Tilak's resignation, but Ranade "thought it my duty to take responsibility on myself and relieve them from a position in which they could neither say yes or no without provoking controversy. If I am sorry for anybody in this connection, it is for those friends who, after having encouraged me with hopes, held back and counselled peace at any price. It is a general weakness of the Nation," he told Rao; "nobody is particularly at fault."[16]

Ranade's decision to succumb to the antisocial reform faction led by Tilak, was the result not only of pressures from within the Congress to avoid a critical split on an issue that had supposedly been settled at earlier sessions, but perhaps also of threats coming from outside. In Poona there was a real possibility of riots, which had broken out before on issues of reform, and a threat was abroad to burn down the Congress pavilion if it was used for the Social Conference. At that time a certain group of young Poona Brahmins was building up through fanatic courage and reckless adventures an atmosphere which was to lead to rioting and several murders in Maharashtra in the ensuing decade. In the extraordinary autobiography of Damodar Hari Chapekar,[17] a young Chitpavan Brahmin who was responsible for murdering

[16] Letter of Dec. 1, 1895, *ibid.*, pp. 250-51.

[17] Translated and included in Govt. of Bombay, *Source Material for a History of the Freedom Movement*, p. 955f; the full text is taken from Bombay Police Abstracts of 1910, pp. 50-107.

a British plague inspector named Rand in June of 1897, are several pages devoted to the secret plans to strike against the social reformers in 1895. The intensity of the resentment toward all reformers manifested in that document has no equal in the published records of the period.

Chapekar had formed a club of militant Poona youths whose aim it was to train men in physical fitness and the use of arms for the ultimate purpose of undermining British rule. Indoctrinating themselves in hatred for officials, missionaries, and social reformers was as much a part of the club's activities as were its military drills. Chapekar noted the proficiency that his group developed in heckling and physically attacking its "implacable enemies," the reformers: "We know the names of all of them, but I need not pollute this memoir by mentioning them in this place."[18] He described an abortive attack on a wedding procession which he instigated because the bride was over 16 years old. In 1895 the Poona Social Conference incited his greatest wrath, and he laid plans to set fire to the Conference pavilion, even after Ranade agreed not to use the Congress facilities. The plot failed since construction work on the new Conference pavilion was constantly in progress.[19] The hatred of reformers felt by Chapekar and his associates was only slightly greater than their distaste for all English-educated Indians, and even Tilak was regarded with suspicion; Vishnu Krishna Chiplunkar came closest to being their mentor. The Ganapati festival, organized by Tilak, suited their uncritical patriotism, but Tilak was "neither a thorough reformer nor is he thoroughly orthodox."[20] However, Chapekar wrote, we "consider him to be a far better man than a reformer. Latterly, he had adapted his manners to the opinions of his community and this had considerably checked his irregular conduct. We hoped that after some time he would be much improved."[21] Tilak's membership in the Congress proved his limited capacity for real

[18] *ibid.*, p. 974.
[19] *ibid.*, p. 981.
[20] *ibid.*, p. 994. Chapekar alleged that Tilak was a member of a widow remarriage association, a fact which I am unable to substantiate, and that he took meals with a nonvegetarian Hindu, Daji Abaji Khare.
[21] *ibid.*, p. 995.

patriotism, as far as Chapekar's group was concerned. The Congress leaders resembled Manmohan Ghose who "though a Hindu by religion . . . dresses like a European from top to toe, and shaves his moustache like a eunuch"; he was a "national hero," Chapekar wrote, because, between warm-water showers and elegant meals, he made arrangements for the Congress and allowed himself to be pampered by the local "patriots."[22]

There is no mention in the published writings of the reformers of Chapekar's undercover movement, which Tilak on later occasions repudiated. But its activities were known to the public through handbills and letters to editors, and they may have influenced Ranade's decision not to press more vigorously for the use of the Congress pavilion.

At the 1895 Poona session Ranade's reputation and stature were embellished, not blemished, by his backing down on the Conference site issue. Surendranath Banerjea, the Congress President, applauded Ranade's "noble sacrifice" made "to restore amity and concord." It "averted a crisis which might have proved disastrous to the best interests of the Congress."[23] In an official letter written earlier to Ranade, Banerjea observed that the demand of the antireformers was "very unreasonable; but we have sometimes to submit to unreasonable demands to avert greater evils."[24] Banerjea was a friend of the social reform movement,[25] but his preeminently political ambitions for the English-educated

[22] In a telling satire on the Congress Chapekar also wrote: "These educated classes have got up a toy regiment, as it were, and have become absorbed in witnessing its unarmed drill. But as it is uninteresting to see girls playing with lifeless dolls, so the feeble display of a regiment without the soul-stirring equipment of arms excites no enthusiasm." *ibid.*, p. 982.

[23] *The Indian National Congresses*, pp. 215-16.

[24] Quoted by Ranade in his speech to the Social Conference. *Miscellaneous Writings*, pp. 152-53.

[25] Banerjea's published writings record nothing but his respect for social reformers and their ideas. See *Speeches and Writings of Babu Surendranath Banerjea*, and his *A Nation in Making*. In the latter book, a primary source for study of the nationalist movement, he extolled the reforming message of Chaitanya and held that Vidyasagar, because of his Widow Remarriage Bill, will "occupy, next to Raja Ram Mohun Roy, the proudest place in our history," p. 8. He lamented that no one carried on Vidyasagar's work in Bengal, but he himself helped on several occasions to find bridegrooms for Hindu widows, pp. 100-01.

214

class kept him out of active social reform associations. As a Bengali he claimed immunity from the Poona controversy and summoned his famous oratory to reinstate the truce between reformers and their opponents. The unwritten customary law of the Congress, he said, proclaimed that "no matter what differences of opinion may exist among us as regards religious beliefs or social usages, they shall be no bar to our acting together in Congress—they shall not be permitted to interrupt the cordiality of our relations as Congressmen."[26] Banerjea's personal loyalty and respect for Ranade and his support of the Social Conference became clear to everyone when the famous nationalist leader appeared on the rostrum of the Conference and delivered a resounding speech on reform. Citing his Brahmin heritage, which he claimed he adhered to with pride, he nevertheless urged that Hindu society must be founded on a new basis to meet the challenge of Western civilization, whose impact on India was "destructive" and "militant." He also said, "It is not with physical forces that we are now called upon to contend, it is a moral force—impalpable, invisible—which escapes the open eyes."[27]

Ranade's address to the Conference sought answers to the question of why the issue of the association of Congress and Conference should have arisen with such force in Poona. He minimized the importance of personal differences, which he said could not fully account "for what we have seen—the loss of temper, the absolute waste of energy . . . ." Instead, he expounded at length on the differences "which mark this part of the country from others."[28] He surveyed the methods of social reform adopted in other major provinces, for example, rebellion and formation of a new "camp" in Bengal and caste reform associations in the North-Western Provinces, and pointed to the fact that Bombay was unique because of its reliance on all methods. The broad-scale attack against traditional customs made by the Bombay reformers, who at the same time refused to consider themselves separate from Hindu society, was more likely to arouse conserva-

[26] *The Indian National Congress*, p. 217.
[27] *Report of Ninth National Social Conference, Poona, 1895*, p. 17.
[28] *Miscellaneous Writings*, pp. 153, 155.

tive opposition, he suggested, than the more restricted thrusts of reformers elsewhere. "If we were distinctly prepared," he explained, "to stand in a camp of our own, leaving the whole community to do what they like, we might be at peace; for this is exactly what our friends—the reactionist and the orthodox community—are desiring us to do."[29] Ranade believed, and with good cause, that western Indian reformers were posing a greater threat to orthodoxy than were their colleagues elsewhere, and hence the hostility they faced—the "cross we must bear," as he sometimes put it—was understandable.

From the Poona episode in 1895, the Social Conference emerged the victor by compromising temporarily for the sake of nationalist unity but ably defending its right to continued recognition by the Congress. In the years following, the Conference was permitted to return to the Congress pavilion, and there is no evidence that the older moderate politicians, so long as their control of Congress remained intact, wavered in their acknowledged support of the social reform movement. C. Sankaran Nair, a Madras reformer, was President of the Congress session at Amraoti in 1897 and there affirmed that "Great as is the necessity of British Rule for the political emancipation of our country, even greater is the necessity for social and religious reform."[30] In 1900 N.G. Chandavarkar, then preparing to assume Ranade's leadership of the Social Conference, presided over the Congress session at Lahore.

The Controversy Grows

The underlying issue of the proper relationship of social reform to political reform and nationalism, however, was not as easily resolved as was the practical question of the Conference's connection with the Congress.

Since the founding of the Conference many social reformers had observed with misgivings Ranade's notable success in linking the social reform movement to the Congress, which they sensed was led by men interested in their own advancement and in

[29] *ibid.*, p. 160.
[30] *The Indian National Congress*, p. 380.

erecting a platform from which to speak to the British rather than to the Indians. For those reformers, the human energy brought into existence through devotion to nationalism should have been directed toward social reform and not dissipated in debates and resolutions on political issues. Leading Madras reformers, speaking through the *Hindu* and the *Social Reformer*, took the view that the Social Conference should break its ties with the Congress. In 1892, for example, the *Reformer* wrote, "If it is still insisted to hold the Conference with the Congress, then the future of the Conference is not hopeful. It is only another way of proclaiming to the world that the Conference cannot stand on its own legs."[31]

The more vigorous reformers felt that the growing interest in politics, sponsored by the Congress, forced into the background the primary aim of social regeneration of the nation; many of them urged the priority of social reform over political reform. Malabari's voice, heard through the *Indian Spectator*, was especially strong in arguing that if Indians wanted to acquire the political institutions of the West they would first have to assimilate, to some extent at least, Western "moral and social usages."[32] R.G. Bhandarkar who was never enthusiastic about the Congress, or in fact about any public body in India, often deplored the "defects and shortcomings of my countrymen" which would have to be overcome "as a necessary preliminary to all progress. . . ." He asserted that "without the acquisition of certain virtues and without a reform of our social Institutions real political advance is impossible."[33] In a Presidential address to the ninth Social Conference, Bhandarkar deplored the condition of the lower castes and said, "If we ask England to remove our disabilities, we must as a necessary preliminary show that we are worthy of the favour by removing the disabilities of the oppressed classes of our society."[34] Narendra Nath Sen, also addressing the Conference, warned that "However we may try to raise ourselves as a nation, we shall find our efforts quite paralysed, because of the crying

[31] S. Natarajan, *Century of Social Reform*, p. 88.
[32] Gidumal, *The Life and Life Work of Behramji M. Malabari*, p. 144.
[33] Bhandarkar, *Collected Works*, I, 453.
[34] Chintamani, *Indian Social Reform*, III, 189-90.

defects in our social system. You will therefore see that social reform is even of more immediate concern to us than political reform."[35] The noted northern Indian reformer, Lala Baijnath expressed the same idea in an essay written in 1891: "The subject of social reform is to my mind even of greater importance than political reform, for political reform can only be useful when those who seek it are physically, mentally and morally capable of using it to the best advantage."[36] The hard-working south Indian reformer, Viresalingam Pantulu, declared in 1902, "How can we clamour for self-government when we are not willing to grant the blessings of higher education to our own women? How can we ask the Government to remove our disabilities when we are not prepared to remove the disabilities of the oppressed classes of our own society? . . . If we do not show earnestness in social reform, will not our attempts at political reform be treated with contempt and disdain?"[37]

In rebuttal to the charges that they were placing unnecessary obstacles in the path of national political advance, social reformers were quick to point to the artificiality of the politicians' programs. Although their own appeals were directed mainly toward educated middle-class Hindus and their program had little relevance to mass uplift, the reformers believed that social reform, even among restricted groups, was directed toward alleviating the nation's fundamental ills more realistically than political reform. They did not scorn constitutional advances but deplored what they considered the waste of energy by influential Indians who spent their spare time only on political speaking and writing.

Reformers often insisted that their task was more difficult, perhaps nobler, than that of persuading the British to grant political concessions: they suffered the ridicule of their own countrymen and thus could claim that they bore a greater burden. N.G. Chandavarkar could tellingly cite the observation of Sir William Wedderburn, that it was easier for an educated Indian to affect the thinking of the Secretary of State than his own mother-in-law.[38]

[35] *ibid.*, p. 191.
[36] Baijnath, "Some Problems of Social Reform," p. 76.
[37] Quoted in *ISR*, June 22, 1902, pp. 349-50.
[38] Chintamani, *op.cit.*, IV, 322.

It was comparatively easy, the *Hindu* once wrote, to criticize the government and urge the British to promulgate constitutional reform: "the task of political reform, so far as the Congress leaders are concerned, is attended with little difficulty." Not so, the newspaper continued, "the task of social reform. The burden of giving effect to the alterations we might suggest is ours. The foreign rulers have nothing to do with them. The social reformer has therefore a more serious and difficult contest before him than the political reformer. If it is this increased responsibility that scares educated men away from social problems, they will hardly receive credit for courage."[39] Politics, many reformers were fond of saying, consisted in seeking gifts from the rulers, whereas social reform meant that Indians were assuming responsibility for their own advancement—the most courageous posture for a nationalist to take.

Most educated and informed Indians probably accepted the idea that social reform was as essential as political reform to India's modern advancement, although they were not prepared to agree on which particular reforms should be undertaken. That group of Indians, most of whom considered themselves nationalists, nevertheless, rejected the idea of the more dedicated social reformers that social progress was a prerequisite to political progress. Even Ranade and Telang, among the reformers, failed to support their colleagues in the Social Conference who urged the priority of social over political reform. Ranade considered the two kinds of advance inseparable, while Telang at one time, in 1886, boldly asserted that Indian nationalists should concentrate on political reform.

Telang's famous speech, "Must Social Reform Precede Political Reform in India?" remained for many years the frankest exposition of the strategy of expediency to be issued by a prominent nationalist. In it he sought to demonstrate that political progress had been made in India under its own rulers in premodern periods and in England in the 17th century without prior social progress, and that in the England of his day "there are still social evils, huge and serious social evils, awaiting remedy" to which "atten-

[39] Quoted (no date cited) in K. Subba Rao, *Revived Memories*, p. 215.

tion is not directed with anything like the force and energy be-
stowed on political affairs."[40] Why, then, the insistence by some
that Indians should grapple first with their social problems and
only later turn their attention to politics? Furthermore, said
Telang expounding the controversial "lines of least resistance"
doctrine in its original form, political progress under the British
is far easier to achieve than social progress, and therefore it ought
to be given more attention. "If we compare the Government and
the Hindu population to two forts facing the army of reform, can
there be any doubt that the wisest course for that army is to turn
its energies first towards the fort represented by the Government,
where we have numerous and powerful friends among the garrison. . . . As to the other fort, the case is as far as possible from
being one of *veni vidi vici*. The soldiers of the old garrison are
not in the least ready to 'give up,' and in some respects we have
yet got even to forge, and to learn to wield, the weapons by which
we have to fight them." And so, he concluded, "Let us then all
devote the bulk of our energies to political reform."[41] The similarity of Telang's position in 1886 to that of Tilak in later years[42]
is beyond question, but the repute in which a man's ideas are held
is determined in the context of human relationships, not the bare,
uncritical recording of his words: Telang's associations made him
a social reformer, while Tilak's associations made him an opponent of the reform movement.

The unwillingness of Telang and Ranade to give unequivocal
priority to social reform as a nationalist endeavor must have provided some comfort to nationalists whose fears of public censure
or private embarrassment checked any expression of their concern for social problems. Two further considerations profoundly
affected the nationalist view of social reform: one, the personal
failings of the reformers themselves in living up to their pro-

[40] Telang, *Selected Writings and Speeches*, 1, 284.
[41] *ibid.*, pp. 288-89, 299.
[42] Of course, Tilak considered it ridiculous that social reform should be a
prerequisite to political progress. The two phenomena were unrelated, he argued,
and at one time cited the position of Burma, where, he noted, society was relatively free from the disabilities noted among Hindus and yet political life was no
further advanced than in India. Cited in Wolpert, "Tilak and Gokhale," *op.cit.*,
p. 208.

testations; and two, the publicized encouragement that the reform movement received from the British.

For every social reformer who stood firmly by his principles and defied caste and even family pressure in order to practice what he preached, there appeared to be another who gave in to threats of community ostracism or family disapproval. Those reformers who, happily, were never faced with cruel decisions—such as whether or not to postpone a daughter's marriage and thus to risk her not marrying at all—could provide none of the moral force of personal example upon which any great movement is based. The National Congress, viewed from within its ranks, gave an appearance of purposeful activity and sometimes even excitement. The Social Conference, on the other hand, was a much less encouraging affair, even to its supporters. While political activity grew in intensity in the latter part of the century, agitation in behalf of social reform at the national level was not, in G. Subramania Iyer's judgment, "vigorous or powerful. At best it has been feeble and spasmodic."[43] Enthusiastic men looking for a cause to support found many social reform leaders unable to harness the full potential strength of their own nominal followings. The confidence of many of the reformers in themselves was failing, and their discouragement affected others. Ranade's second marriage to a young girl in 1873 may have been a dim memory two decades later, but Telang's decision to marry his two daughters, ages ten and eight, in 1893,[44] reinforced a popular impression that most reformers were no more courageous than anyone else in their personal lives. The *Reformer*, commenting on Telang's action, wrote that "A succession of remarkable failures has shaken our faith. . . . We have now learnt never to indulge in high hopes of accomplishing great ends with the materials at present avail-

[43] Speech to Madras Hindu Social Reform Association, 1897, Chintamani, *op.cit.*, IV, 343.

[44] Telang wrote to Chandavarkar that "no one feels more than I do that I have not done the right thing. I plead to the charge—I have no defense; and I must bear calmly what is being said in the papers." Chandavarkar, *Speeches and Writings*, p. 334. It was understood that Telang made the decision to satisfy the desire of his wife, who was close to death at the time. See V. N. Naik, "Telang as a Social Reformer," in Bombay Presidency Social Reform Association, *Social Reform Annual, 1951.*

able in this country."[45] Ranade's decision to make amends, along with Tilak, for his breach of the caste rule against inter-dining, by taking *prāyaścitta*, and Raghunatha Rau's reluctance to attend a wedding ceremony for a widow also brought denunciations from the *Reformer*. Its Bombay correspondent, Chandavarkar, found still another cause for discouragement in the marriage of R.N. Mudholkar, a prominent reformer from Nagpur,[46] to a girl of twelve.[47] Some years later A. Subba Rau, a co-founder of the *Reformer* and the first Secretary of the Madras Hindu Social Reform Association, gave in to family pressure and allowed his daughter to be married under the "proper age."[48] A deviation from reformed ideas on marriage probably kept G.K. Gokhale from lending his full support to the social reform movement. He had married a second wife while the first, an incurable invalid, was still alive and therefore "wished to save the social reform cause from any reflection that would be made against it if he became one of its leaders."[49]

Ranade, always prepared to tolerate compromise, sympathized with the reformers whose will broke under pressure. To his friend, Telang, he wrote in 1884: "People find fault with us, even abuse us, for half-heartedness, for our apparent want of fire and enthusiasm. God only knows that in our households we are perpetually at war with our nearest and dearest. We struggle and strive to do our best, and have perforce to stop at many points, when we fear the strain will cause a rupture."[50] Such words as those from the reformers' national leader and the record of personal failings that they represented did great damage to the reputation of the reform movement. Chandavarkar and a few of the other national leaders could do little to salvage the public's

[45] Quoted (without date) in S. Natarajan, *Century of Social Reform*, p. 90.
[46] Mudholkar, with M.V. Joshi, organized the Berar Sarvajanik Sabha, along the lines of the Poona Sarvajanik Sabha, and worked to stimulate technical education and industrial development. On social reform he favored reforms which could be justified by reference to the shastras, including remarriage of virgin widows. See "Rao Bahadur R.N. Mudholkar; A Sketch of His Life and Services to India."
[47] Natarajan, *op.cit.*, p. 90.   [48] *ISR*, July 19, 1903, pp. 466-67.
[49] R.P. Paranjpe, *Gopal Krishna Gokhale*, p. 27.
[50] Quoted in Kellock, *Mahadev Govind Ranade*, p. 137.

respect for their movement. But they continued to try, arousing their followers to renewed efforts by words that insisted that there was much less to fear from social persecution than some might have imagined. "We fear social ostracism a little too much as children fear to go into the dark," he told the Mangalore Social Reform Association in 1900. "One does not dare because he has a wife and children; another because he has a daughter to marry; a third because he has—well, any difficulty will do where the mind is slow and the heart is weak." He called upon educated Indians to "cultivate a little of manhood" and dispel the childish fears of social innovation.[51] But the vigor of a few could scarcely instill fearlessness in the majority of those who called themselves reformers. By 1891 the inner weakness of the movement was accurately described by a British census reporter commenting on attempts by the Indians to abolish child marriage and permit widow remarriage: "Many cases have occurred within recent years to show that any movement among the literate classes . . . is but mouth deep . . . when the opportunities occur for carrying into practice some of the reforms they have been so strenuously endeavoring to impose upon others, it is remarkable to note what an amount of filial piety and of deference to the feelings of those to whom their respect is due come into play, to prevent them from becoming martyrs to their principles."[52]

If some British observers derided the weak and spasmodic reform movement, others lauded whatever efforts were being made and encouraged Indians to strive harder for social causes. Such British support of social reform, however, became the second—possibly the major—handicap to the movement in the late 19th century. For, as suspicion of official government policy increased among Indians, publicly expressed British interest in social reform gave to the movement the role of an antinationalist influence.

It is probably correct to assume that by the 1890's, if social reformers had been working *against* the wishes of the government they would automatically have been regarded as patriots by a

<hr>

[51] Chandavarkar, *Speeches and Writings*, pp. 89, 91.
[52] From the Report of Mr. Baines on the Indian Census of 1891, quoted in Sir John Strachey, *India; Its Administration and Progress*, p. 493.

great many of the younger groups of educated Indians. The reformers, however, had approved of the Age of Consent Bill and therefore, in principle, appeared willing to collaborate with the government in further social endeavors.[53] After 1887, the government gave increasing evidence of its desire to encourage nationalist unity in behalf of social reform while discouraging the comparable movement for political reform.[54]

The official position on social reform and its relation to political reform received its most cogent and memorable formulation in the 1880's by Sir Auckland Colvin, finance member of the Governor-General's Council and, after 1887, Lieutenant-Governor of the North-Western Provinces. His first pronouncement on the subject came in response to Malabari's "Notes." He wrote at that time that "societies which will not make any combined effort to reform their own shortcomings are not to be much trusted when they combine to reform public affairs. They lay themselves open to the suspicion that in the profession of public zeal, they find an agreeable cloak for the discouragement of private duty."[55] Colvin's reply to Malabari reached the newspapers and elicited considerable resentment among Indian readers. Several years later Lieutenant-Governor Colvin's opinions reached an even wider audience in a

[53] However, the government appeared unwilling to contemplate further reform legislation in view of the unfavorable public reaction and the growth of extremism occasioned by the Age of Consent Bill controversy. In an interview in the *Times of India* in 1899, Malabari cited specific reform legislation that he felt was needed and said that "The impression is gaining ground that Government, growing more and more unpopular on the administrative and economic side, especially with regard to their foreign policy, are constrained to blink their more obvious moral obligation. . . . In this way their critics think they are trying to make up for loss of popularity." Quoted in *ISR*, Jan. 15, 1899, pp. 153-55.

[54] At the least, governmental encouragement came from the ranks of the higher officials. Another state of affairs at the district level, however, was reported by A.O. Hume at the time of the Age of Consent controversy. "Many" district officers, he wrote, sought to discredit the National Congress movement by pointing out to potential followers that its moderate leaders supported social legislation and thus did not truly represent the people. Hume thought that that propaganda was extremely dangerous, because it might alienate nationalists from the Congress, where they were "safe from burning bungalows and murdering Europeans." Hume to Lord Lansdowne, March 5, 1891. Cited in Wolpert, *op.cit.*, p. 93.

[55] Quoted in Gidumal, *The Status of Women in India*, pp. 122-23.

famous exchange of letters with A. O. Hume.[56] His critique of the
first years of the Congress movement stands as a classic statement
of an alien bureaucracy's unsympathetic, suspicious, and somewhat astonished reaction to the nascent yet clearly irresistible
native demands for greater freedom. The bulk of the indictment
stressed the disloyalty and inflammatory character of Congress
propaganda, but in a few sentences Colvin also struck out against
what he felt was the result of the Congress decision to ignore
social problems: "What, I think, people have objected to, is not
so much that the Congress does not deal with social questions, as
that, with social questions so urgently requiring to be dealt with,
a body having for its main object political changes, should have
thrust itself across the path of reform. What, if I understand them
rightly, your critics say, is, not that they expect the Congress team
to draw the ponderous car of social reform, but that they find you
putting your political *char-a-banc* before their social reform horse,
with the result that neither will you progress, nor can they make a
single stride. They fear that the people of India will find it infinitely more agreeable to clamour for place and power; to cry
aloud to all that pass by that they are, in spite of much testimony
to the contrary, aggrieved and neglected; to scramble for the
loaves and dive for the fishes; than to impose upon themselves the
rigorous discipline of social reform. . . . They [the critics] ask of
them only that they should listen to those who appeal to the
physician to commence by healing himself."[57]

Colvin posed anew the perennially intriguing question of
whether Western political institutions can be assimilated by non-
Western societies, without first transforming the social, economic,
and intellectual traditions of those societies. His negative answer
differed little from that of the majority of British observers in
India.[58] The "vast mass of the people," he wrote, ". . . live in the

[56] Reprinted in London in 1888 by Dadabhai Naoroji as "Audi Alteram Partem:
Being Two Letters on Certain Aspects of the Indian National Congress Move-
ment." See discussion of that correspondence in W. Wedderburn, *Allan Octavian
Hume*, p. 66f.

[57] *ibid.*, p. 20.

[58] Nearly every serious British writer on Indian politics in the 19th and early
20th centuries, except those, such as Hume and Wedderburn, who were pleading
the special case of the Congress, viewed India's social condition as an almost

traditions of the Government of their forefathers." They were "as much out of harmony with the political atmosphere breathed by us of English birth, or desired by their own countrymen of English education, as an elephant would be out of his element in Scotch mists, or a Banyan tree in Parliament Street."[59] In short, a social transformation of vast proportions would have to occur before India could undertake to acquire Western political forms of behavior.

Colvin's charges against those engaged in political activities were answered directly by Hume's emphatic denial that the Congress movement was discouraging social reformers. The same nationalist impulse, he wrote, fostered both social and political reform work, as witnessed by the fact that many Congressmen were reformers.[60] Hume's explanation of the exclusively political function of the Congress coincided with that of Dadabhai Naraoji and most of the Congress leaders, all of whom were sensitive to allegations that the Congress was hostile to social reform. In a speech made shortly before his correspondence with Colvin, Hume criticized unnamed people "fatuous enough to urge it as a reproach that the Congress does not directly meddle with social questions." He insisted that anyone "who should endeavor to work out the delicate and intricate questions of social reform by the aid of the rough-and-ready engine of the National Political Congress" would be as foolish as someone using a plough as a vehicle of transportation.[61] Hume's argument and that of most Congressmen, however, served not at all to alleviate concern among British officials—or among the more uncompromising social reformers—about the exclusively political direction of the Congress program.

Official criticism of the increasing preoccupation of educated Indians with political agitation and simultaneous encouragement

insuperable barrier to immediate political progress. See, e.g., Sir John Strachey, *op.cit.*, pp. 492-93; Sir Henry Cotton, *New India* (1907 edn.), pp. 258-59; Sir Walter R. Lawrence, *The India We Served* (1928), p. 282f.

[59] "Audi Alteram . . . ," p. 22.
[60] *ibid.*, p. 66.
[61] A.O. Hume, "A Speech on The Indian National Congress, Its Origin, Aims and Objects . . . ," p. 3.

by the government of the social reform movement, placed reformers in an awkward position; Sir Pherozeshah Mehta, the
noted moderate Congressman, recognized this when he warned
zealous social reformers not to "play into the hands of those officials
who were not favourably inclined toward the Congress."[62] Sir
C. P. Ramaswami Aiyar, in an interview with the author in 1960,
recalled that in the 1890's it was felt that the British had side-
tracked leading men into social reform in order to keep them from
political activities—had encouraged them to wear a "moral top
hat, just as they did a physical top hat!" Chandavarkar observed
that the social reform movement was losing public support because
Indians were troubled by the political implications of engaging in
reform causes: there was ". . . a general feeling among educated
Indians that any criticism or discussion of our social shortcomings
was unwise and impolitic, because it only gave a handle to those
who maintained that no political rights could be extended to us
unless we proved our fitness in other directions."[63] Among politically ambitious Indians any connection with the social reform
movement was becoming an increasingly serious handicap. Indeed, as K. Srinivasa Row noted in 1902, "A certain amount of
pronounced antipathy to social reform and reformers is becoming
a passport to popularity for the Congress politician." He explained
further: "To advise caution in social reform is looked upon as the
perfection of wisdom, while to advise caution in political reform
is resented as cowardice. . . ."[64]

Reformers were at first unimpressed by the suggestion that they
were antinationalist, so long as the political nationalist movement
itself proclaimed its loyalty to British rule and its devotion to the
ideal of Westernized nationhood. But as the political temper
changed toward the end of the century to disillusionment over the
slow pace of constitutional and administrative advance, reformers
began to sense the disadvantages of being identified with the
British design for India's future development. Simultaneously,

[62] Quoted in V.N. Naik, "Telang as a Social Reformer," Bombay Presidency
Social Reform Association, Social Reform Annual, 1951, p. 55.

[63] Chandavarkar, op.cit., pp. 255-56.

[64] From an article in East and West, Feb. 1902, cited in Row, Papers on Social
Reform, p. 61.

the Hindu cultural revival was causing many Indians, reformers included, to place a higher value on their own cultural heritage, in relation to that of the West, than they had previously done. At the Social Conference of 1896 in Calcutta, Narendra Nath Sen's Presidential address included the acknowledgment that "social reform has come to be regarded with the utmost distrust and suspicion. It is viewed in some quarters in the light of something outlandish and foreign." Sen's suggestion for overcoming that popular impression was to gain increasing acceptance among reformers in the years to follow: ". . . social reform should be carried on strictly national, that is Aryan and old Shastraic lines, among those who aspire to be known as good Hindus."[65] "National" in that context meant Hindu, not all-Indian, and it implied a decline in the importance of the Western example of personal morality and social ethics upon which the social reform movement had been founded.

Nationalism's rapidly changing character at the turn of the century produced repercussions in the all-India social reform movement as well as in the political reform movement. One obvious characteristic of the reconstructed nationalism of the 20th century was an increasing disenchantment among educated Indians with Western-style public organizations and their methods of formal debate and resolution and with Western-inspired social ideals. Within the Congress the younger extremists were challenging the liberal moderates for control of the organization, and a serious split soon developed. In contrast, within the Social Conference the older established leaders themselves were adapting their doctrines to the new cultural revivalism. The main challenge to the social reform movement came from outside the Conference, from revivalists such as Annie Besant and Vivekananda, and it was surprisingly well met, largely because of the doctrinal flexibility that Ranade had given to the organization.

Between the Congress and the Conference, relations were never as close after 1895 as they had been before, despite the *pro forma* agreement to hold annual sessions at the same place. Extremist politicians, who had a large public following by the turn

[65] Chintamani, *op.cit.*, III, 191, 193.

of the century in most of the provinces, continued to regard the Social Conference as an instrument to extend British influence and to ridicule the back-sliding of Conference followers. Reformers persisted in their view that social progress, however defined, must underlie any political advance. Thus, at the close of the century the outcome of the social versus political reform controversy appeared to be a partial disengagement of the two movements, as they were represented by the Social Conference and the Congress. The Tilak-led extremist group in the Congress repudiated social reform, partly at least because it was a liability to any movement seeking mass support. Some reformers, on the other hand, urged a break with the Congress and a more strenuous assertion that social progress should be the predominant nationalist activity.

But, in a real sense, nationalism in the first decade of the century was outgrowing both the Social Conference and the Congress in the scope of its popular appeal and in the new conception of the nation which it was offering to Indians. The social versus political reform debate, which was vividly exposed in the relations between Conference and Congress, attracted less attention as the authority of those two forums for the expression of nationalism waned.

THE LOCAL SOCIAL

REFORM MOVEMENTS IN BOMBAY,

MADRAS, AND BENGAL

THE social reform movements at local levels were gaining adherents and expanding their constructive programs all during the period of the controversy described in Chapter IX. The politically motivated controversy over the question of the proper place of social reform in the nationalist movement was occupying the attention of national leaders and publicists, and the all-India debates between reformers and their critics were echoing in the press and on the platform in cities and towns throughout the country while local reform movements were growing in strength. The apparent decline in the stature of the national social reform movement attributable to the attacks upon it by cultural revivalists and extremist politicians did not cause comparable weakening of all the local social reform associations. Bengal was the exception; there the local movement had come to a standstill at the time of Keshub Chandra Sen's abdication of its leadership in the late 1870's.

Several reasons may be suggested for the flourishing of local social reform movements in the 1890's and early 20th century in contrast to the loss of following suffered by the all-India Social Conference. The decline in the prestige of the moderate, liberal Congress leadership toward the end of the century unavoidably affected the Social Conference because of the close relationship of the two in the public mind. This, however, did not affect the local reform movements very much due to the fact that they were not directly involved in the political controversies pursued at the national level. Furthermore, the local reform movements were not expected to and did not follow all of the doctrines and programs of the Social Conference but rather pursued more limited objectives and thus avoided full-scale attacks on their programs. The Social Conference, whose resolutions covered nearly every reform proposal initiated anywhere in India, presented itself as a very large target for opposition attack. In addition, certain local reform movements, especially caste associations, had followings which saw immediate benefits from their reforming activities which they were unwilling to forego merely because powerful national critics ridiculed their efforts. The records of most local social reform organizations active in the 1890's and in the first two decades of the 20th century (if they existed and were made available) would probably show fairly consistent increases in public support during those years.[1]

In addition to the reforming efforts of local groups, and sometimes in response to their suggestions, provincial governments and the administrations in certain princely states continued to enact social reform legislation, in contrast to the hesitancy after 1891 of the Central Government to arouse further orthodox opposition.[2]

Local social reform associations fell into three categories: general (or voluntary) associations; caste reform associations; and the religious reform bodies (generally called Samajes). In Bom-

[1] It must be acknowledged that further investigation needs to be undertaken in all the Indian provinces before this statement can be fully substantiated. The examples given in this Chapter of reform at the local level—cities, districts, and provinces—constitute only part of the evidence presently available and only a small fraction of the evidence which may someday become available of the progress in organized social reform in modern India. These examples should not be regarded in any sense as a complete survey. They were chosen because they provide further accounts of movements introduced earlier in this study and, in some cases, because they provide the background for understanding certain of the changes taking place in India today.

[2] Some of that legislation will be noted, but a complete list awaits a survey of all provincial codes and legislative records and those of the major princely states.

bay and Madras most of the reform associations were of the first type, although caste associations became fairly common in Bombay after the turn of the century. In Bengal whatever reforming endeavor was taking place was in the hands of Brahmos, or those closely associated with the Samaj. The northern provinces presented a unique situation, where caste associations and the Arya Samaj, with its special characteristics, dominated the social reform movement.

The general reform associations—or voluntary associations, as Ranade sometimes called them—were those whose membership was drawn from persons whose common interest was social reform, not religious communion or caste identity. Their purposes, for example, widow remarriage, were often narrowly defined. Along with the standard objectives of improving the position of women and liberating individuals from certain caste restrictions, the general associations frequently took stands on educational and economic questions and occasionally undertook the support of schools and charitable institutions, and eventually entered upon social welfare work.

A compelling concern of the leaders of the social reform movement, especially in the 1880's and 1890's when many reform associations were first being established, was the absence of discipline within the general reform bodies. Caste associations and Samajes had more control over their members than did voluntary associations. As Dayaram Gidumal wrote of the latter in 1888: "These Associations have hitherto failed and become discredited, simply because they have not had the power of keeping men to their word."[3] Indians, unaccustomed to formal collaboration for general public purposes, usually failed to put the interest and prestige of a voluntary public body of which they were members ahead of their private concerns. However enthusiastically they may have initially banded together for social reform purposes, they were often unable to provide for the new body the inner cohesion essential for its bare survival. What kinds of discipline could a reform association enforce upon its members, whose self-discipline, when it came to public concerns, had never

[3] Gidumal, *The Life and Life Work of Behramji M. Malabari*, p. 137.

been developed? Ranade spoke frankly on that issue to the Social Conference of 1889 and introduced a resolution which sought help from the only powerful agency that could be counted on to sympathize with a progressive innovation in Indian life, the government. The resolution asked the government to consider amending Act VI of 1882 (the Indian Companies Act) and Act XXI of 1860 (for the Registration of Literary, Scientific and Charitable Societies), so that there would be special provisions for social reform associations to register themselves as legally constituted bodies.[4] Not only would members of reform associations then consider their pledges of membership more nearly binding, but also the associations would be accountable for funds received and expended and thus be in a better position to launch active programs. Ranade took particular interest in the enforcement of membership pledges, for, he noted, if an association lacks that power "it is the experience of all of us that we are often in our weaker moments tempted to falter and go wrong."[5]

The Hindu Social Reform Association of Sind, under the energetic leadership of Dayaram Gidumal, was the first to register itself as a legal body, and Ranade hoped that the Sind Association's example would be followed by others. In 1886 the Commissioner in Sind had forwarded to the Indian Government a memorial of the Sind Association asking for amendment of Act XXI of 1860 to allow for registration of social reform bodies. The government's reply pointed to the defects of that Act and suggested that the Sind Association incorporate under Section 26 of the Companies Act of 1882, which covered nonprofit associations. The Association's members apparently felt that the technical requirements of incorporation under the Companies Act amounted to an onerous burden, and the Social Conference's resolution asking the government to enact an amendment to facilitate registration of reform bodies came at their behest. The result was that the government reduced the incorporation fees for bodies such as the Sind Association. The latter, then, with its two hundred

---

[4] A similar resolution was passed by the Conference in 1892. See Chintamani, *Indian Social Reform*, II, 9f. and Appendix, p. 368.

[5] Ranade, *Miscellaneous Writings*, p. 99.

thirty charter members, became the first incorporated social reform organization.

The articles of association of the Sind Association showed its purposes to be marriage reform and female education. Penalties were established for breaches of the "first division" membership pledges: 1) not to marry sons below the age of sixteen, 2) to limit dowries taken from brides' families, and 3) to educate female children at least to the level of reading, writing, and simple arithmetic. The fines to be exacted for failure to adhere to pledges were not nominal—from Rupees 500 for breach of the first pledge to Rupees 50 for breaking the third.[6] A fee of Rupees 500 was exacted from pledged members who decided to "retire" from the Association. Several other social reform associations registered themselves as incorporated bodies, with the attendant benefits of having pledges enforceable by law. The Gujarat Hindu Social Reform Association, which was incorporated at Ahmedabad, aimed chiefly at marriage reforms and accepted three divisions of members, according to their respective pledges not to marry sons and daughters before 1) eighteen and fourteen years of age, 2) sixteen and twelve years of age, or 3) sixteen and ten years of age.[7]

But the problems of discipline and organizational structure in local social reform bodies were not always met in the manner that the Sind and Gujarat associations met them. Apparently few social reform societies desired the advantages of legal incorporation, although this practice was recommended by Ranade and Dayaram Gidumal. Gidumal was probably the most effective single organizer of reform associations in the 1880's. Reform society discipline depended upon the strength of individual men, just as founding a society did.

The National Social Conference as an organizational force for

---

[6] See Gidumal, *The Status of Women in India*, p. 271f. The Association permitted four "divisions" of members, including Honorary Members "elected on account of their liberality towards the Association, or for eminent services to the cause of social reform or female education," p. 276. Honorary Members were not bound by pledges and neither were "third division" members, who were merely sympathisers.

[7] *ibid.*, p. 280.

local reform movements provided encouragement, but no real direction. Never, up to the time of the Conference's demise in 1933, was any discipline enforced by it upon local associations or their members, in contrast to what the National Congress did under Gandhi; nor did the Conference organize local reform bodies as the Congress did local units. However, the National Social Conference provided a significant service to local reform associations by opening a channel for their intercommunication. Appended to each year's Conference *Report* were descriptions of local bodies, for example, procedures for establishing a body and getting it registered with the authorities, sample charters, and statements of purpose.

The histories of the local social reform bodies are reflections of the fluctuating enthusiasms and strengths of purpose of leading individuals, who gathered around them somewhat less energetic followers who were aroused from time to time by ideas and happenings that shook their confidence in Hindu social customs. With few exceptions, the general reform associations had little corporate power as organizations. For years at a time some of them might appear moribund and might be revitalized when an issue arose that demanded attention. As inseminators of ideas, however, the associations throughout the country proved more effective than their organizational status would have suggested. Public debates held under their auspices created some enthusiasm for reform, at least among the youth, and their mere existence was an annoying reminder to the more orthodox that society was undergoing rapid changes. Newspapers whose editors were supporters of local reform bodies publicized the speeches and activities of the reformers and frequently constituted the most powerful local transmitters of the reformist doctrines. The mechanism of social change is impossible to analyze thoroughly, but it is arguable that a living individual presenting a personal example of innovation in behavior or in ideas is the only effective means of spreading that innovation. To some extent, at least, social reformers stood out as examples of the changes they wished to promote, and they thus were crucial factors in the process of change.

General Associations and Individual
Reformers in Bombay

Bombay Presidency social reformers in the 20th century could take pride in the fact that their province had the longest and most extensive record of public interest in social reform and of organized reforming activity of any Indian region.[8] Some aspects of that record to the 1880's have been surveyed in Chapter IV of the present study. After the founding of the Congress, in 1885, and the Social Conference, in 1887, the main leadership for both of which came from Bombay, local reforming efforts in that province assume an historical importance secondary to activities on the national level which were dramatically punctuated by the well-publicized debates between men such as Tilak and Ranade. However, work in all parts of the province was proceeding through general associations for social reform, and later for social service.

Social reform societies, often sponsoring girls schools and widows homes, or missions for low caste and tribal communities, as well as putting out literature and holding discussions, were found in the major towns and cities of Bombay. In the province of Berar, which Ranade always (and rightly) referred to as part of Maharashtra, the Berar Association at Akola listed four hundred members in 1895, joined by pledges which covered nearly all the reforms sponsored by the National Social Conference.[9] Bombay reformers tried to organize themselves on a provincial basis when they inaugurated in 1900 the Bombay Provincial Social Conference at Satara, and Ranade made one of his last public addresses on that occasion. In 1903 they founded the Bombay Presidency Social Reform Association. The Conference lapsed in 1907 and was revived in 1912 but made no

[8] The number of reform associations sending reports to the Social Conference was a fair guide to the strength of reform movements in the major provinces: in 1896 the figures were: Bombay, 23; Madras, 11; Mysore, 2; Punjab, 4; Hyderabad (Deccan), 2; C.P. and Berar, 2; N.W. Provinces, 5. Ten Bengal associations sent reports that year, due chiefly to the holding of the Conference at Calcutta; frequently no reports were received from Bengal. See Ranade, *Miscellaneous Writings*, p. 175.

[9] *ibid.*, pp. 167-68.

special contribution. Yet the Bombay Association, whose purpose
it was to foster reform work throughout the year, has survived
to the present day. In spite of a limited membership and very
limited funds, this Association nevertheless has had a significant
record of publicizing social reform ideas, supporting social legislation, and giving financial and organizational support to educational and welfare undertakings. Its main reforming efforts have
been in behalf of women and the depressed classes.[10] N.G. Chandavarkar was the inspiration for the Association and was its
President until his death in 1923; the other original officers were
Lalshankar Umiashankar, K. Natarajan, B.N. Bhajekar, and D.G.
Padhye.

In the years just preceding the First World War social service
or welfare work was advancing in the country, and the more
vigorous and dedicated social reformers made direct contact with
large numbers of needy and backward people in cities as well
as in tribal areas. In Bombay in 1911, a group of young men in
the Social Reform Association created the Social Service League
under Chandavarkar's Presidentship. That organization which is
still active today pioneered numerous activities: running a night
school in the mill area of Bombay; maintaining libraries and
reading rooms; operating a Workingmen's Institute, with an
affiliated Textile Technical School and a Charitable Dispensary;
managing several Industrial Schools for Women; and maintaining as well both recreational facilities for working people
and a Cooperative Credit Society.[11] Bombay also produced the

[10] Including 20 per cent of the population of British India, or some 30 per
cent of the total Hindu population, those classes were at the bottom of the
caste structure and were usually regarded as untouchable because they would
pollute upper-caste Hindus. See *Report of the Indian Statutory Commission*, I,
37. A Widow's Home was maintained by the Bombay Social Reform Association
from 1916 to 1929; a hostel for Hindu women students in Bombay was established
as well as a Female Education Fund. Women's Conferences were started by
the Association as early as 1905. It later took up the cause of the untouchables—
before Gandhi took up that work, and in 1912 joined with the Aryan Brotherhood to hold a public dinner in which caste Hindus and untouchables joined.
Further activities of this group are enumerated in its pamphlet, "Memoir of
Fifty Years of Progress," Bombay, 1952.
[11] See The Social Service League of Bombay, *Annual Reports*. The author of
this study was privileged to discuss the League's activities with Professor T.A.

Seva Sedan which was even more famous because of the spread of its work. In 1908 Malabari and Gidumal established that famous Bombay institution and the next year G.K. Devadhar and Ranade's widow, Ramabai, started the Poona Seva Sedan. Branches of the Seva Sedan were founded throughout the Province and in Madras. The Seva Sedan was established to serve women of all castes and communities, and it marked the shift in social reform endeavor from legislation and liberal education for high-caste women to: welfare, rehabilitation work, education in basic skills, and medical service—all for women of the lower castes.

In the province of Bombay, Poona has always been a center for agitation for social reform ideas, and it has also produced an exceptional number of institutions carrying on active reform work. Homes and educational institutions for widows were an early preoccupation of Hindu reformers in Poona—and of non-Hindus as well. No account of social reform in Poona can be complete without a description of the activities of Pandita Ramabai. A widow whose personality and extensive learning made even her opponents respect her, Pandita Ramabai founded the Sharada Sadan in Poona in 1890. It was a home for high-caste widows, which both Ranade and Bhandarkar supported in spite of the fact that Ramabai had been converted to Christianity. The intense public controversy that broke out in 1894 when several girls under the Pandita's care became Christians, forced the two well-known reformers to give up their support and provided the antireformers with still another propaganda theme about the latent "treachery" of the reform movement.[12] Despite her conversion and the attendant suspicion cast upon her motives, Pandita Ramabai was an inspiration to many Hindus because of the de-

---

Kulkarni (the General Secretary) and K.L.N. Rao (a member of the League) at their offices in the Servants of India Society Building, Bombay.

[12] Ramabai's unusual career has received much attention: Fuller, *The Triumph of an Indian Widow* (a biography); Mrs. Ranade, *Himself*, p. 75f.; Chandavarkar, *Maharshi Karve*, pp. 66-67, 84-86; and Tahmankar, *Lokamanya Tilak*, pp. 42-45. Ramabai studied Sanskrit for a time under Dayananda Saraswati—it seems that she may have imbibed some of his reforming vigor along with her language lessons.

votion of her service to young widows and the tenacity of her struggle for women's rights.

Dhondu Keshave (later Maharshi) Karve was one who admired and assisted the Pandita's crusade.[13] He had come to Poona in 1891 at the behest of Gokhale to fill the mathematics post in the Fergusson College faculty left by the resignation of Tilak, and he soon became a life member of the Deccan Education Society. Unlike his predecessor at Fergusson in nearly every respect (except his Brahmin heritage), Karve in 1893 married a twenty-three year old widow, who had been the first to enter the Sharada Sadan. In the same year he revived the Widow Remarriage Association of Poona,[14] which had been moribund since the death in 1875 of its founder, Vishnu Shastri Pundit. R.G. Bhandarkar became the President of this new Association. For his flouting of orthodox sensibilities in marrying a widow, D.K. Karve was the victim of social ostracism and condemnation—an experience that was not unusual in these circumstances and can only be described as excruciating.[15] Tilak, and this is perhaps indicative of his personal views on social reform, expressed a reluctant approval of the marriage in *Mahratta*, his English-language newspaper: The marriage of Karve to a widow, the newspaper wrote, "was, except being a remarriage, in every way decent, and was performed according to the strict orthodox ritual. Whatever may be our opinion on the general question about the necessity of widow remarriages, we must say that if the thing is worth trying at all, it ought to be made in a way that would make it popular. Mr. Karve, though never known to have been a blustering reformer, has set a practical example

[13] Chandavarkar, *op.cit.*, pp. 61f., 85f.

[14] In 1895 its name was changed to the Association for the Removal of Restrictions to the Marriage of Widows, a modification which more radical reformers deplored.

[15] On visits to Murud which was his native village, Karve and his wife were not allowed to enter the family home, then occupied by his brother and mother; no one would sit or eat with them; scandalous gossip was spread about Mrs. Karve; and they were cut off from the social life of the community—even from normal contacts with Karve's old friends. See Chandavarkar, *op.cit.*, pp. 68-70. In Poona the couple was relatively free from persecution. Also see "Professor Karve's Work in the Cause of Indian Women as Described by Himself," *Modern Review*, XVIII, 5 (Nov., 1915).

of moral courage which not a whole legion of social quacks have shown in their conduct."[16]

After their marriage Karve's wife joined him in his long-lasting work to create a respected and worthwhile place in society for widows and to encourage their remarriage. In 1896 he established an Association to collect funds for a Hindu Widow's Home, Anath Balikashram; this home was to follow the pattern of Pandita Ramabai's Home, as well as those established in Bengal by Sasipada Banerji and in Madras by Viresalingam Pantulu.[17] By 1900 the Home was founded, with eight widows and two unmarried girls in residence. It was exclusively an educational institution and not a boarding place for widows awaiting the opportunity to remarry, and thus it was unrelated to Karve's support of the Widow Remarriage Association. The Home came under attack from reformers, especially in the newspaper, *Sudharak*; they argued that it should try to arrange remarriages for its charges. It was also attacked by the orthodox who were distressed because some widows did remarry after leaving the Home. Karve sought to separate the widow remarriage movement from his major efforts for the education of widows, but, like others who were engaged in social welfare and educational work, he could not escape the responsibilities of the social reformer.

Maharshi Karve, who died at the age of one hundred and four in 1962, spoke and wrote comparatively little on social reform, but he acted according to principles that others spent their energies in proclaiming. Certainly his greatest achievement was in the field of women's education. Like social reformers in every country, he realized that the surest way to create and maintain social progress is through educating women and freeing them

---

[16] *Professor D.F. Karve; A Sketch of His Life and Life-Work*, p. 23. See also Karve's own account in *Looking Backward (An Autobiography)*. He explained that his wife's father was thoroughly orthodox but gave his permission to the marriage because of a humanitarianism stemming from adherence to the bhakti school.

[17] Other widows' Homes were also founded, among them: the Widows' Home in Mysore, 1907; the Mahila Silpasrama in Calcutta, 1907; the Widow's Home in Bangalore, 1910; one in Dacca; the Brahmin Widows' Hostel in Madras, 1912; and the Arya Samaj and Jain homes. S. Natarajan, *A Century of Social Reform*, pp. 123-24.

from customary but valueless restraints. The Mahila Vidyalaya, a girls' school which he founded in 1907 with the assistance of the Deccan Education Society, supplemented in Poona the already existing Girls' High School at Huzurpaga and the Female Training College. In 1915 Karve envisioned the founding of a women's university in Maharashtra, comparable to the Japanese Women's University which he had read about. The idea was presented in his Presidential address to the National Social Conference in Bombay in that year and gained the illustrious support of Annie Besant, Mahatma Gandhi, Chandavarkar, and Dr. Bhandarkar, the latter agreeing to act as chancellor of the proposed university. The institution was founded and the college began to hold classes in 1916. It was not a success, however, until 1919 when Sir Vithaldas D. Thackersey, of the wealthy Bombay industrialist house, provided ample funds for the institution; the name was then changed to Shreemati Nathibai Damodar (S.N.D.) Thackersey Women's University. Still under Karve's direction, the University, with all its subordinate girls' schools throughout western India, became one of the important centers of women's education in the country.

Among the many philanthropic and reform bodies that supported Maharshi Karve's enterprises and the one embodying as well the rapid spread of private educational institutions in western India in the early 20th century, was the Servants of India Society—perhaps the most famous of them all. Carrying forward the theme of self-sacrificing service found among the life members of the Deccan Education Society, Gokhale established the exclusive Servants of India Society in 1905. Impressed, as many Indians were, with the Jesuits and the attitude of the personnel of the American Mission—complete devotion to a principled cause and persistence in the face of meager financial rewards—Gokhale was convinced that India's progress depended upon recruitment of a similar type of person for nation-building work. Much of the labor of national progress, Gokhale wrote in the preamble to the Society's constitution, "must be directed towards building up in the country a higher type of character and capacity than is generally available at present. . . . One essential condition of success in this work is that a sufficient number of our countrymen must now come forward to devote themselves to the cause in the spirit in which religious work is undertaken. Public life must be spiritualized."[18] Beginning with three recruits in 1905, the Society's membership increased slowly to some twenty in 1909 and twenty-six in 1914.[19] The new members had to undergo five years of training under the almost autocratic direction of the "First Member," Gokhale.

Gokhale reasoned that without this rigid training, "there was but small chance, with our disorganized and undisciplined public life, and the want of self-restraint which characterizes most of our young men, of any really useful work being done by the Society."[20] Whether because of the discipline that the Society imposed, its low salaries—subsistence plus professional expenses—the absence of opportunity for acquiring great fame, or its secular and rational methods[21] of inducing national progress, the organization always remained weak in membership. The Society, notwithstanding the prestige it derived from its founder, never became a powerful lever for either political or social change. Politically, it always supported the conservative groups in the Congress, and after 1920 threw its comparatively limited weight against Gandhi's non-cooperation movement and in favor of the National Liberal Federation.

Though few in number, however, individual members of the Servants of India Society made their mark in India's political and social life. Individual service, rather than organizational impact, was said to be Gokhale's own desire: "From the time of its Founder, the Society has not conducted work directly under its own auspices," the Society's *Report* stated in 1926, "but generally through other organizations either already in existence or started

[18] The annual *Report* of the Society, 1958-59, p. ii.

[19] At various times Associates of the Society have been listed in the *Reports*—men who were enrolled to do part-time work in furtherance of the Society's aims. There were 47 Associates in the *Report* for 1917-23. The regular members numbered 17 in 1959, including one member under training.

[20] Gokhale's letter to K. Iyyer, July 31, 1905, cited in Wolpert, *Tilak and Gokhale*, p. 162.

[21] S.R. Venkataraman, a member of the Society in Madras, pointed out to the author in 1960 that his organization received less popular attention than, for instance, the Ramakrishna Mission, because its appeal lacked religious sanction and was thoroughly secular and rational.

242

as occasions arose."[22] Although most members were engaged in approved political work, some were notable social reformers, social workers, and educators. The best known of the Society's social reformers and workers was Gopal Krishna Devadhar of Poona who founded the Seva Sedan. Elsewhere members founded social service leagues, promoted cooperatives, undertook relief work in famines, entered the labor union movement, and worked to uplift depressed classes and tribals. Service organizations, such as the Social Service League of Madras, the Tenants' Associations in Madras and Bombay, the Seva Samiti of Allahabad, and the Bhagini Samaj of Gujarat and Bombay were either organized or led by the Servants of India Society. The Society also established branches in Madras, the Central Provinces, the United Provinces, and Orissa. The philosophy of the Servants of India Society was an unusual example of the attempt to bring about gradual, evolutionary change through moderate liberalism, legalism, and reliance on education and rational persuasion; most Maharashtrian and Gujarati reformers advocated these methods in the periods under consideration.

If religious and humanitarian motives for reform are added to the methods of reform mentioned above, the intellectual image is that of the Prarthana Samaj, discussed in Chapter IV. Although a religious body, the Prarthana Samaj's social reform work was of such a character that it can best be discussed in the context of the work of the general associations. The Samaj's primary direct influence in social reform stemmed from the individual careers of its many illustrious members—Ranade, Bhandarkar, and Chandavarkar, among others—but as a body it also sponsored reform, chiefly through educational work. At an early date, in the 1870's, after an appeal to it from Keshub Chandra Sen, it began establishing night schools for lower-caste Bombay workers, and gradually its program expanded to include a free reading room, an educational ladies' association, women's classes in various fields, an orphanage (at Pandharpur), and several elementary schools in the city of Bombay.

[22] Servants of India Society, *Report of Work (From June 1923 to May 1926)*, pp. 2-3.

In response to Christian missionary work among untouchable and tribal communities, the Prarthana Samaj, as well as several other Indian reform groups, established missions to provide educational and cultural services to those backward people. Notable among the Prarthana Samaj efforts was the work of Vithal Ramji Shinde, who founded the Depressed Classes Mission of India in 1906, with the help of the Bombay Presidency Social Reform Association under Chandavarkar, for work among the "Mahars, Chambhars, Pariahs, Namsudras, Dheds, and all other classes treated as untouchable."[23] The work of the Mission and similar but less extensive endeavors by the Brahmo Samaj were the first examples of non-Christian efforts on an organized basis to improve the outcastes' condition[24]—largely through education, not conversion to a new faith. By 1913 the Depressed Classes Mission, which was a registered charitable body, maintained thirty educational institutions throughout Bombay and Madras provinces. The success of its work stimulated further efforts by the Arya Samaj, the Dev Samaj,[25] the Theosophical Society, Sikh Associations, and certain enlightened maharajas to raise the outcastes' position in Hindu society. In a real sense the Depressed Classes Mission was a forerunner to Gandhian programs for the "harijans."[26]

Perhaps because of the preoccupation of the members of the Prarthana Samaj with social and educational programs, its unique religious life declined in importance and by the early part of this century it was, indeed, little more than its name implies, a prayer

[23] Farquhar, *Modern Religious Movements in India*, p. 372. Chandavarkar was later the President of the Depressed Classes Mission Society.

[24] *ibid.*, p. 372.

[25] The Dev Samaj was founded in Lahore by Shiva Narayana Agnihotri in 1887. Agnihotri had been an energetic member of the Sadharan Brahmo Samaj, but he ultimately became an atheist and led a vigorous attack on the Brahmo, as well as on the Arya Samaj. Agnihotri founded several schools and gave primary attention to education of girls in addition to his other social reform endeavors. Following the example of the Arya Samaj, its greatest rival, the Dev Samaj undertook the work of uplift of depressed classes. *ibid.*, p. 173f.

[26] S. Natarajan cites the veteran social worker, V.A. Sovani's view that without the efforts of Gandhi and the pressure from Dr. Ambedkar the depressed classes would have progressed equally far under the auspices of the Depressed Classes Mission. *A Century of Social Reform*, p. 156. "Harijans" (Children of God) was Gandhi's term for the untouchables.

society. An historian of the Brahmo movement, Manilal C. Parekh, noted in the 1920's that the once-vigorous Prarthana Samaj with its many branches had declined to two units, the Bombay-Poona unit and another in Ahmedabad. In a certain sense, the Samaj movement in western India lost its identity through the results of its own teaching, namely the movements for social reform, social service, and education. Its membership's work for widows, orphans, depressed classes, and education of lower as well as upper castes, left little time for lives of purely religious consecration. But in any case, for India as a whole, the Bengali Brahmos made up for any lack of religious fervor in Bombay.[27]

The attention being given by Hindu reform organizations in the first decade of this century to the condition of the outcastes suggests the beginning of a third period in the history of India's social reform movement, one which is distinguishable from the individualistic and early nationalistic periods partly by its concern for the welfare of the common man, who made up the bulk of the nation's population, in addition to the cultural and political advancement of the high caste and English-educated groups. The political nationalist movement was evolving a strategy of mass appeal at that time, under the auspices of the extremists, which was a powerful reminder to the social reformers of their obligations to all Indians. The Prarthana Samaj had from the start been inspired by humanitarian and religious ideals, such as those of the Maharashtrian bhakti saints,[28] especially Tukaram, to undertake path-breaking work for the depressed classes. The Samaj maintained the connection between religion and social reform during a time when the dominant thrust of the social reform movement stemmed from secular nationalist principles. (Later, Gandhi's message and work reinforced the religious basis for social reform and extended humanitarian and spiritual ideals, like those of the Prarthana Samaj, to the platform of the National Congress. The Ramakrishna Mission and the Theosophical Society also furthered the rejoining of religious with social reform.)

[27] Support for this statement may be found in M.C. Parekh, *The Brahma Samaj*, chap. XI, esp. p. 209.

[28] See Chandavarkar's speech, "The Depressed Classes," in his *Speeches and Writings*, pp. 143-49.

By the turn of the century the major reform bodies were announcing their awareness of the greatest of India's social problems, the condition of the depressed classes. Gokhale's Servants of India Society in 1905 cited the "elevation of the depressed classes" as one of its six major aims. In 1908 the National Social Conference for the first time adopted a resolution calling for the gradual relaxation of caste restrictions. Previously the Conference, led by Brahmins, had been "on the defensive on caste matters,"[29] whether because it feared stronger attacks by the orthodox if it urged the liberalizing of the caste structure or because some members regarded low-caste aspirations as a possible menace to their position, it is difficult to say. Although a Conference resolution in 1896 had cited the duty of Hindus to raise the position of "Pariahs and other outcastes," there was no agreement until a decade later on the need to transform the system which Bhandarkar and Chandavarkar (and Gokhale outside the Conference) regarded as the root of India's social backwardness. To V. R. Shinde (of the Maratha caste), as well as to Chandavarkar, must go much of the credit for the Social Conference's decision to include resolutions favoring the end of caste discriminations in its annual business. Pressing home his crusade at the 1908 Conference session, Shinde called attention to the fact that "the Pariah has no place even in this pandal and even before this national altar . . . the Pariah has been prohibited from attending this national gathering." Alluding to the growing nationalist concern for the depressed classes because of anticipated political necessity, Shinde insisted that "the Pariah is to be elevated not because he is a part of our nation but because he is a human being. . . . This Resolution has been put to you in behalf of righteousness. But who cares for righteousness in these days? . . . I must present myself to you as a Nationalist, then alone I have some opportunity of hearing by you."[30] Gokhale, seldom reported in any active role in a Social Conference session, seconded Shinde's resolution.

The ideals of greater social justice for all Indians which the Conference and other social reform organizations enunciated in

[29] Natarajan, *op.cit.*, p. 109.
[30] *ISR*, Feb. 7, 1909, p. 268.

the 20th century (and which the Prarthana Samaj had urged a decade or two earlier) could scarcely have been included in the narrow 19th century definition of social reform in India. The 20th century movements which those ideals stimulated were led by organizations and men, for example, Gandhi and Dr. B. R. Ambedkar, whose interests and philosophies of social change differed markedly from those of the bulk of the original social reformers. The latter, as represented in the Social Conference and in local reform bodies, were often moved to speech and action in behalf of social unity, that is, the breaking down of caste discriminations or even social equality, but their main energies continued to be directed toward amelioration of social evils and restrictions of a limited kind. The influence of the new ideas of social justice (which, incidentally, were more akin to European social reform doctrines) on the traditional social reform movement originating in the 19th century will be discussed further in Chapter XII. A few words can appropriately be included here, however, on the relationship between the established social reform movement and the new movements for social justice, which only in the broadest sense could be called social reformist,[31] because in Bombay Presidency those relationships could be viewed in clearer outline than was the case elsewhere in India. The movements in Bombay were not, of course, models for movements elsewhere—Hindu social structure in Bombay was unique to that Presidency—nevertheless they illustrated the growing complexity of social reform in 20th century India.

In an oversimplified analysis one might say that there were three reform movements aiming toward social change in Maharashtra by the time of the First World War, each associated with one of the three major caste groupings in Maharashtra. The first was the predominantly Brahmin-led urban-centered movement,

---

[31] Note, e.g., Dr. Ambedkar's analysis: "It is wrong to say that the problem of the Untouchables is a social problem. For, it is quite unlike the problems of dowry, widow remarriage, age of consent, etc., which are illustrations of what are called social problems. Essentially, it is a problem of quite a different nature . . . the problem of the Untouchables is fundamentally a political problem [of minority versus majority groups]." B.R. Ambedkar, *What Congress and Gandhi Have Done to the Untouchables*, p. 190.

which has been the subject of discussion in the present study—the Prarthana Samaj and the National Social Conference as well as their various offshoots, and a few independent undertakings, such as Maharshi Karve's. The next was the non-Brahmin or anti-Brahmin movement begun by Jotiba Phule in the 1870's, whose main purpose came to be the gaining of social and religious recognition for the middle-ranking castes, in particular the Marathas. The third movement was that of the untouchable Mahars, who together with other outcastes made up 11 per cent of the population of the province of Bombay, led vigorously in the 1920's and thereafter by Dr. Ambedkar. The latter two movements, which were concentrated in rural areas, were not so much concerned with alterations, or "purifications" of social customs, nor with cultural elevation of the communities concerned *per se*, as with raising their respective positions *vis-à-vis* the higher caste groups.[32] Those movements, however, incorporated certain elements of the established doctrines of social reform: emancipation of women, breakdown of barriers between subcastes, temperance, and the need to widen educational opportunities. They thereby helped to broaden the appeal of the social reform movement. They did not generally acknowledge the need to adhere to the established social reform doctrines designed solely for the high castes: widow remarriage, improvement of the condition of widows, abolition of infant marriage and purdah, ending restrictions on overseas travel, and abolition of locally respected high-caste customs, such as Kulinism (polygamy) and female infanticide.[33]

[32] The oversimplification of this analysis makes impossible, among other things, the description of the interrelationships between the latter two movements, which initially received their inspiration from the same leaders, e.g., Phule, but which subsequently adhered to different doctrines and political platforms as their separate needs became evident. See the brief analysis of this problem by Dr. D.R. Gadgil in his foreword to Anjilvel V. Matthew, *Bhaurao Patil*, p. xiif. Bhaurao Patil, incidentally, like Phule, tried to raise the conditions of both the Marathas and the untouchable communities through education. His main work was carried on after the First World War.

[33] Evidence can be found of low castes adopting during the last century customs which high castes have specifically discarded in accordance with social reform teachings—e.g. widow non-remarriage, child marriage, purdah, restrictions on inter-dining—in order to improve their social status. However, as high

The non-Brahmin movement of Jotiba Phule, embodied in his
Satyashodhak Samaj (founded in 1873), made little impact in the
19th century, either on the educated Brahmins, who occupied
most of the influential government positions, or on the lower-caste
communities, who were concentrated in rural areas and had not
been exposed to modern education. Some suspicion existed, furthermore, that Phule might have been a Christian,[34] which alone
was enough to deny him a popular following. After Phule's death
the non-Brahmin movement languished until the 1900's, when it
was revived under the resourceful and tenacious Maharaja of
Kolhapur State, a princely remnant of the Maratha domains surrounded on all sides by the province of Bombay. Encouraged by
the British resident, the Maharaja began to raise the status of the
non-Brahmins in his State. In 1902 he reserved 50 per cent of the
civil service posts for communities other than Brahmin, Prabhu,
or Parsi,[35] so as to offset what he regarded as undesirable Brahmin
influences in his administrative system. Because of the lack of
suitable non-Brahmin candidates, however, the bulk of the Kolhapur civil servants remained Brahmin. Recognizing, as Jotiba
Phule had done, that the supremacy of the Brahmins rested on
their monopoly of religious and intellectual life in Maharashtra,
he endeavored to undermine that monopoly by sponsoring non-
Brahmin religious ceremonies and lower-caste education. Kolhapur's underwriting of the non-Brahmin movement was met by

castes have grown more unanimous in their adoption of reformed customs, the
low castes, especially in cities, have received a new image of prestige behavior
and have often "jumped the gap" between their relatively freer (and unorthodox) original customs and those of modernized and reformed high-caste communities and accepted the latter without an intervening stage of Sanskritization.
The author's interviews with Madras social reformers are the basis for this
statement. See also D.N. Majumdar, *Caste and Communication in an Indian
Village*, p. 331f.

[34] A.K. Ghorpade, *Mahatma Phule; Life and Work*, pp. 5-6. According to
Ghorpade, the reason for the popular suspicion that Phule had been converted
to Christianity was his acceptance of European financial assistance in running
a school for untouchables. Ghorpade denies that Phule embraced Christianity,
although he had Christian friends and he openly admired the educational work
of missionaries.

[35] See A. B. Latthe, *Memoirs of His Highness Shri Shahu Chhatrapati Maharaja of Kolhapur*, I, 154.

Brahmin refusal to give him Brahmanic rites, the *Vedokta* ritual, and the assertion that he was a Shudra, eligible only for the *Puranokta* ritual. At that, the Maharaja cut off state subsidies to the pundits, and the lines of opposition were firmly drawn.

The Satyashodhak Samaj was established in Kolhapur State in 1911 and gained the Maharaja's support. At a Samaj school, which the Maharaja founded, Marathas were trained to perform the sacred thread ceremony, chant Vedic hymns, and conduct marriage ceremonies, without the assistance of Brahmin priests. Recognizing that the secular Satyashodhak Samaj could never replace the established religious life of the people and hence their dependence upon Brahmin priests, however, the Maharaja turned his princely favor to the Arya Samaj, the only well developed Hindu religious movement which had successfully eliminated Brahmin leadership.[36] The Baroda Arya Samaj sent a missionary, Pundit Atmaramji, to found a branch in Kolhapur in 1918, and, with the Maharaja's backing, established schools and began to spread its doctrines.

The political impact of the non-Brahmin movement far surpassed its social impact in the post First World War period and is properly the subject for other studies. Though not a social reformer in the usual sense, the Maharaja of Kolhapur, who died in 1922, was a sincere believer in the equality of persons regardless of caste and aided the untouchables as well as his own Maratha community; on several occasions he ate publicly with untouchables. But, like Dr. Ambedkar, he realized that political power, not persuasion by personal example, was the only effective method of advancing the interests of an entire class of depressed communities.

The Maharaja placed himself in opposition not only to Brahmin religious interests in Maharashtra, but also to the advancing political nationalism in that province, led by Tilak and other Brahmins. Just as the Justice Party in Madras, founded in 1916 to represent non-Brahmin communities and precursor to the Dravidian movement, was regarded by many Brahmin Congressmen as

[36] Latthe, *op.cit.*, ii, 461. The Arya Samaj's repudiation of Brahmin leadership was probably a reason for its failure to attract most Maharashtrian social reformers.

anti-national, so also was Kolhapur's increasingly effective non-Brahmin crusade. The Maharaja maintained firm support for the government, not only because his constitutional position demanded it, but also because the government was attempting to squelch the Brahmin-led nationalists, enemies also of Kolhapur.[37]

It is not difficult to argue, as did A.B. Latthe, biographer of the Maharaja and for years the leader of the non-Brahmin movement in Kolhapur, that when faced with a challenge to their social superiority and political power by lower castes, the Maharashtrian Brahmins tended to forget their mutual differences and took a fairly unified stand to protect their status interests.[38] Even Chandavarkar, while urging his fellow Brahmins to do something for the low castes, cautioned the latter's leaders to cease "abusing the Brahmins and denouncing them as the class which has kept for their own aggrandisement the depressed classes out of the pale of Hindu society." He continued, "The Brahmins, like all the higher classes in every country, have their faults and narrowness; but what caste among us can take credit to itself for largeness of heart and breadth of vision?"[39] It was one thing, the Brahmin social reformers might have argued, to persuade the high castes to give up irrational discrimination against lower castes or to strive to improve the condition of the depressed classes, but another, and undesirable, thing for Brahmins to be forced out of their position of leadership. Indeed, most of the Maharashtrian social reformers when they exerted themselves in behalf of the lower orders of society did so in a spirit of humanitarian *noblesse oblige*.

The later movement in Maharashtra for emancipation of the untouchables, led by Dr. Ambedkar, took on still less of a social reformist character than the Kolhapur crusade. According to Ambedkar, the leader of the Scheduled Castes Federation and a Mahar untouchable by birth, there was a brief period when the untouchables looked to the reformers in the Social Conference as possible champions of their grievances. However, faith in the

[37] The revolutionary activities of some Kolhapur extremists in 1910 are cited in Govt. of Bombay, *Source Material for a History of the Freedom Movement*, II, 535-39.

[38] Latthe, *op.cit.*, I, 325.

[39] From a speech made in 1910. Chandavarkar, *Speeches and Writings*, p. 148.

Conference was shaken in 1895 when the antisocial reform faction in the Congress forced to a crisis the question of the priority of social over political reform and succeeded, as he viewed it, in collapsing the position of the reformers.[40] Nevertheless, the Social Conference leader, N.G. Chandavarkar, who was also the President of the Depressed Classes Mission Society, still retained enough influence among the untouchables in 1917 to gain the adherence of some of their representatives in Bombay to the Congress-Muslim League Scheme for post-War constitutional reform. At the time, the untouchables were calling upon the Congress to deviate from established practice and pass a resolution favoring the removal of disabilities imposed on them by Hindu society. The Congress decision in 1917 to pass for the first time such a resolution was interpreted by Ambedkar as a *quid pro quo* for the support to the Congress-Muslim League Scheme given by a Bombay conference of untouchable leaders held under the auspices of the Depressed Classes Mission Society.[41] But for the untouchables the final disillusionment with the nationalist leadership came, according to Ambedkar, when the Congress was under Gandhi's leadership after 1920 and failed to carry out its promises to work seriously for the depressed classes' uplift.[42] Whether or not Ambedkar's explanation of the loss of faith by the untouchables in the social reform movement, especially after that movement was taken over or superseded by Gandhi's Constructive Program, accurately represented the views of most untouchable leaders, he was right in stating that progress for the depressed classes after 1920 was a political, not a social, issue. The Congress

[40] Ambedkar, *op.cit.*, pp. 13-14, 190. Ambedkar mentioned that there was an expression at that time of the untouchables' response to the Congress decision: the burning of an effigy of the Congress in retaliation for the threat to burn the Congress pavilion if the Social Conference were held there. (p. 17) But he cited no evidence for this, and I have found no other specific reference to it. Jotiba Phule, before his death in 1900, made a public display, on behalf of low-caste rural workers, of repudiation of the Congress because of its failure to represent the average Indian peasant.

[41] *ibid.*, p. 18. S. Natarajan agreed with Ambedkar's analysis of the reasons for the Congress action, which he termed "an expedient which was not seriously implemented." *A Century of Social Reform*, p. 145.

[42] Ambedkar, *op.cit.*, chap. II.

and Gandhi saw the need of gaining the political support of untouchables, if only to assure their being counted as Hindus in the calculations for communal representation in the reformed legislatures. Ambedkar's and the untouchables' power increased as they were able to exact benefits from the Congress in return for their political support. Thus, by the end of the First World War the progress of the untouchables—and to an increasing extent all lower castes—became a function of the political power that they could exert. In 1925 the *Indian Social Reformer*, attributing that development to Gandhi's leadership in the Congress, rightly concluded that the current strategy for depressed classes uplift "actually reduced its value and importance as a movement of social, as distinguished from civic and political, equality."[43]

The Local Reform Movement in Madras

Although social reformers from the southern-most Presidency in the latter part of the 19th century made important contributions of individual talent and influence to the national social reform movement, their success in spreading reform ideas and establishing institutions for social purposes in their own region was less impressive, and continued to be so up to the First World War. Indeed, but for the notable work of a few reformers, one might doubt the existence in Madras of an organized social reform movement until well into the 20th century. The number of Madrasis receiving Western education swelled in the closing decades of the 19th century, and the accomplishments of many of them in modern thought and civil administration were widely recognized. But the region produced no reformer of national standing and only a few with lasting local influence.[44]

In 1892 the Madras Hindu Social Reform Association was

---

[43] Quoted by Natarajan, *op.cit.*, pp. 150-51.

[44] Cf. the editorial in the *Indian Social Reformer*, Oct. 7, 1900 (pp. 43-44), which referred to an "apparent depression and retrogression" in the Madras reform movement over the previous five years. One reason for this, the *Reformer* suggested, was the absence of leaders of "great general influence," such as those in other parts of the country. The *Reformer*, at that time, did not include the religious and social influence of the Theosophical Society and Vivekananda in the social reform category.

founded by what Ranade termed "the young Madras party,"[45] which included A. Subba Rau, K. Subba Rao, and B. Varada-charlu. That was the group associated with the *Indian Social Reformer*, which had lent support to the Age of Consent Bill, had agitated in behalf of the Hindu Gains of Learning Bill, and generally stood for radical reform measures.

The Gains of Learning Bill was first introduced into the Madras Legislative Council in 1891 by Sir V. Bhashyam Iyengar, a Council member, who was not counted among the liberal reformers and who was embarrassed by their enthusiastic support. For the latter, the Bill signified possible liberation from the fetters of family tradition, because it provided that a member of a joint family who received professional education at family expense would not be required by law to share with his extended family the earnings resulting from his special training. The attack which the Bill represented on the integrity of the joint family, the repository of upper-caste traditions and values, caused a commotion among the orthodox nine years later, in 1900, when the Madras Council finally passed the measure. By that time, however, the liberal social reform voices remaining in the Presidency had lost most of their audience, and the Governor, Sir Arthur Havelock, vetoed the Bill. (In 1930 a similar measure, sponsored by Dr. M. R. Jayakar, was made law by action of the Central Legislative Council.)

The initial enthusiasm of the young liberal reformers of Madras did not result in a steady expansion of the Hindu Social Reform Association. Its membership was small, and its organization reflected the exclusiveness of the high-caste, educated, reforming group in Madras. Instead of forming an organization with ambitious public purposes and a proliferating set of strong subunits, the reformers, forty-eight of them, bound themselves together by individual pledges to further certain aims: women's education, maintenance of pure personal and ethical standards, for example, abstinence from liquor. "Sympathetic" members were required to pledge not to keep a concubine, not to hire nautch dancers, and to avoid the use of liquor. Further pledges for full members called

[45] Ranade, *Miscellaneous Writings*, p. 120.

for education of girls under a member's direct control; postponement of the marriages of daughters until they reached puberty or
at least ten years of age ("in the case of those with whom marriage before puberty is obligatory"); postponement of the marriages of sons until they reached the age of eighteen; dining with
remarried couples and foreign-travelled Hindus "within the
sphere of [one's] own caste"; and joining in light refreshments
(served by Brahmins) with other caste individuals.[46] That
summed up the common denominator of liberal behavior in
Madras in the 1890's, but some young Brahmins experimented
with reform more boldly by eating openly with low-caste people
and otherwise defying parental and religious authority.

There was little expectation in Madras that the reformers
would attempt to spread their message and influence beyond the
limited circle of the highest castes. Restricted in their conceptions
of the "society" which should be reformed, the Madras reformers
could scarcely foresee the ambitious programs that were shortly
to emerge elsewhere in India. If the Bombay reformers were ex-
cessively judicious in not seeking the early overthrow of traditional
institutions, they did envision an ultimate transformation in
customary practices throughout the entire Hindu society. Madras
reformers, in contrast, seemed aware only of the need gradually to
liberalize and "purify" the lives of the dominant minority communities. Movements were under way to improve the conditions
of the lowest castes and outcastes, chiefly through education, but
they were organized, or at least stimulated, from outside of
Madras, for example, by the Christian missions, the Depressed
Classes Mission Society, the Servants of India Society, the Theosophical Society, and the Ramakrishna Mission.

More in tune with the sentiments of the young educated Madrasis than the Hindu Social Reform Association was the Theosophical Society,[47] whose renowned leader, Mrs. Annie Besant's
arrival in Madras nearly coincided with the formation of the
Society. Madame Blavatsky had moved the headquarters of the

[46] *Report of Eighth National Social Conference, Madras, 1894*, p. 66.
[47] A conveniently brief history of the controversial Society appears in Farquhar,
Modern Religious Movements in India, p. 208f; it might better be termed an
exposé.

255

Theosophical Society to Adyar, near Madras, in 1882, and there followed that notorious sequence of occultist frauds which finally culminated in Madame's hasty departure from India forever in 1885. Despite the tinge of scandal associated with the Society, Colonel Henry Steel Olcott, Madame Blavatsky's co-worker, and C. W. Leadbeater were able to spread its teachings throughout India. In the south, Colonel Olcott took an interest in the untouchables, and the Society began to establish schools for them in the 1890's; four schools were in operation by 1902, under the direction of Miss E. E. Palmer of the University of Minnesota. The number of Olcott Pariah Schools, as they were called, was compared by their founder, in 1902, to the approximately four thousand Christian missionary institutions for pariahs which were then in operation.[48] Olcott and Leadbeater were joined in 1893 by Annie Besant, who within a few years established herself as the outstanding revivalist of Hinduism in south India. The doctrines of Tilak, and later the Bengalis, were superfluous in Madras while Mrs. Besant held forth on the glories of ancient and modern Hinduism in all its facets. Social reformers stood nearly helplessly by while a great-voiced, cultivated Englishwoman besought Hindus to avoid the pitfalls of so-called Western advancement and revere their own great culture. A second powerful encouragement of revivalism in Madras appeared with Vivekananda's visits to the south in 1892 and 1897. No satisfactory reference to the social reform movement in Madras can be made without keeping in mind the extraordinary effects of Annie Besant and Vivekananda on that movement.[49]

By the early 20th century the Madras Hindu Social Reform Association had nothing particular to show for its decade of existence, and one of its few vigorous members, K. Natarajan, had moved to Bombay where the opportunities for propagating reform ideas were ample. A journal, *The Voice of Progress*, which the Association conducted and just managed to keep alive for eight months, reported in December 1901 that "The lack of moral energy, which has always been regarded as one of our defects,

[48] Henry S. Olcott, "The Poor Pariah," p. 23.
[49] A discussion of their contributions appears in Chapter XII.

seems to afford sufficient explanation of the torpor which over-takes so many movements in our country. The Committee [of the Association] has no special reasons to assign for not having done more than was done during the last twelve-month, but will re-iterate the oft-repeated hope that a new year may bring a fresh accession of strength and energy to the Association."[50] The "hope" was realized to some degree, in a possibly unexpected way. In January 1904, almost coinciding with the National Social Con-ference's annual session in Madras the previous month, Mrs. Besant, whose ideas on social reform had recently been altered, launched the Hindu Association in a successful attempt to shift the direction of reform away from rationalistic Western-inspired ideas of social efficiency and progress and toward the goal of "reform along national lines."

Justice Sir S. Subramania, Chairman of the inaugural meeting of the Association, explained that its aims were "substantially the same" as those of the Conference, but its methods differed.[51] The *Social Reformer*, Chandavarkar, and others in the national move-ment saw some danger in tying reform to religious revival. But the direction that Madras was taking could not be altered by that time, because it was also the direction being followed in other provinces as well. Because the Hindu Association adopted most of the planks of the social reformers' program and at the same time gave full expression to resurgent Hindu revivalism, it was an immediate success, and within a few years even the *Social Re-former* favorably noted its meetings and its programs. A major publication which presented the doctrines of the Association, *Hindu Social Progress*,[52] which appeared in Madras in 1904, was probably the most comprehensive and well argued statement ever produced of the case for "reform along national lines." The venerable reformer and founder of the National Social Confer-ence, Raghunatha Rao, gave his support to that doctrine and contributed an essay to *Hindu Social Progress*.

The two outstanding individual reformers in Madras Presi-

[50] *Voice of Progress*, I, 3 (Dec. 1901), p. 16.
[51] *ISR*, Jan. 10, 1904, pp. 234-46.
[52] Edited by N. Subba Row Pantulu.

dency were the Telegu Brahmins, Viresalingam Pantulu and Sir R. Venkata Ratnam Naidu, neither of whom deserted the original social reform movement in Madras despite the obvious appeals of the revivalists. Both men became members of theistic Samajes and both centered their activities outside of the city of Madras— Viresalingam at Rajahmundry and in the Northern Circars and Venkata Ratnam at Cocanada and Masulipatam. The former was a sort of hero among Madras reformers because of his long and devoted work for women's advancement, through education and marriage reform, and his reformed religious beliefs, which denied any religious sanction to the caste system.[53] The founder of the Rajahmundry Social Reform Association in 1878, Viresalingam went on to found the Widow Marriage Association in 1891 and a Widows' Home at Rajahmundry. He later brought to Madras City his efforts to rehabilitate Hindu widows and established there another Widows' Home, which was turned over to the Hindu Social Reform Association in 1902. In those years a message from Viresalingam occasionally appeared in the pages of the *Indian Social Reformer*:

THE HINDU WIDOWS' HOME

Will receive young widows of good character, belonging to castes where widow marriage is prohibited, and willing to be educated in the Presidency Training Institution, Egmore, for at least three years. Board and education will be given free of charge. In the case of minors, consent of parent or guardian will be necessary. Applications to be sent to Rao Bahadur K. Viresalingam Pantulu, Pursewakam, Madras.

Younger than Viresalingam and heavily influenced by him was R. Venkata Ratnam (1862-1939), who began his work in the late 1880's.[54] While a student at Madras Christian College, he had accepted the teachings of the Sadharan Brahmo Samaj missionary, Pundit Siva Nath Sastri, and became a Brahmo and later President

---

[53] For details of his career, see J. Gurunadhan, *Viresalingam: The Founder of Telegu Public Life.*

[54] Factual material on Venkata Ratnam is taken chiefly from K. Suryanarayana, *Sir R. Venkata Ratnam.*

of the Madras Brahmo Samaj. First a teacher in secondary schools and later principal of Mahboob College in Secunderabad, his most important educational work began in 1905 when he became Principal of the Pithapur Rajah (P.R.) College at Cocanada. During his long tenure (1905-1919) he managed to admit into the institution girls and members of the depressed classes. He later (1925) became Vice-Chancellor of Madras University and a nominated member of the Provincial Legislature. Largely due to his efforts, the "social purity movement," as it was called, got its start in Madras, whence it spread to the rest of India. Based on the pledge method of reform adopted by the Madras Hindu Social Reform Association, the movement focused on temperance and the abolition of nautch dancing. "To pursue pleasure as the purpose of life is the animal; to subject pleasure to the purpose of life is man," wrote Venkata Ratnam,[55] for whom the spectacle of public and temple nautch dancing by women (devadasis) of doubtful chastity, and liquor consumption by cultivated men were disgraceful blemishes on Indian society. With religious fervor Venkata Ratnam preached the gospel of purity and challenged all backsliders to renounce their dissolute ways. (One of the backsliders was Eardley Norton, an English lawyer in Madras and supporter of the National Congress, whose privileged position in nationalist circles was fearlessly challenged by Venkata Ratnam on the grounds that Norton had a mistress. The reformer won the day and Norton left Madras.)[56]

Raising to a broader plane the exposé of erotic temple practices which Karsondas Mulji had initiated decades earlier, but to which the reformers had only occasionally alluded, Venkata Ratnam condemned on moral grounds the entire system of popular mythology and representations of established Hindu divinities which seemed to convey sexual licentiousness, or what he called "sanctimonious sin." No wonder, he suggested, that Europeans, the Theosophists excluded, ridiculed and despised Hinduism. In stinging language he wrote that in Hinduism "Devotion, that

[55] In his essay on "Social Purity and the Anti-Nautch Movement," in Chintamani, *Indian Social Reform*, I, 258.
[56] Suryanarayana, *op.cit.*, p. 40; Natarajan, *op.cit.*, p. 100.

rejoicing of the soul in the graces of the Lord, degenerates into vagaries that embody themselves in images and pictures of ruthless realism with dissolute details, and express themselves in song or verse that bigoted partisans alone can mis-name piety. Esotericism, that panacea for all the spiritual ailments of India, would fain galvanise these dead bones into life; but while the subtle apologist points to a mystic inside . . . the simple world accepts the pleading to justify the palpable outside, and vulgar orgies and voluptuous leelas, amorous ditties and 'unholy *holis*' . . . stand out among the main features of the faith of the majority."[57] Venkata Ratnam's crusade against the nautch-girl, or devadasi,[58] was taken up by the National Social Conference and reform associations in all provinces, and it laid the foundations for the disappearance from contemporary India of nautch dancing—a precondition for dances of the classical type, such as the Bharat Natyam, being performed by respectable women.

The temperance movement, joined by missionaries and men of all political and social persuasions, reached truly national proportions when All-India Temperance Conferences were held in the Congress pavilions during the December conference sessions. Local temperance associations sent delegates to the national Conference, which in turn was associated with the Anglo-Indian Temperance Association, founded in London in 1888. The original purpose of Indian temperance societies was to reduce the alcohol consumption of educated, Westernized Indians through nondrinking pledges, but, as S. Natarajan observed, the movement later took on the color of rescuing the working classes.[59]

R. Venkata Ratnam, with a few other Madras reformers, tried to focus public attention on the condition of the depressed classes, especially the untouchable pariahs of the south. K. Ranga Rau had begun a free school for depressed classes at Mangalore in 1897, subsequently taken over by the Depressed Classes Mission,

[57] Chintamani, *op.cit.*, I, 264.

[58] For a convenient description of that institution, see Farquhar, *op.cit.*, p. 407f; also Milton Singer, "The Great Tradition in a Metropolitan Center: Madras," in American Folklore Society, *Traditional India: Structure and Change*, pp. 159-60.

[59] Natarajan, *op.cit.*, p. 158.

which was established in Madras in 1909, and Venkata Ratnam presided over antiuntouchability conferences in the Presidency. Certain princely states (notably Mysore), the Theosophical Society, and Christian missionaries did pioneering work for the depressed classes in the south. To the missionaries, in fact, who were the first to undertake the education of those classes, must go the credit for having begun the movement in all parts of the country. The reformers generally acknowledged that the successes of Christian missionary conversions from among the outcaste groups was the initial incentive for Hindus to come to the rescue of their dishonored countrymen.

In Madras, as in Bombay, some of the most influential social reformers were lawyers and judges, who occasionally were given nonofficial seats in legislative councils, where they might assist in the making of social legislation. Of a stature among Madras reformers comparable to Justice Telang's in Bombay was Justice C. (later Sir C.) Sankaran Nair. The movement for marriage reform among the Nayars (or Nairs) of the Malabar coast received its major encouragement from Sankaran Nair, whose caste and local origin gave him a personal concern in the matter. From his place in the Madras Legislative Council he introduced the bill which, after its passage in 1896, legalized marriages among the Nayars. An eminent Congress member (its President in 1897), he also helped to chart the new course for the Social Conference and the Madras Hindu Social Reform Association when, toward the end of the century, he insisted that reformers take a strong stand against the caste system and that reforming bodies resolve to undermine its inequities.

While taking into account the work of several devoted and influential social reformers in Madras during the late 19th and early 20th century, it seems fair to say that peninsular India awakened to the reformers' messages later than did regions to the north. Social conservatism, stemming from the rigidity of the caste system, has been cited as one reason for the delay.[60] Perhaps

[60] See Chap. IV for a discussion of this point. Other reasons for the relative weakness of social reform movements in Madras might lead one into a discussion of the psychological characteristics of south Indian Brahmins, the peculiar-

related to the unwillingness to move rapidly and experimentally in social matters was the hesitation to push forward with vigor and haste in political matters. An observer once wrote gratefully of the fact that Madras was quiet, politically, until as late as 1907, when Bipin Chandra Pal arrived and presented a lecture series which finally aroused Madrasis to the nationalist agitation going on in the rest of the country.[61] A review of the literature on social reform in Madras will show that the liberal, secular nationalist motive for social reform, so strongly expressed in Bombay and elsewhere, was not as strong in Madras. However, toward the end of the century the national leadership was beginning to swing away, in the reformer's jargon, from "rational" to "national" reform, and soon the Madras reformers, most of them Brahmin intellectuals, found the new philosophy of social change to their liking. The movement for "reform along national lines," which included Mrs. Besant, marked a break in the 19th century tradition and therefore will be dealt with separately.

The greatest social transformations in southern India and the Deccan in the 20th century have unquestionably resulted from the rising power and status of the low-caste communities, which have come about through political, not social reform movements. Madras reformers, like those in Bombay adapted their programs to the needs and demands of the depressed classes. Indeed, by the early 20th century it was scarcely plausible for a reformer from the south to propagate any relatively minor reform, for example, widow remarriage or prohibition of nautch dancing, unless he also demonstrated awareness of the massive injustices which were inherent in the very structure of society. Much of the active reforming work in behalf of those classes before the First World War, however, was of a social-service and educational variety rather than actual social reform; the bulk of it was done through organizations which were not essentially parts of the social reform movement.

---

ities of British administration in Madras, and the economic condition of the province—the length and complexity of which might not justify the conjectural ideas thereby brought out.

[61] *Notes on the Administration of the Hon'ble Sir Arthur Lawley, Governor of Madras, 1906-1911*, pp. 54-55.

In the social service field Madras may very well have led the rest of India by the First World War. Organizations from outside, including Christian missions, provided Madras with the example and the financial means of providing service, chiefly to the depressed classes and urban working people. The Theosophical Society under Colonel Olcott, the Depressed Classes Mission, the Servants of India Society, the Ramakrishna Mission, and even a small Arya Samaj mission were all engaged in educating and otherwise raising the cultural levels of the lowest classes before the War. After 1920, Gandhi's immense prestige was thrown into the struggle. A possibly significant aspect of social service work in Madras was the relatively large contribution made there by Europeans and Americans; the careers of Mrs. Besant and Mrs. Margaret Cousins were notable examples of the influence that foreigners have had in Madras.[62]

The Failing Reform Movement in Bengal

By the 1880's Bengal had achieved the reputation among reformers as the province least hospitable to the social reform movement. When Social Conferences were held in Calcutta a group of sympathetic spectators could ordinarily[63] be gathered together by Narendra Nath Sen, the Bengali Conference stalwart and editor of the *Indian Mirror*, but few men from his province could be found to report that constructive reform work was being done. Perplexed about why the most intellectually advanced province should be lagging behind, Ranade, Chandavarkar, and other national reform leaders rebuked the Bengalis for failing to live up to the standards set by Rammohun Roy and Vidyasagar. But

[62] Further study might fruitfully be made on the relations between Europeans and Indians in various parts of the country and the impact of their relations on the nationalist movement. The Madrasi, Prof. S. Satthianadhan, could write at the end of the last century that "the relations between the Natives and Europeans in our Presidency is far more cordial than in any other part of India. At all events there is more sympathy between the two races here than in Bengal. We natives of the benighted Presidency had our equilibrium undisturbed even during the discussions of the Ilbert Bill." Chintamani, *op.cit.*, I, 246.

[63] In 1896 hardly a respectable showing was produced when only two or three score students and less than a score of elderly men made up the audience for Ranade's inaugural address. S. Natarajan, *op.cit.*, p. 93.

none of them ventured to do missionary work in Bengal, as they did in Madras and elsewhere—Bengali intellectual life was too formidable and Bengalis too unreceptive to preachers from outside for anyone to adopt that course.

Bengalis themselves seemed to be divided on the question of whether or not their province was backward in social reform. Surendranath Banerjea, who always showed respect to the reformers and occasionally lent his prestige to a reform endeavor, acknowledged in 1904 the moribund state of Bengal's reform movement. In a Calcutta speech honoring Rammohun Roy Banerjea felt "bound to say that the social reform movement in Bengal is going down. . . . Whatever is being done is done through the slow operation of time and beneficent influences. No effort is made to energize the movement. I fear the falling-off in this respect is largely due to the revival movement which has inspired us with a sort of belief that everything in our institutions is perfect. . . . I yield to none in my veneration of my native land. . . . But no ancient system can long endure without the necessary changes. A system without the means of change is without the means of conservation."[64] No better evidence of the state of the social reform movement in Bengal can be found than in Banerjea's remarks, although the reason given for the "falling-off," the revival movement, is only part of the explanation—the political life of Bengal must be included.

But there was another side of the coin to be examined in assaying the status of reform in Bengal, namely the social changes taking place there without the prodding and advice of local social reformers. The *Indian Messenger* tried in 1906 to reverse the usual image of the local reform movement in these words: "There is an impression abroad that social reform is not making any progress in Bengal. This is not correct. Though it is true that no organized systematic effort has been made recently in Bengal to further the cause of reform, in actual practical reform no other province can yet even approach Bengal. The Hindu society of Bengal has been silently but thoroughly leavened with the spirit of reform." The article went on to note that nowhere else but

[64] *ISR*, Oct. 16, 1904, p. 78.

Bengal could a great dinner be held at which Hindus, Muslims, and Europeans all ate together; that Bengal sent many more young men abroad for study than other provinces; and that higher education for women had made more progress there than elsewhere.[65] Similar views were expressed by other Bengalis who argued that the earlier social progress of the province was so genuine and widespread that a decline in social reform endeavors toward the end of the century did not mean that Bengal was backward, compared with the rest of India, in social matters. The *New India*, Bipin Chandra Pal's newspaper, lamented in 1902 that "Bengal, which, only a few years back, led the army of social reform, should have fallen into a sort of torpor and inactivity and should look on coldly and dreamily while the other provinces are showing praiseworthy signs of activity." But, it continued, "the work done in years past . . . has not been in vain. Notwithstanding Bengal's present inactivity, it will be found that in actual progress in social matters—in liberal ideas and ways of living— she is still far ahead of her sister provinces."[66]

The divergent views on Bengali social reform can be explained. One comparatively small group of Bengalis, made up of Westernized men, most of them Brahmos, was indeed more "advanced" (in the reformer's sense) than any group elsewhere in the country. It had more completely abandoned customary restrictions on social intercourse, and especially on the freedom of women, than most reformers had done in other provinces, and its reformed religious practices and educational advancement set the standard for the rest of India. But in reaching that position the Brahmos had left the bulk of Hindu society far behind and virtually unaffected by the new ways. Narendra Nath Sen defended the Bengali reform movement in the Calcutta Social Conference of 1896 by citing his province's progress, especially in female education,

---

[65] Article reproduced in *ISR*, Oct. 21, 1906, p. 89. The figures on Indian students in England would probably bear out the assertion that Bengalis were more numerous than others. In 1896 Ranade cited the following numbers of Hindus studying in England, by provinces: Bengal, 56; Bombay and C.P., 42; Madras, 13; Punjab, 36; Mysore, 1; Kathiawar, 1; Hyderabad, 5. *op.cit.*, p. 177.

[66] Issue of Dec. 18, 1902, as quoted in S. Tattvabhushan, *Social Reform in Bengal*, p. 2.

but he then added that his assessment "holds good chiefly of the Indian Christian, Brahmo, and the England-returned classes."[67]

The cultural and religious revival movement cited by Banerjea, was emerging in Bengal in the 1870's, and its negating effects on the social reform movement were immense. The then leading reformer, Keshub Chandra Sen, who had founded the Indian Reform Association in 1870, could scarcely have maintained the standing and influence of the movement in the face of the new forces in Bengali intellectual life, even if he had remained faithful to his own cause and had kept his followers united. Sen's ideas on social reform, acquired partly in England, were too Westernized to be acceptable to most Bengalis, who were then enthusiastically discovering for the first time the refinements and grandeur of their traditional heritage. Among Brahmos his social reform leadership was destroyed after the Kutch-Behar marriage alliance in 1878.[68] By the 1880's Bengal had no social reformer whose personality and prestige were powerful enough to stem the revivalist and antireformist tide.

The close association in Bengal of social reform and Westernization—closer than in any other province—aroused a suspicion of reform based on political grounds, even before a similar suspicion and open hostility to reform developed in Bombay under the influence of Tilak. It was true that leading political figures in Bengal, such as Banerjea, W.C. Bonnerjee, Ananda Mohan Bose, and Bipin Chandra Pal, sympathized and even actively supported social reform causes in their own province. Although none of them chose to participate actively in the Social Conference, they did not set out to undermine it, as Tilak was doing. But Bengali politics, dominated by Brahmos and others who could scarcely be distinguished from Brahmos, skirted around the problem of the relationship of social to political reform; social and religious innovation, as the Brahmos had demonstrated, were private matters and need not become subjects for public political controversy. In the political echelons below the nationally known Bengali leaders, in many newspapers, on the stage, and among

[67] Presidential address, Chintamani, op.cit., III, 193.
[68] See M.C. Parekh, The Brahma Samaj, p. 100f. and p. 211.

students opposition to social reform and the reformers was growing unchecked in the latter decades of the century. The Age of Consent Bill served to release much of the potential antagonism toward the reform movement and toward the government which favored it—antagonism based partly on the desire to conserve and protect Hindu religion and culture against alien influences and partly on an assertion of national political self-respect. As Bipin Chandra Pal explained, "This spirit of self-assertion and this growing anti-British feeling materially changed the angle of our thoughts and activities in every department of life, religious and social, no less [than] political."[69] When the reformers in the 20th century revised their doctrines to conform to the ideas of cultural and political nationalism, they met not vigorous opposition but, perhaps worse, indifference. For by that time, notably after the Partition of 1905, most Bengali nationalists had given themselves over completely to politics, and with a puissance never before seen in India.

One further line of analysis suggestive of the conditions underlying the social reform movement in Bengal—as opposed to Bombay, the center of the national reform movement—appears in the writings of Bipin Chandra Pal, whose sensitivity to the intellectual and social currents of his day was unmatched among Bengalis writing in English. In 1881 he passed through Bombay en route to Madras and made the following observations, which deserve reproduction without further comment.

"Bombay was socially far ahead of Bengal. Bengal, or the new Bengal which was building before our eyes, was the creation, really of the British. All our progressive movements had been born of the inspiration of freedom and democracy taught to us from our contact with modern European, particularly modern British, culture through our schools and colleges. But Bombay was different. Bombay had very recently a national state and Administration. In Maharashtra the Peshwas governed the people to almost the middle of the nineteenth century, that is, about fifty years or thereabout before I first saw it. And this national State had developed certain traits in the Mahratta people and called

[69] Pal, *Memories of My Life and Times*, II, lxi.

into being certain social institutions and customs under pressure of what can best be described as the biological requirements of the Mahratta society, which we had no knowledge of in Bengal. Female education and the freedom of social intercourse and movement of respectable Mahratta ladies was a new and inspiring experience which I had in Bombay. Both the Parsis and the Mahrattas did not observe the *zenana* seclusion or the *purdah*, which is universal among higher class Hindus and Moslems in Bengal and Upper India. While we in Bengal were fighting even in the Brahmo Samaj for higher education of ladies and the removal of the *purdah*, these social evils were practically absent from the Indian community of Bombay. And all this made a very profound impression upon me during my first visit to this city."[70]

The leadership of the 19th and early 20th century social reform movement in Bengal was chiefly in the hands of members of the Brahmo Samaj, in particular the Sadharan branch, which broke away from Keshub Chandra Sen after the Kutch-Behar marriage and tried to maintain the social consciousness and reforming impulse which Sen had given to many Brahmos. Keshub Chandra himself, after the 1878 split and the inauguration of his New Dispensation, no longer included social reform as an important aspect of his religious leadership.[71] Charitable and educational enterprises were continued by Sen's faction, but the social reform activities subsequently carried on by Brahmos were undertaken by the larger faction, the Sadharan Brahmo Samaj. Ananda Mohan Bose, a founding member of the Sadharan Brahmo Samaj, led the new body in several of its reform and service endeavors. Yet he was recognized then, and is today, chiefly as a political leader of the nationalist movement. Bose

[70] *ibid.*, I, 392.
[71] Even before 1878, as M.C. Parekh pointed out, Sen "came to see clearly that the Brahma Samaj was more a social community than a Church of God, that it was busy with outward forms and organizations borrowed from the West . . . , and that it was identified principally with social reform and rationalism rather than with higher religion." Sen therefore aimed at restoring the predominantly spiritual meaning of the Samaj, which, he reasoned, would also widen its popular appeal. Parekh, *op.cit.*, p. 147.

and his colleagues, including Dwarkanath Ganguli, Siva Nath Sastri, and Durgamohan Das, took a serious interest in education for girls and women. The Sadharan Brahmo Samaj added to the number of girls' schools already under Brahmo direction, and daughters of Sadharan Brahmos made up the bulk of the early women graduates from Calcutta University. The literacy rate among Brahmo women was the highest of any community in India.[72] Boys' schools were also founded, and a Brahmo College, the City College in Calcutta, in the 1880's set a new educational standard by introducing courses in carpentry and instruction in physical and moral development.[73] Philanthropic work had been a feature of the Brahmo Samaj since 1832, and the Sadharan branch greatly expanded the endeavors in relieving famines and meeting similar public crises. Schools, dispensaries, orphanages, and a deaf and dumb training program were some of its achievements in behalf of lower castes in Bengal. Siva Nath Sastri began social work for the depressed classes in the 1890's, and in 1908 a Depressed Classes Mission was started. Much of the Samaj's work was among tribal people in Bengal and Assam, who were urged to attend Brahmo schools established for them and even to embrace Brahmoism.[74]

The Sadharan Brahmo Samaj's practical social work was an impressive reminder of the continuing dedication of some Brahmos to the welfare of society. However, the Samaj did not extend its educational and social service drives into social reform crusades or organizational work. With the exception of Bipin Chandra Pal, who could not be regarded as an active Samajist, Brahmos almost ignored, in their public careers, the issues which reformers elsewhere considered crucial.

In a unique category among Bengali social reformers was Sasipada Banerji, whose endeavors appear more nearly like those of Maharshi Karve or the Prarthana Samajists than those of his

[72] Gupta, *Studies in the Bengal Renaissance*, p. 502.

[73] The latter were introduced in response to the great criticism among educated Indians of the overwhelmingly academic curricula of the government schools— the "moral poverty" that they represented. Many Indians felt that higher education should include more than mere training of the mind.

[74] Parekh, *op.cit.*, p. 247.

Brahmo contemporaries, who were chiefly engaged in furthering the religious gospel of their Samaj. Banerji regarded himself as a reformed Hindu, rather than a Brahmo and in 1873 established his own religious body, the Sadharan Dharma Sabha, many years later called the Devalaya.[75] Banerji was closely associated with the Sadharan Brahmo Samaj and received his inspiration for reform from Keshub Chandra, but his work was his own and cannot properly be included under the reforming work of the Brahmo Samaj. His career spanned the last four decades of the century.[76]

In the 1860's Sasipada Banerji began private efforts to educate young girls, including widows, and soon he was running a small girls' school in Baranagore, near Calcutta, with the aid of his wife, whom he had taught to read and write. Mary Carpenter, an Englishwoman who took up the cause of Indian female education, gave Banerji encouragement, and together they tried unsuccessfully to gain government support for normal school education of adult women, so that the latter could then teach Hindu girls, even in the zenana (the women's section of high-caste households). Vidyasagar, more conservative than Banerji in his attitude toward female emancipation, opposed the idea, and Keshub Chandra gave it no encouragement, and therefore the scheme languished in Bengal. But the Madras and Bombay governments were able to move ahead with the normal school proposal, which, according to the Bengali, Tattvabhushan, in 1904, "helped them to be so much ahead of this province at the present time."[77] Finally, in 1873, Banerji saw his normal school project realized with the establishment of the Hindu Mahila Vidyalaya

[75] *ibid.*, pp. 255-57.

[76] See Chapter ix for his connection with the widow remarriage movement. Accounts of Banerji's career may be found in B.N. Motiwala, "The Life and Career of Mr. Sasipada Banerji"; Tattvabhushan, *Social Reform in Bengal*; and A. Gupta, *Studies in the Bengal Renaissance*, pp. 492-93. Banerji, a Brahmin, born in 1840, was from a modestly situated family; his career was in government service.

[77] S. Tattvabhushan, *op.cit.*, p. 62. Due chiefly to the Parsis, Bombay city advanced more swiftly than Calcutta or Madras in female education through the high school level, having in 1913, 10 high schools for girls (8 run by Parsis) to 2 in Calcutta (both Brahmo), and none in Madras. O'Malley, *Modern India and the West*, p. 456.

near Calcutta. A similar institution, the Banga Mahila Vidyalaya, was founded in 1876 by Durgamohan Das and Ananda Mohan Bose. By the 1880's in Bengal the education of high-caste girls and women was no longer a novelty, and even Keshub Chandra supported a normal school.

Simultaneously with his high-caste female education crusade Banerji strove to ameliorate the condition of the low-caste working people of Calcutta, then in the early stages of its development of the jute industry. He set up a night school for factory workers in the 1860's, an inspiration for similar schools founded later in Bombay, and in 1870 a Workingmen's Club. In 1871 he journeyed to England, accompanied by his wife, probably the first Brahmin lady to visit that country. A year earlier Keshub Chandra Sen had stimulated interest among English men and women in Indian female education, and the National Association in Aid of Social Progress and Education in India had been founded in England to direct support for Indian education. Banerji's visit encouraged further English help, both financial and with teaching personnel, and the reformer himself returned to India with new enthusiasm for female education and the improvement of the laboring classes. He began to publish the *Bharat Sramajivi* (Indian Laborer), a monthly illustrated paper selling for one pice—said to have been the first labor journal in India—[78] and in 1873 a weekly journal publicizing workers' grievances was started.

Banerji's preoccupation, however, was to improve the treatment that Hindu society gave to women, and especially to widows. When his first wife died, he married a widow, and together, through persuasion and plotting, they managed to arrange remarriages for scores of Hindu widows. In one case Banerji's arrangements shocked even his Brahmo friends: in 1868 he sponsored the remarriage of his widowed niece to a non-Brahmin man, a match regarded as "among the most violently radical that have as yet been performed among the most radical followers of Babu Kesavchandra Sen."[79] More far-reaching than remarriage was ed-

[78] Gupta, *op.cit.*, p. 493.
[79] Tattvabhushan, *op.cit.*, pp. 88-89.

ucation for the otherwise statusless widow. Banerji's female schools admitted widows, but the latter's complete rehabilitation as useful members of society did not begin until he founded the Widows' Home in 1887 in Calcutta, the first such institution in India. With a curriculum of home economics in addition to academic subjects, the Home was conducted along orthodox lines, which the Sadharan Brahmo Samaj regarded as unenlightened. When Banerji was forced to give up his connection with the Home in 1902 the Samaj refused to take charge of it because of its orthodox character and instead set up its own institution. But special education for Hindu widows and efforts to remarry them virtually ceased in Bengal after Banerji's withdrawal from active life after 1903.

By the end of the century in Bengal, social reform by individual crusaders was virtually at an end and the National Social Conference was making no headway. Rather desperately searching for evidence of reform in that province Ranade cited the "right earnest" efforts being made to persuade caste leaders to readmit men who had crossed the seas,[80] hardly a major crusade in view of Bengal's already notable record of sending men abroad for study. The sea-voyage movement, as it was called, sprang up in each province as the problem of foreign-traveled, high-caste Hindus became acute. Relying on the formula, "reform along lines of least resistance," reformers could press for readmission to their castes of overseas travelers with good assurance of success, because even the orthodox pundits recognized that their sanctions against travel abroad were of little avail. After a few celebrated cases in each province of refusal of caste panchayats to readmit returning men, the pundits usually gave way. *Pro forma* ceremonies to readmit men after a trip abroad became standard practice in all communities, so that, as Bhandarkar once put it, Hindus gave up their castes at Apollo bunder when they left for England and reassumed them upon their return.[81] Pressure from the National Social Conference and local associations, strongest

[80] Ranade, *op.cit.*, p. 131.
[81] Bombay Social Conference Presidential address, 1912, in Social Conference Addresses, p. 44.

in the 1890's and early 20th century, probably had the effect of at least reducing the formal penalties imposed on sea voyagers.[82]

Narendra Nath Sen, President of the Tenth Social Conference, could defend Bengal's recent record in social reform by mentioning only the sea-voyage movement and an agitation to reduce marriage expenses and by citing the Bengali (chiefly Brahmo) record in female education.[83] Sen was President of the Bengal Social Reform Association and apparently was in charge of arrangements for Social Conference sessions held in Calcutta. His reminders to Bengalis that their province was the birthplace of Rammohun Roy, Vidyasagar, and Keshub Chandra Sen were not enough to recruit a significant following for either the provincial association or the National Conference. What saved appearances for Bengal at the latter's sessions was the willingness of Bengali Congressmen at least to put in appearances. As for the Social Reform Association, the very year of its establishment, long after similar bodies had been set up in other provinces, marks the *coup de grace* of the faltering social reform movement in Bengal. For 1905 was the year of Lord Curzon's partition of the province. The first *Report* of the Association announced its reform program of urging free mass education, female education, moral instruction in schools, a rise in the marriage age and curtailment of dowries, and then acknowledged that "It is a matter of great regret that the Bengal Social Reform Association have not been able to take any active steps in furtherance of any of the objects above stated owing principally to the great absorption of public interest and attention in Bengal in the great Partition and Swadeshi questions."[84]

[82] A great many tracts on the overseas travel question appeared; fair examples were: "The Hindu Sea-Voyage Movement in Bengal," by The Standing Committee on the Hindu Sea-Voyage Question; A. Mahadeva Sastri, "The Hindu Sea-Voyage Problem." A lengthy plea by Bishan Narayen Dar that residence in England improves the character and manners of young Hindus appeared in Chintamani, *op.cit.*, I, 188.

[83] Chintamani, *op.cit.*, III, 193. The near absence in Bengal of organized social reform endeavors, outside of the Brahmo Samaj, was confirmed in the *Report of the 6th National Social Conference, 1893*, p. 52f.

[84] Quoted in *ISR*, Jan. 14, 1906, p. 233.

Professor R.C. Majumdar[85] and other Indian historians have traced the demise of active social reform in Bengal to its source in the political nationalist and cultural revivalist teachings of influential men such as Raj Narain Bose and Bankim Chandra Chatterjee, and there seems to be no evidence that would cast doubt on that analysis. Reformers and their sympathizers in late 19th century Bengal saw what was happening and were powerless to affect it. Raj Narain Bose of the conservative Adi Brahmo Samaj had already enunciated in the 1860's the argument which no liberal reformer could easily refute: in Bipin Chandra Pal's words, that social reform, imitative of Western ways, "if not checked very definitely . . . would strengthen the hold of the alien political authority established in the country by adding to it the moral and spiritual hold which the introduction of European customs and institutions in our society would inevitably bring about."[86] By the end of the century Mano Mohan Ghose, founder of the *Indian Mirror,* attested to the fact that there was "a decided reactionary tendency among a large and influential section of my educated countrymen in Bengal, whose well-meaning efforts have been directed towards opposing any further influx of European civilization into the country."[87] Reform movements in other provinces partially escaped the fate of the Bengali movement because elsewhere cultural revivalism was less intense, political thought less radical, and reformers less committed than the Brahmo Samaj to the assimilation of Western social ideals.

A Note on the Princely States

The more enlightened of the Indian princes, notably in Mysore, Baroda, and Travancore, took some interest in promoting social reform in their domains and occasionally in British India. Their record is by no means impressive when it is evaluated in terms of their often immense influence and capacity to evoke responses from their subjects. Their achievements were mostly legislative, but in a few cases they extended their patronages to local reform

[85] See his *Glimpses of Bengal in the Nineteenth Century,* Lect. III, esp. p. 74.
[86] Pal, *Memories of My Life and Times,* I, 263.
[87] Chintamani, *op.cit.,* IV, 237.

associations. The amount of legislation on social matters passed by the various states around the turn of the century probably exceeded that passed by British Indian governments; the princes had little worry over political repercussions. This social legislation, however, was seldom enforced and had little immediate effect.

Mysore was the first of the states to enact social legislation. Its Government, after obtaining a favorable opinion from the Representative Assembly, passed a law in 1894 regulating the age of marriage: no girl below the age of eight could be legally married, and ill-assorted marriages were forbidden. In 1909 a law was enacted prohibiting the dedication of girls as devadasis in temples. The Mysore Government gave special support to the State's social reform body, the Aryadharmmajjvini Sabha, which propagandized for marriage reform and the breakdown of caste discrimination.

By the beginning of this century Baroda moved into first place among states, so far as social reform was concerned, and retained that position. In 1901 a Hindu Widow Remarriage Act was enacted, modeled on the 1856 Act of British India. In 1904 the Baroda Government enacted an Age of Consent Act and a marriage law, far in advance of public support for any such reform, which fixed the minimum ages at sixteen and twelve.[88] A Civil Marriage Act, with features similar to the Brahmo Marriage Act, was enacted in 1908. Baroda's marriage legislation continued to be in advance of British India's until after Independence. The Gaekwar of Baroda took a more than formal interest in social reform, and especially pressed for women's education and emancipation. He gave an address to the National Social Conference in 1904 and patronized social reform organizations in Gujarat. V.R. Shinde's Depressed Classes Mission got its start in Baroda, where the Government instituted schools for untouchables.

The states of Indore, Travancore, and even Kashmir, as well as a few smaller domains, would figure in any full account of the social reform movements in princely India.

[88] Predictably, it had to be loosely enforced and was of little consequence to most of the Gaekwar's subjects; its educational effect on literate Hindus, however, was probably important. See Farquhar, op.cit., p. 399.

XI

THE LOCAL SOCIAL REFORM MOVEMENTS

IN NORTHERN INDIA

The North-Western Provinces[1] and the Punjab were the remaining two provinces of British India in which local social reform movements flourished in the period preceding the First World War. In those provinces the movements were uniquely organized, and voluntary or general associations assumed a relatively minor place in them. Instead, organized social reform by Indians was carried on primarily under the auspices of caste organizations and the Arya Samaj, with minor additional support coming from religious and cultural associations, such as the Brahmo Samaj.

In the years under review the Punjabis appeared to be more receptive to reform ideas than the educated inhabitants of the provinces to the south. The Social Conference Report for 1894 summed up the Punjab reforming activity in these words: "Reform work in Punjab is carried on through the agency of Baradari or Caste Associations, which are established in all large towns, their action being confined to their respective castes. This action is not steady, but at times is supplemented by the activity of Arya Samajes, the Brahmo Samaj, the Singh [Sikh] Sabha, the Sanatana Dharma Sabha, and other societies."[2] In 1895 Ranade con-

[1] In 1877 the North-Western Province (corresponding with the province of Agra) and Oudh were united under the same administration, and in 1902 the name was changed to United Provinces of Agra and Oudh. In 1901 the Punjab lost its frontier districts, beyond the Indus, which were formed into the new Northwest Frontier Province.

[2] *Report of the Eighth National Social Conference*, p. 80. By 1912, when this pattern of reform endeavors had spread to the United Provinces, Ganga Prasad

cluded that the Punjab—because of the reforming influence there
of the Sikhs—was more advanced than the North-Western Provinces, where, he said, "neither the Brahmo Samaj nor the Arya
Samaj has produced any effect." He continued remorsefully, "They
are a very slow mass to move. The present condition of the North-
west Provinces with all their natural advantages of position and
climate is characterized by lethargy and backwardness. . . . But
the rising generation and the fruit of the University education
[Allahabad University was incorporated in 1889] are devoting
their best attention to this question and are trying to reform the
usages of their caste."[3]

In both the Punjab and the North-Western Provinces the National Social Conference had its outposts of influence, the local
general reform associations, and in the North-Western Provinces
Provincial Social Conferences were held. With few exceptions,
the participants in the Conference and in local voluntary associations were active members of the Arya (or sometimes the Brahmo)
Samaj or one of the caste reform bodies. Lala Devraj, Lala Munshi Ram, Lala Hans Raj and Lala Lajpat Rai of the Punjab; and
Lala Baijnath of the North-Western Provinces were some of the
chief Social Conference supporters.

Social Reform in the Caste Movements

The constructive and progressive functions which castes, as
organized groups, could perform were recognized by British
administrators in the north Indian plains early in the 19th century. Some of the earliest and most effective British efforts to
promote social reform were directed toward caste organizations
in the Punjab, Rajputana, and the North-Western Provinces and
took place by persuasion rather than legislation.[4] In Bengal, the

told the U. P. Social Conference at Cawnpore that "The work of social reform in
these provinces centres round the Arya Samaj and the several caste conferences. . . ." Social Conference Addresses, p. 88.

[3] Ranade, *Miscellaneous Writings*, pp. 156-57. At the same Conference session
Ranade attributed the "backward" conditions in the N.-W. Provinces to the delay
in establishing Western education in those regions. *ibid.*, pp. 165-66.

[4] The efforts to abolish infanticide of Charles Raikes of North-Western Prov-

Deccan, and peninsular India, on the other hand, the caste system had nothing to recommend itself in the estimations of most Western observers; it appeared to be an antiquated and often diabolical means of subjugating the majority of Hindus to hereditary servitude and degradation and simultaneously a repository for superstitious ideas. Indian reformers also recognized the differences in the structure of castes between the Hindustani region and those further south. While they came to condemn the caste system as it operated in most of the country, some of them at least saw its possible virtues in the north, where the bulk of the Hindu population was composed of intermediate level castes, where the authority of the Brahmins was weakest, and where the lowest castes or outcastes had some opportunities of improving their condition.

In no small measure due to the emergence of Western-style corporate caste bodies in both north and south India, the function of caste in Hindu society has radically altered in the last century, as many writers have endeavored to show.[5] The Indian political arena today provides the setting for the most effective assertion of the interests of particular castes. It is likely also that caste interests and loyalties are the most influential factors in current Indian political life.[6] One half century ago, however, most caste

---

inces, M.R. Gubbins of Agra, and John Lawrence of the Punjab have been surveyed in M.N. Das, *Studies in the Economic and Social Development of Modern India*, chap. IX.

[5] e.g., M.N. Srinivas, "Caste in Modern India," *Journal of Asian Studies*, XVI, in which the author shows that strengthening of caste ties and the new functions which castes perform are the result of British rule, in particular the expansion of communications and the development of a representative political system. See also F.G. Bailey, *Caste and the Economic Frontier*.

[6] The new political importance of caste, operating within the limits of linguistically defined regions, has been unquestionably established in Selig Harrison's *India: The Most Dangerous Decades*. Harrison's sober conclusions might be tempered if read in conjunction with the ideas presented by Lloyd I. and Susan H. Rudolph in "The Political Role of India's Caste Associations," *Pacific Affairs*, XXXIII, 1, esp. p. 9: "The caste association brings political democracy to Indian villages through the familiar and accepted institution of caste. In the process, it is changing the meaning of caste. By creating conditions in which a caste's significance and power is [*sic*] beginning to depend on its numbers, rather than its ritual and social status, and by encouraging egalitarian aspirations among its members, the caste association is exerting a liberating influence. . . . its successful

groups were directing their primary attention to improvements in their social and economic status; indeed, political questions were barred from consideration by the important caste conferences and sabhas. Many of the caste associations which were formed initially for nonpolitical purposes later assumed political importance, while retaining their earlier interest in social and economic advancement.

The creation of caste associations was itself a radical departure from the traditional patterns of caste organization, because the new associations had to depend to a large extent on voluntary, rather than ascriptive, membership, at least by the caste leaders.[7] Relying on persuasion and education to recruit members of the same caste into a sabha or samiti, they often collected dues and demanded adherence to new regulations adopted by leading representatives at caste conferences. The new regulations to which caste members were asked to subscribe did not always reflect a prime concern by the conferences or sabhas in social reform, as it was currently defined. Some caste bodies—this held true chiefly for the lowest castes—urged on their members the adoption of traditional Brahmanic customs in order to emulate higher caste behavior and thus possibly improve their status. But the largest and most influential of the associations, which emerged in northern India, incorporated into their programs for caste advancement many of the principles advocated by social reformers. The leaders of the National Social Conference acknowledged the caste associations as social reform societies, and several caste leaders became prominent in Conference proceedings (although it does not seem likely that the caste associations received the inspiration for their founding from the Social Conference, as Lala Baijnath, the Vaishya leader, once suggested).[8]

An important minority of social reformers always urged that

---

assertions of privilege and rights are in many ways comparable to the extension of corporate feudal liberties which characterize the development of English liberalism. They are perhaps more truly indigenous assertions of liberties than the liberalism of the modern Indian middle classes."

[7] Rudolphs, op.cit., p. 8.

[8] In his Presidential address to the National Social Conference, Lucknow, 1900, Chintamani, *Indian Social Reform*, III, 209.

the proper and most effective vehicles for reform were the established religious and caste leaders in any Hindu community. This "reform from within" doctrine was occasionally in evidence when reformers persuaded a pundit to lend his support to a reform proposal. But the judgments of a liberal pundit could easily be assailed by the pronouncements of other religious authorities—or even by the reforming pundit's followers.[9] The disorganized structure of religious leadership alone would discourage any systematic efforts to impregnate popular religious teachings with social reform ideas. The traditional institutions of caste leadership, for example, caste panchayats, were also not the most convenient vehicles for social advancement, although limited social reform measures were often introduced under their auspices. Most of the new caste organizations which were established in the late 19th century drew their leadership and their following initially not from traditional caste leaders, but from Western-educated caste members, men who were aware of the social reform movement and for whom advancement of their castes implied adoption of modern social ideals.

At the second annual National Social Conference, at Allahabad in 1888, Ranade welcomed the representatives of "the great Kayastha conference" which had met in that city two months earlier. At subsequent Social Conferences representatives and reports were acknowledged from other caste and subcaste bodies: the Walterkrit Rajputra Hitkarini Sabha; sabhas and conferences of the Vaishya, Jat, Bhargava, and Sarin (the Punjabi Khatri) communities of northern India; the Nayar community of Malabar; the Khalsa (Sikh) and the Jain sabhas (which operated much like caste reform bodies); more localized caste organizations, such as the various Brahmin castes and the Prabhu and Oswal communities in Bombay; and the Kunbis in Berar.

By the 1890's the advantages, if only in prestige, accruing to those castes which had organizations representing their interests

<hr />

[9] An example of the latter occurred when the Sankaracharya of Western India ordered that several high-caste Hindus be readmitted to their caste after returning from overseas. His nominal followers, the caste leaders and pundits, opposed his judgment. See K.M. Jhaveri, "An Interview with Shri Shankaracharya," *Indian Review*, VI, 3, 159-60.

were so obvious that most of the major castes of intermediate or high rank with memberships in the urban centers of northern India had some kind of body claiming to represent them, if only in the form of periodic conferences. But even before the new caste bodies had firmly established their influence, Ranade and other reformers began to recognize certain deficiencies in that manner of social advancement. In 1895 Ranade observed that "For certain purposes these caste organizations are very valuable, but they have their own weakness. They cramp and narrow the sympathies of those who belong to them, and the sphere of action is restricted within very defined limits."[10] Nevertheless, he admitted two years later that "As regards Conference work generally, it may be noted that caste Conferences are the order of the day in parts of India."[11] Indeed they already were, and were to become by the early 20th century the mainstay of the secular social reform movement.

The model for many new caste organizations, especially in northern India, was the Kayastha Conference, whose first session took place in Lucknow in November 1887. Kayastha is a general name for a group of castes (or subcastes, depending on one's definition)[12] of roughly comparable status located chiefly in upper India, Bihar, Bengal, and also in Bombay. Their traditional occupation was that of writer, and therefore their position in society was and is relatively high, although they were regarded, for caste ranking purposes, in some regions as Shudras, in others as Vaishyas, and in still others as Kshatriyas. A major purpose of the Kayastha Conference and the various sabhas associated with it was to gain public acceptance of all Kayasthas as twice-born.[13] But of equal, and to some Kayastha leaders, greater value was the Conference's support of modern education and social reform. In 1873 Munshi Kali Prasad had founded the Kayas-

[10] Ranade, op.cit., p. 165.
[11] ibid., p. 187.
[12] Technically, caste is an endogamous group; because no subcaste or section of the Kayastha community would inter-marry or inter-dine with another, each was a separate caste.
[13] Note the resolution passed at the Kayastha Conference in December 1906 urging upon all Kayasthas "the necessity of observing Dwijdharma rites." Hindustan Review, xv, 102.

tha Pathshala, a school for Kayastha children, which was raised to high school status in 1882 and in 1895 affiliated to the Allahabad University as an intermediate standard school.[14] The Kayastha Conference gave considerable attention to the strengthening of the Pathshala as a major means of training young Kayasthas and thereby improving the level of the community in general. But adequate financial support for the institution, which could only be expected to come from Kayasthas, was not easily obtained, and in 1914 the Pathshala was still not on a par with the Hindu College at Benaras or the Dayananda Anglo-Vedic College.

The Kayastha Conference, like the National Social Conference, depended upon the voluntary support that it might receive from local Kayastha sabhas, some of which were inclined to further the needs of their local membership more than the only theoretically united all-India community. Reports of the National Social Conference indicate the existence of several hundred local Kayastha sabhas by the 1890's, and the establishment of ten Provincial Representative Sabhas was recommended by the Fourth Kayastha Conference to coordinate activities under the guidance of a Kayastha Sadar Sabha of India or "supreme governing body."[15] The latter was established, and the caste found itself strong enough to send a pundit to represent it at the Chicago Parliament of Religions in 1893.[16]

In addition to raising funds for the spread of education among members of the already widely literate community, the Conference's original purposes were to encourage homogeneity within the caste, to spread social reform (vaguely defined) among Kayasthas, and to promote Kayasthas in commercial and industrial occupations where the material rewards were greater than in the service pursuits associated with a caste of writers.[17] Local sabhas were not agreed among themselves even on the basic issue of the homogeneity of Kayasthas, much less on practical social reform

[14] The *Hindustan Review*, xxix, 469-78, provided a survey of the Pathshala's history.

[15] "Fourth Kayastha Conference Report," in *Report of the Fourth National Social Conference*, Calcutta, 1890.

[16] *Report of the Seventh National Social Conference*, Lahore, 1893, p. 57.

[17] "Fourth Kayastha Conference Report," *op.cit.*

questions. Kayastha communities did not inter-marry, nor did they inter-dine. The Conference's attempts to break down those inhibitions and unite all Kayasthas was, in a sense, analogous to some social reformers' attempts to break down all caste distinctions among Hindus. Neither had much effect.

A major split soon developed, comparable to the split in the National Congress, on whether or not the Kayastha Conference should concern itself with social reform, as well as with economic and educational matters, and the Conference continued for years to harbor two sections, the orthodox and the liberal. The latter sought Conference sanction for progressive stands on marriage ages, ceremonial expenses, overseas travel, widow remarriage, inter-dining and inter-marriage among Kayasthas, and on temperance, but on all such questions they were frequently outvoted by the more conservative representatives. The liberal Kayasthas' methods of spreading social reform, therefore, were by working through local sabhas over which they had control and by propaganda, often carried on through several Kayastha journals, which were published in English and in vernaculars. The *Hindustan Review* of Allahabad (in English) was the most sophisticated and liberal of the journals which publicized Kayastha affairs, and it strongly supported the social reform approach to the advancement of the caste.

In January 1907, Kayastha social reformers staged a symbolic dinner of the traditional eight subsections of their community,[18] in which one hundred sixty Kayasthas—"the greater number was that of graduates and undergraduates"—from Hyderabad, C.P., Bihar, and the Punjab "came forward boldly to inter-dine with and embrace one another as brothers."[19] That episode, and another which centered on the dining of Kayasthas with a caste member who had returned from England, caused a major revolt of the conservative group at the next Conference. The conservatives seized control of the organization, eliminated all references to social reform from its stated purposes, and then reorganized the

[18] Lala Baijnath, not a Kayastha, listed twelve subsections, Chintamani, *op.cit.*, I, 159; there was obviously some confusion on this matter.

[19] The *Hindustan Review*, xv, 104.

body as the Kayastha Educational Conference, urging the reformers to set up another organization if they liked.[20] The reformers would not consent to be thrown out, but they did establish a Kayastha Intermarriage Society in December 1907 to promote mingling of Kayasthas at that basic level, and the struggle continued to flourish.

In 1909 the Conference, with the reformers in control, reinstated social reform, passed a resolution favoring the readmission to caste of Kayasthas who had traveled abroad, and another resolution urging inter-marriage of subcastes of Kayasthas.[21] In 1912 the antisocial reformers, regaining their voting power, managed again to change the name of the Conference, but a compromise was finally reached whereby joint Conferences were sanctioned; as President of the conservative Educational Conference a Bengali Kayastha, appropriately, was elected, while a Kayastha from Oudh was made President of the Social Conference. Kayasthas henceforth remained split on the reform question, which adversely affected the management of the Pathshala, and they have never achieved real unity extending to inter-marriage between subsections. The *Hindustan Review* commented: "It is outrageous that men frankly hostile to social reform, join bodies like the Kayastha Conference and abuse their position to thwart the work that these organizations wish to accomplish."[22] One result of the stormy 1912 session and the election of a Bengali president, however, was the forming of a superficial bond between Kayasthas of upper India (Hindustan) and Bengal, which had not previously been achieved. As late as 1929 the Prabhu Kayasthas of Maharashtra could still not be brought into the Conference.[23]

Like the Kayasthas, castes regarding themselves as Vaishya successfully established a Conference in 1891. The Vaishyas were castes chiefly engaged in trades, all of whom inter-dined but did

---

[20] The *Hindustan Review*, XVII, 104f.

[21] *ibid.*, XIX, 453-54.

[22] XXV, 505. Despite the split at the 1912 Conference, Kayasthas managed to stage a grand public display publicizing their gathering and increasing their fame; a parade of elephants, carriages, flag-bearers, and a military band marked the opening of the session, which was held in Fyzabad.

[23] Sachchidananda Sinha, "Caste Conferences and National Progress," Presidential address at 35th All-India Kayastha Conference, March 29, 1929.

not inter-marry.[24] Perhaps because of the illustrious leadership in the Vaishya Conference and Vaishya Maha Sabha of Lala Baijnath, the noted social reform advocate and judge of the Small Causes Court of Allahabad, the Vaishyas apparently avoided the serious split which marred the progress of the Kayastha organization. By 1900 there were over one hundred sabhas associated with the Vaishya Conference, many of which were strong advocates of reform in age of marriage, elimination of extravagant dowries, prohibition of nautch dancing, and the like. The Vaishya Conference, unlike the Kayastha Conference, was able to pass resolutions favoring minimum marriage ages of sixteen and twelve, opposing ill-assorted marriages and polygamy, and authorizing its Maha Sabha to distribute social reform tracts, although like the Kayasthas it took no position on widow remarriage, inter-marriage of subcastes, or, not surprisingly, on the inequities of caste discrimination.[25] The Vaishyas supported a caste newspaper, the *Vaishya Hitkari*, and their sabhas and lower schools laid great stress on the encouragement of Hindi and the use of devanagri script. Encouragement of the community's economic advancement was a prime function of the sabhas and the Conference, which resolved that, among other economic policies, "All members of the caste who own manufacturing, trading or banking firms may be requested to train a certain number of youths of the caste in the respective business."[26]

Before the First World War the Kayastha and Vaishya Sabhas and Conferences stood in advance of all other caste bodies in their geographical extension and in the influence of some of their leaders in the social reform movement in northern India. Most of the remaining conferences and sabhas, hundreds of whose reports appeared in the pages of the Social Conference *Reports* and in newspapers such as the *Indian Social Reformer*, were organized on the models of the Kayastha and Vaishya bodies, and their concern with social reform varied according to the local require-

[24] Baijnath in Chintamani, *op.cit.*, I, 159.
[25] *ISR*, Feb. 12, 1899, p. 187. On the marriage age question the 7th Vaishya Conference Report stated, "There being some difference of opinion among the Delhi people about the age, they will settle this question among themselves."
[26] *ibid.*, p. 187.

ments of each caste group. The Nayars of Malabar, for example, had a peculiar family system, and all Nayar social reform was directed toward altering it. The Marriage Act passed by the Madras Government in 1896 on the instigation of Sir C. Sankaran Nair provided for legal registration of Nayar marriages and gave children an inheritance share of the father's personal property. It was therefore an initial move toward reforming the marriage customs in Malabar by breaking down the matriarchal, often polyandrous, system and establishing a nuclear family with the father at its head. The Act was ineffective, and few marriages were registered, but the marriage reform movement had been launched, and Nayar social reform bodies were soon formed to carry forward its message. The first Nayar Social Conference was held in 1903 at Shertally and took up at once the problems of inheritance and legal recognition of monogamous marriages. For the Nayars, "The period between the latter half of the 19th century and the third decade of the 20th century can be treated as a period of acute stress and strain through which the institution of marriage has passed."[27] Changes in Nayar marriage customs, due only in part to the direct effects of social reform propaganda, have in fact been so great in this century that disagreement exists over what those customs were previously. Among Nambootri Brahmins in the same region marriage customs have also changed, again partly under the aegis of a reform drive, the Yogakshema movement.[28]

A Jat Conference at Meerut in 1890 stressed reform in marriage customs;[29] an agitation was under way in 1898 among Sikhs, who had formed some forty sabhas in the Punjab, to allow widow remarriage;[30] many caste associations put pressure on members to

---

[27] M.S.A. Rao, *Social Change in Malabar*, p. 99. The all-India Hindu Marriage Code currently applicable to Nayars was preceded by provincial and state enactments which required registration of marriages and inheritance from the husband and father: the Madras Marumakkattayam Act of 1933 and the Cochin Nayar Act of 1937.

[28] *ibid.*, p. 106.

[29] *Report of the Sixth National Social Conference*, Allahabad, 1892. The Jat reformers had a newspaper, the *Jat Samachar*, at their disposal.

[30] "Summary of the Reports from Social Reform Associations for the Year 1898," p. 80.

raise marriage ages and allow widow remarriage;[31] measures to educate girls were undertaken by almost all of the sabhas, usually by financing girls' schools;[32] and many castes founded and maintained orphanages, established benevolent and educational funds, and sent out preachers who acted as vehicles for spreading ideas of social improvement as well as organizers of the caste sabhas.

But all caste bodies were not organized on the models just described. In the case of the Rajput castes or clans in the princely states of Rajputana the movement for reform emerged not from Western-educated leaders but under the aegis of the traditional rulers or chiefs in that region, where aristocratic feudal society still survived in the late 19th century. Actually, reform among the Rajputs, though sanctioned by the ruling chiefs, apparently came as a result of the influence of British officers attached as Residents in the various states of Rajputana. The recognized social evils in Rajput society had long been due to marriage customs, which required such enormous outlays of wealth by families marrying their daughters that impoverishment or female infanticide were often the only two alternatives open to Rajputs of high standing. The crusade against female infanticide was carried on, primarily by the British, in Rajputana, the Punjab, and the North-Western Provinces during the entire period of their rule in those territories with only gradually appearing signs of success. In 1870 an act had been passed in an unsuccessful effort to suppress the custom. In 1888 Colonel C.K.M. Walter, agent to the Governor-General in Rajputana, produced some excitement in British and Indian circles by successfully persuading a group of the most powerful Rajput princes to agree for the first time on measures aimed ultimately at undermining the causes of female infanticide. The British Parliament, whose *Papers* are singularly devoid of references to the broader aspects of the Indian social reform movement, published the account of Colonel Walter's successes, and Lord Cross, the Secretary of State for India, was reported to have cited the achievement as "the greatest advance made in the present century."[33]

[31] Ranade, address at the Eighth Social Conference, *op.cit.*, p. 141.
[32] Ranade, *op.cit.*, p. 182.
[33] Quoted in Gidumal, *The Status of Women in India*, p. 289. See also House

At Ajmer in March 1888, representatives of the major Rajput states gathered and reached unanimous decisions on the reform of marriage customs. On betrothal and marriage ceremonial expenditures, as well as on funeral costs, tables (similar to life insurance tables) were soon devised showing what amounts could be spent, in proportion to the annual income of the family, ranging from one Rupee to a lakh (100,000) of Rupees. Exchanges of money and presents at the time that the marriage agreement was reached were outlawed, and limits were placed on the distribution of "Tyag" (financial outlays to participants in weddings). Finally, limits were set for ages of marriage, eighteen for boys and fourteen for girls. A reservation which applied to all of the new regulations disclosed the true spirit in which the reforms were introduced: ruling chiefs were exempt from adhering to the new regulations; on all other Rajputs they were binding.[34]

In 1889 the Walterkrit Rajputra Hitkarini Sabha was formed with a full-time paid secretary, the British Agent was President, and local sabhas were set up in each of the states. The central Sabha and its subunits were to maintain records of the Rajputs' success in abiding by the new rules and impose fines, if necessary, on offenders. Though systematically organized, Rajput social reform was not a notable success; there was much overlooking of offenses against the rules and ignoring of fines. Among non-

---

of Lords, *Accounts and Papers, 1888*, xix, No. 227, "Correspondence regarding the adoption by the States of Rajputana of Reforms in connection with Marriage and Funeral Customs." An earlier British-inspired effort at social reform took place in 1859 and involved many of the same marriage ceremonial customs that affected the Rajputs in the 1880's. In forwarding to the Bombay Governor a report on the efforts of James Gibbs to reform marriage customs in his area, Sir H.B.E. Frere, Commissioner in Sind, wrote: "As a general rule, we cannot, I think, be too cautious in applying the influence of Government in this country to effect any change, however obviously beneficial, in the domestic habits of a people, which do not lead to any direct breach of law. But in this case, the reform has been commenced and worked out from among the people themselves, and a great good has been effected with very little direct interference on the part of Government." Govt. of Bombay, *Selections from the Records*, No. LV, New Series, "Correspondence showing the Measures Taken by the Synds of Tatta in Sind to Reduce the Expenses of their Birth, Marriage, and Funeral Ceremonies."

[34] Gidumal, *op.cit.*, p. 289.

Rajput castes in Rajputana the Arya Samaj carried the burden of reform work.

Still another type of caste reform centered around neither the Westernized sabhas nor the traditional caste leadership, but was the product of religious movements. In north India the Arya Samaj frequently combined social reform with religious conversion, particularly among low castes: sacred threadgiving ceremonies were performed for castes seeking to raise their status, and caste members were thus brought under the social reforming influences of the Samaj. A more narrowly focused religious caste reform movement emerged in Malabar early in the 20th century under the inspiration of Guru Narayana. Born an untouchable Exhava (or Elava) in Travancore, Guru Narayana (as he was later called) managed to become educated and something of a Sanskrit scholar. Thus specially endowed he took up the leadership of the so-called temple-entry movement, a crusade to permit untouchables to partake in Hindu temple worship, which Gandhi later supported. In 1903 the Guru formed the Sri Narayan Dharma Paripalana (S.N.D.P.) Yogam, assisted by Dr. Palpu, who had already been conducting political agitation for the betterment of the Exhavas. The purposes of the S.N.D.P. were to initiate education for the untouchables and to provide them with religious ceremonies involving hitherto forbidden Brahmanic rituals. The movement spread through the Malayalam-speaking region and in the 1920's and 1930's was one of the most politically powerful factions in southern India. Its importance today as a bulwark of the Communist Party in Kerala has been discussed by Selig Harrison.[35] But Sanskritization of religious life, the elimination of inequalities based on caste, and political power were not the only aims of the Guru Narayana movement. According to the Communist leader, E. M. S. Namboodripad, "It also demanded the total overhauling of the family system, i.e. conversion of the family system from a matriarchal to a patriarchal one; prohibition of polygamy, polyandry and other forms of sexual relationships that have been handed down to us from ancient tribal society; an end to the impartible [economically indivisible] character of the joint fam-

[35] Harrison, op.cit., pp. 196-99.

ily (both patriarchal and matriarchal). At the same time, this movement encouraged and advocated marriages on the basis of love and not on the basis of the will of the parents. The objective of the movement was thus the establishment of the bourgeois family."[36]

Social reform under the auspices of caste organizations, thus, took several forms, though the secular, Westernized sabhas and conferences outnumbered the other forms. While admitting that social reform through disciplined caste bodies often aroused more enthusiasm and proved more lasting, than through general associations, social reformers who were not associated with the caste reform movements came to dispute their value for Hindu society as a whole. Ranade saw the disunifying implications of the increasingly popular caste-reform movements but acknowledged that in the North-Western Provinces the Kayastha community and its Conference and sabhas supplied the main leadership of the social reform movement.[87] The discipline of castes appealed particularly to him. The following episode could scarcely have taken place in a general reform association: a Kayastha vakil of Gya who had pledged a limitation on the acceptance of wedding gifts weakened and took Rupees two thousand on the marriage of his son. The caste association exposed his deed and forced him to turn over all of the money to a fund for education of poor Kayasthas.[88]

But such effective pressure on faltering caste brethren was not frequently recorded, and in any case it illustrated the limitations of caste reform as a lever for general social advancement: while instituting its own reforms, a caste became increasingly less aware of general social problems, and the possibilities of developing corporate social consciousness among all Indians receded even further. As a system of social organization, caste was greatly strengthened when modern communications between caste members and new organizational techniques were brought into play within any community. Bhandarkar, one of the strongest critics of the caste system in his day, issued a warning in 1895: "Reform

---

[36] Namboodripad, *The National Question in Kerala*, p. 111. See also article on Guru Narayana in the *Times of India*, Aug. 29, 1960.

[87] Ranade, *op.cit.*, p. 129.

[88] *ISR*, May 6, 1900, p. 281.

through the agency of caste, which is attempted in some parts of the country, is very unsatisfactory. Very little can be effected in this way. The reduction of marriage expenses and measures of this nature only can be carried out by its means, and the great danger of this method is that caste which has corroded the vitals of this country will be strengthened by it."[39] A decade later, when more evidence was available, the *Hindustan Review* published an analysis of the caste-reform movements which substantiated Bhandarkar's fears: ". . . the greatest disadvantage of the caste-conference method is that of sharpening social distinctions, of breeding a sense of exclusiveness and animosity among various communities, and dividing and disuniting Indian people at a time when united cooperation was most needed. The exponents of the movement will assure me that all such thoughts are unreal and that each community is striving to reach the common goal. But I am no believer in mere words. The feeling that I am a Brahman, that you are a Vaishya, and that he is a Kayastha, and that each should make improvement at the expense of another, is gaining ground."[40]

But, in defense of the caste-reform movements, it could be pointed out that if social reform had to carry the burden of creating inter-caste harmony and to await the day of unity of all Hindus before promoting lesser goals, the outlook for a reformer was bleak. Caste reformers, Lala Baijnath argued, "take society as we find it, and are beginning the work of reform in the only way in which it could possibly begin, i.e. from the bottom upwards."[41] Any practical reformer's program had to accept certain given social conditions, however undesirable, before trying to reform others; no complete undoing of the social structure and then rebuilding was possible, except in a reformer's rhetorical fancy. Most social practices which reformers had always sought to alter were underwritten by caste regulations which were often enforced more effectively than the official legal codes. An obvious means of encouraging a desired social change was to obtain sanctions for it

[39] Chintamani, *op.cit.*, III, 187. In later years Bhandarkar would have noted other reform measures taken by caste bodies.

[40] Narayen Prasad Ashthana, *Hindustan Review*, XIV, 381.

[41] Presidential address, National Social Conference, 1899, Chintamani, *op.cit.*, III, 212.

from caste groups. Indeed, without the sanction or at least the toleration of caste elders or associations, deviations by individuals from traditional customs often resulted in little more than a growing number of excommunicated persons. In any case, organizing for educational, economic, and social prestige purposes was an irreversible drive among caste groups, and whatever social reforms could be fused into that process contributed something to the reform of the entire Hindu community.[42]

To have condemned the caste reformers because the scope of their efforts was restricted, one should have logically condemned all reformers, whose contacts and range of influence reached only those with whom they formed natural bonds—based on educational or professional experience or religious interests, as well as on caste ties. Societies advance, Sachchidananda Sinha, a president of the Kayastha Conference, once noted, as their component parts advance. As long as Hindu society was divided into castes, whose rules of behavior were accepted by their members, social advance had to be a function of the progress made by each caste component.[43]

The Arya Samaj as a Local Social Reform Movement

Although the Brahmo Samaj has had a longer continuous history, the Arya Samaj has had a greater direct impact on Indians over a longer period of time than any other religious or social reform movement in modern times. The practical wisdom of its founder was bequeathed to his followers, who, for several generations, displayed a versatility in adjusting the Samaj's creed and methods to contemporary needs and a steadfast enthusiasm

[42] The formation of caste conferences, sabhas, and educational institutions continued at an increasing rate in the 20th century, and that development was deplored by many Indians whose main loyalty was to the nation, not to a caste brotherhood. One such Indian observer wrote in 1933: "So, beginning with a general Social Conference, intended to reform, reorganize, and reunify all Indian society and social life, we are now having scores upon scores of Conferences of the most miserable little sub-castes, even the names of which one had not come across before, unless one had occasion to wade through a Census Report." Bhagavan Das in Sarda, ed., *Dayanand Commemoration Volume*, p. 95.

[43] Sinha, "Caste Conferences and National Progress."

for strengthening their movement that were unmatched in any other reform body. A review of the Arya Samaj's history from the death of Dayananda in 1883 to the First World War shows that the Samaj combined a religious zeal comparable to the Brahmo Samaj with a liberalizing social program comparable to the Prarthana Samaj, and cemented its members together by an organizational tie which was not unlike that of some caste sabhas. If the practical effects of the social reform movement in India are ever accurately evaluated, the record of the Arya Samaj will serve as strong evidence that the spread of ideas, as well as the extension of economic and technological changes, has resulted in social advancement.

Dayananda Saraswati's first efforts to organize his movement around Vedic schools and his original Arya Samajes in Bombay and Gujarat proved to be unsuccessful instruments of the reform that he was determined to set in motion. In 1877 the Lahore Arya Samaj was founded, and the movement was truly under way. The ten principles, or Niyams, making up the Creed of the Lahore Samaj had advantages over the nebulous liberalism of much of the educated thought of the day by setting forth a determinate religious and social philosophy. But at the same time the Creed did not embody the complex and controversial substance of Dayananda's writings and was simple and flexible enough to allow for reinterpretation by later Arya Samajists.[44] It became the doctrinal basis for the entire Arya Samaj movement.

From Lahore the movement spread rapidly through western Punjab and into the United Provinces by the method of establishing local samajes with some semblance of contact with the original unit. The chief bond among members of any Arya Samaj was their common worship, of a congregational form similar to Brahmo Samaj and Christian services.[45] At the time of Daya-

[44] The 28 rules of the earlier Bombay Samaj were greatly simplified at Lahore, with the result that both orthodox and liberal members could subscribe to them without compromising their beliefs. Cf. J. Reid Graham, whose extensive research and first-hand observations on the Arya Samaj movement must be reviewed by anyone pursuing this topic, in "The Arya Samaj as a Reformation in Hinduism with Specific Reference to Caste," p. 197.

[45] It involved (and still does) a ceremonial *havana*, a fire into which ghee (melted butter) was poured in order to "purify" the air. J.N. Farquhar described

nanda's death there were 132 such samajes; in 1885, 200; in 1886, 265.[46] According to the Swami's instructions, representative provincial Sabhas, Pratinidhi Sabhas, were established, the first in the Punjab in 1885, to oversee the work of local samajes, although the latter were permitted a degree of autonomy suited to India's diversity of religious and social life. Crucial to the success of the Arya Samaj organization after Dayananda's death was the fact that he had refused to construct the new religious movement on the basis of personal devotion to himself; thus, the Creed, not the Swami, was the principal focus of loyalty. As an additional bonus to followers left temporarily leaderless in 1883, Dayananda's estate provided funds to carry on the work and a well-endowed printing press out of which tracts continued to pour.

Within a decade after the Swami's death, when the membership of the Samaj had risen to over 40,000, a rupture appeared within the movement, despite all precautions taken in framing its Creed and organizational structure. The dispute formally centered on this question: did adherence to the Lahore Creed alone qualify one for full membership in the Samaj. A liberal faction argued that it should, and a conservative faction held that membership also required adoption of other standards set by Dayananda. At least two important concrete issues were involved. One was vegetarianism, which the conservative, or orthodox, faction insisted upon, both because Dayananda had done so[47] and also because the

---

an Arya service which he attended in 1912: after the *havana* ceremony, "It was just like a Protestant service, and totally unlike any Vedic observance." Farquhar, *Modern Religious Movements in India*, p. 123. See also the description of the impact of the Samaj and its form of worship on one who was nurtured in that religious atmosphere in Prakash Tandon, *Punjabi Century 1857-1947*, pp. 33-34.

[46] Graham, *op.cit.*, p. 400n.

[47] A movement which Dayananda founded, and around which subsequently much Hindu communal aggressiveness centered, urged an end to slaughter of cattle. Dayananda set up Gaurakshini Sabhas, or Cow Protection Societies, which expanded their propaganda against Muslim and Christian cattle slaughtering in the decades after his death. Har Bilas Sarda explained that Dayananda urged cow protection on grounds of the economic usefulness of the cow and *"nowhere* assigned sacerdotal character to the cow." (Sarda, *Life of Dayanand Saraswati*, chap. xxviii.) However, orthodox Hindu associations did attach religious significance to the cow-protection movement and claimed that it was a vital part of upholding Hindu dharma.

norms of many high-caste Hindus demanded it. The liberals, who could argue that meat-eating added to a peoples' vigor and in any case should not interfere with religion, relied on the absence in the Lahore Creed of any reference to vegetarianism and refused to accept uncritically all the teachings of Dayananda. The meat-eating issue, sometimes debated in terms of the infallibility of the Swami, led to great bitterness, with the meat-eating faction, called the "Flesh Party" or the "Vultures," somewhat on the defensive because of the deep revulsion against a nonvegetarian diet among many Hindus.[48]

The second issue turned on the educational policy of the Arya Samaj. At Lahore, the main center of the Samaj's strength, a group of liberal Samajists had managed to establish a high school in 1886 in memory of their deceased leader. By 1888 college classes were added, and the famous Dayananda Anglo-Vedic (D.A.V.) College began to make its mark on higher education in north India. The College was the pride of the young, Western-educated Arya Samajists whose enthusiasm for a revival of classical Hindu learning was tempered by their respect for Western science and technology; it "became the backbone of the progressive section of the Punjabi Hindu community."[49] Its rapid rise to prominence was due chiefly to Hans Raj, a graduate of Punjab University in 1886, who donated his services without pay as Headmaster of the high school and became honorary Principal of the College, and his equally young and vigorous associates, Guru Datta Vidyarthi and Lala Lajpat Rai. The D.A.V. College curriculum stressed San-skrit studies (eliminating the "degenerate" post-Vedic works which were despised by Dayananda but which were read at the Lahore Oriental College), English literature, and science and technology. Conservative Samajists accused Hans Raj, a non-vegetarian, of neglecting Sanskrit studies and molding the College's curriculum according to the standards which the government had set down for the Universities.[50] Indeed, the D.A.V. College

[48] In 1918 the liberal faction of the Samaj finally bowed to the pressure for vegetarianism and passed a resolution stating that meat-eating was opposed to the Vedic religion. Graham, *op.cit.*, p. 524.

[49] Prakash Tandon, *op.cit.*, p. 33.

[50] See Sri Ram Sharma, *Mahatma Hansraj; Maker of the Modern Punjab*, p. 61.

met those standards and became a part of the University system. Supporters of the College insisted that Dayananda's ideas on education, as some of his other ideas, were not infallible and need not be carried out literally; education had to meet the needs of modern times.

In 1893 the two factions, each claiming to embody the true spirit of the Arya Samaj, formally split by holding separate annual conventions in Lahore, and within a short time "what had been a Lahore conflict spread to the whole of the Arya Samaj movement,"[51] although the split was never as deep elsewhere as it was in the Punjab. Because the liberals, or "College Party," led by Lajpat Rai, retained control of the D.A.V. College, the conservatives, or "Mahatma Party," planned to create their own school on the classical Hindu model for education. According to that model students should follow a rigid pattern of life, under the supervision of gurus, from the age at which they undertook their studies until they were prepared to enter active community affairs.[52]

In 1902 Mahatma Munshi Ram, the leader of the conservative Arya Samajists, founded the famous Gurukula at Hardwar, near the source of the Ganges. Generally regarded as an extraordinary experiment in education, the Gurukula flourished, and similar institutions were established elsewhere. Though its specialty was the training of Sanskrit scholars, and though it was not affiliated with any University, courses included English language and literature, modern sciences, history, and social science; classes were conducted in Hindi, and a degree equivalent to a B.A. was offered. Boys only were admitted—other gurukulas were established for girls—at ages six to eight, on condition that their parents would not have them married before they had completed their course of study at the age of twenty-five. A high degree of physical fitness and discipline was required of the students, in line with Daya-

[51] Graham, op.cit., p. 410.
[52] Dayananda's ideal scheme of education provided that upon completion of studies at a gurukula a Hindu would take an examination to determine to which of the four varnas he belonged, and he would henceforth occupy that caste or varna status. But that procedure was never followed at the Arya Samaj Gurukula. Graham, op.cit., pp. 379, 423n.

nanda's admonition that the Hindu "race" lacked vigor and courage; one Indian visitor found the boys bathing in the icy waters of the Ganges at 4:30 a.m., when he visited the place in 1913.[53] No women could distract the students by their presence at the Gurukula, and vegetarianism was enforced. In 1907 the institution had 187 students.[54]

Despite the split in the parent religious movement the educational work of the Arya Samaj moved ahead in the 1890's and in the 20th century, and soon rivalled Christian missionary endeavors in the field of private education.[55] Indeed, by the mid-twentieth century the emphasis which the Arya Samaj in its early years placed on education for both boys and girls can be seen as a major element in the intellectual advancement of northern India.[56]

Swami Dayananda's unceasing attacks on the "degenerate" social practices of Hindus were accepted as valid by later Arya Samajists, but the latter did not promote crusades against social evils with the same persistence that characterized their educational programs. Nor did local Arya Samajes constitute a body of families separate from Hindu society like the Brahmo Samajes, which had liberated themselves from caste customs and were living isolated, Westernized lives. Proposals around the turn of the century to make a break with Hindu society and establish an Arya Bhratri Sabha, or Aryan Brotherhood Society, wherein Samajists could live completely reformed lives according to Dayananda's teachings, did not succeed.[57] Aryas themselves were divided on several matters, in-

[53] G.A. Chandavarkar, "The Gurukula Academy at Kangri," *The Indian Review*, XIV, 8, 641-49.

[54] "The Quinquennial Report of the Gurukula Academy" (1901-1907).

[55] See Fred B. Fisher, *India's Silent Revolution*, p. 85.

[56] The author and other visitors to Arya Samaj schools have been impressed by their approach to education, which can only be described as character-building, as well as by their academic qualifications. In 1947 the Samaj managed: 30 Gurukulas for boys; 10 Gurukulas for girls; 15 D.A.V. Colleges; 192 primary schools, 151 middle schools, and 200 high schools for boys; 700 primary schools and 10 high schools for girls; 142 night schools; and 322 schools for depressed classes, according to Ganga Prasad Upadhyaya, "The Aryasamaj and the International Aryan League," pp. 13-14. Arya Samaj schools are open to children from non-Arya families, and these constitute the bulk of the students now enrolled.

[57] See Graham, *op.cit.*, pp. 415-16, 475f.

cluding vegetarianism, and in addition they recognized the fact that the aim of strengthening Hindu society, *vis-à-vis* Muslims and Christians, would be undermined if Hindu reformers were to renounce their community and the leadership of it.

Nevertheless, the Arya Samaj, as Ranade acknowledged in his day, was the chief exponent of social and religious reform in the Punjab.[58] Attacks similar to Dayananda's on idolatry, polytheism, religious pilgrimages, and various caste and sect rituals, especially marriage and funeral rites, continued to hold a prominent place in the Arya Samaj tracts and newspapers. Dayananda's advocacy of later ages for marriage of girls and boys—sixteen to twenty-four for girls, twenty-five to forty-eight for men—may have had more effect ultimately on his followers than similar preachings of other reformers, if one may judge from the statistics on marriage among Aryas.[59] Partly as a result of postponing marriages, the literacy rates among Arya women were considerably above those of the general population.[60] Foreign travel received the support of the Samaj as a part of its educational programs. Release of women from the seclusion of purdah and their qualification for participation in religious and public life were other prescriptions which Dayananda had insisted upon and which Aryas tried to follow. Dayananda's *niyoga* doctrine, however, which advocated informal conjugal relationships by widows, was never promulgated by the Arya leaders, who instead took up the widow remarriage movement. Widow remarriages under Arya Samaj auspices were not uncommon in northern India. In social service work the Samaj excelled, and it was especially noted for its founding of orphanages during the famines of 1896-1902 and 1907-8, when thousands of

[58] After listing the Samaj's achievements Ranade told the Eighth Social Conference that the Arya Samajes "in a word constitute all that is most hopeful and worth living in the new life of the Punjab." Ranade, *op.cit.*, p. 138.

[59] e.g. E.A.H. Blunt, a census officer in 1911, wrote that "whilst the number of married or widowed Hindu girls under 10 is 61 per 1,000 [in northern India], the similar number of Aryas is only 21, and of those a majority were probably married before conversion." Blunt, *The Caste System of Northern India*, p. 331.

[60] In 1911 "The literacy of Arya women in the Punjab was 80 per thousand as compared with 6 literate women per thousand of the general population; and 230 Arya Samajist men as against 63 of the general population." E.A. Gait in *Census of India*, 1911, I., Pt. I, 306-07; cited in Graham, *op.cit.*, p. 424n.

children might otherwise have been taken into Christian orphanages and their numbers thus subtracted from the Hindu community's numerical strength.[61] J. Reid Graham concluded from his probing study of the Arya Samaj that Aryas were losing some of their initial drive for social reform by the turn of the century, as they and the orthodox Hindu groups moved closer together "to form a close politico-religious unity against Muslims and all non-Hindus."[62] When that observation is made, however, the fact should be kept in mind that all of the social reform bodies were making necessary adjustments to Hindu nationalism and cultural revivalism at that time. The Arya Samaj, notwithstanding its increasingly sympathetic view of some orthodox movements, still remained in the 20th century the most active social reform body in the country. "Being within the fold of Hinduism," a British resident concluded about the Aryas, "they are silently undermining it. . . ."[63]

The greatest obstacles which Arya Samajists, in common with all social reformers, had to overcome in order to give practical meaning, as individuals, to their professed creed were the constraints of caste customs. Those customs and the orthodox religious sanctions which supported them also constituted a major barrier to the spread of the Samaj's ideals throughout the Hindu population. When Aryas refused to break with Hindu society and form a separate community, as the Brahmos had done, in practice that meant that they continued to respect caste customs, particularly in matters of marriage alliances, which form the matrix of the caste system. Aryas might worship together according to nonidolatrous rites as well as join in postponing the marriages of their sons and daughters; as long as they did not inter-marry (unless they belonged to the same caste) they could ordinarily escape excommunication for their unorthodox beliefs and behavior. The Lahore Creed did not repudiate caste practices specifically, and Dayananda "did not propose the abolition of the caste system, but rather the introduc-

[61] See Lajpat Rai's description of his own work for the Samaj in famine relief. Rai, *The Arya Samaj*, pp. 238-47.
[62] Graham, *op.cit.*, p. 435.
[63] Alfred Nundy, "The Gurukul," *Hindustan Review*, XIX, 465.

tion of a new caste [varna] system the classes of which would be founded on merit. . . ."[64]

The *Arya Patrika*, the major organ of the Samaj, explained the Samaj's position on caste in 1889: "The Arya Samaj believes only in caste by merit, but it is not a body of brainless firebrands. It is resolved to exterminate caste as it at present exists root and branch, but it will do it slowly and imperceptibly though surely." In an even more revealing statement of the Samaj's position on social reform, the *Patrika* wrote: "To eat with Churas [sweepers] and Chamars [leather workers] or to sit at the same table with white Europeans, a thing which in the opinion of our biscuit reformers is the outward expression of the highest development of the feeling of humanity in a person, has certainly no weight with the Arya Samaj. . . . The Arya Samaj is not prepared to advocate promiscuous eating and drinking on the infinitely more important consideration of retaining the sympathies and confidence of the nation; if that is lost the Arya Samaj is frustrated."[65]

A certain uneasiness, however, lingered in the minds of some Aryas because of their continued loyalty to their respective castes, which resulted in the abortive effort to form an Aryan Brotherhood.[66] However undesirable the formation of a separate Arya community seemed, Arya Samajists were constantly reminded by their own literature that social progress for themselves and for Hindu society in general was blocked at a certain point by caste. Graham concluded that "the Samaj cannot be said to have undertaken any aspect of caste reform to any appreciable extent in the first twenty years of its existence—a fact that was commencing to

[64] Graham, *op.cit.*, p. 387.

[65] *Arya Patrika*, May 7, 1889, p. 1; and Dec. 31, 1889, p. 2; quoted in Graham, *op.cit.*, pp. 469, 470.

[66] The *Arya Patrika* contained one of the many suggestions along that line: "It is time that we cut the orthodox caste conventions and form a living connection between Aryas. We think alike, but fear the excommunication of the biradri [caste brotherhood]. . . . Our standard of honour at the present time is not the Arya Samaj but the orthodox biradri, for the membership of the Arya Samaj does not disqualify one for membership of the biradri, the disobedience of whose laws brings troubles." Jan. 16, 1897, p. 6. Quoted in Graham, *op.cit.*, p. 477. The Samaj was not transformed into a new caste biradri, but Aryan Brotherhood units were established by individual Samajists, and non-Aryas as well, to help undermine the caste system.

trouble certain members of the organization."[67] Of greater weight, perhaps, than even the concern for social reform, was the fact that low caste groups were attracted to Islam and Christianity, and therefore the caste system was resulting in the strengthening of non-Hindu communities.

The specific proposals for an Aryan Brotherhood, regarded as daring and fraught with dangers, lost their force shortly after the turn of the century, and demands for reform of the entire caste system, heard among reformers throughout India, began to animate the thinking of many Aryas who had previously thought in terms of radical reform only for those who could fully appreciate the advanced doctrines of the Samaj. The result of that reassessment of the purposes of the Samaj by its members produced a movement for caste reform which had incalculably far-reaching results in northern India. Both factions of the Samaj sponsored it, but, as Lajpat Rai acknowledged, the conservative, or Guru-kula section was its most active supporter.[68] Beginning in 1900, low caste groups were recruited for the first time as members of the Arya Samaj in ceremonies which formally raised their status to the level of twice-born castes and made them, technically, according to the doctrine of the Samaj, eligible to inter-dine and inter-marry with high caste Aryas. Until that time and despite the fact that Samajists themselves remained split along caste lines, the Samaj was overwhelmingly a body of educated, upper-caste individuals and families, similar to other religious and social reform associations throughout the country.

Discussing the question of admitting low caste sweepers into the Samaj the editor of the *Arya Patrika* had confessed in 1896 "that no one has yet thought of turning the direction of the Samaj toward these matters. The very idea of converting such low and downtrodden people seems abominable. We live amongst people who would not tolerate such conduct on our part for a moment, and our instinct too treats it with utter repugnance. Yet the Christians do it."[69] Four years later the Lahore Samaj inducted, or

[67] Graham, *op.cit.*, p. 474.
[68] Rai, *op.cit.*, pp. 271-72.
[69] *Arya Patrika*, Aug. 8, 1896, p. 5. Quoted in Graham, *op.cit.*, p. 490.

converted, a group of low-caste Rahtias, and the movement at once developed a momentum which must have surprised the Arya Samajists themselves. "There was of course danger that orthodox biradris might excommunicate a few of the first Samajists who took food at the hand of the newly purified low castes [often a part of the conversion ceremony], but there could be nothing like the stir that would have resulted had the experiment of the Arya Bhratri [Aryan Brotherhood] Sabha been carried into action. Thus a conservative [i.e. defensive] movement was substituted for a radical one, the energies of the Arya Bhratri leaders were employed in purifying the low castes, and the personal caste affiliations of Arya Samajists remained undisturbed."[70]

A few months after the Rahtias were converted came Ods, Meghs, and later Jats, not singly but in bodies numbering scores of hundreds. The movement spread from the Punjab to Kashmir and the United Provinces, where entire communities, ranging from the lowest untouchables to higher agricultural castes, were brought into the Arya Samaj. An extraordinary number of Arya missionaries and volunteers was mobilized to do the work of conversion. Lajpat Rai, one of the more famous workers, recorded that in 1913 or 1914 he "succeeded in making a big hole in the orthodox fortress by reclaiming a number of [untouchable] Doms and admitting them into the Arya Samaj. I went to their houses in the interior of the hills and along with a number of high caste Arya Samajists ate food cooked by them and drank water brought by them. Last year I went to Benaras and addressed a large meeting on this question and challenged them to excommunicate me for this activity."[71] As a result of the movement to Aryanize low castes, the census figures showed great increases in the numbers of Indians calling themselves Aryas. The rate of growth of the Samaj from 1891 to 1901—a 131 per cent increase with over 92,000 Samajists counted in 1901—rose over the next decade to 163 per cent and levelled off at a 100 per cent increase in the succeeding ten-year period, 1911 to 1921. In the latter year almost one-half million Aryas were enumerated, and by 1931 there were nearly one mil-

[70] *ibid.*, p. 491.
[71] Rai, *op.cit.*, p. 231.

lion.[72] The early stronghold of the Samaj, the Punjab, had only one-quarter of the membership by 1901, while the United Provinces had nearly three-quarters. However by 1921 the Punjab surpassed the United Provinces in numbers of Aryas.

The ceremony by which low castes and outcastes were brought into the Arya Samaj religious community was virtually the same as that by which errant Muslims and Christians were "reclaimed"[73] from their respective religious faiths. Accounts of it vary, but it always included indoctrination in Vedic rituals and usually ritual purification by bathing and, for men, shaving of the head. Inter-dining with high caste persons—joining in eating sweets or sherbet or the like—the taking of water from a well previously reserved for high castes, and investiture with the sacred thread of the twice-born castes were also often parts of the ceremony, and those rituals were specifically intended to challenge the social superiority of high castes. The challenge to orthodoxy was not as profound as it could have been, however, had high-caste Aryas insisted on eliminating all caste distinctions among themselves and between themselves and the purified low caste groups.[74] But in any case the Samaj was undermining the religious justification of the caste system by throwing open to everyone participation in previously exclusive, even secret, rituals. The orthodoxy, as represented by formal associations as well as by individual village leaders, did not vigorously oppose the movement, for several possible reasons: the Arya Samaj's services to Hinduism in its cultural, and later political, opposition to Islam were understood by all Hindus; and the Samaj's reforming message, which could not easily be rejected as an alien invention, gained the respect of

[72] Cited in Graham, *op.cit.*, pp. 417, 432n, 442n, 444n. Increases for other religious communities were far lower during all of those decades; e.g., from 1901 to 1911, the percentage increases were: Brahmos 35, Hindus 5, Sikhs 37, Muslims 6, and Christians 32.

[73] Dayananda and the Samaj argued that Muslims and Christians had originally been converts from Hinduism, and they were merely returning to their ancestral faith.

[74] Regarding the latter, Graham observed: "When groups from the lower strata of society are purified, they retain their old caste or social group, but simply advance up the caste scale so that they are within the pale of respectability and touchability." *op.cit.*, p. 522.

Hindus and led many of them to modify their own caste prejudices.[75]

The effects of "purification" on low castes, outcastes, and tribal peoples were hard to judge, but Graham was undoubtedly right in observing that the religious motives did not enter significantly into the joining of the Samaj by low caste communities.[76] The desire to rise socially has frequently been seen as the chief, if not the only, reason for low-caste groups to embrace the Arya Samaj,[77] as well as the Christian and Islamic faiths. In many cases the progress that those communities made in economic and political terms was sanctified, so to speak, by the ritual acknowledgment of their status provided by the Arya Samaj. But the meager results of their conversion in terms of brotherhood ties with high-caste Aryas continued to exist, as did restrictions on inter-marriage between high-caste Aryas themselves. In 1922, when Gandhi's caste reform ideas were gaining attention, a group of Samajists, led by Bhai Parmanand, a Professor at the D.A.V. College, founded the Jat Pat Todak Mandal in Lahore to work for elimination of caste distinctions within the Samaj,[78] and in 1937, after a decade of effort by Samajists, an Arya Marriage Validation Act (XIX of 1937) was passed by the Central Legislature to assure the legality of inter-caste marriages among Aryas, which were still, however, few in number.

The Arya Samaj's recruitment of low castes and outcastes grew out of its earlier crusade, known as the Shuddhi movement, for the conversion and "purification" of Muslims and Christians. The political foundations of the Shuddhi movement could not be concealed from anyone who had read Dayananda's aggressively

[75] *ibid.*, pp. 516-18.

[76] *ibid.*, p. 515.

[77] In 1960 the author interviewed Pundit Anandpriya of the Arya Samaj in Baroda, who told of his plan to invest 5,000 tribal Bhils with the sacred thread. "It is not religious, but social, appeal," said the Pundit, which led the Bhils to agree to the forthcoming ceremony. He noted that as the government takes over welfare and educational work among the depressed classes the opportunities for the Samaj diminish. "Our specialty is gone," he remarked. For a contemporary account of Samaj activities in breaking down caste barriers and refuting superstitious ideas, see Oscar Lewis, *Village Life in Northern India*, Index.

[78] Graham, *op.cit.*, pp. 537-38.

Hindu nationalist writings, which clearly stated that the political future of India rested in large measure on the reconstruction of the entire society according to a Hindu religious pattern. Starting with Pundit Tulsi Ram's "purification" of converts from Islam and Christianity at Amritsar in the 1880's the movement grew to include depressed classes among Hindus, as just noted, and in 1909 the All-India Shuddhi Sabha was established to carry the work to all parts of the country, if opportunities for expansion presented themselves. The Shuddhi movement placed the Samaj in league with orthodox bodies, such as the Hindu Mahasabha,[79] and created for it an inescapable involvement in communal tension and disputes, and hence in politics.

Official statements of the Arya Samaj and its various local subdivisions always proclaimed the Samaj's policy of not taking part in politics, a policy laid down by Dayananda himself. Yet Samajists never denied that the Samaj was one of the most powerful agencies for the spread of nationalist ideas in northern India. Lala Lajpat Rai admitted that he received political guidance through his association with the Arya Samaj, and he wrote: "that the Arya Samaj is one of the most potent nationalizing forces no one should or need deny. The Arya Samaj aims at radical changes in the thought and life of the people. It aims at the formation of a new national character on the fundamental basis of Vedic thought and Vedic life."[80] In Rai's work, *The Arya Samaj*, a prime source for study of the movement, he constantly used political nationalist arguments to explain the Samaj's work in education, social reform, and Shuddhi. Bipin Chandra Pal, as a Bengali journalist working in Lahore in the late 1880's, passed an outsider's judgment on the Arya Samaj, that "The movement, at least in those days, seemed to me, in fact, far more political than religious or spiritual." Its militancy, in contrast to the piety of Pal's Brahmo Samaj, shocked

[79] See *Indian Social Reformer*, June 14, 1924, p. 658: "The Shuddhi Movement has largely bridged the gap between the Arya Samaj and the orthodox Hindus."

[80] Rai, *op.cit.*, p. 254. See also Har Bilas Sarda, *Hindu Superiority: An Attempt to Determine the Position of the Hindu Race in the Scale of Nations*, in which the author demonstrated in 454 pages the brilliance of Hindu civilization, excelling all others. Sarda's was one of scores of such works by Samajists, in English and vernaculars, which followed Dayananda's pattern of exaggerated assertion of the achievements of Hindus.

him, and in any case he was intellectually unable to accept the Samaj's doctrine of Vedic infallibility.[81]

Because of its vigorous anti-Christian message, as well as the political record of some of its membership, the Samaj struck many British observers as a movement which held a greater threat to the established rule in the Punjab than any other development in the 20th century. Valentine Chirol's famous exposé, *Indian Unrest*, contained such a pointed analysis of the Samaj's political implications, notably at the time of the Punjab disturbances of 1907, that defenders of the Samaj felt it necessary to answer his allegations for years thereafter. Chirol found it anomalous that "the Arya Samaj, which shows the impress of Western influence in so much of its social work, should at the same time have associated itself so intimately with a political movement directed against British rule." Many Aryas, he noted, "have played a conspicuous part in the seditious agitation of the last few years, both in the Punjab and in the neighboring United Provinces."[82] What made the Samaj more dangerous than other movements, for Chirol, was that "Although the Arya leaders are generally men of education and sometimes of great culture, they know how to present their creed in a popular form that appeals to the lower classes and especially to the agriculture population."[83]

The Samaj's arousing of communal hostilities created an immediate administrative problem for the British which alone would have set many of them against the organization. Replies to such charges as those of Chirol were often impassioned denials by Samajists of the involvement of their body in political activities, but in them too were significant signs of pride that a national movement had finally emerged which could challenge the government on all levels of society. In a letter to the *Vedic Magazine and Gurukula Samachar* one writer took satisfaction in the effects which the Samaj had on the Indian, who "was ready to kneel

[81] Pal, *Memories* . . . , II, 71. Several decades later Pal revised part of his evaluation of the Samaj: "Both morally and spiritually the Arya Samaj has advanced very considerably from what I found it in the late eighties of the last century." *ibid.*, p. 83.

[82] Chirol, *Indian Unrest*, pp. 111-12.

[83] *ibid.*, pp. 116-17.

down before any and every body that he thought was armed with some authority whether natural or supernatural. Even before stones and stalks he stood with bowed head and folded hands. . . ." The writer could not deny that "The complete overthrow of un-questioning obedience to spiritual power was followed by a partial diminution of the excessive awe felt by the Indian toward temporal authority."[84]

The chief inspiration for political involvement by Aryas was the example of Lala Lajpat Rai, a Congress leader who devoted a great share of his time to the educational and social program of the Samaj. At the time of his arrest and deportation in 1907 he was a member of the executive committee of the Lahore Arya Samaj and a Vice President of the D.A.V. College. Rai's acknowledgment of the political role of the Samaj brought quick disclaimers from several leading Samaj leaders, including Munshi Ram and Hans Raj, and the latter tried to keep D.A.V. College students away from political activities. Lajpat Rai was accused by his associates of having drawn the Samaj into politics, where, as Dayananda had stipulated, it did not belong. The *Arya Patrika* supported their view that "The Vedas are the truth for all the world; Lajpat Rai and the D.A.V. leaders are localizing and nationalizing a universal movement."[85] The sincerity of the Arya Samaj leaders in re-pudiating Rai's activities, in 1907 and later, and the official Samaj policy of not supporting political causes, as a body, could not be fairly disputed. Yet, as individuals, Aryas were specially motivated to political action, and in the Punjab disorders and the Patiala State Conspiracy Case during the First World War many of them were linked together as conspirators or, at least, as men of un-settling influence. A revolutionary colleague of Tilak, Krishna Varma, who was also one of Dayananda's chosen agents for the executing of his Will, founded the Home Rule League in London in 1905 and, later, from his exile in Paris, he wrote approvingly of the murder of Sir William Curzon Wyllie of the India Office in 1909.[86] Although he had resigned from the Arya Samaj, its leaders

[84] Madan Mohan Seth, "The Arya Samaj; A Political Body . . . ," p. 70.

[85] Quoted in Graham, *op.cit.*, p. 431. D.A.V. here referred to the section of the Samaj, not the College itself, headed by Hans Raj.

[86] The alliance between Arya Samajists and certain of the followers of Tilak,

were called upon to repudiate any connection with him or his views.[87]

The Arya Samaj, in short, was informally split on the issue of political nationalism, with the College branch somewhat more anxious than the Gurukula branch to support nationalist anti-British activities.[88] But, despite that split, the Arya Samaj movement as a whole has had the effect of uniting social reform and (Hindu) nationalism, in a manner unlike that of other 20th century reform movements. Social reform for Aryas, which includes education and the rehabilitation of the depressed classes, was a precondition for the re-emergence of Hinduism (purified and invigorated) as the dominant social and political force in modern India, which naturally implied its hostility toward the Muslim and Christian cultures. The irony, which Chirol sensed, of Westernized, enlightened reformers opposing British rule and asserting a doctrine which, in a self-governing India, was bound to deny Muslims—a political minority—legitimate expression of their cultural autonomy, concealed a more profound dilemma. The dilemma was produced by the unresolved conflict between the desire for a revitalization of Hindu society, which the Arya Samaj and similar bodies indeed could produce, and the desire for an independent India achieved without bloodshed or partition. Even after Partition, the dilemma remained for Hindus in India—and a comparable dilemma was posed for Muslims in Pakistan.

---

and the oversimplified slogan, "Lal-Pal-Bal," should not by any means suggest parallel interests between the Samaj and Maharashtrian (or Bengali) extremism. Many Aryas found Tilak's resort to popular religious prejudices an insult to any true Hindu revival. See, e.g., The *Vedic Magazine*, I, 12, 12, as cited in Graham, *op.cit.*, p. 128.

[87] See Munshi Ram, Jijyasu and Rama Deva, *The Arya Samaj and Its Detractors: A Vindication*. The present author learned that the Baroda Arya Samaj mission gave secret refuge to Bhagat Singh after Singh had been involved in the plot to kill the Viceroy, Lord Hardinge, in 1912.

[88] When the Congress adopted platforms of Hindu-Muslim cooperation, especially after Gandhi assumed control in 1920, the more orthodox and Hindu nationalist Samajists, to be found chiefly in the Gurukula branch, found it impossible to accept Congress leadership. The controversial evidence, compiled by the government and the Muslim League, of Arya Samajist communal activities before Independence requires fresh, objective study.

THE RECONSTRUCTION OF INDIAN

NATIONALISM

IT WAS SIGNIFICANT that the first great Hindu revivalist, Dayananda Saraswati, was also a social reformer of major rank. The extremist nationalists who were trained in the Arya Samaj, including Lajpat Rai, made a close connection in their thinking and action between revivalism and the reformation of Hindu society. However, they regarded the established social reform movement, as it was enunciated by the National Social Conference, as "denationalizing," or antinationalist, and for a decade or more around the turn of the century they battled with the leading reformers. Out of that controversy both sides came to recognize and indeed to overcome the primary source of their disagreement—the reformers' reliance on Western inspiration for their ideals. The Arya Samaj movement demonstrated that social reform could have meaning and attraction for Indians if the society which the reformers wished to create seemed authentically Indian. The fact that the specific aims of the Samajist social reform program coincided at nearly every point with the aims of the Social Conference did not lessen their appeal when those aims were stated as ideals of traditional Hinduism.

A new stage of intellectual development came into prominent focus in the first decade of the 20th century as the reconstruction of Indian nationalism assumed form under the leadership of Hindu revivalists. The pressures for cultural and religious revival came partly from political leaders, who saw the Congress movement collapsing from want of popular support.[1] The nationalist movement of the Indian National Congress had tried to define a new India in terms borrowed from European political experience and Western social ethics, but the results had never been entirely satisfying even to the moderates. By the end of the 19th century they, as well as the extremists, discovered that the ideals and methods of the Congress neither conveyed hope to the people at large nor stimulated real devotion from their limited followings. A reconstructed, Hindu nationalism, therefore, emerged, which was expected to lead to a more rapid and a more widespread advancement. One result of this third stage of modern intellectual development was a new alignment of political and social reform movements which the expediencies of an exclusively secular nationalism had thrust apart. Both social reformers and political leaders found that they could agree when their aims were defined in Indian, rather than in Western, terms.

The Political Reconstruction

By the turn of the century the moderates in the Congress appeared to have lost faith in their own prescriptions and had certainly lost the bulk of their following; the extremists, on the other hand, offered a vague program for political progress and had no organization to spread their embryonic doctrines of swaraj, swadeshi, and boycott. The stagnant political life, reflected in the stand-off between the moderates and extremists, discouraged Indians and may have encouraged Lord Curzon to push ahead with his administrative reforms without consulting the wishes of national leaders. In 1903 Allan O. Hume, who had fostered the political nationalist movement, addressed a message to Congressmen in which he accused them of being "never more

---

[1] One of the earliest cogent analyses of the failure of the Congress to present a program and a leadership that could reach the general public was Aurobindo Ghose's series in the *Indu Prakash*, "New Lamps for Old," written in 1893. Rightly, Aurobindo saw that the Congress did not truly represent the nation at large, and for that reason could bring about no fundamental alteration in British rule. The articles are reprinted in Mukherjees, *Sri Aurobindo's Political Thought*, p. 63f. Lajpat Rai, Tilak, and B.C. Pal were also writing similar criticisms in the 1890's.

than half earnest in your fight" and unwilling to devote "any earnest thought or any day's real work to poor India's public business!" And he continued, "Years ago I called on you to be up and doing; years ago I warned you that 'Nations by themselves are made'. . . . Can you suppose that a race is to be won by merely looking at the course and talking brilliantly about it? Can you fancy that any despotic government . . . *will willingly* yield to you. . . . Do you dream that the British nation here . . . will go out of their way to insist on justice being done to you simply because it *is* justice . . . ?"[2]

The answer to Hume—indeed, the response to their own critiques of their failings—came from Indian nationalists in forms that Hume himself repudiated. It came as terrorism built up from literary appeals to race hatred and from secret political organizations. The answer came also in the form of the increasingly popular nationalist ideology of cultural and religious revival. What Hume, and the moderate leaders in Congress, wanted was a greatly strengthened democratic Congress organization for mass political involvement. However, the Congress, again under the control of the moderates after the crisis at Surat in 1907, had ceased to be the major vehicle of nationalism. J. Ramsay Macdonald, after a visit to India in 1910, wrote with a remarkable accuracy that at Surat "the Nationalist movement as such broke away from the movement for political reform."[3] Political reform was represented by the continuing agitation of the Congress and its responsiveness to the Morley-Minto Reform Act and other British gestures of conciliation under Lord Minto and Lord Hardinge. Nationalism, not bound by the requirements of organized endeavor, expressed itself through terrorism and through cultural revival. In the latter form it grew rapidly in the richness of its intellectual context, in the intensity of its grip on those who understood it, and in the scope of its contacts with the public at large.

---

[2] Reprinted in *Hindustan Review*, xxvii, pp. 597-600. One month before Hume delivered his remarks the journal, *East and West*, aptly referred to him as "the chivalrous Englishman whose only fault was that he mistook poor old-world India for a modern British or American constituency on a huge scale." ii, 25, 1,307.

[3] Macdonald, *Awakening of India*, p. 200.

By 1915-1916 the Home Rule movement, led by Annie Besant and Tilak,[4] was attempting to give form and strength to the new nationalism as a useful political weapon, but that effort largely failed; the attempt was again made in 1920 by Gandhi, that time with greater success.

An important symptom of the breakdown in nationalist *organization* at the very time when intellectual formulations of nationalism were gaining strength was the formation of the Muslim League in 1906. Until that time the Congress could claim to represent Hindu and Muslim nationalists, but thereafter a certain body of influential Muslims was always to be found in an organization whose origins and ultimate purposes testified to the existence of Muslim nationalism. The theory that Indian society embodied two separate and distinct nations undercut in a fundamental way the integrity of Congress nationalism and caused a dilemma for Hindu Congress leaders which was still unresolved at the time of the Partition in 1947.[5] Indian nationalism had in fact become by the first decade of this century Hindu nationalism among the Hindu leaders of the movement. The moderate constitutionalists, such as Naoroji, Gokhale, Pherozeshah Mehta, and Banerjea, no longer commanded their earlier following; instead men such as Lajpat Rai, Tilak, B.C. Pal, and Aurobindo, all of whom identified the nation with the religious tradition of Hinduism, were taking over the leadership.

The Surat Congress of 1907 provided the opportunity for Aurobindo Ghose, an extremist, to make his political debut. Following the split at Surat, Aurobindo made a brief speaking tour of western India and analyzed the meaning of these events. Nationalism, he said, is a "new religion," which cannot be subdued either by the British rulers or by the erstwhile monopolizers of India's political life. To a Bombay audience he declared, "You call yourselves Nationalists. What is Nationalism? Nationalism is not a mere political programme; Nationalism is a religion that has come from God; Nationalism is a creed in which you shall

---

[4] The movement, in fact, consisted of two separate Home Rule Leagues, with Besant controlling one and Tilak the other. See Wolpert, *Tilak and Gokhale*, pp. 276, 288.

[5] That dilemma was noted at the conclusion of Chapter XI.

have to live. . . . Nationalism is immortal; Nationalism cannot die. . . . God cannot be killed, God cannot be sent to jail."[6] Finally returning to his native Bengal, where he and Bipin Chandra Pal edited the extremist paper, *Bande Mataram*, Aurobindo pressed the challenge which his circle was presenting to the public and to moderate Congressmen. His desire was not to break with the Congress leaders, but he said to them, "we have our path to follow and our work to do, and if you will not allow us a place in the assembly you call National, we will make one for ourselves out of it and around it, until one day you will find us knocking at your doors with the nation at our back and in the name of an authority even you will not dare to deny."[7]

Aurobindo and Bipin Chandra exemplified the reconstruction of nationalism, which followed two new lines of thought and action: 1) the incorporation into the nation of the "masses" (all Indian political writers refer in this way to the illiterate peasantry and workers—Aurobindo used the term "proletariat"); and 2) the identification of the nation with the religious ideals which were summarized, for Aurobindo, in the idea of the "Mother." The two elements were inseparably linked because only through religion could the masses understand the nation and give it their loyalty and their energy. As *Bande Mataram* (Hail to the Mother) explained, "Swaraj as a sort of European ideal, political liberty for the sake of political self-assertion, will not awaken India. Swaraj as the fulfillment of the ancient life of India under modern conditions, the return of the *Satyayuga* [era of truth] of national greatness, the resumption by her of her great *role* of teacher and guide, self-liberation of the people for the final fulfillment of the Vedantic ideal in politics, this is the true Swaraj for India."[8]

That ideal and those words could scarcely appeal to Muslims— they clearly proclaimed a Hindu nation. The point was later glossed over by certain Hindu leaders, but in the early, exuberant

[6] Iyengar, *Sri Aurobindo*, p. 142.
[7] *Bande Mataram*, Dec. 8, 1907; quoted in Mukherjees, *"Bande Mataram" and Indian Nationalism*, p. 60.
[8] *Bande Mataram*, May 3, 1908; quoted in Mukherjees, pp. 84-85.

years of the new nationalist period, it was stated with candor. "The ground work of what may well be called the composite culture of India is undoubtedly Hindu," wrote *Bande Mataram*. "Though the present Indian nationality is composed of many races, and the present Indian culture of more than one world civilization, yet it must be admitted that the Hindu forms its base and center. . . . The dominant note of Hindu culture, its sense of the spiritual and universal, will, therefore, be the peculiar feature of this composite Indian nationality. . . . And the type of spirituality that it seeks to develop, is essentially Hindu."[9] Muslims and Christians would be tolerated and respected, but they must recognize their essential "Indianness," which meant the essential Hindu quality of their particular beliefs and practices. After reviewing the evolution of the new nationalist doctrines, Bipin Chandra Pal in 1916 summed up his findings: "The Nationalist Movement in India, which, so far, is essentially a Hindu Movement, stands, ideally, for 1) Hindu Nationalism; 2) Federal Internationalism; 3) Universal Federation." In practice those ideals should lead first to the "Preservation of the distinctive genius and character of Hindu Culture and Civilization," and second to the "Promotion of sympathetic and reverent study of other world cultures . . . represented in the composite life of modern India, and the Cultivation of the spirit of mutual understanding and helpful cooperation with them."[10]

The Bengali inspiration for the new nationalism did not undermine the appeal of its ideas to other Indians, although the terrorism into which many Bengali youths translated the more activist and chauvinist elements in the doctrines was repudiated by most political leaders in all provinces. Ideas of a religious resurgence among the Indian people had always attracted national leaders. The Prarthana Samajists of western India, for instance, believed fundamentally that a religious spirit had to awaken Indians before they could revive their civilization. Ranade repudiated an unthinking revival of useless Hindu traditions, but, echoing Keshub Chandra Sen, he declared in the 1880's that there

[9] *Bande Mataram*, June 14, 1908; quoted in Mukherjees, pp. 93-94.
[10] Pal, *Nationality and Empire*, pp. 47-48.

was no chance of genuine reform unless the "heart of the nation . . . is regenerated, not by cold calculations of utility, but by the cleansing fire of a religious revival."[11] Ranade and his political and social reform followers in western India, however, refused to carry the religious message forward, partly because of its obvious irrelevance and even repugnance to part of India's population, and partly because of its seeming lack of clarity as a guide to social reform.

The conservative branch of the Arya Samaj was forthright in its zeal for a Hindu revival, and even Lajpat Rai, a liberal Arya who often sought genuine reconciliation with the Muslim community, wrote, "In my opinion, the problem before us is in the main a religious problem—religious not in the sense of doctrines and dogmas—but religious in so far as to evoke the highest devotion and the greatest sacrifice from us."[12] The "highest devotion" for Lajpat Rai would scarcely be the same for a Muslim; Rai noted on one occasion that "The spiritual note of the present Nationalist Movement in India is entirely derived from . . . Vedantic thought."[13] In south India the Theosophical movement and Mrs. Besant proclaimed the ideals of revival and specifically linked them to nationalism. Mrs. Besant's handbook for nationalists, a series of articles published under the title, *Nation Building*, acknowledged the religious divisions in India but urged that they be merged "by the theosophical recognition of the spiritual unity of all religions."[14] This was a nominally universal ideal but was closely linked to the Hindu mystic tradition, as was the Theosophical Society. On other occasions Mrs. Besant encouraged a frank conjunction of politics and religion. "If there is to be an Indian nation," she wrote enthusiastically, "Patriotism and Religion must join hands in India."[15]

Thus the reconstruction of nationalism, a necessity if the movement were to penetrate beneath the English-educated intellectual groups and an Indian rather than a neo-Western nation were to

[11] Ranade, *Religious and Social Reform*, p. 93.
[12] Gupta, *Studies in the Bengal Renaissance*, p. 195.
[13] Rai, *Young India*, p. 193.
[14] *Nation Building*, p. 22.
[15] *Hindustan Review*, xv, 545.

be created, took place from cultural and religious materials of essentially Hindu origin.

Political nationalism was enormously enriched in its meanings and strengthened by increased popular response as a result of the reconstruction of nationalist ideas which took place in the early 20th century. The demand for full independence was for the first time understood by great numbers of Indians, and a sincere pride in the Indian heritage made that demand into more than an academic assertion of natural rights. Complete reliance on petitions directed at the government and propaganda directed at British public opinion was forsworn by almost all nationalist leaders. But despite its increased popularity and its many brilliant exponents the new nationalism failed to embody itself in a political organization which might spread the doctrines and offer a practical program of swaraj. Aurobindo's warning, or threat, that the nationalists would come knocking at the door of the Congress with a nation behind them never materialized; the nation as a whole remained dormant politically until new techniques for rousing it were tried in the 1920's by Gandhi. Various reasons can be suggested for the failure—at least during the first two decades of the century—of reconstructed nationalism to produce a nationally organized political program. One was the steadfast grip on the Congress organization maintained by the moderates, whose conception of the nation remained essentially what it had been in the 1880's. Another was the fairly successful repression by the government of the radical nationalist spokesmen—Aurobindo's retirement to the Pondicherry ashram saved the government the trouble of further silencing the most intellectually formidable of all Indian nationalists. Finally, the new nationalists, even if they had succeeded in organizing themselves, had no program for constructive action. In Bengal, where the swadeshi movement for several years produced an organized and popular response, active politics meant revolutionary overthrow of British rule and very little more.[16]

[16] See H. and U. Mukherjee, *India's Fight for Freedom or the Swadeshi Movement.* The Mukherjees, incidentally, have sought to demonstrate that the new nationalist movement did not emphasize a Hindu revival, except occa-

In contrast to the ineffectiveness of reconstructed nationalism in producing a political program, it had a creative, constructive effect on the social reform movement. That effect was summarized in 1911 by the editor of the *Indian Social Reformer*, K. Natarajan. He keenly observed that the political leaders, whether moderate or extremist, had to depend almost exclusively on Western ideas for the substance of their reform programs; the Indian tradition of politics had virtually nothing in it that could be used as a base for the advance the politicians desired. On the other hand, in reforming social institutions Indians could find support in their own traditions—either the intellectual traditions or the living social institutions—for all of their reform doctrines. Thus, for Natarajan, revivalism "has had a wonderfully steadying effect on the national character. It has made us more deliberate and self-respecting in our progress . . . and has invested the work of reform with a dignity which does not belong to mere imitation."[17]

Reconstructed Nationalism and Social Reform

Under the influence of the new nationalist ideas the social reform movement in the early 20th century altered its creed and shifted the focus of its practical programs so as to bring both into line with the movement for national cultural revival. Initially, however, the reformers and the new nationalists were in conflict.

The original opposition to the social reform movement came from individuals and groups that represented established orthodox views in Hindu society. For every social reform association

---

sionally as a political expedient and then in no way aggressively enough to have alienated Muslims. In contrast to their usually sound scholarship, that conclusion has not been adequately documented. The confusion in their analysis appears to lie in their effort to disassociate revivalism from social and religious reaction. Revivalism did not imply reaction, as the Mukherjees have shown. But by showing that, they have by no means also shown that revivalism was not a genuine effort to reassert Hindu values and to promote them as the standard of loyalty to the nation. *ibid.*, pp. 206-212. For a very detailed account of the nationalist movement in Bengal following the Partition of 1905, see John R. McLane, "The Development of Nationalist Ideas and Tactics and the Policies of the Government of India: 1897-1905," chap. VI.

[17] "The Working Faith of the Indian Reformer," *Hindustan Review*, XXIII, 13.

established, at least one orthodox body was founded to counter whatever influence the reformers were thought to have. The founding of the Dharma Sabha in 1830 to counter Roy's Brahmo Sabha and defend Hindu religion and society from alien influences, was followed by the establishment of an increasing number of public associations in Bengal during the 19th and 20th centuries to check the spread of Western ideas and their undermining effects on Hinduism. The Sanatana Dharma Rakshini Sabha (Society for Defense of the Eternal Religion), founded in Calcutta in 1873, and the Dharma Mahamandali (Great Religious Association) established two decades later, were two of the more vital orthodox bodies. In western India similar developments occurred. The Hindu Dharma Vyavasthapaka Mandali (Association for the Preservation of the Hindu Religion) was formed in the mid-1860's to oppose the Widow Remarriage Association. Much later, following the passage of the Age of Consent Bill, Tilak and his followers formed several associations to popularize Hindu, and specifically Marathi Hindu, traditions. In south India the Theosophical Society in its early years performed the function of increasing confidence in orthodox ideas and customs, and less famous societies, such as the Bharata Dharma Mahaparishad (Great Indian Religious Association), led by Indians, did the same. The Punjab had Pundit Din Dayal Sarma, whose vigorous attacks on the Arya Samaj gained enough strength so that his circle founded the Sanatana Dharma Sabha (Eternal Religion Society) in 1895 in Delhi and at Hardwar. A decade later Lala Lal Chand, an ex-Arya, began forming Hindu Sabhas, chiefly to counter the Muslim League's units in north India.

The culmination of the movement to strengthen Hindu orthodoxy was the formation in 1900 of the Bharata Dharma Mahamandala (Great Indian Religious Organization), which by 1910 "had been recognized as a body representing the whole Hindu community by the heads of the chief Hindu sects and religious orders."[18] After the retirement of its first leader, Swami Gyananan-

---

[18] Farquhar, *Modern Religious Movements in India*, p. 319. The date of its founding is taken as Aug. 8, 1900, when the first comprehensive conference of the movement's 700 sabhas took place at Delhi. *ISR*, Aug. 19, 1900, p. 401.

daji, a leading congressman from the United Provinces, Pundit Madan Mohan Malaviya, undertook to strengthen the society's work in spreading the doctrines of Hinduism and showing their relevance for contemporary times. During the First World War, or shortly thereafter, Malaviya and Lajpat Rai organized the Hindu Mahasabha, which to the present day has maintained with considerable success an orthodox response to Western ideas, with persuasive force for many educated Hindus.[19]

Support for orthodox religious beliefs—often termed Sanatana Dharma[20]—came not only from voluntary associations. Religious sects which were already a part of Hindu life became more active in their own defense as the religious and social reform movements gained ground. The Madhva (Vaishnava) sect in south India found support in the Madhva Siddhantonnahini Sabha (Society for Strengthening the Madhva System), founded in 1877 by an English-educated government official. Also in the south, educated followers of the Sri Vaishnava sect formed the Ubhaya-vedanta Pravartana Sabha (Society for Promotion of Both Forms of Vedanta) in 1902. In 1911 four major Vaishnava sects flourishing in various parts of India held a general conference at Allahabad. South Indian Shaivism produced a movement based on Shaiva Sabhas which, after 1906, held annual conferences. Bombay Shaivites also formed new organizations in the late 19th century that were connected with the Lingayat sect and began to promote the education of youth, much as caste associations were doing. Bengali Chaitanyas began to create a defensive, but somewhat modernized, neo-Vaishnava movement in the late 1880's, based chiefly on a literary revival of the Krishna legend and the

---

[19] Few good accounts of the Mahasabha exist in English and there is disagreement even on the date of its founding. See, however, a brief account in Myron Weiner, *Party Politics in India*, p. 166f.

[20] A modern term which generally can be said "to indicate the eternal principles of religion and conduct considered to be fundamental truths of Hinduism. The term has largely come into use in Hindu revivalist circles and an appeal is made to Sanatana Dharma for the purpose of resisting changes in the Hindu law." Sir P.S. Sivaswamy Aiyar, *Evolution of Hindu Moral Ideas*, pp. 132-33. Aiyar continued: "Even the most ardent champions of Sanatana Dharma must shrink from any proposal to enforce the entire body of rules contained in the *Smṛtis*."

Bhagavad-Gita. Orissa and the northern Telegu country also experienced a neo-Vaishnava revival.[21]

The orthodox bodies opposed the social reform movement as a defensive measure against the threat to the established order that they knew the spread of Western ideas entailed. Defensiveness could be seen in a typical criticism of the social reform movement which came from one respondent to the "Notes" of Behramji Malabari. The writer called the reformers "denationalized," and he continued, "Our reformers attack everything. . . . They assail religion, caste, and all that is dear to the Hindu . . . and they invoke the aid of Government in matters in which it should least interfere. The result is that they set the whole country against themselves and their measures of reformation, and make it impossible for the people to consider dispassionately the merits of the particular measure which is proposed for the good of the nation."[22] The reaction taking place against the reform doctrines was analyzed in 1889 by Bipin Chandra Pal in a lecture to the Bethune Society in Calcutta, entitled "The Present Social Reaction, What Does It Mean?"[23] Pal deplored the sudden turn away from the rationalism and liberalism of the 1870's and 1880's to the "narrow patriotism" and "race hatred" of his day. But the reasons for it, he thought, were understandable, namely the "freaks and fancies" of the early reformers. He continued: "The first batch of our English-educated young men were so dazzled with the new light they received from the West, that in their zeal for reform they sadly overdid their part. They saw no good in anything belonging to their own country, and sought to transplant English institutions bodily into the Indian soil. Such violent actions were sure, sooner or later, to lead to as violent a reaction in the opposite direction."[24] Thirty years later Aurobindo drew the same lesson from the "false method" of the early reformers: "an anglicised India is a thing we can no longer view as either possible or desirable,—and it could only, if pursued to

[21] More detailed accounts of those movements appear in Farquhar, *op.cit.*, p. 291f.
[22] Rai Mulraj, in Gidumal, *Status of Women in India*, p. 116.
[23] The lecture took place Dec. 5, 1889 and was later published in Calcutta.
[24] *ibid.*, pp. 4-5.

the end, have made us painful copyists, clumsy followers always stumbling in the wake of European evolution and always fifty years behind it. This movement of thought did not and could not endure. . . ."[25]

By the end of the century the reactionaries and orthodox critics of the social reform movement were overtaken by the revivalists, whose aims were not to oppose advancement but to create changes in Hindu society—changes as radical as those of the social reformers but based on Indian, not alien, ideals. In some respects revivalism, in its multitude of forms, could be likened to a counter-reformation, because along with its reassertion of the old faiths went their reconstruction through doctrines and practices which made them more acceptable to enlightened Hindus.[26] In the first decade of the 20th century no clear-cut distinction could be made between the major revivalist movements (except for Tilak's)[27] and the social reform movements in terms of the objectives that they both set for Hindu advancement.

One of the outstanding features of intellectual life in India in the years around the turn of the century was the dialogue between the social reformers and the revivalists. Although much of it initially centered around the conflicts between them, it increasingly revealed the essential agreement that existed between the social reform movement and revivalism on issues of significance for nationalists.

Lala Lajpat Rai, whose revivalism was channeled through the Arya Samaj, ardently supported the most radical social reform doctrines but he criticized the leaders of the national social reform movement, the "eminent Hindus of the Western Presi-

[25] Aurobindo, *Renaissance in India*, articles reprinted from the *Arya* of 1918, p. 35.

[26] Bipin Chandra Pal wrote of Bengal, "All these revivals and reactions were more directly the fruit of the previous movement of religious and social revolt led by the Brahmo Samaj itself. In this sense, they were not merely destructive of the Brahmo propaganda, but also at the same time, partially corrective of and supplementary to it. Most, if not all of the protagonists of this new Hindu religious revival and social reaction had been in their early life connected with the Brahmo Samaj." *Memories of My Life and Times*, vol. 1, 427-28.

[27] Tilak's revivalist endeavors were specifically directed against social reformists chiefly because of the peculiar personal hostility which Tilak himself nourished toward the reformers of Poona.

dency" who based their reform on "rationality" instead of "nationality." He agreed that social reform was a matter of "paramount national importance. There can be no doubt that the whole future of the nation depends upon the amounts of social efficiency we secure and display, but I do not at the same time share the general belief that socially, the ancient Hindus were a very inferior people and had no, or very poor, notion of social or national responsibilities." Lajpat Rai doubted "the possibility of a wholesale bringing back or revival of the past such as perhaps some of the Theosophists and also some of the Arya Samajists contemplate. . . ." But he recognized "a great deal in our past which can rightly inspire or guide us in building up our future social edifice. . . ." In the manner of many other Indians at the turn of the century, Lajpat Rai found Western society much less inspiring than it had appeared to an earlier generation, and he doubted that a "wholesale imitation of the West" would solve India's problems.[28]

The usually conciliatory Ranade intensified the debate with the revivalists in a famous speech at Amraoti in 1897, which is quoted even today by reformers. "When we are asked to revive our institutions and customs," Ranade said, "people seem to be very much at sea to what it is they [wish] to revive. . . . Shall we revive the old habits of our people when the most sacred of our caste indulged in all the abominations as we now understand them of animal food and drink which exhausted every section of our country's Zoology and Botany? The men and the Gods of those old days ate and drank forbidden things to excess in a way no revivalist will now venture to recommend. Shall we revive the twelve forms of sons, or eight forms of marriage, which included capture, and recognized mixed and illegitimate intercourse? Shall we revive the Niyoga system of procreating sons on our brother's wives when widowed? . . . Shall we revive the hecatombs of animals sacrificed from year's end to year's end, and in which human beings were not spared as propitiatory offerings? Shall we revive the Shakti worship of the left hand with its indecencies and practical debaucheries? Shall we revive the *Sati* and infanti-

[28] *Lala Lajpat Rai: The Man in His Word*, pp. 67-74.

cide customs, or the flinging of living men into the rivers, or over rocks, or hookswinging, or the crushing beneath Jagannath car? . . . Shall we require our Brahmins to cease to be landlords and gentlemen and turn into beggars and dependents upon the king as in olden times? These instances will suffice to show that the plan of reviving the ancient usages and customs will not work our salvation, and is not practicable."[29] Lajpat Rai appeared to be answering Ranade, with an equal amount of sarcasm, when he asked the reformers "into what they wish to reform us? Whether they want us to be reformed on the patterns of the English or the French? Whether they want us to accept the divorce laws of Christian society or the temporary marriages that are now so much in favour in France or American [sic]? Whether they want to make men of our women by putting them into those associations for which nature never meant them? . . . Whether they want us to reform into Sunday drinkers of brandy and promiscuous eaters of beef? In short, whether they want to revolutionize our society by an outlandish imitation of European customs and manners and an undiminished adoption of European vices?" Lajpat Rai acknowledged that in posing such questions he was assuming an extreme posture, but he suggested that many social reformers were doing the same.[30]

By the early 20th century Lajpat Rai said that he was convinced that the revivalists and reformers had reached an essential accord on social questions; differences remained on religious matters, but those should not be allowed to conceal the real similarity of views. He knew that Ranade and others did not desire a break with religion. Thus, despite the sharpest of surface disagreements, the only real dispute between reformers and revivalists was over the authorities from which they derived their inspiration.

Bipin Chandra Pal, the Bengali Brahmo Samajist and revivalist, possessed a religious background and a mystic temperament which raised his nationalist proclamations to a level of fervent inspiration that Lajpat Rai, the Punjabi Arya, could never equal.

[29] Ranade, *Miscellaneous Writings*, pp. 190-91.
[30] *Lala Lajpat Rai* . . . , op.cit., pp. 123-27.

More than any other political leader, Pal constructed the philosophy of the new nationalism in Bengal and brought the rest of
India to an understanding of its spirit.[31] Patriotism was for Pal a
religion and the standard by which all secular advancement had
to be judged. Indian nationalism, in its early stage, Pal correctly
understood, had been based on a European image of the nation.
"In the name of India," he said, "we loved Europe. . . . We loved
the abstraction we called India, but, yes, we hated the thing it
actually was. . . . Our love for our people was something like
the pious love of the Christian missionaries for the heathens. . . ."
When nationalists saw India as a society in evolution toward the
Western example of a nation, "every patriot was a reformer. And
reformers can never be true lovers of their country. . . . Reformers,
by the very necessities of their vocation, dwell constantly on the
darkness, the ugliness, the evil and the ignorance [that they see]
about them." The true patriot, Pal insisted, "loves his Fatherland,
not simply because of the good that is in it, but, yes, also even
the very evils of it."[32] The original nationalists of the Congress were
able to combine political and social reform in their thinking
(though not in their organization) because the standards for
both were derived from the West. The new nationalists, Pal observed, had to repudiate not only the political ideals and methods
of the Congress, but also the social inspiration and methods of
reform of the National Social Conference, because both were admittedly of alien inspiration.

But for Bipin Chandra Pal that repudiation merely cleared the
stage for the entrance of the appropriate nationalist doctrines; it
did not indicate a reaction against the ideas of liberal advancement. Reformers and their opponents, the reactionaries, were both
condemned by Pal. Neither could support true nationalism because neither had "any real and correct appreciation of their own
country and culture." The reformers, "applying the untested
canons of imported European enlightenment to the examination
of the surface values of Indian life and institutions," saw in them

[31] See H. and U. Mukherjee, *Bipin Chandra Pal and India's Struggle For
Swaraj.*
[32] Pal, *The New Spirit*, pp. 200-05.

"signs of almost universal degradation and decadence." Judging Indians "in the light of the history and achievements of Europe, [the reformer] constantly condemns his own country and culture, and with the relentless pity of the missionary propagandist seeks to ruthlessly improve them more or less after these alien ideals." The reactionary, Pal knowingly pointed out, "from a different motive, and pursuing quite an opposite method, also applies unconsciously the standards of Europe." The reactionary wanted to claim for Hindu society precisely what he saw as the strengths of Western society. His endeavors to construct an infallible and absolute religious creed, comparable to the Christian or Islamic, were based on Western inspiration and denied the spirit of tolerance and universalism in Hinduism. The reactionary's tenacious desire to preserve Hindu social institutions just as he found them revealed his alien-inspired faith in the lifeless, formal, and materialistic aspects of Hindu culture, rather than a true understanding of the "soul of India" and its ever-changing manifestations. The real India, Pal said, was understood by the sage and philosopher who was neither a reformer, in the usual sense, nor a reactionary, but who lived in the religious spirit of his country.[33]

The task of building a nation, Pal thought, was one of reconstructing Hindu society, not replacing it or tolerating it as it then was. The reconstruction would result from a re-infusion of religious spirit. India's most serious problem, he wrote, had always been its separation of real spiritual illumination from social life, which was responsible "for the curious spectacle of a highly rational and spiritual people like the Hindus subjecting themselves to material symbols in the religious, and irrational institutions in the social life." That "divorce" between spirit and social practice was due, Pal thought, to an overemphasis on the individual's path to salvation, with little recognition given to his social environment or the salvation of the whole society. Concomitantly, detachment of the individual from the world meant a "divorce between spirit and nature" and explained the fact of India's economic backwardness; the highest minds always looked toward their spiritual welfare, and nature was neglected.[34] The

[33] Pal, *The Soul of India*, pp. 52-56.
[34] Pal, *The New Spirit*, pp. 177-86.

proper duties of a nationalist did not end with his proclaiming political emancipation from British rule, Pal insisted. Of prior importance was the duty to lead the nation through social and religious reform into a "new synthesis of life," which would become the basis of political freedom. Political leaders who failed to acknowledge that duty and act accordingly received Pal's censure.

Throughout Pal's prolific outpourings of prose[35] the urgent need for a rebirth of India's social life was always an important theme. At one point he felt it necessary to answer men, such as Telang, who had once argued that because England had social evils and yet had produced a politically advanced system, India could expect to do likewise. "There are, I admit, social evils in England," he wrote, "but these evils . . . are altogether different in kind from the evils which are eating into the very vitals of the Indian nation at the present moment. Drinking or poverty, or other evils of the same nature do not war against the fundamental principles of democracy, but caste, and the train of monstrous customs connected with it do so in this country. Our religion preaches not the equality of men but their inequality. . . . The social evils under which we groan are based upon a synthesis of life of which inequality, caste, moral servitude, and spiritual slavery form the flesh, the marrow, and the bones." Perhaps exaggerating or revealing his own preconceptions of a West which he had not yet visited, Pal went on to say that, in contrast to the situation in India, both Europe and America find that "political progress may be possible without social reform, for there, as in almost all Christian, and especially in all Protestant countries, democracy is a native of the soil. . . ."[36] Bipin Chandra's early image of Western society contracted by the turn of the century under the weight of his political frustrations, but this only led him to a more complete reliance on Indian ideas as

[35] See the bibliography of Pal's writings in Gupta, *Studies in the Bengal Renaissance*, which also includes a nice sketch of Pal's career.

[36] From "The Basis of Political Reform," a lecture in Calcutta, 1889, pp. 10-11. It was apparently aimed at refuting Telang's 1886 address, "Must Social Reform Precede Political Reform in India?"

foundations for the reforms in Indian society that he insisted upon.[37]

The social reformers had no basic quarrel with either Bipin Chandra Pal or Lala Lajpat Rai—both Samajists who enunciated reform doctrines from their incontestable political platforms with more vigor than most other participants in the National Social Conference. Another revivalist, however, of different background and apparently with other motives, elicited for a time their severest criticisms. Mrs. Annie Besant, the Theosophical leader, had begun to win favor for her movement in the 1890's by extolling the blessings of Hindu culture and urging a revival of ancient learning.[38] Her chief targets for ridicule were the social reformers, whose influence she regarded as debilitating. The center of Mrs. Besant's influence was in south India, from whose educated group had come several eminent leaders of the Social Conference. The latter led the attack against her, correctly regarding her as a major threat to their cause.

Against Mrs. Besant's persistent evocation of India's spiritual heritage the *Indian Social Reformer*, while still located in Madras, wrote, "We do not understand the claim of spiritual supremacy that is made on behalf of India." On the contrary, "We hold that India's deterioration is due to a variety of causes, the chief of which was over-spirituality. . . ."[39] The *Reformer* attributed to Mrs. Besant's influence "much of the mischievous results of the reactionary movement. She upheld the most grotesque practices, she idealized some of the least useful customs of Hindu society. Her sex, her eloquence, her antecedents, her nationality, all told in her favour. The educated person who fled from action could point with pride to the approbation of a cultured woman, a member of the ruling race . . . in exculpation of the strategic movement he had ignominiously executed to the

---

[37] See, e.g., his speech to the Madras Hindu Social Reform Association, Dec. 13, 1902; in *ISR*, Dec. 21, 1902, pp. 150-51.

[38] Even before her advent, there existed a "mania of the educated Hindus for Theosophy. Their minds are now too fully occupied by it to pay any attention to social reforms." C. Ramachandra Aiyar, Subordinate Judge of Madura, to the Govt. of Madras, Dec. 17, 1884; in Govt. of India, Home Dept., *Selections from the Records*, No. ccxxiii, Ser. No. 3, p. 18.

[39] *ISR*, Jan. 29, 1899, p. 170.

rear."[40] Mrs. Besant's claims for mysticism did not satisfy all educated Madrasis. The reformer, K. Srinivasa Row, produced an essay on "The Dangers of Spiritualism, or The Advent of Theosophy," which called upon Mrs. Besant to become a social reformer to assist India out of its physical miseries.[41] In northern India, Theosophy had little following, and Mrs. Besant was attacked by many revivalists, as well as by reformers, for her irrational approach to religion. Har Dayal, the extremist leader from Delhi, warned Indians of the dangers of being taught the shastras by a European. "Mark the sad spectacle," he wrote, "ponder over its deep significance. It is the death-knell of the Hindu race."[42] The *Hindustan Review* of Allahabad observed that "The people of Hindustan are coming to realize, and chafe at the incongruity of an English woman teaching the Hindus Hinduism, and are talking of putting a period to this grotesque anomaly."[43] Hans Raj, the principal of the D.A.V. College, took issue with Mrs. Besant's refusal to sanction widow remarriage; significantly, both based their cases on shastric authorities.[44]

Like most of Mrs. Besant's convictions, her views on social reform were subject to change. Shortly after she had taken the leading part in founding the Central Hindu College at Benaras, in the year 1898—it later became Hindu University—reformers noted a perceptible shift in the direction of her thinking about social reform. The *Reformer*, probably relieved, wrote in 1901 that "Mrs. Besant is slowly coming round. The fit of 'spirituality' is passing away, and she is opening her eyes to the hard facts which surround mankind in their mundane existence." It reported that the educated Englishwoman was advocating the education of Hindu girls and that married boys were being refused admission to the Hindu College.[45] In the same year she published in Benaras her *Ancient Ideals in Modern Life*, in which she took notice of the "scandals and evils that we see around us."

[40] *ISR*, Aug. 11, 1901, p. 395.
[41] Row, *Papers on Social Reform*, p. 46.
[42] *Hindustan Review*, XXI, 125, 125.
[43] *loc.cit.*
[44] *ISR*, Jan. 31, 1904, p. 271.
[45] *ISR*, March 17, 1901, p. 21.

Although she still regarded the four-varna system as the "best . . . that was ever organized," she condemned the proliferation of castes in contemporary Hindu society. "These sub-divisions," she wrote, "go against the possibility of national spirit, against the growing up of national unity; they make it almost impossible to weld the people into one. . . ." She noted other areas where reforms were needed, such as in foreign travel restrictions, marriage ages, and the practice of untouchability, and wrote, "I know that these social changes are perhaps the most difficult of all, because they are so mixed up with family traditions, with social customs, with the whole fabric of ordinary daily life; yet the question is one of life or death, one of progress or extinction."[46]

Indeed, Mrs. Besant was "coming round." In 1904 she and her many associates founded the Madras Hindu Association, "to promote Hindu social and religious advancement on national lines in harmony with the spirit of Hindu civilization." To a crowded gathering at Victoria Town Hall, under the chairmanship of Justice Sir S. Subramania Iyer, Mrs. Besant explained the Association's position. It desired to advance along "the old lines" and thus to "carry with it those classes of the population that are still a vast majority." Reform meant a resurgence of purified Hinduism, because "Without Hinduism there is no future for India. I do not mean Hinduism narrow, unenlightened, dogmatic; I mean Ancient Hinduism enlightened, intellectual, full of vigour and strength. . . ." The platform of the new Hindu Association specified the need for: educating Hindu girls and women, bringing Western enlightenment to Hindu priests, introducing religious education in schools and colleges, raising the ages of marriage for girls and boys, educating of widows (not their remarriage), and encouraging foreign travel.[47] The Hindu Association flourished and was soon looked upon by reformers as a welcome addition to their cause. More than any other public body in India it served to enunciate the doctrine of "reform along national lines"—a doctrine which admirably reconciled revivalists and social reformers.

[46] *Ancient Ideals. . .* , pp. 89-90, 104.
[47] *ISR*, Jan. 10, 1904.

By 1913 Mrs. Besant had become one of the outstanding social reformers in India. Her book, *Wake Up, India: A Plea for Social Reform*, published that year, announced her complete repudiation of the four-varna ideal and all aspects of the caste system as it then existed. She described frankly the "first eleven years of my working in India, [when] I worked perpetually at the attempt to revive the idea of dharma, of function, in relation to the four great castes. By 1905, I had come to the conclusion that it was hopeless; . . . from that time onwards I have been working, solely to form an opinion in favour of change."[48] Her new viewpoint included vehement advocacy of all the major planks of the social reformers' program, including remarriage of virgin widows and the emancipation of the depressed classes, notably the pariahs of south India.

Orthodox spokesmen were plainly disillusioned by Mrs. Besant's social reform pronouncements. Benaras pundits had for years criticized the deviations from orthodox practices, notably in interdining, at the Hindu College.[49] After the publication of *Wake Up, India*, her orthodox critics increased in numbers and in their open hostility to the erstwhile defender of Hinduism.[50] But most of the educated Indians who had already welcomed such advice from the nationally recognized Hindu revivalists greeted Mrs. Besant's new crusade (conducted by the pledge method familiar to Madrasis) with understanding, if not enthusiasm. With the colorful style of a Malabari, Mrs. Besant described India's social evils, differing from the late Parsi reformer only in not advocating legislative cures for the ills she identified. No longer limiting herself to reform on shastric lines, she appealed to the laws of nature, which should determine the age of marriage, traditional prescriptions notwithstanding. "So much nonsense is talked about karma," she told a Madras audience. "If you determine to marry your children—the

<hr />

[48] *Wake Up, India*, p. 286.
[49] *ISR*, Feb. 28, 1904, p. 318.
[50] In 1915 a Madrasi published a pamphlet which suggested that there was still plenty of malice felt against reformers. What Mrs. Besant wanted for Indian women—individual liberty and education—her antagonist wrote, "would mean . . . the status of whoredom and brothel, not the sanctuary of hearth and home." M.V. Srinivasa Aiyangar, "An Open Letter to Mrs. Annie Besant; Being a Reply to Her Attacks on Hinduism," p. 38.

virgin widows you have made—marry them, and then you will
see that karma does not interfere with the proceeding."[51]

During the remainder of Mrs. Besant's eventful career, during
which she became one of the most remarkable figures in Indian
national politics, she increased her interest in social reform, and
the Theosophical Society carried her concern into practical endeavors of a social service and educational nature. Madras reformers and social workers today recall her vigorous advocacy of
freedom for Indian women and her appeals to the highest patriotism in behalf of modern liberal social ideals with respect to low-
caste communities.

In the closing years of the 19th century, when Mrs. Besant was
still bolstering the orthodox position on social reform with the
weight of her influence and that of the Theosophical Society,
another figure appeared in south India to cause discomfort to the
reformers. Swami Vivekananda's first visit to Madras had taken
place in 1893, when, after five years of wandering throughout
India, he had finally determined to announce the beginning of his
new mission. The chosen disciple of Ramakrishna Paramahansa,
who had died in 1886, Vivekananda had inherited the mystic
insight into the truth of Vedanta from his guru but had discovered
for himself, by living close to the Indian people, their misery and
their ignorance. The solution for India's condition, he had decided,
could be found in the West; India's poverty made the teaching of
religion impossible without first rectifying the physical ills of the
country. Madras had given him his first group of devoted disciples
and the financial support he needed to begin his journey to the
Chicago Parliament of Religions, which met in 1893. Vivekananda
had stayed in America, and then in England and Europe, until
1896, proclaiming to large audiences and intimate parlor gatherings the message of India's spiritual heritage—and describing the
current physical needs of his country.[52] He had recruited several

[51] *Wake Up, India*, p. 68.

[52] A fully documented account of the Swami's American visit has been compiled by Marie Louise Burke, in *Swami Vivekananda in America; New Discoveries*. The author concludes from her extensive research that Vivekananda's
practical purpose in touring the United States was to collect funds for his
constructive educational and social service work in India (pp. 330-34). He was

Western followers, including Margaret Noble (Sister Nivedita), and had launched the Vedanta movement in America and England. The fame that he had acquired in the West and the luster which he had given there to the image of India's intellectual and religious heritage assured him a triumphal welcome when he reached Madras again in 1897.

The Madras reformers, at that time wary of the efforts of revivalism on their influence, attacked Vivekananda through their newspapers.[53] The Swami, not unaccustomed to public debate at any level, answered his critics in a Madras lecture: "Let any one of our reformers bring out that life, ready to cleanse the W. C. of a Pariah, and wipe it with his hair [as Ramakrishna had done], and then I sit at his feet and learn, and not before that. One ounce of practice is worth twenty-thousand tons of big talk."[54] Vivekananda continued, in a trenchant analysis of the social reform movement, which the reformers never forgot, "I do not dare to put myself in the position of God and dictate unto our society, 'This way you should move and not that way.'" And then, "Boys, mustached babies, who never went out of Madras, standing up and wanting to dictate laws to three hundred millions of people, with thousands of traditions at their back! . . . Irreverent boys, simply because you can scrawl a few lines upon a paper and get some fool to publish it for you, you think you are the educators of the world, you think you are the public opinion of India!"[55] Vivekananda acknowledged that he had no plan for India's future, that he knew not where India was going. But he declared his purpose of

only slightly hindered in that objective by the hostility of the Brahmo representative then in the United States, P.C. Mozoomdar; Vivekananda had been a Brahmo and later had renounced the association (pp. 396-97). According to Burke, the two most remarkable discoveries made by Vivekananda in America were the position and influence in society of American women and the voluntary organization of American hospitals and welfare services (p. 247).

[53] The *Indian Social Reformer* kept up the attacks for several years, at one time ridiculing "the Anandas, as we shall for brevity's sake call the Sanyasis who always delight in names ending in that happy word, [who] dwell in season, if not out of it, on our spiritual heritage and our predestined appointment as the spiritual teachers of the world." Feb. 5, 1899, p. 174.
[54] *From Colombo to Almora* (Seventeen Lectures), p. 126.
[55] *ibid.*, p. 133.

strengthening, physically and morally, the lives of India's people so that they, not a small educated leadership, could be free to determine their own future.

The social reform movement, Vivekananda declared, had been active in India for a century.[56] But "What good has been done," he asked, "excepting the creation of a most vituperative, and most condemnatory literature?" The reformers, he said, "have criticized, condemned, abused the orthodox until the orthodox have caught their tone, and paid them back in their own coin, and the result is the creation of a literature in every vernacular which is the shame of the race, the shame of the country. Is this reform? Is this leading the nation to glory?"[57] His criticism, he said, was not so much directed against the Madras reformers, who, he acknowledged, were producing "steady and slow progress," but against the Bengalis, drifting between Westernization and orthodox reaction. Yet he could not sanction the Madras movement, because it was based essentially on destroying social customs, not rebuilding a new society. Furthermore, "Most of the reforms that have been agitated for during the last century have been ornamental. Every one of these reforms only touches the first two castes [—he cited widow remarriage—]. . . . Every effort has been spent in cleaning [the reformers'] own houses, making themselves nice and in looking pretty before foreigners. That is no reformation."

What Vivekananda demanded was to "go down to the basis of the thing, to the very roots. That is what I call radical reformation. Put the fire there [at the level of the masses] and let it burn upwards and make an Indian nation."[58] Vivekananda's hope for India's reformation rested on education for all, mostly secular, along with a massive spiritual rejuvenation. He claimed to be a "greater reformer" than any of those associated with the social reform movement, because his aim was to touch all Indians, through love for them, and spread afresh the true religious message of Hinduism.

[56] In April, 1897 he wrote, "Travelling through the various places of India these last ten years, I observed the country full of social reform associations. . . ." *Selections from Swami Vivekananda,* p. 561.

[57] *ibid.,* p. 129.

[58] *ibid.,* p. 130.

The shock of Vivekananda's repudiation of the social reform movement was telling on the reformers, and they never recovered from it to proclaim again their Westernized doctrines of "social utility." But no real damage to the cause of reform was done by Vivekananda. Instead, his authority was added at once to the advocacy of the most basic ideas which reformers had long been enunciating. With the image of physically strong and morally certain Western societies,[59] which he had visited, presented more clearly to him than to any of the contemporary reformers, Vivekananda called upon Indians first to liberate and educate their women as the requirement most crucial, after religious faith, to the development of the nation.[60] He did not oppose widow remarriage, and on the age of consent question he called the opponents of the measure "religious hypocrites." "The rulers passed the Age of Consent Bill," he told a questioner, "and at once all these so-called leaders of your religion raised a tremendous hue and cry against it, sounding the alarm, 'Alas, our religion is lost!' As if religion consists in making a girl a mother at the age of twelve or thirteen! So the rulers also naturally think, 'Goodness gracious! What a religion is theirs!'"[61] As Dayananda did, Vivekananda argued that Hindu social customs were not based on the true religious teachings of Hinduism. Let true religion stand, he told those, especially Brahmos, who advocated a new faith for the sake of a reformed society,[62] but shake off customs which have weakened the nation and which have no relationship to true religion.

Unimpressed by the "ornamental" reforms advocated by the Social Conference, he called for a new life for *all* of India's women and for the low castes. Anticipating by many years the views on the caste system that the national reform movement ultimately adopted, Vivekananda told his Madras audiences that the miseries of the depressed classes must end and that Brahmin superiority

[59] Vivekananda thought the West was spiritually impoverished, but in worldly accomplishments and in practical humanism far ahead of India.

[60] Vivekananda, *Speeches and Writings*, pp. 748-49.

[61] *Selections from Swami Vivekananda*, pp. 474-75.

[62] He argued that all reformers, from Buddha to Rammohun Roy, had gone astray because they confused social evils, such as caste, with religious teachings. See *India and Her Problems*, p. 26; and *Speeches and Writings*, p. 89.

over other castes was a dying cause. His solution to the caste problem, however, was not pulling the Brahmins down from their high position, but the Brahmins' raising up the rest of society.[63] "So long as the millions live in hunger and ignorance," he wrote to his disciples while in America, "I hold every man a traitor, who having been educated at their expense, pays not the least heed to them!"[64]

The heated exchanges between Vivekananda and the social reformers following his return from the West were not easily forgotten. But the reformers, at least, recognized by the turn of the century that in Vivekananda's revivalism—a meek word for the vigor of the Swami's message and his decade of public activity— they had found the strongest possible ally. As rebellious against his own society as the strongest of the reformers, Vivekananda's inspiration for the secular changes he desired was, like theirs, the West—American society, however, more than the European society which the reformers so admired. He frankly told his followers that American society was "very superior to ours."[65] India's young men, he said, had need of "a little strong blood"; to make the point still clearer, he advised them: "You will be nearer to Heaven through football, than through the study of the Gita."[66] Vivekananda's practical work, furthermore, was possibly of more far-reaching benefit to Indian society than that of any single reformer in the national movement, although it was much less than he might have accomplished if ill-health had not begun to plague him following his return to India.[67] He founded the

[63] *Speeches and Writings*, pp. 658-65.
[64] Romain Rolland, *Life of Vivekananda*, p. 72.
[65] *ibid.*, p. 74n.   [66] *India and Her Problems*, p. 26.
[67] His affliction with asthma, ulcers, and later diabetes, noticeably slowed down his pace and weakened his organizational efforts from 1897 until his death in 1902. In a paper on this subject, written by a student at the American University, George Dunham, the author presented the case for Vivekananda's discouragement, toward the end of his life, due to his physical ailments and the fact that only his Western disciples seemed capable of understanding what he desired for his constructive Indian mission. After getting the work started, "his will failed" when he faced the difficulties of persuading Indian disciples to carry on his programs. He relied increasingly on his Western associates, as he had always done on Western financing, but they could not do the practical village-level work that he knew must be done.

Ramakrishna Mission in 1897, and later the Math, defined their complementary spiritual and mundane objectives, and traveled to America again in 1899. The Math's rules included the following summary of Vivekananda's aims: "The first and foremost task in India is the propagation of education and spirituality among the masses. It is impossible for hungry men to become spiritual, unless food is provided for them. Hence our paramount duty lies in showing them new ways of food supply." Furthermore, "The Math will not pay much attention to social reform. For social evils are a sort of disease in the social body, and if that body be nourished by education and food, those evils will die out of themselves."[68] Vivekananda's second return to India at the end of the year 1900, stimulated the organizing of several branches of his organizations for relief work, education, and social service. But sickness was his constant companion, and he died, at the age of forty, in mid-1902. In 1901 the *Indian Social Reformer* welcomed Vivekananda's message of national awakening and strength and credited him with "evoking in the minds of his followers an earnest feeling of practical philanthropy that is not very common among us."[69] The Math's work expanded and has continued to the present day along lines which reinforced the efforts of the national social reform movement.

In the first decade of the 20th century the ideas of social advancement for Hindus which were held by social reformers in the national social reform movement merged into those being enunciated by the revivalists.[70] Some reformers saw that their social gospel could be forwarded, as they felt Vivekananda was doing, by coating the pills "with the sugar of Vedantism."[71] But most of

---

[68] *History of the Ramakrishna Math and Mission*, p. 136.

[69] *ISR*, Aug. 11, 1901, p. 395.

[70] G. Subramania Iyer in 1897 had, wistfully perhaps, asked the Madras Hindu Social Reform Association, "Cannot the Reformers install Swami Vivekanada or some spiritual hero like him into a reform Sankarachari as there was a second Pope for some time in Europe!" Chintamani, *Indian Social Reform*, IV, 363.

[71] K. Srinivasa Row, in *East and West*, Feb., 1903; quoted in Row, *Papers on Social Reform*, p. 70. The *Indian Social Reformer* noted that Swami Abhedananda, a disciple of Vivekananda, was carrying forth the social reformers' proposals while

them recognized that, in the *Reformer's* words, "The only reaction which may really be said to exist among us is a reaction against the tendency towards self-humiliation. . . . The reaction of the present day is nothing more than a revolt against the constant assertion of our worthlessness."[72] Reformers in the National Social Conference, led by (the Anglicized and later knighted) N.G. Chandavarkar, imperceptibly replaced Western by Indian sources of inspiration. They did so not by hypocritically divesting themselves of unpopular slogans, but by achieving for themselves a fresh confidence in their own national heritage.

The President of the National Social Conference in 1897, Narendra Nath Sen, had told his colleagues that "Social reform . . . means nothing more than a return to the social structure that was built up in Ancient India."[73] When Chandavarkar took over the leadership of the Conference, after Ranade's death in 1900, it was soon clear that the new vigor that he wished to instill into that body was expected to come not only from a rededication of its members to practical social work, but also from a revival of their faith in the spirit of the nation. To the Conference in 1904 Chandavarkar said that if social reformers were following borrowed ideals, instead of "proceeding strictly on what are called national lines," he would repudiate their movement.[74] Reform, he said, must be directed toward restoring India's ancient ideals, and the reformers' programs were in fact aimed only at that. In 1905 the Conference in Benaras heard its leader extolling the Sanatana Dharma and linking the major reform doctrines to that principle.[75] At the meeting in 1907 the Chairman of the Reception Committee defined again for his associates the new aims of the Social Conference: "Reform is not revolution," he explained, "it is not innovation, or an apish imitation of foreign ideals. To be effective with the general masses it must aim at ideals which we call our

---

pleading that he was not a reformer, because there "always seems to be a lurking conviction in his mind that the ideals of the social reformer are gross and worldly and [are] merely the slavish imitation of the social system of the West." Sept. 30, 1906, p. 53.
[72] *ISR*, Feb. 12, 1899, p. 182. [73] Chintamani, *op.cit.*, III, 192.
[74] *Speeches and Writings*, p. 125. [75] *ibid.*, p. 133f.

own."[76] The local and provincial associations throughout the country followed the newly expressed objective of "advance along national lines."[77] But nothing in their specific programs had changed.[78]

The impact of the new nationalism, embodying revivalism, on the social reform movement had more significance than the revision in the reformers' terminology alone suggests. The new nationalists, inspired by Lajpat Rai, Bipin Chandra Pal, Mrs. Besant, and Vivekananda, stimulated and reinforced the reformers' beliefs that all groups in society must benefit from the advances that modern India was making. That ideal was accepted by the Social Conference early in this century and by all of India's nationalist organizations before the end of the First World War. The advancement of the lower classes in society called for an enlargement of the "meaning and scope of social reform," as Chandavarkar expressed it in a message to the Conference of 1919, to include "such questions as the education of the masses, the sanitation of the country, the housing of the poor, the care of the sick and feeble, the employment of labour . . . , and rural education, instead of confining social reform as we have hitherto confined it to female education, widow remarriage, removal of caste restrictions and such other items." The Conference of that year responded to this new definition of social reform, and K. Natarajan introduced a resolution incorporating Chandavarkar's new vision of the social progress of India.[79]

[76] *ISR*, Jan. 12, 1908, pp. 233-34.

[77] e.g. the Madras Provincial Conference in 1912 was advised in a welcoming address by A.S. Balasubramanya Iyer that none of the resolutions to be introduced conflicted with the shastras. But he welcomed the possibly few remaining "rational" reformers, "those that trust to their own reason even as against the Shastras. . . ." He felt that even the orthodox could accept the "resolutions on female education, elevation of low castes, amelioration of widows, marriage reform, Dasis [devadasis], and temperance, [which] are not in the least against the Shastras. . . ." Social Conference Addresses, 1912, pp. 167-68, 174-75.

[78] For many years the widow remarriage movement had virtually ceased its propaganda for remarriage of adult widows and was concentrating on virgin or child widows. Shastric principles were interpreted to permit that practice.

[79] *ISR*, Jan. 4, 1920, pp. 286-87.

EPILOGUE

THE new focus of attention on the backwardness of India's lower classes by the social reform movement in the 20th century might be interpreted as evidence of a degree of satisfaction on the part of the reformers that many of their original, limited objectives were in sight. A class of Indians that had been liberated from traditional social bonds was firmly and permanently established and was to assume the dominant role in a politically advancing country. Most social reformers assessed their own contributions to the process of India's social progress as minimal, however, and credited instead the spread of education and the almost unconscious adaptations made to outside forces—chiefly modern economic institutions—impinging on Indian culture. At the turn of the century the *Indian Social Reformer* acknowledged the changes taking place in Hindu society and advised its readers to consult the proprietor of the YMCA restaurant in Madras about the steady increase in his Brahmin clientele; it judged, however, that the National Social Conference could take very little responsibility for them. "The Conference has noted with pleasure many little things that were done during the year," the *Reformer* wrote in 1899. "Changes for the better are taking place, and they will take place whether the Conference notes them with pleasure or no."[1] N. G. Chandavarkar once said that the Parsi soda water seller at the Bombay railway station was known as "the best because the most efficient social reformer in India," since by providing drinks to any buyer, regardless of caste, he was unostentatiously breaking down that barrier.[2] The education of girls, their later marriages, increasing travel abroad, liberation of individuals from control by family and caste elders, and relaxation of prohibitions on inter-caste relations were only a few changes that appeared to many as inevitable, with or without the conscious efforts of reformers to induce them.

[1] *ISR*, Feb. 5, 1899, p. 176.
[2] Chandavarkar, *Speeches and Writings*, p. 9.

The measure of the effectiveness of an intellectual movement surely must exist in the actual spread of the ideas that it advocates in society; its impact cannot be judged only by its popularity or the number of its acknowledged adherents. Nearly all of the social reforms advocated in the 19th century—widow remarriage is the notable exception—form in part the ethical and social ideals of modern Indians. The Hindu social reform movement did not merely "ride the tide" of social change; it supplemented the gravitational pull of ideas and examples that produced the tide.

Many reformers were misled about the influence of their efforts because leadership of the social reform movement was always diffuse and never powerful. In India all unified and effective public endeavor rests heavily on strong leadership—whether it is a religious movement or a political crusade.[3] The social reform movement produced few powerful leaders, and those that did appear, such as Keshub Chandra Sen and M.G. Ranade, often faltered at some points in their careers. Never, therefore, did the movement recruit a popular following, and its brief successes in terms of arousing public awareness were always followed by periods of apathy or hostility. Nonetheless, social reformers exerted a strong influence as individuals, personifying the new ways that many Indians knew were irresistible; as a group (sometimes existing only in the abstract), the movement seemed to be blazing a new trail and encouraging others to follow. Aurobindo Ghose thus summed up the careers of Ranade and Vivekananda: they created few definite works, but their influence was gigantic, "so wide and formless that it has little relation to any formal work

[3] India is an overorganized society. New leadership, to be effective, must transcend the structure of normal social organization; the most successful leaders, therefore, are those who can raise themselves above the ordinary life of society, as religious leaders traditionally did. What in the West might be accomplished through impersonal organization, in India is accomplished by the personal magnetism of a guru-like leader. "Guru worship" replaces organization as a means of mass persuasion: an individual who embodies certain ideas and traits is venerated and followed, and thus the ideas and traits themselves become popular. As V.N. Naik wrote, "It is men that make institutions live, grow, and prosper. In India they are always a one man's show, a tent raised on a single, central pole." Bombay Presidency Social Reform Association, *Social Reform Annual, 1951*, p. 44.

that they have left behind them."[4] Men's minds were imperceptibly altered by the words and deeds of reformers such as these, and thus the spirit of modern India came into existence as one recognizes it today.

But "modern India" represents only a small wedge being driven into the larger society of the subcontinent. Social reformers, often at the penetrating points of that wedge, are no longer occupied with the fashioning of the instruments of change (legal, economic, educational) as much as with the speed with which those instruments can have their effect on the bulk of the people. In the three decades preceding Independence, the social reform movement in India increasingly directed itself toward the betterment of the lives of Indians who would never have been affected by the reform crusades before the First World War. In order to achieve this purpose the movement dispersed itself into various social service endeavors, which the National Social Conference under Chanda-varkar recognized as the logical extension of social reform to the uneducated groups in the country. The Conference in 1916 recom-mended that, henceforth, there be two sessions of the body, one concerned entirely with social service, and in 1917 the first Social Service Conference was held. The Bengal Social Service League was founded in 1915, indicating an increased concern in that province for the kind of mass uplift that had motivated reformers elsewhere. Throughout the country, women's organizations were set up, partly at least to work for underprivileged women and children.[5] The All-India Women's Conference, brought into exist-ence through the efforts of Margaret Cousins in 1927, established a permanent office and staff in the 1930's and gave to women's societies a degree of national coordination, especially on questions of marriage and inheritance. S. Natarajan concluded that the

[4] Ghose, *Bankim-Tilak-Dayananda*, pp. 41-42.

[5] Evaluating these women's groups, Neera Desai wrote, probably too pessi-mistically, "In contrast to the women's organizations of the West which orient to higher civic, political, academic and class issues, of national and international significance, we find the women's organizations in India either as mere paper bodies, passing resolutions, or as a few grim rescue centers which attempt to provide a very ineffectual shelter home for distressed women." Desai, *Woman in Modern India*, p. 165.

A.I.W.C. became "the successor of the Social Conference,"[6] which held no further sessions after 1933. The social reformers had always focused their attention on the condition of women and their place in the family; it was appropriate that Indian women themselves should assume the predominant burden of education and propaganda in their own behalf. In this respect the social reform movement was turned over to the leadership of women, whose prestige in society was increasing markedly as a result of their participation in political agitation under Gandhi.

Social service work also spread further among the untouchables in the inter-war period, with Gandhi's Harijan Sevak Sangh supplementing the work of the Depressed Classes Mission Society and the various religious bodies, native and foreign. However, the main hope of improving the position of those classes lay in their political strength, as Dr. Ambedkar rightly judged. After the First World War service organizations began for the first time to make a visible, though scarcely influential, effort to change patterns of social and economic behavior among rural inhabitants. Village development schemes, such as the private Khed Shivapur in Poona District under the auspices of the Deccan Agricultural Association and those conducted by provincial governments, began to experiment in a task that the post-Independence Community Development Projects later undertook.[7] The labor union movement rapidly assumed importance after the First World War and devoted some of its still undeveloped strength to the cause of urban working class betterment.

The increased activities of social workers and reformers was the result, to some degree, of the unprecedented recognition which such endeavors received from the Congress. In 1917 under the presidency of Mrs. Besant, the Congress broke its long-standing rule of ignoring social questions;[8] under Gandhi's leadership, after 1920, the Congress continued to pass resolutions on social reform at its annual sessions. Thus, nominally at least, the rift between the two national reform movements ended, and social reform became part of the political program for national advancement.

[6] Natarajan, *A Century of Social Reform*, p. 178.
[7] See E. Blunt, *Social Service in India*, p. 385f.
[8] *ibid.*, p. 284.

But politics still dominated the thinking and public lives of most nationalists, whose support of Gandhi was not translated into any more fervent efforts to overcome India's social ills. Perhaps ironically, the National Social Conference had less reason for existing after the Congress went on record supporting social reform, not because its work was being transferred to newer, more competent hands, but because its work *appeared* to have been incorporated into the increasingly popular Gandhian political program. As an organization, the National Social Conference was further weakened by the split away from the Congress of the moderate constitutionalists of the National Liberal Federation in 1919. From 1922 until 1927 the Liberal Federation sponsored its own annual Social Conference, under the leadership of G.K. Deodhar and D.G. Dalvi. The proceedings of the new Conference had much in common with those of the original body (Kamakshi Natarajan was General Secretary after the death of Chandavarkar). Both concentrated increased attention on the elevation of the depressed classes. After 1933 no significant backing could be found for the holding of annual National Social Conferences, and no further sessions were held.[9]

When, in 1929, Gandhi was asked to preside over the National Social Conference he declined, because, as he put it, his way "was often different from those of orthodox reformers."[10] Gandhi was as firm as the social reformers in insisting that social progress, especially for the untouchables, was a condition for political progress. "To postpone social reform til after the attainment of Swaraj," he said, "is not to know the meaning of Swaraj."[11] But his methods of social reform, like his techniques of political action, departed from the established patterns of the national organizations, and he refused to associate himself with any movement which he could not direct personally. Gandhi's methods of promoting the transformations in Indian society that he considered basic to national revival differed from the traditional methods of the social reformers in several ways. He used propaganda (or education) as they did, but his message was that Indians should

[9] *A Century of Social Reform, op.cit.*, p. 172.   [10] *ibid.*, p. 137.
[11] Quoted in Sarma, *Studies in the Renaissance of Hinduism . . .* , p. 576.

343

abide by moral laws, divinely inspired, and thus avoid sin;[12] the reformers based their cases chiefly on reason and empirical evidences of the need for reform. Personal example, Gandhi felt, was the most powerful argument for any desirable change in behavior, and his personal life—also virtually his public life— provided a perpetual reminder of the kind of action that he advocated. Unlike most social reformers and social workers, who tried to teach by the spread of ideas, Gandhi taught through the impact that his own life had on others. Finally, he broke completely with the earlier movements for both social and political reform by undertaking the satyagraha campaigns, notably in behalf of untouchables.[13] By placing the burden of initiating the struggle for social reform on the people who stood to benefit from it, instead of on the higher classes in society, Gandhi charted the only possible path to social advancement for untouchables and other abused communities. By openly violating the law, as well as social customs, by great public demonstrations Gandhi showed the moral wrongness (or departure from truth—satya) of the established order. Most social reformers were unprepared to move either that rapidly or illegally toward the goals they advocated and were accustomed to relying on verbal arguments, individual conversions to reformed practices, and gradual changes in the social and legal environments. Furthermore, men associated with the main Hindu social reform tradition looked to the government as an ally, not an opponent, in their efforts to promote progress.

If Gandhi's methods differed from those of the orthodox reformers, so also did some of his objectives. Although he disapproved emphatically of child marriages (he thought sixteen should be the minimum age for girls, but he sometimes mentioned twenty) and supported widow remarriage,[14] his views on

[12] See, e.g., his article arguing against child marriage in *Young India*, Aug. 26, 1926; in Gandhi, *Hindu Dharma*, p. 354.

[13] For a thorough analysis of satyagraha, or "truth force," see Joan V. Bondurant, *Conquest of Violence; The Gandhian Philosophy of Conflict*. Chapter III includes a discussion of the campaigns to gain entrance by untouchables to Hindu temples and presents case studies of the Gandhian method of social reform.

[14] "To force widowhood upon little girls," he wrote, "is a brutal crime for which we Hindus are daily paying dearly. . . . we must rid ourselves of this

the caste system deviated substantially from those of most social reformers. Probably the basic reason for this deviation lay in Gandhi's vision of the ideal Indian society as centered in small rural communities, where relatively unchanging, hereditary status could continue to determine social relations. Gandhi supported the varna system of four ideal classes as a natural and proper division of society. Varnashramadharma, or adherence to the patterns of class (varna) structure and the sequence of traditional stages of life (ashrama), "satisfied the religious, social and economic needs of a community," Gandhi wrote in 1933.[15] Accordingly, he struck out against many grotesque caste practices, including untouchability, which have no justification under the ideal varna system. The social reformers had to reject Gandhi's position—to give up caste and retain the four varnas—just as they had rejected the identical position taken by Dayananda Saraswati; they knew that most Hindus would never understand, much less act on the basis of, such a subtle distinction. The reformers realized that nothing practical would be gained if Hindus were to re-classify themselves into varnas, and in any case it would be impossible to give real effect to such a procedure.

Thus, in S. Natarajan's estimate, "Gandhi's entry into the social reform field was . . . a somewhat ambiguous one; and his insistence that he had differences with 'orthodox' reformers was more than justified."[16] Gandhi's views on the breakdown of customary barriers between castes illustrates this estimate. In the early 1920's he opposed inter-dining and inter-marriage between castes; in the early 1930's he shifted to a somewhat neutral stand on both.[17] He was never able to accept the reformers' argument that true national unity could only be achieved by the complete removal of caste barriers to social intercourse. Gandhi and the reformers reinforced each other's views on the position that women should assume in society, which had always been the most important

---

poison of enforced widowhood." *Young India*, Aug. 5, 1926; in Gandhi, *Hindu Dharma*, pp. 252-53.

[15] *ibid.*, p. 334. At another time he wrote, "Everyone will admit that Hinduism is nothing without the law of *varna* and *ashrama*." *ibid.*, p. 336.

[16] *A Century of Social Reform, op.cit.*, p. 151.

[17] See M.V. Shah, "Social Philosophy of Gandhiji," pp. 66-67.

practical ideal of the social reform movement. But the nature of the new Indian society, its social and economic structure and its spirit, remained in dispute between them.

The new linkage established between social and political reform at the time of the First World War was partly a result of Gandhi's insistence on their interconnection. Most other political leaders also adopted that position, chiefly because they recognized the wisdom of making at least verbal concessions to the lower castes and untouchables; nominal acceptance by educated Indians of increased rights for women was already fairly general. B.G. Tilak's Congress Democratic Party, organized in 1920 to promote the election of Congressmen to provincial legislatures under the provisions of the Montford Reform Act, gave its support to "the removal of all civic, secular, or social disabilities based on caste and custom."[18] The conversion of Tilak to the reformers' camp was viewed by some as opportunistic;[19] in any case it signified that political nationalists could no longer ignore, much less oppose, social reform. The reformed legislative bodies, provincial and central, after 1919 offered Indian politicians ample opportunities to give legal backing to social reform ideals. The government, which had already shown itself unwilling to promote public hostility by passing further social reform measures, divested itself of all responsibility for India's social progress.

Earlier in this century an attempt had been made by reformers to pass a new civil marriage law under which a Hindu could marry someone not of his caste or religious community. The bill had been introduced into the Central Legislative Council in 1911 by Bhupendranath Basu and had been defeated. A similar measure had been introduced by Vithalbhai Patel in 1918 and had also been turned down. Finally, after the new legislative councils were formed a bill drafted by Dr. Hari Singh Gour was passed, which amended the 1872 Special Marriage Act by eliminating the necessity to deny affiliation with established religious communities. In the provinces and princely states from the 1920's to Independence, a considerable amount of legislation was passed affecting marriage

[18] *ISR*, April 25, 1920.
[19] e.g. the *Indian Messenger*, as quoted in *ISR*, May 9, 1920.

and inheritance, the position of women and children, vagrancy and begging, immoral traffic, and penal institutions, which had its origin in agitation by social reform and social welfare workers. British observers and Indians themselves have frequently judged that the Indian-sponsored legislation on social and economic matters before the transfer of power represented the most constructive use of newly tested capacities for self-rule.

In the Central Legislature the most highly publicized social reform measure of this period was the Child Marriage Restraint Act XIX of 1929, known as the Sarda Act, from the name of its sponsor, the Arya Samajist, Har Bilas Sarda. Since 1911 pressure in the Central Legislature for an act to raise the age of consent above that established in 1891 had been building up, with the government aligning itself with the orthodox representatives in opposition.[20] After 1922, when the issue was again raised, the government at first followed a neutral policy and then itself introduced a measure in 1925 to raise the age of consent to thirteen for married and fourteen for unmarried girls. Delays followed, and Dr. Gour brought forth another age of consent bill in 1927. By that time opinions outside of India and England were being publicly expressed against the Indian Government's apathy toward the social condition of the country. Katherine Mayo's book, *Mother India*, published in New York in 1927 and translated into dozens of languages (including Indian vernaculars) was by itself an embarrassing enough indictment of the condition of Indian women to cause renewed government and private action.[21] The

[20] The government's reasons for opposition were later officially revealed as concern that another age of consent bill would lead to unrest, Government of India, *Report of the Age of Consent Committee*, p. 11.

[21] The book, written chiefly as a muckraking piece to earn its author money and fame, was extensively read in India. Gandhi, who had given an interview to Miss Mayo, wrote in *Young India*, "While I consider the book to be unfit to be placed before Americans and Englishmen (for it can do no good to them), it is a book that every Indian can read with some degree of profit." (Quoted in the *Statesman* [Calcutta], Aug. 16, 1927). Many Indians were furious over *Mother India*; public demonstrations were held to protest it, one presided over by the Mayor of Calcutta, and a resolution was introduced in the legislature asking the government to ban its distribution in India. Several rejoinders to the book were published, one by K. Natarajan, entitled *Miss Mayo's Mother India*. At the National Social Conference in Madras, Dec. 1927, the book caused

Sarda bill, introduced a few months prior to the publication of Miss Mayo's book, soon received attention by the government's Age of Consent Committee, which had been appointed to consider the facts and report on the Gour bill.[22] The Committee recommended passage of a new law on age of consent and added the weight of its approval to a law establishing minimum ages for marriage, which would be the first such law with general applicability throughout British India. The Sarda Act, passed on the centenary of Lord Bentinck's regulation abolishing suttee, was hailed by reformers as the most advanced piece of legislation enacted by the Central Government in recent times. It established minimum ages for marriage: eighteen for males, and fourteen for females. The Act had great "educative" force in the succeeding decades, but it was at first ignored and could be flouted by many parents wishing to marry their offspring at earlier ages. The fine for disregarding the law (Rupees 1000) could be regarded as an additional expense of a marriage; several princely states with lower marriage ages could be visited for purposes of holding marriage ceremonies; imprecise data existed on the ages of children—such were the obstacles to enforcement of the law.

By the 1920's social reformers recognized that the future of reform in India lay with the government, in which they were steadily gaining more influence. Despite Gandhi's pleas for voluntary work and reliance on alterations in men's conceptions of right and wrong, nationalist leaders and followers turned increasingly toward the government for the solution of all India's problems. The secular, welfare state became the ideal of the advanced sections of the Congress, led by Jawaharlal Nehru. The state, they argued, must seek to regulate individual lives, at least in matters affecting social order and progress; such matters must

---

heated discussion and a plea from one delegate to stop "indulging any longer in vain protests against Miss Mayo's *Mother India* and . . . wasting our energy and intellect in giving tit for tat. . . ." (As reported in the *Hindu*, Dec. 27, 1927.)

[22] The Committee's *Report* is one of the few thorough pre-Independence official Indian studies on any social question. Its comment on the impact of the 1891 Age of Consent Act was: "It must be candidly admitted that the Law of Age of Consent has not been effective . . . the law is to a large extent unknown." pp. 119-20.

be treated without reference to religion, which should be restricted to men's spiritual lives. The more radical political leaders of the 1930's and 1940's no longer challenged the government's right to interfere with social customs, as the extremists had done at the turn of the century, because the modern radicals did not derive their power from orthodox, revivalist groups and because, too, they favored the precedent of strong state leadership in all matters. They joined Gandhi, but for somewhat different reasons, in advocating the close relationship of social and political progress.

Since Independence, social reformers are still heard pressing the case for awareness of India's social ills. Echoing earlier demands for a higher priority for social reform, V. N. Naik wrote in 1951, "We realize today that the Congress had won independence for India during the course of 62 years, while in vital matters of religious and social reform, with all the soul force of the Mahatma, the promised land is not yet in sight."[23] The Nehru Government has lent its weight to the reformers' programs, by pressing forward the legal and economic instruments of social change. The republican Constitution of 1950 incorporates into its Directive Principles of State Policy (goals of the State unenforceable by the courts) a statement generally regarded as signaling the government's intention to carry out social reform, at least among Hindus, in the face of whatever orthodox opposition may develop. Article 38 proclaims, "The State shall strive to promote the welfare of the people by securing and protecting as effectively as it may a social order in which justice, social, economic and political, shall inform all the institutions of the national life." Among the Fundamental (enforceable) Rights which the Constitution strives to protect are the right of an individual to state employment without regard to his religion, race, caste, or sex; his right of access to "shops, public restaurants, hotels and places of public entertainment"; and his use of "wells, tanks, bathing ghats. . . ." A more sweeping clause seeks to transform the position of the untouchables: " 'Untouchability' is abolished and its practice in any form is forbidden. The enforcement of any disability arising

[23] Bombay Presidency Social Reform Association, *Social Reform Annual, 1951*, p. 37.

349

out of 'Untouchability' shall be an offense punishable in accordance with law." Thus, the goals of the new state have been pronounced, and the legal mechanisms are in order to carry them out. The process of prodding the people to assert their newly granted rights is under way, and progress can be measured in certain areas.

The leaders of the independent Indian state acknowledge, as M. C. Chagla wrote, that "All social legislation, to a very large extent, must operate as restraints upon the various freedoms guaranteed to the citizens under our Constitution."[24] Thus far the major thrust of social legislation has been in the direction of regulating individual behavior in matters of marriage and family relations, areas in which the government can exercise authority more effectively than in the area of inter-caste relations. The so-called Hindu Code Bill has been in process of evolution since 1941, when the Hindu law committee was appointed, under the direction of Sir Benegal N. Rau. The intervention of World War II and the exceedingly thorough review which the Bill received by the committee and the Legislative Assembly postponed any action until after Independence. The Constitutent Assembly and a select committee debated the issue from 1947 to 1952 with increasing indications that the Bill might be shelved. Finally after Prime Minister Nehru had made the issue one of Congress prestige, and the 1952 elections had confirmed the Congress Party's strength (over contending orthodox Hindu parties), the Bill, separated into parts, was enacted.[25] A Special Marriage Act, a civil code, was enacted in 1954 and was followed by the Hindu Marriage Act of 1955 and laws affecting adoption and inheritance. Reformers are still not satisfied that the government is determined to throw its full legal weight behind even marriage reform. The fact that the penalties in the Hindu Marriage Act for marrying a girl under the age of fifteen or a boy under eighteen may not deter breaking the law is, for S. Natarajan, "a clear sign that the Congress support of reforms is half-hearted, a submission to Mr. Nehru's instance which the party tries to keep to the minimum

[24] Chagla, *The Individual and the State*, p. 17.
[25] For further discussion see *A Century of Social Reform, op.cit.*, p. 192f.

necessary and which Mr. Nehru and his supporters are not vigi-
lant enough or interested enough to ensure is real."[26]

But legal codes, however well enforced, have never been the
most powerful instruments of social change, in India or elsewhere.
The chief inducement that the Indian Government can bring to
bear on the process of social change is its capacity to create economic changes, as most reformers themselves recognize. Many
Indians now rightly insist that social progress depends directly on
the success of the government's Five-Year Plans, in particular
the industrialization programs. A modern society, as they conceive it, can only be one founded on a modern economy resembling those of the already industrialized states. Urbanization,
mass communications, mechanization of economic processes, and
a growing surplus of manufactures for reinvestment purposes are
the ingredients of the kind of economy which can extend and
support mass education, housing, and public health facilities,
and can induce social mobility and unity. Social reform is no less
important to India's present government than it is to reformers,
but advancement in the modern economic sector is correctly seen
as the surest and swiftest means of bringing it about.

In the rural, less modern areas, the processes of social and economic change are not as well understood as in that sector of the
economy already in rapid transition. The government's Community Development Projects sought to induce the social changes
that are essential to a transformation of village economic life,
with less success than the planners expected. The seemingly inescapable circle of traditional social relationships and attitudes
leading to economic stagnation which in turn inhibits social
changes could not be broken merely by the introduction of technical knowledge and propaganda. In the early 1960's a more
powerful lever to move rural communities out of their supine
immobility was created by increasing participation in local political life through the Panchayati Raj schemes of the state governments. Their success, or lack of it, will be a modern judgment,
in a new context, on the efficacy of linking political and social
reform.

All significant changes in modern India have a crucial bear-

[26] *ibid.*, p. 196.

ing on the still emerging phenomenon of nationalism. Social reform and nationalism are irrevocably linked as living processes and as organized movements, in India and elsewhere. Nationalism is "a product of the breach with the old order of which a part is the disruption of traditional communities."[27] This disruption, necessary to the creation of the nation, is evident above all else in the transfer of individual loyalties from the family, the village, the caste to the greater societies of the city, the region, and the nation. For those involved in nationalism, participation in these larger societies gradually replaces, or takes precedence over, participation in the traditional communities and requires changes in social values. Daniel Lerner's study of transformation in a traditional society focuses on the extension of an individual's "participation" in society from mutually isolated communities to the nation. With this extension comes a new "consensus" of values that is conducive to still further changes,[28] all of which imply the breakdown of certain social norms rooted in traditional life. Social reform is brought about by the spread of this consensus of values that is an essential aspect of nationalism.

The 19th century social reformers strove for the emergence and the success of nationalism and social reform together. Social reform was considered a prerequisite to political advancement. Equally important, the unity of the nation would hasten social progress through the creation of what reformers called "corporate consciousness." N. G. Chandavarkar once described the process, which is visibly under way in India today: "We leave our homes either in search of employment or for trade, and imbibe new ideas, contract new sympathies, and learn to form new connections. A newer and wider kind of sympathy [Lerner calls it empathy] is being generated than that to which the confined atmosphere of caste in the old days accustomed our ancestors."[29] The broadening of participation at all levels of Indian life in the 20th century, culminating in the spreading awareness of national identity, is at least a partial preparation for the fulfillment of the social reformer's aspirations for modern India.

[27] Rupert Emerson, *From Empire to Nation*, p. 188.
[28] Daniel Lerner, *The Passing of Traditional Society; Modernizing the Middle East*, p. 50.
[29] *Speeches and Writings, op.cit.*, p. 59.

APPENDIX I

The Treatment of Widows Urged by a 19th Century Bhakti Sect (From the *Shiksha Patri* [Epistle of Precepts] of Swami Narayana. See Chapter 11.)

"Widows shall serve the Lord Krishna with minds intent on Him as their only husband, and they shall live under the control of their father or other male members of their family, and never in independence. They shall never touch at any time any men except their nearest relations, and when young they shall never without necessity engage in conversation with young men. If any infant male child touch them no blame attaches to them any more than from contact with a dumb animal, nor if they are compelled from necessity to talk with or touch an old man. They shall never receive instructions of any kind from any men except their nearest relations, and they shall often mortify their flesh by vows and fasts. They shall never give away to others the money required for their own support and they may give away only that which is in excess. They shall eat only one meal a day and shall sleep on the ground. They shall never look at animals engaged in the sexual act. Widows shall never dress like married women, nor like a female ascetic, nor like a mendicant nor in any unbecoming attire. . . . They shall never join in the frolics practiced at the Holi festival, nor shall they put on ornaments or finely woven clothes composed of cotton or metal threads." (Quoted in M. C. Parekh, *Sri Swami Narayana*, p. 345.)

APPENDIX II

A Proclamation of Caste Excommunication by the Kapole Banyas Against Madhowdas Rugnathdas for His Marriage to a Widow, Issued May 14, 1871 in Bombay

1. That as the custom of widow remarriage is not in our caste, and as such remarriage is contrary to the immemorial practice of our caste, and is opposed to what we conscientiously believe to be the law enjoined by our religious Shastras, the said Madhowdas Rugnathdas having married the said widow, Dhunkorebai, they have rendered themselves ineligible for such social intercourse as that of eating and drinking with the caste, and of giving and receiving in marriage. Therefore, no member of the caste shall hold such intercourse with them.

2. That if any member of the Kapole caste will eat or drink with the said Madhowdas Rugnathdas or Bai Dhunkore, or hold such intercourse with them as that of giving and receiving in marriage, such member shall render himself equally ineligible for holding such intercourse with the caste, and no such intercourse shall be held with him.

3. That if it be proved hereafter that any member or members of our caste had aided, or taken part in, the remarriage of Madhowdas Rugnathdas with Dhunkorebai, the caste shall not hold with such member or members any such intercourse as is stated above. (From Madhowdas Rugnathdas, *Story of a Widow Remarriage*, p. 54.)

GLOSSARY

advaita—non-dualism, monism
ashrama—stages of life
atman—the soul, the self, Universal Spirit
bhakti—devotion based on love of God
bhakta—devotee, who worships God through love
biradri—caste brotherhood
dharma—proper way of life or code of conduct
guru—a traditional Hindu teacher
gurukula—a traditional Hindu school
jnanin—one who seeks salvation through intellectual comprehension of God
maharaja—a ruler of high rank
Manavadharmashastras—sacred writings on proper conduct by Manu, the traditional Hindu law giver
maya—delusion, the metaphysical cause of the physical world
moksha—spiritual release or salvation
mukti—release from worldly experience (same as moksha)
nautch-dancing—performances by professional girls often suggestive of or leading to sexual involvement
panchayat—committee of village or caste leaders to regulate community affairs
pathshala—a Hindu school
prāyaścitta—a penance
pundit—a Hindu learned man
purdah—seclusion of women
sadhu—a Hindu ascetic or holy man
samaj—a society
samiti—a society
Sanatana Dharma—Eternal Religion or the traditional way of life
Sankara—greatest exponent of the advaita Vedanta philosophy, who lived in the 9th century, A.D.
sannyasi—a celibate member of a Hindu religious order, one who has renounced the world

shastras—Hindu scriptures

suttee—widows' self-immolation by fire

swadeshi—the production and use of home manufactures

swami—literally, "lord," a title conferred on sannyasis

swaraj—self-rule

varna—one of the four traditional classes of Hindu society (Brahmin, Kshatriya, Vaishya, or Shudra)

Vedanta—a monistic philosophical system underlying much Hindu religious thought

zenana—women's section of a house

BIBLIOGRAPHY OF WORKS CITED

I. *Writings of Social Reformers and Contemporary Accounts of Reform Movements*

Agarkar, Gopal Ganesh, *Sampurna Agarkar* (in Marathi), Poona, 1940, 3 vols.

Aiyangar, M. V. Srinivasa, "An Open Letter to Mrs. Annie Besant; Being a Reply to Her Attacks on Hinduism" (pamphlet), Madras, 1915.

Aiyar, A. Subramanya, "A Lecture on State Interference in Social Matters in India" (pamphlet), Madras, 1891.

Ambedkar, Bhimrao Ramji, "Ranade, Gandhi and Jinnah; Address Delivered on 101st Celebration of Ranade's Birthday, Jan. 18, 1943" (pamphlet), Bombay, 1943.

——, *What Congress and Gandhi Have Done to the Untouchables*, Bombay, 1946.

An Indian, *Essays on Indian Social Reform*, Bombay, 1893.

"The Arya Samaj from the Outsider's Point of View" (pamphlet), Lahore, 1902.

Baijnath, Rai Bahadur Lala, "Social Reform for the N.W. Provinces; Proceedings of Public Meetings, with two papers and a preface" (pamphlet), Bombay, 1886.

——, "Some Problems of Social Reform" (pamphlet), Aligarh, 1891.

——, "Suggestions for Religious Education and Other Reforms in Hindu Society . . ." (pamphlet), Agra, 1909.

Banerjea, Surendranath, *A Nation in Making*, London, 1925.

——, *Speeches*, Calcutta, 1896, vol. 5.

——, *Speeches and Writings of Babu Surendranath Banerjea*, Madras, 1st edn. n.d.

Besant, Annie, *Ancient Ideals in Modern Life*, Benaras, 1901.

——, *For India's Uplift: A Collection of Speeches and Writings on Indian Questions*, Madras, 2nd edn., 1917.

——, *How India Wrought for Freedom*, Madras, 1915.

——, *Nation Building*, Madras, 4th edn., 1917.

——, *Wake Up, India; A Plea for Social Reform*, Madras, 1913.

Bhandarkar, Sir R.G., *Collected Works of Sir R.G. Bhandarkar*, Poona, 1927-33, 4 vols.

———, "A Note on the Age of Marriage and Its Consummation. According to Hindu Religious Law" (pamphlet), Poona, 1891.

Bombay, Government of, Selections from the Records, CXLVII, New Series: *Repression of Female Infanticide in the Bombay Presidency*, Bombay, 1875.

———, Selections from the Records, LV, New Series: *Correspondence Showing the Measures Taken by the Synds of Tatta in Sind to Reduce the Expenses of Their Birth, Marriage, and Funeral Ceremonies*, Bombay, 1859.

———, *Source Material for a History of the Freedom Movement in India (Collected from Bombay Government Records)*, I, 1818-1885; II, 1885-1920, Bombay, 1957, 1958.

Bombay Prarthana Samaj, *Ninety-first Annual Report for 1957-58*, Bombay, 1958.

Bombay Presidency Social Reform Association, *Memoir of Fifty Years of Progress, including Report for 1949 to 1951*, Bombay, 1952.

———, *Report for the Years 1952, 1953, and 1954*, Bombay, 1955.

———, *Social Reform Annual, 1942 (Ranade Centenary Number)*.

———, *Social Reform Annual, 1951 (Telang Centenary Number)*.

Bose, Shib Chunder, *The Hindoos As They Are; A Description of the Manners, Customs and Inner Life of Hindoo Society in Bengal*, Calcutta, 1881.

Burke, Marie Louise, *Swami Vivekananda in America; New Discoveries*, Calcutta, 1958.

Chand, Diwan, *The Arya Samaj; What It Is and What It Stands For*, Lahore, 1942.

Chandavarkar, Ganesh L. (ed.), *The Religion for Modern India*, Bombay, 1960.

Chandavarkar, Sir Narayen G., *The Speeches and Writings of Sir Narayen G. Chandavarkar*, Bombay, 1911.

Chintamani, C. Yajnesvara, *Indian Social Reform*, Madras, 1901.

Collet, Sophia Dobson (ed.), *Brahmo Year-Book for 1879; Brief Records of Work and Life in the Theistic Churches of India*, London, 1879.

Cotton, Sir Henry, *New India*, London, 1907.

Das, Chitta Ranjan, *India for Indians*, Madras, 3rd edn., 1921.

Dayananda Anglo-Vedic College Golden Jubilee Commemoration Volume, Lahore, 1936.

Ganapati, Lakshmana, *Essay on the Promotion of Domestic Reform among the Natives of India*, Bombay, 1843.

358

Gandhi, Mohandas K., *Hindu Dharma*, Ahmedabad, 1950.

Ghose, Sri Aurobindo, *Ideals and Progress*, Pondicherry, 4th edn., 1951.

——, *The Renaissance in India*, Pondicherry, 4th edn., 1951.

——, *Uttarpara Speech*, Ponicherry, 5th edn., 1950.

Gidumal, Dayaram, *The Status of Women in India, or a Hand-book for Hindu Social Reformers*, Bombay, 1889.

Govindacharya, Alkondavilli, *The Divine Wisdom of the Dravida Saints*, Madras, 1902.

Great Britain, House of Lords, *Accounts and Papers, 1888*, xix, No. 227: "Correspondence regarding the adoption by the States of Rajputana of Reforms in connection with Marriage and Funeral Customs."

Guild of Service (Central), *36th Annual Report*, Madras, 1959.

Gurukula Academy (Hardwar), "The Quinquennial Report (1901-1907)", Lahore, n.d.

"The Hindu Sea-Voyage Movement in Bengal" (pamphlet), Calcutta, 1894.

Hume, Allan Octavian, "A Speech on the Indian National Congress, Its Origin, Aims, and Objectives, Delivered at a Great Public Meeting Held at Allahabad . . . , 30 April, 1888," Calcutta, 1888.

——, and Sir Auckland Colvin, "Audi Alteram Partem: Being Two Letters on Certain Aspects of the Indian National Congress Movement" (pamphlet), London, 1888.

India, Government, *Imperial Census of 1881: Operations and Results in the Presidency of Bombay*, 1, Bombay, 1882.

——, *Report of Age of Consent Committee, 1928-1929*, Calcutta, 1929.

——, Council of the Governor-General for the Purpose of Making Laws . . . , *Proceedings, 1891*, Calcutta, 1892.

——, Home Department, *Public Proceedings, Nov. 1886*, Numbers 131 to 138E.

——, *Selections from Records*, No. liv, "Note on the State of Education in India, 1865-66," by A.M. Monteath, Calcutta, 1867.

——, *Selections from Records*, No. lxvii, "Note on the State of Education in India During 1866-67," by A. P. Howell, Calcutta, 1868.

——, *Selections from Records*, No. ccxxiii, No. 3, "Papers relating to Infant Marriage and Enforced Widowhood in India," Calcutta, 1886.

———, Imperial Record Department, *Selections from Vernacular* (or *Native*) *Newspapers*, as follows: Bengal, 1868-1891; Madras, 1872-1891; Bombay, 1868-1891; Punjab, 1891; N.W. Provinces, Oudh, Central Provinces, and Rajputana, 1891.

———, Legislative Council, *Proceedings from Jan. to Dec. 1856*, II, Calcutta, 1857.

"India in 1906, or A Collection of Presidential Addresses Delivered at the National Congress and other Conferences Held in Calcutta in December, 1906 . . ." (pamphlet), Poona, 1907.

The Indian National Congress, Madras, publ. by Natesan, n.d. (1909?).

Indian Politics, Madras, 1898.

Infant Marriage and Enforced Widowhood in India, Being a Collection of Opinions for and Against, Received by Mr. Behramji M. Malabari, from Representative Hindu Gentlemen and Official and Other Authorities, Bombay, 1887.

Johns, William, *A Collection of facts and opinions relative to the burning of widows with the dead bodies of their husbands, and other destructive customs prevalent in British India*, Birmingham, 1816.

Karkaria, R.P., "The Late K.T. Telang and the Present Political Movement in India" (pamphlet), Bombay, 1895.

Macnicol, Nicol, *Psalms of Maratha Saints*, Calcutta, 1919.

Majumdar, Jotindra Kumar (ed.), *Indian Speeches and Documents on British Rule, 1821-1918*, Calcutta, 1937.

———, (ed.), *Raja Rammohun Roy and Progressive Movements in India; A Selection from Records (1775-1845)*, Calcutta, 1941.

Mandlik, V.N., *Writings and Speeches of the Late Honourable Rao Saheb Vishvanath Narayan Mandlik, C.S.I.* (ed., Narayan Vishvanath Mandlik), Bombay, 1896.

"A Memorial to His Grace the Duke of Argyll, Her Majesty's Secretary of State for India in Council from the Hindu Inhabitants of Madras, together with Proceedings of the Public Meeting Held for Adopting the Same, on the 17th June, 1872" (pamphlet), Madras, 1872.

Mozoomdar, Protap Chunder, *Faith and Progress of Brahmo Samaj*, Calcutta, 1882.

Murdoch, J., *Papers on Indian Religious Reform*, Madras, 1890.

Naoroji, Dadabhai, *Essays, Speeches, Addresses, and Writings* (ed., C. L. Parekh), Bombay, 1887.

Nirvedananda, Swami, *Swami Vivekananda on India and Her Problems*, Almora, 4th edn., 1946.

Olcott, Henry S., "The Poor Pariah" (pamphlet), Madras, 1902.

Pal, Bipin Chandra, "The Basis of Political Reform" (pamphlet), Calcutta, 1889.

——, *An Introduction to the Study of Hinduism*, Calcutta, 2nd edn., 1951.

——, *Nationality and Empire*, Calcutta, 1916.

——, *The New Spirit*, Calcutta, 1907.

——, "The Present Social Reaction—What Does It Mean?" (pamphlet), Calcutta, n.d. (1889?).

——, *The Soul of India*, Calcutta, 4th edn., 1958.

——, *Speeches of Bipin Chandra Pal*, Madras, 1907.

——, *Swadeshi and Swaraj*, Calcutta, 1954.

Pantulu, N. Subba Row (ed.), *Hindu Social Progress*, Madras, 1904.

Peggs, James, *India's Cries to British Humanity, Relative to Infanticide, British Connection with Idolatry, Ghant Murders, Suttee, Slavery, and Colonization in India; to which are added Humane Hints for the Melioration of the State of Society in British India*, London, 1832.

Pherwani, S., *Social Efficiency, India's Greatest Need*, Bombay, 1923.

A Punjabi Brahmo, "The Arya Samaj and a Refutation of Its Tenets" (pamphlet), Lahore, 1883.

Rai, Lala Lajpat, *The Arya Samaj*, Lahore, 1932.

——, *Lal Lajpat Rai; The Man in His Word*, Madras, 1907.

——, *The Political Future of India*, New York, 1919.

——, *Young India*, New York, 1917.

Ram, Munshi, Jijyasu and Rama Deva, *The Arya Samaj and Its Detractors; A Vindication*, Dayanandabad, 1910.

Ramakrishna Math and Mission, *General Report for 1958*, Calcutta, 1959.

Sri Ramakrishna Math and Charitable Dispensary, *Report for the Year 1959*, Madras, 1960.

Ranade, Mahadev Govind, *The Miscellaneous Writings of Mr. Justice M.G. Ranade*, Bombay, 1915.

——, *Religious and Social Reform; A Collection of Essays and Speeches* (compiled by M. B. Kolaskar), Bombay, 1902.

——, *Rise of the Maratha Power*, Bombay, 1900.

Row, K. Srinivasa, *Papers on Social Reform; Being the Speeches and Writings of K. Srinivasa Row*, Madras, 1906.

Row, R. Ragoonath (R. Raghunatha Rau), *A Review of the Progress of Knowledge of Hindu Law and Custom, Made among Our British Rulers, During the Past Hundred Years*, Madras, 1885.

361

Roy, Rammohun, *The English Works of Rammohun Roy* (ed., Jogendra Chunder Ghose), Allahabad, 1906.

Rugnathdas, Madhowdas, *Story of a Widow Remarriage; Being the Experiences of Madhowdas Rugnathdas*, Bombay, 1890.

Saraswati, Swami Dayananda, *Light of Truth; or an English Translation of the Satyarth Prakash*, by Dr. Chiranjiva Bharadwaja, Allahabad, 2nd edn., 1915.

——, *The Ocean of Mercy; an English Translation of Gocaruna Nidhi*, by Durga Prasad, Amritsar, 1886.

Sarda, Har Bilas (ed.), *Dayanand Commemoration Volume*, Ajmer, 1933.

——, *Hindu Superiority; an Attempt to Determine the Position of the Hindu Race in the Scale of Nations*, Ajmer, 1906.

——, *Speeches and Writings*, Ajmer, 1935.

Sastri, Pandit A. Mahadeva, *Collected Essays of Pandit A. Mahadeva-Sastri on Vedic Religion and Social Reform*, 1: *The Vedic Law of Marriage or the Emancipation of Women*, Madras, 1918.

Sen, Keshub Chandra, *Lectures in India*, London, 1901, 1904, 2 vols.

The Servants of India Society, *Report of Work (from June 1923 to May 1926)*, Poona, 1926.

——, *Report for 1958-59*, Poona, 1959.

Seth, Madan Mohan, "The Arya Samaj, a Political Body; Being Open Letters to Viscount Morley. . ." (pamphlet), Allahabad, 1912.

Singh, Saint Nihal, *Messages of Uplift for India*, Madras, n.d. (1900?).

Sinha, Sachchidananda, "Caste Conferences and National Progress," Presidential address at 35th All-India Kayastha Conference, 29 March, 1929.

Social Conference Addresses, 1912 (a conjectured title since title page is missing), publ. by Messrs. M. R. Krishna Ras and Co. (1914?).

The Social Service League of Bombay, *Forty-Seventh Annual Report for the Year 1958-59*, Bombay, 1959.

"The Students' Miscellany; containing a Selection of the Essays Read at the Students' Literary and Scientific Society, Bombay, 1850," No. 1, Bombay, 1850.

Tattvabhushan, Sitanath, *Hindu Theism: A Defense and Exposition*, Calcutta, 1898.

——, *The Philosophy of Brahmaism*, Madras, 1909.

——, *Social Reform in Bengal*, Calcutta, 1904.

Telang, Kashinath Trimbak, *Selected Writings and Speeches*, Bombay, (1916?), 2 vols.

Tilak, Bal Gangadhar, *His Writings and Speeches* (with an appreciation by Aurobindo Ghose), Madras, n.d.

Upadhyaya, Ganga Prasad, "The Aryasamaj and the International Aryan League" (pamphlet), Delhi, 1947.

Vaidya, C.V., *Social Reform Series No. 1. On the History of Hindu Social Reform Agitation and the Proper Methods of Carrying It On*, Poona, 1890.

Vaidya, Pandit Narayan Kesab (ed.), *A Collection Containing the Proceedings which led to the passing of Act XV of 1856, an Act to remove all legal obstacles to the Marriage of Widows*, Bombay, 1885.

Vidyasagar, Eshwar Chandra, *Marriage of Hindu Widows*, Calcutta, 1856.

Vivekananda, Swami, *From Colombo to Almora; Seventeen Lectures*, Madras, 1897.

———, *The Complete Works of Swami Vivekananda*, Calcutta, 10th edn., 1957.

———, *The East and the West*, Calcutta, 1955.

———, *India and Her Problems*, Almora, 4th edn., 1946.

———, *The Letters of Swami Vivekananda*, Almora, 4th edn., 1948.

———, *Our Women*, Almora, 1953.

———, *Salvation and Service*, Almora, 1949.

———, *Selections from Swami Vivekananda*, Almora, 2nd edn., 1946.

———, *Speeches and Writings*, Madras, 7th edn., 1927.

II. *Biographies and Autobiographies of Reformers*

Bhan, Suraj, *Dayanand; His Life and Work*, Jullundur, 1956.

Bharati, Shuddhananda, *Mahatma Ramalingam and His Revelations*, Pondicherry, 1936.

Bomanji, Framji, *Lights and Shades of the East; or a Study of the Life of Baboo Harrischander*, Bombay, 1863.

Chaitanya to Vivekananda; Lives of the Saints of Bengal, Madras, 2nd edn., 1949.

Chandavarkar, Ganesh L., *Maharshi Karve*, Bombay, 1958.

———, *A Wrestling Soul; Story of the Life of Sir Narayan Chandavarkar*, Bombay, 1956.

Chapman, E. F., *Sketches of Some Distinguished Indian Women*, London, 1891.

Chaudhuri, Nirad C., *The Autobiography of an Unknown Indian*, New York, 1951.

Collet, Sophia Dobson, *Life and Letters of Raja Rammohun Roy*, (ed., Hem Chandra Sarkar), Calcutta, 1913.

Das Gupta, Hemendranath, *Deshbandhu Chittaranjan Das*, Delhi, 1960.

Famous Parsis: Biographical and Critical Sketches, Madras, 1st edn., 1930.

Fraser, J. Nelson, *The Life and Teaching of Tukaram*, Madras, 1922.

Fuller, Mary Lucia Bierce, *The Triumph of an Indian Widow; The Life of Pandita Ramabai*, Philadelphia, n.d. (1939?).

Ghorpade, A. K., *Mahatma Phule* (in Marathi), Poona, 2nd edn., 1959.

Ghose, Sri Aurobindo, *Bankim Chandra Chatterji*, Pondicherry, 1954.

——, *Bankim-Tilak-Dayananda*, Pondicherry, 1955.

Gidumal, Dayaram, *The Life and Life Work of Behramji M. Malabari*, Bombay, 1888.

Gopal, Ram, *Lokamanya Tilak*, Bombay, 1956.

Gurunadhan, J., *Viresalingam; The Founder of Telegu Public Life*, Rajahmundry, 1911.

Hoyland, John S., *Gopal Krishna Gokhale; His Life and Speeches*, Calcutta, 1933.

Indian Judges; Biographical and Critical Sketches, Madras, 1932.

Iyengar, K. R. Srinivasa, *Sri Aurobindo*, Calcutta, 1945.

Jambhekar, Ganesh G. (ed.), *Memoirs and Writings of Acharya Bal Shastri Jambhekar*, Poona, 1950, 4 vols.

Karkaria, R.P., *India; Forty Years of Progress and Reform, being a sketch of the Life and Times of Behramji M. Malabari*, London, 1896.

Karmarkar, D. P., *Bal Gangadhar Tilak; A Study*, Bombay, 1956.

Karve, D.G., *Ranade; The Prophet of Liberated India*, Poona, 1942.

Karve, Dhondo Keshav, *Looking Back (An Autobiography)*, Poona, 1936.

Professor D. K. Karve; A Sketch of His Life and Life-Work (from a work by Professor Paranjpye), Madras, 1918.

Kelkar, N.C., *Life and Times of Lokamanya Tilak*, Madras, 1928.

Kellock, James, *Mahadev Govind Ranade*, Calcutta, 1926.

Latthe, A. B., *Memoirs of His Highness Shri Shahu Chhatrapati Maharja of Kolhapur*, Bombay, 1924, 2 vols.

Behramji M. Malabari; A Sketch of His Life and an Appreciation of His Works, Madras, 1914.

Matthew, Anjilvel V. *Karmaveer Bhaurao Patil*, Satara, 1957.

Motivala, B. N., *Karsondas Mulji; A Biographical Study*, Bombay, 1935.

364

———, *Karsondas Mulji; A Short Sketch of a Great Indian Social Servant*, Bombay, n.d. (1931?).

———, "The Romance of a Great Indian Social Servant, or The Life and Career of Mr. Sasipada Banerji" (pamphlet), Bombay, 1915.

"Rao Bahadur R. N. Mudholkar; A Sketch of His Life and His Services to India" (pamphlet), Madras, n.d.

Müller, F. Max, *Ramakrishna; His Life and Sayings*, New York, 1899.

———, *Rammohan to Ramakrishna*, Calcutta, 1952.

Naik, Vasant N., *Kashinath Trimbak Telang; The Man and His Times*, Madras, n.d.

North Indian Saints, Madras, 2nd edn., 1947.

Pal, Bipin Chandra, *Memories of My Life and Times*, Calcutta, 1932, 1951, 2 vols.

———, *Mrs. Annie Besant; A Psychological Study*, Madras, n.d. (1918?).

Pantulu, Rao Bahadur Veerasalingam, *Autobiography*, translated by N.C. Narasinha Acharya, Bombay, n.d. (a fragment).

Paranjpe, R.P., *Gopal Krishna Gokhale*, Poona, 1915.

Parekh, Manilal C., *Sri Swami Narayana*, Rajkot, 1937.

Parvate, T. V., *Gopal Krishna Gokhale*, Ahmedabad, 1959.

Pillai, G., Paramaswaran, *Representative Indians*, London, 1902.

Prakasa, Sri, *Annie Besant*, Bombay, 2nd edn., 1954.

Raja Ram Mohun Roy; His Life, Writings, and Speeches, Madras, 1925.

Life of Sri Ramakrishna; Compiled from Various Authentic Sources, Calcutta, 1955.

Ramanand to Ram Tirath: Lives of the Saints of Northern India, Including the Sikh Gurus, Madras, 2nd edn., 1947.

Ranade, Mrs. Rambai, *Himself, the Autobiography of a Hindu Lady*, New York, 1938.

Rao, K. Subba, *Revived Memories*, Madras, 1933.

Rao, V. Ramakrishna (ed.), *The Message and Ministrations of Dewan Bahadur R. Venkata Ratnam*, Madras, 1922-24, 3 vols.

Ratcliffe, S., *William Wedderburn and the Indian Reform Movement*, London, 1923.

Rolland, Romain, *The Life of Ramakrishna*, Almora, 3rd edn., 1944.

———, *The Life of Vivekananda and the Universal Gospel*, Almora, 1953.

Saraswati, Dayananda, *Autobiography of Pandit Dayanand Saraswati*, written for *The Theosophist* (ed., H.P. Blavatsky), Madras, 1952.

Sarda, Har Bilas, *Life of Dayanand Saraswati*, Ajmer, 1946.

365

Shahani, Tejumal K., *Gopal Krishna Gokhale; A Historical Biography*, Bombay, 1929.

Sharma, Sri Ram, *Mahatma Hansraj; Maker of the Modern Punjab*, Lahore, n.d. (1941?).

Shay, Theodore L., *The Legacy of the Lokamanya*, New York, 1956.

Singh, Bawa Chhajju, *The Life and Teaching of Swami Dayanand Saraswati*, Lahore, 1903.

Suryanarayana, K., *Sir R. Venkata Ratnam*, Rajahmundry, 1952.

Tagore, Debendranath, *Autobiography of Maharshi Davendranath Tagore*, translated by Satyendranath Tagore and Indira Devi, London, 1914.

Tahmankar, D.V., *Lokamanya Tilak*, London, 1956.

Tandon, Prakash, *Punjabi Century, 1857-1947*, New York, 1961.

Wedderburn, Sir William, *Allan Octavian Hume, C.B.*, London, 1913.

III. *General Works*

Aiyer, Sir P.S. Sivaswamy, *Evolution of Hindu Moral Ideas*, Calcutta, 1935.

Andrews, C. F. and Girija Mukerji, *The Rise and Growth of the Congress in India*, London, 1938.

Appasamy, Paul, *Legal Aspects of Social Reform* (with a lecture on Hindu Law reform by Sir P. S. Sivaswami Aiyar), Madras, 1929.

Bagal, Jogesh Chandra, *History of Indian Association, 1876-1951*, Calcutta, 1953.

Ball, Upendra Nall, *A Century of Service; A Survey of the Services Rendered by the Brahma Samaj in First Hundred Years (1828-1928)*, Lahore, 1928.

Ballhatchet, Kenneth, *Social Policy and Social Change in Western India, 1817-1830*, London, 1957.

Bevan, Edwyn, *Indian Nationalism*, London, 1913.

Blunt, Sir Edward A. H., *The Caste System of Northern India*, London, 1931.

——, *Social Service in India*, London, 1938.

Bose, Nemai Sadhan, *The Indian Awakening and Bengal*, Calcutta, 1960.

Bose, Nirmal Kumar, "Modern Bengal" (pamphlet), Berkeley, 1959.

Bose, Pramatha Nath, *A History of Hindu Civilization During British Rule*, Calcutta, 1894, 4 vols.

Bose, Ram Chandra, *Brahmoism; or History of Reformed Hinduism*, New York, 1884.

366

Buch, Maganlal A., *The Principles of Hindu Ethics*, Baroda, 1921.
———, *Rise and Growth of Indian Liberalism*, Baroda, 1938.
Buckland, Charles Edward, *Bengal Under the Lieutenant-Governors*, Calcutta, 1902.
Cave-Brown, John, *Indian Infanticide; Its Origin, Progress, and Repression*, London, 1857.
Corvan, Minna G., *The Education of the Women of India*, New York, 1912.
Das, Babu Govinda, *Hindu Ethics; Principles of Hindu Religio-Social Regeneration*, Madras, n.d. (1928?).
Das, Manmath Nath, *Studies in the Economic and Social Development of Modern India: 1848-56*, Calcutta, 1959.
Datta, Kalikinkar, *Survey of India's Social Life and Economic Condition in the Eighteenth Century* (1707-1813), Calcutta, 1961.
Desai, A. R., *Social Background of Indian Nationalism*, Bombay, 2nd edn., 1954.
Desai, Neera A., "The Impact of the British Rule on the Position of Indian Women," M.A. thesis, University of Bombay, 1951.
———, *Woman in Modern India*, Bombay, 1957.
Emerson, Rupert, *From Empire to Nation*, Cambridge, 1960.
Farquhar, J. N., *Modern Religious Movements in India*, New York, 1924.
———, *An Outline of the Religious Literature of India*, London, 1920.
Gambhirananda, Swami, *History of the Ramakrishna Math and Mission*, Calcutta, 1957.
Ghurye, G.S., *Caste and Class in India*, Bombay, 1950.
Gilchrist, R.N., *Indian Nationality*, London, 1920.
A Glossary of the Tribes and Castes of the Punjab and North-West Frontier Province, II, Lahore, 1911.
Graham, J. Reid, "The Arya Samaj as a Reformation in Hinduism with Special Reference to Caste," Ph.D. dissertation, Yale University, 1942, 2 vols.
Griffiths, Sir Percival, *The British Impact on India*, London, 1952.
Griswold, H.D., *The Religious Quest of India: The Religion of the Rigveda*, London, 1923.
Gupta, Atulchandra (ed.), *Studies in the Bengal Renaissance*, Calcutta, 1958.
Harrison, Selig S. (ed.), *India and the United States*, New York, 1961.
———, *India; The Most Dangerous Decades*, Princeton, 1960.

Hayes, Carlton J.H., *Essays on Nationalism*, New York, 1926.
——, *The Historical Evolution of Modern Nationalism*, New York, 1931.
India, Government, Planning Commission, *Social Legislation; Its Role in Social Welfare*, New Delhi, 1956.
Ingham, Kenneth, *Reformers in India, 1793-1833; An Account of the Work of Christian Missionaries in Behalf of Social Reform*, Cambridge, England, 1956.
Joglekar, J.G., "Evolution of Social Life and Ideals in Maharashtra During the 19th Century and After," M.A. thesis, University of Bombay, 1928.
Kane, Pandurang Vaman, *History of Dharmaśāstra*, II, Part I, Poona, 1941.
Kennedy, Melville T., *The Chaitanya Movement; A Study of the Vaishnavism of Bengal*, Calcutta, 1925.
Kohn, Hans, *The Idea of Nationalism*, New York, 1944.
Lillingston, Frank, *The Brahmo Samaj and Arya Samaj in Their Bearing upon Christianity*, London, 1901.
Lovett, Sir Verney, *A History of the Indian Nationalist Movement*, London, 1920.
McCully, Bruce Tiebout, *English Education and the Origins of Indian Nationalism*, New York, 1940.
McLane, John R., "The Development of Nationalist Ideas and Tactics and the Policies of the Government of India: 1897-1905," Ph.D. dissertation, University of London, 1961.
MacDonald, J. Ramsay, *Awakening of India*, London, 1910.
——, *The Government of India*, London, 1919.
Macnicol, Nicol, *Indian Theism from the Vedic to the Muhammadan Period*, London, 1915.
——, *The Making of Modern India*, London, 1924.
Majumdar, Amvika Charan, *Indian National Evolution*, Madras, 2nd edn., 1917.
Majumdar, Bimanbehari, *History of Political Thought from Rammohun to Dayananda (1821-84), 1: Bengal*, Calcutta, 1934.
Majumdar, Ramesh Chandra, *Glimpses of Bengal in the Nineteenth Century*, Calcutta, 1960.
——, *History of the Freedom Movement in India*, 1, Calcutta, 1962.
Meston, Lord, *Nationhood for India*, New Haven, 1931.
Misra, B.B., *The Indian Middle Classes; Their Growth in Modern Times*, London, 1961.

368

Monier-Williams, M., *Hinduism*, Calcutta, 1951 (reprint).

———, *Religious Thought and Life in India*, London, 1885.

Mookerjee, Kanye Lall, *Hindu Society*, Calcutta, 1902.

Mookerji, Radhakumud, *The Fundamental Unity of India*, New York, 1914.

Morrison, John, *New Ideas in India*, London, 1907.

Mostofi, Khosrow, *Aspects of Nationalism; A Sociology of Colonial Revolt*, Salt Lake City, 1959.

Mukherjee, Haridas and Uma, *"Bande Mataram" and Indian Nationalism 1906-1908*, Calcutta, 1957.

———, *Bipin Chandra Pal and India's Struggle for Swaraj*, Calcutta, 1958.

———, *The Growth of Nationalism in India (1857-1905)*, Calcutta, 1957.

———, *India's Fight for Freedom; or The Swadeshi Movement*, Calcutta, 1958.

———, *Sri Aurobindo's Political Thought (1893-1908)*, Calcutta, 1958.

Mukerji, Dhurjati Prasad, *Modern Indian Culture*, Bombay, 2nd edn., 1948.

Murdoch, John, *Education in India: A Letter to His Excellency the Most Honorable the Marquis of Ripon*, Madras, 1881.

Namboodripad, E.M.S., *The National Question in Kerala*, Bombay, 1952.

Natarajan, S., *A Century of Social Reform in India*, Bombay, 1959.

Nevison, Henry W., *The New Spirit in India*, London, 1908.

Notes on the Administration of the Hon'ble Sir Arthur Lawley, Governor of Madras 1906 to 1911, Madras, 1912.

O'Malley, L.S.S., *India's Social Heritage*, Oxford, 1934.

———, *Modern India and the West*, London, 1941.

Panikkar, K.M., *Hindu Society at Cross Roads*, Bombay, 2nd edn., 1956.

Parekh, Manilal C., *The Brahma Samaj*, Rajkot, 1929.

Park, Richard L., "The Rise of Militant Nationalism in Bengal: A Regional Study of Indian Nationalism," Ph.D. dissertation, Harvard, 1950.

Patterson, Maureen L.P., "A Preliminary Study of the Brahman versus Non-Brahman Conflict in Maharashtra," M.A. thesis, South Asian Regional Studies, University of Pennsylvania, 1952.

Prakash, Satya, *A Critical Study of Philosophy of Dayananda*, Ajmer, 1938.

Radhakrishnan, Sarvepalli, *Eastern Religions and Western Thought*, London, 2nd edn., 1940.

Raghuvanshi, V.P.S., *Indian Nationalist Movement and Thought*, Agra, 2nd edn., 1959.

Rao, M.S.A., *Social Change in Malabar*, Bombay, 1957.

Rao, M.V. Krishna, *The Growth of Indian Liberalism in the Nineteenth Century*, Mysore, 1951.

Ranganathananda, Swami, *The Ramakrishna Mission; Its Ideals and Activities*, Madras, 5th edn., 1956.

Report of the Indian Statutory Commission, London, 1930, 2 vols.

Sarasvati, Pundita Ramabai, *The High-Caste Hindu Woman*, Philadelphia, 1888.

Sarkar, Benoy Kumar, *Villages and Towns as Social Patterns*, Calcutta, 1941.

Sarma, D.S., *Studies in the Renaissance of Hinduism in the 19th and 20th Centuries*, Benaras, 1944.

Sastri, K.A. Nilakanta, *History of India, Part III: Modern India*, Madras, 1952.

Scott, Roland W., *Social Ethics in Modern Hinduism*, Calcutta, 1953.

Shah, M.V., "Social Philosophy of Gandhiji," Ph.D. dissertation, University of Bombay, 1953.

Shay, Theodore L., *The Legacy of the Lokamanya; The Political Philosophy of Bal Gangadhar Tilak*, London, 1956.

Sinha, Sasadhar, *Tagore's Approach to Social Problems*, Calcutta, 1947.

Snyder, Louis L., *The Meaning of Nationalism*, New Brunswick, 1954.

Stokes, Eric, *The English Utilitarians and India*, Oxford, 1957.

Strachey, Sir John, *India: Its Administration and Progress*, London, 1903.

Sulzbach, Walter, *National Consciousness*, Washington, 1943.

Topa, Ishwar Nath, *The Growth and Development of National Thought in India,* Hamburg, 1928.

Upadyaya, Ganga Prasad, *The Origin, Scope, and Mission of the Arya Samaj*, Allahabad, 1940.

———, *Philosophy of Dayananda*, Allahabad, 1955.

———, *Swami Dayanand's Contribution to Hindu Solidarity*, Allahabad, 1939.

Vidyavachaspati, Indra, *Aryasamaj ka Ithias* (in Hindi), Delhi, 1957, 2 vols.

Vyas, K.C., *The Social Renaissance in India*, Bombay, 1957.

Wilson, Horace Hayman, *Religious Sects of the Hindus*, Calcutta, 2nd edn., 1958.

Wolpert, Stanley A., *Tilak and Gokhale*, Berkeley, 1962.

———, "Tilak and Gokhale: A Comparative Analysis of Their Social and Political Philosophies," Ph.D. dissertation, University of Pennsylvania, 1959.

Younghusband, Sir Francis, *Dawn in India*, London, 1930.

Zutshi, Manohar Lal, *Gleanings*, Allahabad, 1933.

IV. *Serials*

East and West, Bombay, vol. I (1901)—vol. IV (1904).

Hindustan Review, Allahabad, vol. XV (1907)—vol. XXXII (1915).

The Indian Social Reformer, Madras and Bombay, vol. IX (1898)—vol. XIX (1909), vol. XXX (1919), vol. XXXI (1920).

Indian Review, Madras, vol. VI (1905)—vol. IX (1908).

Madras Review, Madras, vol. II (1896), vol. III (1897).

National Social Conference, *Reports*, Poona, 1889-1901.

Times, London, 1890, 1891.

The Indian Magazine and Review, issued by the National Indian Association in Aid of Social Progress and Education in India, London, vol. XXI (1890), vol. XXII (1891).

The Voice of Progress, Madras, vol. I (1901-1902).

INDEX

374

INDEX

New India, 265
Noble, Margaret, 332
Norton, Eardley, 259
Nulkar, Krishnaji Lakshman, 172
Nundy, Alfred, 299n

Olcott, Henry S., 256, 263
O'Malley, L. S. S., 126n, 270n
outcastes, *see* untouchables
overseas travel, 24, 103, 120f, 248, 255, 272-73, 329, 339

Padhye, D. G., 191, 237
Pal, Bipin Chandra, 35, 66f, 72n, 140, 169n, 262, 265, 266, 267f, 274, 305, 312f, 320, 323f, 338
Pal, Kristodas, 44n
Palmer, E. E. (Miss), 256
Pandurang, Dadoba, 178
Panikkar, K. M., 205n
Pantulu, B. Subba Row, 23n
Pantulu, M. Butchiah, 109
Pantulu, N. Subba Row, 88n, 199n, 257n
Pantulu, Viresalingam, 87, 88n, 110, 112, 218, 240, 258
Paramahans Mandali, 99
Paranjpe, R. P., 222n
Parekh, Manilal C., 39n, 78n, 95n, 109, 245, 266n, 268n, 269n, 353
Park, R. L., 143n
Parmanand, Bhai, 304
Parsi Benevolent Institution, 148
Parsi Marriage and Divorce Act, 149
Parsis, 13n, 92, 148f, 155, 189, 194, 268, 270n
Patel, Framjee Nusserwanjee, 149
Patel, Vithalbhai, 346
Patiala State Conspiracy Case, 307
Patwardhan, W. B., 34
Petit, Dinshaw Manockjee, 149
Phatak, N. R., 35
Phule, Jotiba Govind, 102f, 109, 248f
Pioneer, 116
Pocock, D. F., 139
Potter, Karl H., 31n
Prarthana Samaj, 30, 105f, 110, 124, 125, 192, 243f, 248, 269, 293, 314
Prasad, Munshi Kali, 281
prāyaścitta, 24, 185, 222
princely states, social reform in, 274-75
Pundit, Vishnu Shastri, 86f, 124, 178, 179, 184-85, 239

Rai, Lala Lajpat, 53, 113, 277, 295, 296, 299n, 301, 302, 305, 307, 309, 312, 315, 319, 321f, 338
Radhakrishnan, S., 28n, 31
Rajahmundry Social Reform Association, 87, 110, 258
Ram, Munshi, 277, 296, 307, 308n
Ram, Pundit Tulsi, 305
Ramabai, Pandita, 238f
Ramakrishna Paramahansa, 42f, 95, 331, 332
Ramakrishna Math and Mission, 44, 242n, 245, 255, 263, 336
Ramalingam, Mahatma, 41f, 45
Ramananda, 33, 126
Rangachariar, M., 23
Ranade, Mahadev Govind, 17, 18, 19, 21, 35, 52, 65, 85n, 86, 98, 106n, 108, 124, 143, 150, 154, 164, 165-66, 176f, 188, 190f, 197f, 203, 204, 208, 211f, 220, 221, 222, 228, 232, 233, 236, 238, 243, 254n, 263, 272, 276, 277n, 280, 281, 287n, 290, 298, 314, 322-23, 340
Ranade, Mrs. Ramabai, 184, 238
Rast Goftar, 149, 189
Ratcliffe, S. K., 50
Rao, K. L. N., 238n
Rao, K. Subba, 211, 212, 219n, 254
Rao, M. S. A., 286n
Rao, T. Madhava, 112, 163, 193
Rau, A. Subba, 222, 254
Rau, Benegal N., 350
Rau, K. Ranga, 260
Rau, Raghunatha, 112, 163, 167, 170, 188, 190, 193, 201, 222, 257
"reform along national lines," 187, 228, 257, 262, 329, 337-38
restitution of conjugal rights, 170, 195
revivalism (Hindu), 25, 139f, 187, 191, 192, 206, 228, 257, 264, 266, 274, 299, 309f, 321f, 329, 333f
Ripon, Lord, 68f, 158
Risley, H. H., 156
Rolland, Romain, 42n, 43n, 97n, 335n
Row, K. Srinivasa, 227, 328, 336n
Roy, Rammohun, 7, 10f, 14, 16, 18, 19, 21, 29, 33, 39, 43, 47, 51, 57n, 73f, 82, 89, 91, 101, 102, 112, 183, 203, 214n, 263, 264, 273, 334n
Rukhmabai, 170
Rupram, Mahipatram, 101

Sadharan Brahmo Samaj, 97, 109, 244n, 258, 268-70, 272